Mastering the
Game of Thrones

MASTERING THE GAME OF THRONES

Essays on George R.R. Martin's
A Song of Ice and Fire

EDITED BY Jes Battis
AND Susan Johnston

McFarland & Company, Inc., Publishers
Jefferson, North Carolina

ALSO OF INTEREST

Blood Relations: Chosen Families in Buffy the Vampire Slayer *and* Angel, by Jes Battis (McFarland, 2005)

LIBRARY OF CONGRESS CATALOGUING-IN-PUBLICATION DATA

Mastering the Game of thrones : essays on George R.R. Martin's
  A song of ice and fire / edited by Jes Battis and Susan Johnston.
      p.   cm.
  Includes bibliographical references and index.

  ISBN 978-0-7864-9631-0 (softcover : acid free paper) ∞
  ISBN 978-1-4766-1962-0 (ebook)

  1. Martin, George R. R. Song of ice and fire.   I. Battis, Jes,
1979– editor.   II. Johnston, Susan, 1964– editor.   III. Game
of thrones (Television program)

PS3563.A7239S5935 2015
813'.54—dc23   2014044427

BRITISH LIBRARY CATALOGUING DATA ARE AVAILABLE

Cover images © 2015 iStock/Thinkstock

Printed in the United States of America

McFarland & Company, Inc., Publishers
  Box 611, Jefferson, North Carolina 28640
    www.mcfarlandpub.com

For my mother, who watches from beneath her wolf blanket.—Jes

For Marcel, shekh ma shieraki anni.—Susan

Acknowledgments

As the first of its kind, this volume was a challenging if rewarding endeavor. There are a number of people whose support and patience made it possible. Thanks to all of our colleagues in the Department of English at the University of Regina, who offered guidance and kept us sane while we worked. Thanks as well to our extraordinary contributors, who shared their ideas with us, and responded to our queries with grace. It is a privilege and a pleasure to present their fascinating work. Jes would like to thank Bea for keeping him in one piece, Lynda Mae for her medieval knowledge, and Alexis for the many spirited conversations at the Fireside Pub (where we own the leather couches). Susan would like to thank Marcel, for never letting it show that he was sick of the whole thing, for the insights, and for the coffee; Katy, Elizabeth, and Maggie, for the patience; Nick Ruddick, for unflagging encouragement and holding the oxygen bottle; and Brian and Bridget and David and Susan and all the rest of the Albuquerque gang. These acknowledgments would not be complete without the folks at *Tower of the Hand*, *The Citadel*, and the *Wiki of Ice and Fire*, whose unfailing and unpaid work has made the impossible task of fact-checking merely improbable. To David Benioff and D.B. Weiss: thanks for transforming adaptation and bringing our imaginations to life. And to George R.R. Martin himself: thank you. *Now write like the wind.*

Table of Contents

Bodies

Intimacies

Adaptations

A Note on Editions

For ease of reference, we have used the U.S. first edition of each novel of *A Song of Ice and Fire*, as follows (in order of publication), and abbreviated each title as such:

Martin, George R.R. *A Game of Thrones.* New York: Bantam, 1996.	*GoT*
_____. *A Clash of Kings.* New York: Bantam, 1999.	*CoK*
_____. *A Storm of Swords.* New York: Bantam, 2000.	*SoS*
_____. *A Feast for Crows.* New York: Bantam, 2005.	*FfC*
_____. *A Dance with Dragons.* New York: Bantam, 2011.	*DwD*

In addition, all references to the novels will be presented as follows:

GoT 42 Jon 5: 376

First is the novel, then the chapter number, the name of the character from whose point of view the chapter is written, the count of the chapter from that character's point of view, then the page number. In the example above, the quote is from page 376 in Chapter 42 of *A Game of Thrones*, in the fifth chapter narrated by Jon. The initial chapter numbers (e.g., *GoT* 42) are based on the chapter tables from Tower of the Hand: http://towerofthehand.com/books/101/.

References to HBO's *Game of Thrones*, the television series, are abbreviated *Thrones* and followed by season number and episode number, then episode title, as follows:

Thrones S1: Ep.6, "A Golden Crown."

Introduction: On Knowing Nothing

Susan Johnston and Jes Battis

"You know nothing, Jon Snow"—*A Clash of Kings*

In George R.R. Martin's universe of ice and fire, the learned men of the Citadel wear great chains of office, to mark them as "maesters": as scholars, scientists, teachers, statesmen. Their ponderous chains are "forge[d]"—as is this book—"with study" and "[t]he different metals are each a different kind of learning" (*GoT* 42 Jon 5: 376), from history to herbalism, "but two links can't make a chain.... A chain needs all sorts of metals, and a land needs all sorts of people" (376). This is also, we propose, both the purpose and the practice of this book; we wanted to bind together different kinds of learning and, like the maesters themselves, to serve with them the realm. And like the novices of Oldtown's Citadel, we have discovered in the process that the realm is larger and more various even than we had dreamed of in our philosophies, from the show-firsters who belatedly jumped on board the HBO adaptation in spring of 2013 just in time to reel in horror from the thirteen-year-old Red Wedding, to the undergraduate who has clutched his signed first edition of *A Game of Thrones* itself ever since the mid-nineties, to the linguists, the Shakespeareans, the psychologists who inhabit both Martin's world and our own. That is the audience, the disparate realm, we hope this book will serve.

If we have learned a great deal of the reach of our subject here, though, we have also learned, in view of this reach, humility. This too is as it should be: as Brian Cowlishaw notes in his essay here, "What Maesters Knew: Narrating Knowing," the potent learning of the maesters is, in the end, barren.

> What they "know" doesn't matter much, and what they *should* know, they don't. This is so despite the important fact that they are precisely the people *designated* in their world *to know things*. Thus they are singularly incompetent at what they do. After all, farmers know farming, blacksmiths smithing; septons know theology, soldiers warfare. Maesters fail spectacularly at their culturally designated specialty. Maesters, you know nothing [Cowlishaw].

1

Cowlishaw, importantly, reads the maesters' ignorance in terms of the interplay of power and knowledge, and here his work intersects with that of Marc Napolitano, whose "'Sing for your little life': Story, Discourse and Character" remarks upon the ways that the point-of-view characters control the presentation of the story but are nonetheless rendered powerless in the face of that story's progression. They appear to have power because they seem to control what readers know, but their power is limited to discourse; they do not control their own stories. Yet, as Napolitano shows, discursive power is vital to the meaning of *A Song of Ice and Fire*.

Outside of the Citadel, where George R.R. Martin's universe of ice and fire stretches for thousands of years back in time and thousands of miles to hint at its own unexplored margins, the maesters are too often reduced to the stature of the adolescent Jon Snow, on the wrong side of the Wall, the wrong side of knowledge, perhaps even the wrong side of history. Like Jon, like the maesters, we have learned enough to know that after all, we know nothing. This is so, of course, in part because of the sheer complexity of Martin's world: with well over a thousand named characters, hundreds of place names, and a fictive history stretching back into the mists of millennium-old legends, the problem of fact-checking alone becomes nearly as insurmountable as the Wall itself.

And the Martinverse is growing. David J. Peterson's essay on "The Languages of Ice and Fire" details his own role as a conlanger—language creator—in developing Dothraki and Valyrian from the bare bones Martin gives in the novels into actual languages that could be spoken by main characters on screen and by secondary characters in the background. While already an experienced language creator, Peterson nonetheless had to come to grips with a whole range of new challenges, including leaving significant elements of the languages unfinished in order to accommodate potential developments in a book series not yet finished.

But it is also so, as Cowlishaw demonstrates, that "to read *A Song of Ice and Fire* is to be dragged sequentially through all the possible ways of knowing nothing"; we come to this series from our experience of fantasy, experience that, for many readers, takes in much of that vast terrain of fantasy over which, as Martin reminds us, Tolkien looms "like a mountain" (Ippolito). It is this experience that has trained us to embrace Martin's complex world—and which Martin repeatedly subverts, by turning its tropes and conventions on its head. Indeed, it is difficult to locate *A Song of Ice and Fire* within the fantasy tradition, because Martin's novels have been celebrated for being precisely unlike most fantasy literature. In *A Short History of Fantasy*, for example, Farah Mendlesohn describes the series as "hardcore" (146), an adjective that few readers would disagree with. Martin himself, in an online interview with John Hodgman, criticizes other medievalist fantasy writers for creating "a sort of Disneyland middle ages, where they had castles and princesses and all that. The trappings of a class system, but they didn't seem to understand what a class system actually meant." The series has garnered much praise for going against the conventions of the fantasy genre, although many of these conventions—the happy ending, the safety of primary characters, the sanctity of oaths—are not only the province of fantasy literature. In fact, *A Song of Ice and Fire* quite skillfully mines the fantasy tradition, by including unexpected elements from much earlier texts: the blood-curdling horror of *Beowulf*, the dark satire of *Don Quijote*, and perhaps even the liminal magic of *Gilgamesh*.

In the same sense that Tolkien's *The Lord of the Rings* is difficult to classify as a result of its scope, *A Song of Ice and Fire* remains in a class of its own. Martin's epic is based largely on the work of European writers, such as Tolkien and Maurice Druon, yet it also incorporates and revises traditions that have become central to American mass-market fantasy (in particular, a serial format that defies the trilogy model put forth by writers such as C.J. Cherryh[1]). And the Martinverse takes place in what could be a plausible medieval world, complete with the outrageous inequalities and prejudices that would have driven overlapping societies within the high middle ages. This commitment to realism is likely what makes the series attractive to readers (and viewers) who would normally eschew the fantasy genre, but Martin's work is also replete with the uncanny and the marvelous.

In "'All men must serve': Religion and Free Will from the Seven to the Faceless Men," Ryan Mitchell Wittingslow examines the relationships between some aspects of the marvelous, specifically in terms of the religions of the Martinverse and their analogues in the primary world. From the priestess of R'hllor, kindling the nightfires on Dragonstone, to the greenseers in their cavern far beyond the Wall, Wittingslow asks if the devotees of these varied gods are ever truly free—and, if they are, what that suggests about the view of necessity and freedom that permeates the series as a whole. This tension between freedom and necessity, between the supernatural and the natural, reflects the complexity of a work that lies somewhere along a spectrum that moves between historical fiction and epic fantasy. Even the most learned inhabitants of Westeros—the maesters—have little to no understanding of how the supernatural functions within their world. As Brian Cowlishaw points out in his essay, the maesters are often wrong about what they firmly believe to be empirical. As academics seeking to analyze Martin's series before it has concluded,[2] we also encounter gaps within the chain of knowledge. But these gaps and moments of speculation can be thrilling, just as the fantastic is thrilling because it exists as a "hesitation between genres" (Todorov 31), a moment of indrawn breath that signals exquisite doubt.

What are the Others? Is Dragonglass merely obsidian? What is the secret of warging? *A Song of Ice and Fire* presents its readers with magic that hovers on the verge of explication, just as medieval bestiaries conveyed information about real and mythical animals, side by side. The essays in this volume offer a series of perspectives on Westeros and its inhabitants, but as editors, we understand that these perspectives may be challenged as the series progresses. Indeed we recognize that all our conclusions may themselves be left in smoking ruins. As we write, the publication dates of the last two novels in *A Song of Ice and Fire* remain unannounced[3]; like our contributors, we remain rather chary of pronouncing on the fate of characters and worlds whose creator has not yet done so. This is so not least because George R.R. Martin has shown himself entirely willing to kill off everything we love. It is also because, in the face of the complex and creative mastery Martin has already shown in offering up the world of ice and fire, our own attempts at maestery seem doomed to incompletion. We fear, in other words, that we will get everything that really matters wrong. And yet we welcome such reversals and surprises, because they signal that we are examining a living text of astonishing complexity, a maester's chain of stories—both heroic and quotidian—which will alter the landscape of contemporary fantasy.

It is astonishing now to look back and recall that when it was published in 1996, *A Game of Thrones* was not a best-seller (in a 2011 article, "The Fantasy King," James Hibberd goes so far as to call it a "disappointment"). At the time, *A Crown of Swords*, the seventh book in Robert Jordan's *Wheel of Time* sequence, was on the New York Times Bestsellers List. *A Song of Ice and Fire*, with its focus on medieval politics, is radically different from *The Wheel of Time*, which Farah Mendlesohn describes as "an eternal champion tale" (*Short History* 145). However, Martin acknowledges the influence of Jordan's work in a 2007 interview:

> Jordan essentially broke the trilogy template that Tolkien helped set up. He showed us how to do a book that's bigger than a trilogy. I don't think my series would've been possible without *The Wheel of Time* being as successful as it was [Kirschling].

Rather than concentrating solely on Martin's break with the fantasy canon, it may be more useful to contextualize Martin's work alongside Jordan and his other forerunners. *The Wheel of Time* was the cutting-edge fantasy series that defined the 1990s, just as *The Belgariad*, by David and Leigh Eddings, defined the 1980s.

Although their styles may seem incompatible, there are some intriguing similarities present in the work of Eddings (both David and his wife and co-writer, Leigh) and Martin. Both *The Belgariad* and *A Song of Ice and Fire* offer us the perspective of young boys—Garion and Bran—who have been relatively sheltered from a hostile medieval world. Bran's context is widened after witnessing the execution of a deserter from the Night's Watch (*GoT* 2 Bran 1:15), and Garion begins to doubt the safety of his surroundings after he nearly drowns (Eddings 44). Both boys follow the trajectory of the traditional "portal fantasy," which Mendlesohn defines in *Rhetorics of Fantasy*: "In both portal and quest fantasies, a character leaves her familiar surroundings and passes through a portal into an unknown place" (1). Unlike Bran, Garion is not pushed out of a tower window. Martin's adaptation of the portal fantasy involves destroying Bran's home, rather than exposing him to violence on the road. While Garion leaves Faldor's Farm to explore the world with his aunt and grandfather, Bran must eventually flee Winterfell to escape death at the hands of Theon Greyjoy, the fosterling who has betrayed the Stark family, though not before surviving two unrelated assassination attempts.

In the transition from *The Belgariad* to *The Wheel of Time*, whose final volume was published in 2013, over five years after Robert Jordan's death in 2007, readers noticed an increase in scope and word count. *The Wheel of Time* spans fourteen novels, the longest of which is *The Shadow Rising*, clocking in at over a thousand pages. Although David and Leigh Eddings were some of the first writers to break away from the trilogy model, Jordan was the first to create such a sprawling epic. Jordan's work has come to define contemporary fantasy literature, which now strives for soaring word counts. There are still plenty of fantasy novels that are 300–350 pages in length, but the exceptions[4]—like Martin's epic—have attracted a massive fan base. Martin has noted in interviews that: "I wanted to do something with a cast of thousands, and not worry how long it was. I wanted to write a big novel, something epic in scale" (Kirschling). It was Jordan's *Wheel of Time* sequence that made such a goal possible. And while Jordan's work tends to be largely uncritical of fantastic conventions, Mendlesohn notes that its predecessor, *The Belgariad*, has "acerbic comments to make about feudalism" (*Short History* 121). Both writers have essentially paved the way for a dark fantasy epic like *A Song of Ice and Fire*.

Martin also cites the author Maurice Druon as an important influence, and indeed he echoes a number of stylistic elements visible in Druon's literary-historical series about the Hundred Years War—*Les Rois Maudits*/*The Accursed Kings*. Druon incorporates multiple points of view, including Queen Isabella (who shares certain personality traits with Cersei), and Jacques Molay, the disgraced Grand Master of the Knights Templar, who is falsely imprisoned. While Molay bides his time in the dungeon, he whispers to God the names of his accusers—"Clément, Guillaume, Philippe"[5]—repeating them over and over, in much the same way that Arya repeats the names of those she wishes were dead. Since the medieval cultures of Westeros tend to mirror the high middle ages, the Hundred Years War serves as a fitting analogue for Martin's world as well. Yet the

War of the Roses is generally cited as the inspiration for *A Game of Thrones*, and Shakespeare scholar Jessica Walker, in her chapter "'Just songs in the end': Historical Discourses in Shakespeare and Martin," provides a novel take on that inspiration, reading not history itself but Shakespeare's history plays, particularly the Henriad cycles, as the key sources for Martin's appropriation of the Wars of the Roses. Here, too, the question of knowing comes into play, as Walker focuses on how these texts retell, and comment on their own retelling of, a nation's history. Like Michail Zontos, for whom the critical historical encounter of *A Song of Ice and Fire* is not the battle between the Yorkists and the Lancastrians but the shifting borderline of the American frontier, Walker sees Martin's history as a kind of historiography, an encounter in and of the text. For Zontos, however, the historical text is Frederick Jackson Turner's proclamation of the frontier thesis in 1893, and in reading Martin's epic in terms of a dwindling civilization and a robustly primitive frontier, Zontos accounts for what he terms the essential Americanness of *A Song of Ice and Fire*.

Maurice Druon also presents Edward II's relationship with Piers Gaveston in an overt (if not entirely sympathetic) manner, which set something of a precedent for the inclusion of homosexuality within popular historical literature. Although not nearly as nuanced as Marguerite Yourcenar's treatment of Hadrian, Druon's conflicted portrayal of Edward II is perhaps an early analogue to a character such as Renly Baratheon, proving that alternative sexualities do exist within the feudal economy. Nor are some of these sexualities, and the economy they reproduce, necessarily palatable to modern sensibilities. D. Marcel DeCoste has provided an important analysis of Craster and his daughter-wives, suggesting in "Beyond the Pale? Craster and the Pathological Reproduction of Houses in Westeros" that Craster's self-reproduction and destructive culling of his own offspring discloses the true economy of Westeros as a near-universal social narcissism. Identity in Martin's medievalist universe is bound up, as it was in the middle ages themselves, with kinship, and the incest that DeCoste argues characterizes the great Houses can thus be understood in terms of the tyranny of kin, a view that can only be countered by the fraternal bonds of the Night's Watch and of the order of the maesters.

Charles H. Hackney examines a different sort of order, the order of chivalry, in his essay "'Silk ribbons tied around a sword': Knighthood and the Chivalric Virtues in Westeros." He notes that while it could be argued that George R.R. Martin presents chivalry purely as a failed ethical ideal, he sees instead a slow decline, a hollowing-out, of the knightly virtues, so that in the end most of the noble sers are devoted not to service but to cynical self-advancement. Yet several characters for whom chivalry is not yet entirely dead—Brienne, Davos, Barristan, even Jaime Lannister—hint that in the end these ideals may not be entirely lost.

David C. Nel, in "Sex and the Citadel: Adapting Same Sex Desire from Martin's Westeros to HBO's Bedrooms," emphasizes, quite differently, the homo-eroticism of the fraternal bond of chivalry, particularly through the character of Ser Loras Tyrell and the Renly/Loras pairing. Visualized by HBO's *Game of Thrones*, this pairing represents a significant amplification of Martin's source-text. A survey of online message boards reveals a lively debate between long-time fans who never suspected that the two characters were involved, and other fans who felt that it was obvious from the very beginning. Much hangs on a short exchange between Loras and Tyrion in *A Storm of Swords*, which is perhaps the only proof of their relationship. Loras explains to Tyrion that, as a third son, he is not pressured "to wed, or breed." Tyrion responds teasingly that "some find it pleasant," and asks, "what of love?" Loras responds: "When the sun has set, no candle can replace it" (*SoS* 13 Tyrion 2: 137). Tyrion mocks Loras for being young and sentimental, but adds: "I had my own love once, and we had a song as well" (137). Although we do not know whom the sun represents, Tyrion's admission does place this occluded romance alongside his own, which is also non-traditional (given that he was in love with Tysha, whom he believes to be a prostitute).

The treatment of gender and sexuality, as well as other modes of identity, in contemporary fantasy literature is varied, and the overlapping genres of science-fiction and fantasy have provided fertile ground for the exploration of identity and diversity. From the early inclusion of gay and gender-variant characters in the work of Marion Zimmer Bradley and Ursula Le Guin, to Mercedes Lackey's treatment of queer and at-risk youth in her urban fantasy novels of the late 1980s, the genre has never conformed wholly to a set of stereotypes. Its medieval roots, after all, are a riot of glorious difference, uncommon bodies, and a polyphony of voices which includes what we would now describe as marginal narratives. Lackey's novel *Magic's Pawn* (1989) was one of the first fantasy novels to include a queer protagonist, the wizard Vanyel, who "comes out" within a medieval environment when he is barely sixteen. Following the success of *A Song of Ice and Fire*, and its subtle presentation of the Renly/Loras pairing, Chaz Brenchley wrote about an erotic relationship between a knight and his squire in *Tower of the King's Daughter* (2000). Lynn Flewelling has also written about a charismatic queer thief, Seregil, in *Luck in the Shadows* (1996).

Martin's series has been both celebrated and criticized for its treatment of sexuality, which is all the more prominent on HBO's *Game of Thrones*. The show incorporates a variety of non-canonical sex scenes (Renly/Loras), in addition to altering canonical scenes (such as Dany's loss of virginity, which the pilot episode renders as non-consensual). The show makes copious use of Littlefinger's brothel, in order to illustrate what it considers to be a medieval economy of sexuality. Recent episodes have also enlarged the scope of the bisexual Prince Oberyn. In "A Bisexual's Requiem for *Game of Thrones,*" C.A. Pinkham calls Oberyn "the most important male bisexual character in TV history." The sexual diversity on the show also takes place within a medieval historical context (with a few creative embellishments). Martin points out that he is "not writing about contemporary sex—it's medieval" (Brown). Although Ned and Catelyn have a companionate marriage, Robert and Cersei do not, and sex within the series remains inseparable from feudal structures of power. These structures do not, however, exclude the possibility of sexual transgression. In an interview with Brent Hartinger, Martin notes: "I try to reflect a whole spectrum of humanity as best I can" (Hartinger). This spectrum includes a variety of characters who are either in same-sex relationships, or who seek out same-sex encounters.

The Renly/Loras pairing is often described as "subtextual" within the novels, but Martin's description points to it as a kind of open secret, easily legible. "I never meant to make it a mystery," he says in an interview. "I like to handle things subtly.... But I thought it was pretty clear in context," and also points out that "there are other gay characters in the books that are villainous or that are bad in various ways ... I try to portray a variety" (Hartinger). Both Cersei and Dany engage in same-sex encounters, and these tend to occur within the interstices of medieval power. Although we have no way of knowing the sexuality of Varys, the eunuch does admit to Tyrion that he worked as a prostitute on the streets of Myr ("I sold what parts of my body still remained to me" [*CoK* 45 Tyrion 10: 486]). In *A Storm of Swords,* while informing Tyrion of Cersei's flirtations, Varys asks: "What would a eunuch know of such things?" Then: "The tip of his tongue ran across his lower lip like a shy pink animal" (*SoS* 13 Tyrion 2: 135). Varys eludes categories, and indeed this may be the key to his power.

Daenerys Targaryen, mother of dragons, is also a category-defying grotesque, according to Karin Gresham's "Cursed Womb, Bulging Thighs and Bald Scalp: George R.R. Martin's Grotesque Queen." Reading Dany through Russian theorist Mikhail Bakhtin's theory of grotesque realism, Gresham sees Dany as emblematic of Martin's redefinition of the heroic: both monstrous and mother, leader and other. And in "'A thousand bloodstained hands': The Malleability of Flesh and Identity," Beth Kozinsky documents the powerful figuration of the multiplicity of identity in Martin's characters through disfigurement and disability, particularly through the amputation of hands. The medieval world from which Martin draws, she notes, offers numerous examples of lost hands, notably as punishment for thievery or treason; this medieval idea of physical retribution, the writing of punishment on the body, becomes for Martin a way of articulating, or indeed assigning, identity.

The series also presents us with Brienne of Tarth, a female knight whose disruption of medieval gender invites ruthless mockery, as well as threats of sexual violence. Jaime Lannister is particularly cruel to her (it doesn't help that she defeats him in battle). He is amused by her unrequited love for Renly. In "Dark Wings, Dark Words" (S3: Ep.2), Jaime tells Brienne that "you weren't [Renly's] type, I'm afraid. He preferred curly-haired little girls, like Loras Tyrell." It's important to note that while Renly's same-sex desire is never made explicit in the novels, HBO's *Game of Thrones* presents it as common knowledge. Yet Jaime, in this scene, realizes that he has gone too far. He relents by saying: "We can't choose who we love." This enigmatic comment might refer to Brienne, to Renly, or to Jaime himself, who has only ever loved his sister. The show chooses to soften this moment, largely due to its collapsed time-frame, and the need to accelerate Jaime's transformation as a character. Here, we see another gap in knowledge: Jaime's somewhat generous comment is mediated by his own proscribed desires, which Brienne cannot know first-hand. Martin's diversity of perspectives reminds us that the game of thrones is also a game of knowing, a puzzling chain of views that are sometimes linked, but which often fail to make contact at crucial points, just as our own perspective as readers cannot possibly hold everything together.

Perspective, and its link to identity, comes to the fore in T.A. Leederman's "A Thousand Westerosi Plateaus: Wargs, Wolves and Ways of Being." Following Deleuze and Guattari, Leederman suggests that the Stark children's construction of wolf selves lets them apprehend themselves as part of something larger, connected over the land, and indeed, as in the case of Bran's greensinging, connected through it. Such connections change our perspectives as they change our ways of being in the world, and provide the last, best hope for driving back the Long Night, even as those who refuse to open themselves to others and to other ways of being have risked the end of all the world.

This idea of limitations in our perspectives is significant, particularly as Martin studies moves from the online world of the fan to the more rigorously patrolled terrain of the classroom; for whatever else it may be, teaching is also, and always, an exercise in the limitations of what we ourselves can know, and how we know it. Thus, for example, when in September of 2012, the University of Regina offered a senior single-author course in George R.R. Martin—a course in *A Song of Ice and Fire*—professor Susan Johnston described the class as "dancing without a net": so few models were available, so few sources, and the primary "text" itself, Martin's epic series, was unfinished. It was not the first such course; that summer, Drexel University's Donald Riggs had offered an honors seminar in *A Game of Thrones*: part influence study, part adaptation study, part close reading. By fall 2013, similar courses were available at the University of Texas at Austin, the University of North Florida, and California State University

Sacramento. In Sacramento particularly, Susan Fanetti's students exceeded the cap on a senior seminar class by 50 percent for the chance to examine the first three books and the first two television seasons of the HBO series through the lens of fan studies as well as Marxist and feminist literary criticism. Elsewhere, courses in medieval literature and history were being tied to HBO's *Game of Thrones* or to Martin's work as professors sought to capitalize on renewed interest in their areas, as with Oxford University's announcement of an online history course for 2015, entitled "From Westeros to Westminster: *Game of Thrones* and English History." Here too the work of this book intersects with the broader world of Martin studies, for in the classroom, as in this volume, scholarship in a variety of disciplines intersects with fandom: at the University of Regina, that first George R.R. Martin course was attended by a front page story in the local paper (Graney) and followed by a student-run, one-day Conference of Ice and Fire in February 2013, at which both editors were in attendance.

We may say, in other words, that Martin studies has entered that precarious but thrilling space of aca-fandom (Jenkins, *Confessions*) in which "popular culture demands our passionate engagement and active participation" (Jenkins, McPherson, and Shattuc 6)—our fandom—but also our discipline, our research, our scholarship (Coker and Benefiel). And while we don't mean to take up here the cudgels on either side of the debate over the very idea of "aca-fandom," it is nonetheless true that our very project is informed by a sense of our own positioning as scholars in love with our subject, and our longing to speak in these pages to others who love what we do. This is, we hope, valuable in particular because as yet the field of Martin studies has been dominated by the fan rather than the academic, and, as teachers of the newly minted Martin courses are discovering, in consequence the resources available to students and faculty are simultaneously voluminous—websites like *Tower of the Hand* and the *Wiki of Ice and Fire*—and very sparse indeed, with very few articles as yet appearing in the traditional refereed journals of academe. This may, indeed, be all to the good: fandom, like aca-fandom, may have reason to fear co-optation by the tweedy hordes,[6] but at the same time we may say that the role of the academy is memory: what survives, survives not just because its cult status as the loved object allows it to become real (Jenkins, *Textual Poachers* esp. 50–85), but because its academic status makes it part of that institutional memory of "lost causes, and forsaken beliefs, and unpopular names, and impossible loyalties!" (Arnold xi). Indeed, we agree with Jenkins that the importance of the aca-fan is, in this way, less the bridging of two worlds, but the multivalence with which we come to the text. Like this book, the aca-fan must do the policing in different voices if we are to be heard by both, or either.

In this sense, if *Mastering the Game of Thrones* has been a lesson in humility, it has also been a lesson in translation. We come to this project in Season Four of HBO's game-changing *Game of Thrones*. If Peter Jackson's epic three-part treatment of Tolkien's *The Lord of the Rings* was, as Bogstad and Keveny remark, the "'gold standard' for Tolkien's cinematic presence" (Bogstad and Kaveny 8), it also transformed the practice of adaptation through its capacious trilogic form—though even there the films are marked and even marred, for fans and scholars alike, by the compressions, abridgements, elisions, and exclusions, for "even ten hours of screen time [are] insufficient to convey all the story, setting, characters, and incidents in Tolkien's twelve hundred pages" (Rateliff 54). George R.R. Martin recalls knowing that Jackson's approach couldn't work for his own series:

> Huge castles, vast dramatic landscapes, deserts and mountains and swamps, dragons, dire-wolves, gigantic battles with thousands to a side, glittering armor, gorgeous heraldry, swordfights and tournaments, characters who were complicated, conflicted, flawed, a whole imaginary world and a cast of thousands. Absolutely unfilmable, of course [Martin 5].

Showrunners David Benioff and D.B. Weiss, whom Martin describes as "brave men or mad men" (4), however, refused to believe it was impossible—and convinced HBO. They took ten hours of screen time in the first two seasons to render the first two books, and in Season Three departed from this highly successful formula to show roughly half of Martin's 924-page *A Storm of Swords* in the same ten hours, treating the second half in Season Four. Only such scope could begin to do justice to Martin's epic world, though it did not, of course, elide entirely the problem of translation from page to screen. Zack Handlen et al., in the wake of Season Four's controversial fourth episode, "Oathkeeper," have worked to document the major differences between page and small screen, some of which are the inevitable result of moving from text to television. Benioff, speaking of the wildly expensive "Blackwater" (S2: Ep.9), remarks that

> we went pleading to HBO for more money. We made our case why we needed the battle and they obliged. That allowed us to do a battle. It did not allow us to do the battle from *A Clash of Kings*. It would be difficult for a $200 million feature to do justice to the battle from the book [Hibberd, "Game of Thrones"].

If "Blackwater" did not do justice to the battle from the book, though, it has done justice to Martin's books and Martin's vision. David Benioff insists, "We fell in love with the books. We fell in love with the world [Martin] created, with the sprawl of Westeros and Essos. ... We fell in love with the brutality of the narrative" (Cogman, "Seven Questions" 7). And their professed goal? "We're going to make viewers all over the world fall in love with these characters" (Benioff, qtd. in Cogman, "Epilogue" 192). This they have done. Indeed, as the audience has grown—in Season Three, to an average of 4.9 million viewers, approximately double the 2.5 million who tuned in during the first season, in 2011, and which, by the time all the viewing numbers, from PVR playbacks to HBO streaming, are in, reaches 13.6 million *per episode* (Adalian)—it has evinced exactly the passionate engagement Benioff and Weiss sought. In part this is because the showrunners have succeeded in retaining mystery as a central experience of the ice and fire story, even, astonishingly, for those who know the books so well. We, too, know nothing, in the face of such "faithful departures" as the delayed introduction of Jojen and Meera Reed, the presence of Robb Stark's wife at the Red Wedding, or "Oathkeeper's" dramatic reveal of the fates of Craster's sons.

And as Andrew Howe and Zoë Shacklock argue in this volume, the adaptation of and participation in the Martinverse, the world of ice and fire, is not restricted to the one-way transmission of page to screen. Examining the representation of central characters in fan art from aesthetic, cultural, political, and economic points of view in "The Hand of the Artist: Fan Art in the Martinverse," Howe explores the differences between the fan art associated with the novels and with the "cult of images" that arose with the success of HBO's *Game of Thrones*. As Shacklock shows in "'A reader lives a thousand lives before he dies': Transmedia Textuality and the Flows of Adaptation," the thousand lives of Martin's narrative, and its afterlives, are not limited to text or television, but multiply endlessly through the active readings of the fan audience. As she observes, such adaptation practices insist that we re-examine the politics of adaptation and of fan engagement, particularly as that engagement is in part driven by the social marketing of HBO. In this sense do we engage the material culture of fandom, from fan art to YouTube mashups and parodies to *Thrones*-inspired medieval feasts, which testifies to the way the world of ice and fire "sticks to the skin" (Jenkins, McPherson, and Shattuc). Working in this emergent field, then, we hope that this book will become part of the open and participatory reception of *A Song of Ice and Fire*, reception that in a new world of new media, of show-firsters and book-firsters and, indeed, meme-firsters, seeks to cut across the profound epistemological gaps of both critic and fan to travel joyfully through to Martin's much-anticipated ending.

Notes

1. When Mercedes Lackey was beginning her career as a fantasist, Cherryh advised her to "commit trilogy" with her work (Lackey, "Mercedes Lackey").

2. At the time of this volume's publication, it is rumored that the HBO series will continue for seven to eight seasons (Windolf). As it's still unclear when the print series will end, the possibilities for reversing our own expectations seem endless.

3. In a recent interview with *The Guardian* (June 3, 2014), Martin's editor Anne Groell

states: "7 [books] is what we currently have under contract.... When I have a [publication] date, you will have a date" (Beaumont-Thomas). It is also suggested in this article that Martin could release an eighth book.

4. Another example is the *Kushiel's Legacy* series (2001–11), by Jacqueline Carey, which followed on the heels of *ASoIaF*. In many ways, Carey's series is an erotic adaptation of Martin's work. She also employs an unstable political backdrop, although this tends to give way to a focus on the relationships between her characters. Rather than serving as feudal communities, her "houses" are enclaves of sex-workers, each adopting a particular specialty in accordance with her world's quasi–Semitic religion of *Naamah*.

5. "'Seigneur mon Dieu, donnez-mois la force,' murmurait-il, intérieurement ... 'donnez-mois un peu de force.' Et pour trouver cette force, il se répétait les noms de ses trois ennemis: 'Clément, Guillaume, Philippe'" ["'O Lord my God, give me strength,' he whispered to himself ... 'give me a little strength.' And to find that strength, he repeated the names of his three enemies: 'Clément, Guillaume, Philippe'"—trans. S. Johnston] (Druon 44).

6. Mark Sample remarks, "A musicologist friend of mine has attended every Slayage conference since the inaugural *Buffy the Vampire Slayer* conference in 2004. The first several years were huge, drawing academics and fans alike, both groups often dressed in *Buffy*-inspired costumes. Every year, however, the conference shrinks, and the attendees in 2010 were mostly media scholars, wearing that strangest of costumes, tweed."

Works Cited

Adalian, Josef. "For HBO, *Game of Thrones* Ratings Second Only to *The Sopranos*." 6 June 2013. *Vulture*. Web. 20 June 2013.

Arnold, Matthew. *Essays in Criticism, First Series*. London: Macmillan, 1902. Print.

Beaumont-Thomas, Ben. "George R.R. Martin's editor hints at eighth *Game of Thrones* book." *Theguardian.com*. 3 June 2014. Web. 26 June 2014.

Bogstad, Janice M., and Philip E. Kaveny. "Introduction." *Picturing Tolkien: Essays on Peter Jackson's The Lord of the Tings Film Trilogy*. Ed. Janice M. Bogstad and Philip E. Kaveny. Jefferson, NC: McFarland, 2011. 5–23. Print.

Brenchley, Chaz. *Tower of the King's Daughter*. London: Orbit, 2000. Print.

Brown, Rachel. "George R.R. Martin on Sex, Fantasy, and *A Dance With Dragons*." Interview. *The Atlantic*. 11 July 2011. Web. 20 June 2013.

Carey, Jacqueline. *Kushiel's Dart*. New York: Tor, 2001. Print.

Cogman, Bryan. "Epilogue: Reflections on *Game of Thrones*." *Inside HBO's Game of Thrones*. By Cogman. San Francisco: Chronicle Books, 2012. 190–92. Print.

____. "Seven Questions with David Benioff and D.B. Weiss." Interview. *Inside HBO's Game of Thrones*. By Cogman. San Francisco: Chronicle Books, 2012. 6–7. Print.

Coker, Catherine, and Candace Benefiel. "We Have Met the Fans, and They Are Us: In Defense of Aca-Fans and Scholars." *Flowtv* 13.5 (2010): 3 pp. 17 December 2010. Web. 6 June 2013.

Druon, Maurice. *Le roi de fer*. Paris: Del Duca, 1955. Print.

Eddings, David. *Pawn of Prophecy*. New York: Del Rey, 1982. Print.

Flewelling, Lynn, and Gary Ruddell. *Luck in the Shadows*. New York: Bantam Spectra, 1996. Print.

Graney, Emma. "Game of Thrones Enters Academia." *Leader Post*. 9 June 2012. A1. Print.

Handlen, Zack, Rowan Kaiser, Todd VanDerWuff, Myles McNutt and Sonia Saraiya. "'Well, actually, in the books...': 15 Differences from Text to TV in *Game of Thrones*." *A.V. Club*. 28 April 2014. Web. 30 May 2014.

Hartinger, Brent. "Gays Go Medieval in Upcoming *A Game of Thrones* Fantasy Series." *The Backlot: Logo Online*. 19 January 2011. Web. 26 June 2014.

Hibberd, James. "The Fantasy King." *Entertainment Weekly* 1165 (29 July 2011): 44–6. Print.

_____. "*Game of Thrones*: Blackwater Battle has 'dramatically exceeded our expectations.'" *EW.com*. Interview. 20 May 2012. Web. 26 June 2014.

Hills, Matt. "'Proper Distance' in the Ethical Positioning of Scholar-Fandoms: Between Academics' and Fans' Moral Economies?" *Fan Culture: Theory/Practice*. Ed. Katherine Larsen and Lynn Zubernis. Newcastle: Cambridge Scholars, 2012. 14–37. Print.

Hodgman, John. "George R.R. Martin, Author of *A Song of Ice and Fire* Series." Interview. *The Sound of Young America*. Transcribed by Sean Sampson. 19 September 2011. Web. 8 September 2012.

Ippolito, Toni-Marie. "George R.R. Martin Talks to Fans About the Making of Game of Thrones and What Inspired His Best-selling Book Series." Interview. *The Lifestyle Report*. 13 March 2012. Web. 20 September 2012.

Jenkins, Henry. *Confessions of an Aca-Fan*. Blog. 2006–2014. Web. 20 June 2013.

_____. *Textual Poachers: Television Fans and Participatory Culture*. London: Routledge, 1992. Print.

Jenkins, Henry, Tara McPherson and Jane Shattuc. "The Culture That Sticks to Your Skin: A Manifesto for a New Cultural Studies." *Hop on Pop: The Politics and Pleasures of Popular Culture*. Ed. Henry Jenkins, Tara McPherson and Jane Shattuc. Durham: Duke University Press, 2002. 3–26. Print.

Jordan, Robert. *The Shadow Rising*. New York: Tor, 1992.

Kirschling, Gregory. "By George!" Interview with George R.R. Martin. *EW.com*. 27 November 2007. Web. 6 September 2012.

Lackey, Mercedes. *Magic's Pawn*. New York: Daw Books, 1989. Print.

_____. "Mercedes Lackey." Author Biography. *Penguin Group*. 2001. Web. 26 June 2013.

Martin, George R.R. "Preface: From Page to Screen." *Inside HBO's Game of Thrones*. By Bryan Cogman. San Francisco: Chronicle Books, 2012. 4–5. Print.

Mendlesohn, Farah. *Rhetorics of Fantasy*. Middletown, CT: Wesleyan University Press, 2008. Print.

Mendlesohn, Farah, and Edward James. *A Short History of Fantasy*. London: Middlesex University Press, 2009. Print.

Pinkham, C.A. "A Bisexual's Requiem for *Game of Thrones*." *Jezebel.com*. 2 June 2014. Web. 26 June 2014.

Rateliff, John D. "Two Kinds of Absence: Elision and Exclusion in Peter Jackson's *The Lord of the Rings*." *Picturing Tolkien: Essays on Peter Jackson's The Lord of the Rings Trilogy*. Ed. Janice M. Bogstad and Philip E. Kaveny. Jefferson, NC: McFarland, 2011. 54–69. Print.

Sample, Mark. "Comment # 59508 RE: Ian Bogost—Against Aca-Fandom." *Bogost.com*. 29 July 2010. Web. 23 June 2013.

Todorov, Tzvetan. *The Fantastic: A Structural Approach to a Literary Genre*. Trans. Robert Scholes. Ithaca: Cornell University Press, 1975. Print.

Windolf, Jim. "The Gathering Storm." *Vanityfair.com*. April 2014. Web. 26 June 2014.

LANGUAGE AND NARRATION

The Languages of Ice and Fire[1]

DAVID J. PETERSON

"The language of Pao was derived from Waydalic, but molded into peculiar forms"—Jack Vance, *The Languages of Pao* (6)

Jack Vance was an idol of George R.R. Martin's, and his influence on Martin's style is evident. In *The Languages of Pao*, Vance sets up a test case for the Sapir-Whorf hypothesis, which suggests that consciousness is structured by language: a single, invariant culture for a planet of nine billion people, all of whom speak the same language. Though these conditions had to hold for the experiment to work, many science fiction and fantasy writers have unwittingly followed suit when it comes to language. The various planets of the *Star Trek* universe are some of the more salient examples, where the crew of the *Enterprise* (or *Voyager*) encounters planet after planet of homogenous beings who all have one culture, one government, one religion, and one style of dress—and who, of course, all speak the same language (usually rendered as English, thanks to the fantastical Universal Translator). In a word, the result is unnatural.

Part of what distinguishes a natural language[2] from other non-natural or non-human languages (computer languages, auxiliary languages like Esperanto, animal communication systems, etc.) is the way in which natural languages evolve and adapt based on the needs of their communities of speakers. Natural languages are replete with irregularities (e.g., goose~geese vs. block~blocks), but these irregularities aren't random: they can be explained by examining the history of the language. A naturalistic created language is one that tries to mimic this evolution. It's not something that had been done with any language created for a show or film (Pakuni for *Land of the Lost*, Klingon for *Star Trek* or Na'vi for *Avatar*), but it's something that's existed within the constructed languages community for quite some time.

It's an approach that comes from a long tradition beginning with Tolkien (amongst documented examples), and I learned what I know from the members of the Conlang Listserv, an e-mail-based forum whose membership comprised the first online language creation community. Standouts from the community who've worked in the naturalist tradition include pioneers like Matt Pearson, Sylvia Sotomayor, Doug Ball, David Bell, Jan van Steenbergen, Christophe Grandsire-Koevoets, Andrew Smith and Henrik Theiling, among many, many others.

The dictates of naturalism hold that nothing in the language be purely "off the cuff." Every word, every grammatical change, every sound change must be grounded in sound evolutionary principles—and the same is supposed to hold for the culture and world the language inhabits.

Yet, in the realm of science fiction, one might allow for a little leeway. After all, though at present our planet's residents speak between six and seven thousand languages (depending on whose estimates one reads), the number of languages is decreasing daily, and who knows if two or three thousand years from now we'll be left with but one language that everyone on Earth will speak? It's a possibility, and one science fiction writers should feel free to explore. Fantasy, though, tends to look backward—especially the subgenres of high fantasy (or epic fantasy) and historic fantasy. Whether it's to a familiar place with unfamiliar characters, or to a place that might have been had things gone differently in a bygone era, fantasy, as a genre, tends to focus on times before the present. In fantasy one might expect to find an exploration and proliferation of linguistic diversity—especially given the influence of the works of J.R.R. Tolkien. Instead, one often finds exactly the opposite.

One of the more common tropes in fantasy is the language of the protagonist and the protagonist's people versus the language of the Other. In Jennifer Roberson's *Shapechangers*, the protagonist Alix comes from a fair-skinned people whose culture mirrors the kind of idealized medieval English culture seen often in fantasy, who speak Common. She is abducted by a brutish race of dark-skinned shapeshifters called the Cheysuli who speak a language called Cheysuli, replete with harsh-seeming consonants and apostrophes. As far as the reader knows, though, these are the only two languages that exist in the world (that is, until another nation or people is introduced, in which case the number of languages will increase by one).

On Earth, the situation is rarely that simple. Some languages span broad expanses, with little or no current cultural or geographic ties between their various speakers (consider English, a first language of many in the United States, Canada, the United Kingdom, Ireland, India, Australia, New Zealand and Pakistan, among others). Conversely, most countries are home to at least two languages spoken by at least a plurality of its citizens—some, like Papua New Guinea, boasting more than 800 (Lewis). And though the number of languages on Earth is decreasing as we move forward in time, the linguistic diversity described herein increases the further back in time one goes. A fantasy realm which, in other important respects, appears to mirror (or mimic) many of the traits of our world at a time in the distant past ought to be expected to reproduce this linguistic diversity.

In many ways, George R.R. Martin's *A Song of Ice and Fire* series seeks to subvert many of the tropes prevalent in the epic fantasy series of the latter half of the twentieth century. In *A Game of Thrones*, several characters meet with bad ends, but the one character readers are trained to identify as the hero—Eddard "Ned" Stark, the one whose cause is always righteous, and whose missteps are the result of ill fortune or adherence to a Western sense of honor—appears to be safe. If allies of Eddard are felled by their enemies, the reader can be assured that, at the very least, the hero Ned will survive and ultimately exact vengeance. Martin pushes the reader's faith to its limit when Ned is executed by the arbitrary young king Joffrey—an act which shocks and horrifies even the king's own supporters. The lesson here (one of many Martin teaches his readers) is multifaceted. First, Martin demonstrates his understanding of the tropes of the genre—tropes which must be familiar to the reader to produce the desired effect. These tropes, as Martin shows us, are common ground, known even to his characters, as Sansa Stark, a kind of avatar for the reader, makes clear in her reactions to the action of the plot. Like Sansa, the reader learns that traditional expectations will not be borne out in *A Song of Ice and Fire*. By acknowledging the trope, though, Martin shows the reader that their instincts did not, in fact, betray them. That is, there isn't a strong argument that Eddard Stark was, in fact, the antagonist the whole time, and that the reader was being tricked into believing he was the hero. Martin wants the reader to feel betrayed—to feel that, indeed, something very wrong has happened.

The most important element in this lesson is one of realism, or authenticity. By its very nature, fantasy is supposed to be unreal, but unreal in what sense? Fantasy literature often takes impossible elements, be they unreal beings (elves, ogres, trolls), unreal beasts (dragons, unicorns, gryphons), unreal forces (magic, telepathy, midichlorians) or unreal places (Atlantis, Avalon, Lilliput), and builds a story around them. Tolkien held that the "fairy-story" defies usual convention—that it is the product of a land where almost anything goes, save that "the magic itself ... must ... be taken seriously, neither laughed at nor explained away" (*Reader* 10). Martin's world features unreal beasts, unreal beings, unreal forces, and a bit of the indescribable, but otherwise the action involves humans not unlike the humans of our world, and a world that's not unlike ours. The fantasy of *A Song of Ice and Fire*, then, is confined to the setting. The scope of the series allows Martin to present quite a different argument: That sometimes truly terrible things happen, and that, despite this misfortune, the course of history moves inexorably forward. As a result, though *A Song of Ice and Fire* is a work of fantasy, fantasy has been banished from the plot (i.e., fantasies prevalent in older works[3] like the righteous always triumph over the wicked, or that events can always be interpreted as objectively good or objectively bad).

The level of authenticity present in the series extends to the linguistic diversity of the peoples of Westeros and Essos. Though George R.R. Martin has stated on numerous occasions that he isn't a language creator and didn't set out to create any of the languages in his work, the fictional status of the languages in *A Song of Ice and Fire* bespeaks a complexity not found in many comparable works of fantasy. Indeed, though Martin created no languages, he did create language families. Based mainly on the spread of Indo-European languages, Martin has a working knowledge of how many of the languages mentioned in *A Song of Ice and Fire* evolved, where they evolved from, and where they spread to. The most developed of these families is the Valyrian family of languages, which Martin based on Romance.

High Valyrian (akin to Latin), the language of the Valyrian Empire, sits at the top of the Valyrian family tree. Some five thousand years before the action of the novels, the Valyrian Empire laid waste to and overran the Ghiscari Empire to the east, supplanting the language there (Ghiscari) with High Valyrian. Over

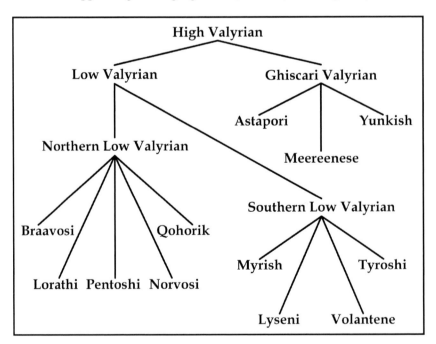

Figure 1: A potential sketch of the Valyrian language family.

the centuries, High Valyrian evolved into Low Valyrian within the empire, and the High Valyrian of the Ghiscari Empire itself evolved, mixing partially with the Ghiscari language, the result likely resembling a creole language with High Valyrian as its main superstrate, and Ghiscari its substrate. Valyria's Low Valyrian, then, was spread to the Free Cities to the north and west, producing other mixed languages akin to modern Romance languages (French, Spanish, Italian, Catalan, Romanian, etc.). Even though the details of these languages were never worked out, their presence is remarked upon, and the details of the evolution were planned. It's true that they mirror the spread of the Romance languages almost exactly, but the mere presence of a detailed language history elevates *A Song of Ice and Fire* above comparable works in regard to language (a notable exception, of course, being Tolkien).

Given the detailed histories—linguistic or otherwise—present in *A Song of Ice and Fire*, a new reader could be excused for believing that George R.R. Martin has boxes stuffed with files detailing the histories of every family of Westeros and Essos, every war that's ever taken place, every plant and animal that exists or has existed in the past—and that he's created every single language mentioned in the books. Such a thing certainly wouldn't be unprecedented. J.R.R. Tolkien created an entire language family, complete with phonological and semantic changes, detailed grammars, and loads of lexical entries well before he ever wrote his first book set in Middle Earth. Though they share a pair of middle initials, Martin differs from Tolkien sharply in this regard. Though Tolkien wrote "To me a name comes first and the story follows" (*Letters* 233), Martin believes the story comes first, and that all other elements should bow to it. Of High Valyrian, for example, Martin once famously wrote (in response to an e-mail request from a fan), "[A]ll I know about High Valyrian is the seven words I've made up to date. When I need an eighth, I'll make that up too" (*Not a Blog*). The bits of language used in the books, along with the numerous references made to other languages and language families, are there to serve one of the primary goals of the work as a whole: to establish the authenticity of an otherwise fantastical realm. To this end, the references are well placed and well researched. Though some of Martin's fans would be disappointed to learn that there isn't a High Valyrian grammar sitting in his desk drawer, even a linguistically-minded reader such as myself will vouch that what elements there are contribute to the larger creation, and the fact that they don't spring from a larger linguistic work doesn't detract from the series in any way.

A unique problem arose when David Benioff and Dan Weiss's pilot for their adaptation of Martin's *A Game of Thrones* got the green light from HBO. The pilot was to feature action from the book's first two Daenerys chapters: The sale and marriage of Daenerys to Khal Drogo. And while in the books

Martin, as author, has the power of narrative convention to focus the reader's attention where he will, and to pass over non–English phrases in the course of narration, the camera has a much wider scope. In order to create a believable setting, Benioff and Weiss needed to have an actual Dothraki language to draw from. When they learned that Martin had created nothing of Dothraki beyond what was in the books, they realized they were in a bit of a bind.

On the face of it—and in a different era—this reality might have posed no problem at all. As late as 1967, it was still considered uncontroversial for non–Chinese actors to play Chinese characters in film, and for their language to be rendered as utter gibberish (as evidenced by *Thoroughly Modern Millie*). For an entirely fictional race speaking an entirely fictional language (in more than one sense), who could possibly be offended by the actors speaking gibberish—or even accented English?

As it turns out, the problem proves to be much more complex than it seems. In order to delve into the issues behind it, I'd like to examine the potential avenues open to Benioff and Weiss when they were faced with the problem of creating Dothraki dialogue.

First, consider one option that gets raised any time a language is needed for a fictional people in a television show or film: Why not have them speak some non–English language? A majority of English-speaking viewers can't tell the difference between Turkish, Georgian, Thai and gibberish. It's simple enough to find a translator, as there are millions of speakers of any number of natural languages spoken on Earth, which would mean translating dialogue—and voice coaching—would pose no real problem. And, if the production is popular, it might raise awareness of the language and its speakers.

With Dothraki, the prospect of using a natural language as a stand-in raises one important question: Which language? How one answers this question may betray one's own linguistic biases. The bits of language Martin devised were intended to be harsh-sounding (or harsh-seeming, as the language appears in print), but what does "harsh-sounding" mean? To an English speaker, it often means a language that makes use of a number of "throaty" consonants—roughly, fricatives and approximants whose points of contact in the vocal tract are the velum, the uvula and the pharynx, none of which exist in English (one of the keys to understanding what "harsh-sounding" means to a speaker of a given language). In choosing a natural language to stand in for Dothraki, Arabic would seem to fit the bill—or if Arabic seemed too familiar, Tashelhit Berber.

But if Benioff and Weiss were to choose a natural language to use as Dothraki, what would it say about that language and those people? Martin's Dothraki are portrayed as a violent, warlike people. They steal what they will and rape who they will, and do so often, in the course of the story. In the pilot episode, in fact, there is an extremely controversial change from the book, whereby Daenerys, after being sold and forced to marry Khal Drogo, is raped by her new husband (in the book, the act is, according to most readings, consensual). It would seem, at the least, culturally insensitive, and at the most, downright offensive to have the only occurrence of a non–English natural language in the show be introduced by such acts. Whatever the language chosen, the resulting controversy that would have arisen after the very first episode aired would have drawn unwanted—and avoidable—negative attention to the series. Perhaps there might be a television show that could successfully appropriate the language of a human society for use with a fictional race, but *Game of Thrones* was simply not that show.

Of course, if the Dothraki weren't going to be speaking a non–English language, what's wrong with English? The pros should be evident enough. If the Dothraki spoke English, there would be no need for subtitles: English-speaking fans would be able to follow all the action. Having the Dothraki actors speak English would cut down on translation costs, freeing up that area of the budget for other things.

The first problem with this approach is the same problem raised by using a non–English natural language. There is no such thing as unaccented English. If the Dothraki were to speak English, which accent would they use? Dialect coach Brendan Gunn worked closely with the actors portraying Westerosi characters to help them develop regional accents (hence, all the characters born in the North sound like they come from the same place, which is distinctly different from those born in the South, etc.). Presumably he could have taught the Dothraki actors to speak English with another accent, but which? An English speaking audience would hardly accept, for example, a standard American accent. It would have to be a "foreign" accent, but were it identifiable, it might very well cause offense.

There's also another snag, and that's verisimilitude. Benioff and Weiss have the utmost respect for Martin's books, and want to do their best to realize his vision of a realistic epic fantasy. Readers of the books would know the Dothraki are supposed to be speaking a different language, and having them simply speak English would tax the credulity of even a new audience. The precedents set by the *Lord of the Rings* film trilogy, and even *The Passion of the Christ*, whose dialogue consists almost entirely of subtitled Aramaic, elevated the expectations of the audience to a significant degree: If a production wished to present itself as authentic, it must be linguistically authentic. Anything less would break the show's Tolkienian sense of "magic"—would distance the audience from the new reality to which they've been introduced. Furthermore, part of the isolation Daenerys suffers from is a direct result of the language barrier. She grows closer to Jorah Mormont and her handmaidens in the early part of the series simply because she's able to talk to them. If Dany were able to converse with Drogo at length in English, that element of the story would be lost.

But this, it turns out, is only half the story. There was another option, of course, that would have satisfied all objections raised thus far: The actors could have spoken gibberish. Using the key phrases Martin included in the books where they were necessary, the actors or the writers could have come up with some language-like utterances on the spot and passed that off as Dothraki. True, the audience may have cried foul, but if it didn't interfere with the flow of the show, it could have worked. And this is, in fact, precisely what Benioff and Weiss tried at first.

What came next, though, is the truly astonishing part. Well before the pilot began and audience concerns were even taken into consideration, Benioff and Weiss decided that using gibberish for the Dothraki language was *artistically unsatisfactory*. The concern wasn't necessarily that using gibberish wouldn't be authentic enough, or that the audience wouldn't accept it, or anything of the kind: it simply didn't sound right. It didn't fit their artistic vision for the show. It was at this point that the other options (and other drawbacks) came into play, and Benioff and Weiss decided that the safest and most artistically satisfactory solution was to hire someone to create an actual Dothraki language to use in translation.

When Benioff and Weiss first decided they wanted a full Dothraki language, they weren't sure where to turn. This has been the case with every major language construction project for a production (Pakuni, Klingon, Na'vi, Kryptonian, etc.), but unlike their predecessors, who blindly reached out to nearby linguistics departments, Benioff and Weiss had a lead. In May of 2009, Arika Okrent published her book *In the Land of Invented Languages*, and it made a bit of press—enough to catch Benioff and Weiss's attention. Instead of turning to a linguistics department, then, they sought her out. Okrent, in turn, sent them to the Language Creation Society (LCS), sponsor of the Second Language Creation Conference in 2007 which Okrent had attended. This led to the LCS-sponsored contest from which, ultimately, my Dothraki proposal was selected by the producers amongst an initial pool of about thirty applicants.

In constructing the language itself, I was operating under a series of constraints (both linguistic and otherwise), each of which contributed in an important way to the final product. Having been a language creator (or conlanger) for a decade, I was well familiar with the linguistic challenges one faces in creating a new language. The challenges posed by working on a television show which itself is an adaptation of an existing book series were entirely new to me, though.

The first challenge I faced was creating what was, essentially, a conlang adaptation. The Dothraki language is supposed to exist within the universe of *A Song of Ice and Fire*, but the only pieces of it we see are a few words, phrases and names spread across the first three books of the series. Given Martin's attitude towards the use of invented languages in his works in general, I likely could have invented a system that was radically different from what was present in the books, so long as it met with the approval of Benioff and Weiss. I decided to take what I view as a more conservative route for a number of reasons.

At the time I joined the project, *Game of Thrones* had had a pilot greenlit by HBO, but there was no guarantee that they would pick up the series. The overwhelming consensus at the time was that a series order was imminent, but still, it wasn't a certainty. What was a certainty was that the books existed and had a huge fanbase—and that the series wasn't finished. If *Game of Thrones* never took off as a series, it would have a viewership within the fan community of *A Song of Ice and Fire*. Furthermore, I felt that the presence of the show would never be capable of diminishing the original fanbase of the book series. As a result, I felt like the best way to ensure the success of the Dothraki language was to design it with the fan community in mind—specifically, the book series' fan community. What would lend legitimacy to the language more than anything else would be if George R.R. Martin himself were to use it in a future book in the series—something that was (and, at the time of writing, remains) a possibility.

Consequently, I felt it was in my best interest to, first and foremost, account for all the material in the books without changing any of it. The more the end product matched the scant material in the books, the better it would be accepted by the fans and Martin himself. In order to achieve this, I first incorporated all the extant vocabulary, and then analyzed the phrases to derive grammar. The first phrase I started with was this one: *Rakh! Rakh! Rakh haj!* This is translated as "A boy! A boy! A strong boy!" (*GoT* 47 Daenerys 5: 410) The only elements repeated three times in both the Dothraki and the English translation are *rakh* and "boy." The easiest solution here is to posit that *rakh*, then, is the word for "boy." This leaves *haj* to correspond with "strong." At this point, a number of things could be said. For example, *rakh haj* could be a binominal compound that simply means "strong boy." *Haj* could be a verb (either finite or a participle), rendering the translation a kind of English paraphrase. *Haj* could in fact be a classifier of some kind that only classifies strong or exceptional objects. The simplest explanation, though, is that *haj* is an adjective, and that adjectives follow the nouns they modify, as happens in Spanish. This is the type of linguistic alternation that would be accessible to one who doesn't have a lot of foreign language experience, and seemed like Martin's most likely intention with the composition of the phrase.

It's important to point out at this juncture that George R.R. Martin didn't have any input in the creation of Dothraki (or subsequent creations like High Valyrian). His input would have been welcome, but both Martin and the producers were content to let me do as I saw fit. In order to justify the freedom I was given, I wanted to try to guess Martin's intentions as nearly as possible.

Back to *rakh haj*, then, notice that the indefinite article "a" also has no reflex in the Dothraki translation. There are natural languages that have a definite article and no indefinite article (Arabic, for example), but moving on without any articles simplified things quite a bit; it's easier to account for something that isn't present than to have no account for something that is. Information like this helped me to round the Dothraki grammar into form. So, for example, if adjectives follow the nouns they modify, that's indicative (but not definitively predictive) of a head-initial language, one in which the most important word of a phrase tends to come first.[4]

Another piece of evidence (*Khalakka dothrae mr'anha*, "A prince rides inside me"; *GoT* 47 Daenerys 5: 410) pointed towards the potential use of prepositions as opposed to postpositions. It's established early on that the leader of a band of Dothraki is a *khal*, and a Dothraki band is referred to as a *khalasar* (the latter evidently derived from the former via a suffix). While it's certainly possible to argue that the sentence works in a different way, the simplest explanation is that the equivalent of "prince" would be *khalakka* (likewise deriving from *khal* as does *khalasar* and *khaleesi*). Of the remaining bits, identifying the major word order of the language as subject-object-verb is relatively uncontroversial, as it makes sense for the word *dothrae* to correspond with "rides" (it seems to come from the same root as *Dothraki* and *Dothrak*, giving the term for the people themselves, *Dothraki*, the meaning "riders"), leaving *mr'anha* to correspond with "inside me." Of this phrase, when a preposition and a pronoun come into contact, it's possible for the preposition to reduce (cf. French *de elle > d'elle*), for the pronoun to reduce (cf. English *with them > with'em*) or for both to reduce or conflate (cf. Arabic *bi ana > bii*). In this case, it's hard to imagine the *anha* element being reduced, as it's still quite large; if it were to reduce, one would expect it to do so more—at the very least to *ana*. At the same time, it's quite common for a smaller element ending in a vowel to reduce before a word beginning with a vowel. As Martin is an English speaker, the odds seemed to be in favor of there being some preposition like *mra* which means "in" reducing before a first person pronoun *anha*. The opposite may have been true, with *mra* being the pronoun, but it seemed unlikely to me for Martin to have intended that, as such constructions are rather uncommon in foreign languages with which Americans generally become familiar (Japanese being the only likely candidate).

Deciding that *mra* was, in fact, a preposition nearly cemented Dothraki as a head-initial language. The remaining elements generally included in word order discussions are the orders of possessors and possessees and the position of relative clauses with respect to the nouns they modify. I decided early on that I wanted Dothraki to be a case language (like Latin or Russian), where one modifies a noun to indicate what role it plays in a sentence. Most case languages have some sort of genitive case (a case used to identify the possessor in a possessive clause), and I figured this would be the easiest way to set up a possessee-possessor relationship. Finally, head-final relative clauses are completely alien to speakers of Western languages. Whereas in English one might say "The man who gave flowers to my daughter is decent," in a true head-final language, it would come out as something like "The to my daughter flowers gave man is decent." Such a construction seems entirely unlikely to have occurred to one unfamiliar with a head-final language like Japanese or Turkish, and so deciding to go with a relative clause structure more familiar to Western speakers was a simple enough decision.

The result was a more or less fully head-initial language (see Table 1 below). Thus, in Dothraki, the most important part of a given clause will occur on the left (i.e., in a noun phrase, the noun is of greater import than the adjective, so the noun, identified as the head, will appear to the left of the adjective, identified as the dependent). Most importantly, this structure was determined from the few elements in the book (mainly the two clauses cited, in fact, with the rest being used for corroboration), without resorting to any invention (save the conclusion that, as a case language, the genitive case would exist, and possessors would follow possessees).

ELEMENT	HEAD	DEPENDENT	ORDER	EXAMPLE
Clause	V	O	SVO	*Anha tih yera.* "I *saw you.*"
Noun Phrase	N	A	NA	*rakh haj* "*strong* boy"
Possessive Phrase	N	G	NG	*sajo anni* "*my* mount"
Adpositional Phrase	P	N	PN	*she rayan* "*at* the summit"
Relative Clause	N	R	NR	*mahrazh fin tih anna* "the man *who saw me*"

Table 1: A summary of headedness in Dothraki.[5]

In addition to culling grammatical information from the material in the books, I also took the phonology (the sound system) of Dothraki from the words in the books, and also word shape. Word shape, I felt, was crucial in making the extant Dothraki vocabulary feel as if it had sprung from the larger work. For example, given the phonotactics of English—the particular combinations of sounds that the language allows—*kanibunaki, angmeeloo, haborbori* are all licit potential words, because they follow English syllable patterns, but they simply do not look like English words, especially when compared to other licit examples like *cring, runk, dilk* and *hean*. A language will often admit a much wider variety of potential word shapes than it ultimately makes use of.

In order to match Dothraki's phonotactics, I took the words in the text and created words like them—both words matching the shape, and words making use of the same consonantal clusters found throughout the book's vocabulary (see Table 2). Names were fairly easy, with all male names ending in *-o* (and many featuring doubled consonants), and the only two female names ending in *-i*. Other cues I took were the overrepresentation of consonant clusters featuring *h*. Ultimately I decided that combinations which were commonly used as digraphs for single sounds in romanizations around the world (*th, sh, kh*) would become representations of single sounds, while others (*rh, hr, mh*) would become consonant clusters (an unenviable task for the actors, I lamented at the time). Otherwise, I made a few key decisions when it came to the phonology of the language. The consonant *q* is used several times without a following *u*, and the vowel *u* is only ever used when following *q*. As a result, I decided to add the voiceless uvular stop [q] (found in Arabic, Georgian and Inuvialuk, among oth-

Book Word(s)	Pattern(s)	Derived Coinages
tolorro "bone(s)" *khalakka* "prince"	CVCVCCV	*jorokkeya* "corn husk," *Kovarro* "man's name," *varanna* "(s/he) will be neglected"
arakh "sword"	(C)VCVC	*eyel* "rain," *jalan* "moon," *oyof* "clay," *qazat* "nine," *tokik* "fool," *zajikh* "refusal"
hranna "grass" *hrakkar* "lion"	hr-, hr, hC [+liquid]	*hrazef* "horse," *hrelki* "mushroom," *hlofa* "wrist," *mahrazh* "man"
mhar "sore" *anha* "I"	mh-, mh, nh C[+nasal]h	*mhotha* "barley," *mhegga* "dried dung," *nhare* "head," *janha* "blanket"
rhae "foot" *dothrae* "rides"	ae, VV	*aena* "dawn," *lahklae* "(s/he) pants," *lathoe* "(s/he) wakes up," *khaor* "waist"

Table 2: Examples of Dothraki words based on vocabulary from *A Song of Ice and Fire*.

ers), and remove the vowel [u]. At the same time, with *p* and *b* only evidenced in two names (Pono and Bharbo), I decided to remove *p* and *b* from Dothraki— a kind of addition by omission—to give Dothraki a unique sound.[6]

As mentioned before, I considered it important to maintain the vocabulary present in the books. This was a primary concern; however there was an over-riding criterion that ended up affecting one lexical item, and that criterion is the speakability of Dothraki by English-speaking actors. Though the pilot was shot in Morocco, the main actors who would have Dothraki speaking parts (Jason Momoa as Drogo; Iain Glen as Jorah; Roger Allem as Illyrio; Tamzin Merchant as Daenerys[7]) were all English speakers. In order to ensure the sound of it came out right, I wanted to make the language as easy as possible to pro-nounce for an English speaker (while, at the same time, keeping with the material in the books). In one instance I felt one of Martin's Dothraki lexical items needed to be changed—that item *jaqqa rhan.*

In *A Game of Thrones*, the *jaqqa rhan* (translated as "mercy men") are described as men who go through a battlefield after combat has finished remov-ing the heads of the wounded. According to the rules I'd come up with—no matter whether *rhan* was treated as an adjective or noun—*jaqqa* must corre-spond with "men" and *rhan* must correspond with "mercy." The word *jaqqa* fea-tures a geminate voiceless uvular stop (i.e., *qq*), which is *quite* difficult for an English speaker to pronounce. As "man" is such a common word, I figured it would come up in scripts (and would also be commonly used by fans if the lan-guage ever developed a fanbase), and so, for the sake of the actors, I decided to change it. Ultimately I decided on *mahrazh* for "man" (primarily because I liked the sound of it), and decided that *jaqqa rhan* would translate to "merciful exe-cutioner." I felt that "mercy men" could be considered a snappier paraphrase of the longer literal translation.

Concessions such as this one were inevitable, given the nature of the job, and, indeed, several of those who submitted Dothraki proposals during the ini-tial application process developed intentionally simpler linguistic systems than they might otherwise have, reasoning that it should be easy to learn for the actors. Though I did my best to simplify the phonology while adhering to the phonotactics of the extant material, I in no way felt it was warranted to simplify the grammar. Though Westeros and Essos are fictional lands, their peoples are (more or less) human, displaying all the traits of ordinary humans found on Earth. As a result, their linguistic systems should reflect the full range of alter-nations and eccentricities found in natural languages. Artistically, an authentic naturalistic language was called for. But most importantly, I entertained no illu-sions that any of the actors would *ever* learn anything of the Dothraki language. Learning *any* language is a mammoth undertaking, and requires dedication and, more importantly, motivation. Anyone's second language skills will deteriorate if they're not put into practice. The practicality of learning a conlang whose vocabulary is minuscule compared to modern natural languages is nil. Furthermore, it's entirely unnecessary. If a character like Tyrion has a deep scar on his face, makeup will do; it's not necessary to actually cut a scar into the actor's face. Similarly, as long as an actor *sounds* like a native speaker of a given language, it matters little whether they speak anything of the language in real life. Were such a requirement taken seriously in Hollywood, actors would, of necessity, be the world's most astonishing polyglots.

Certain physical practicalities of working on a television show did end up affecting the construction of the Dothraki language. Ordinarily conlangers work in a vacuum, with an entire lifetime to flesh out and perfect their creations. The demands of translations (and deadlines) necessitated that I streamline my process. I correctly determined that having a cache of vocabulary developed ahead of time would greatly simplify the translation process. While a conlang of mine like Kamakawi had accrued just over 2,000 words in the eight years I'd been working on it, Dothraki had over 1,700 words after the initial two month application process. To help generate vocabulary, I modeled the dictionary after another language of mine, Zhyler, which builds words up based on roots to which noun class suffixes are added (see Table 3). Although Dothraki doesn't have noun classes to the same extent, it uses roots to create nouns, adjectives and verbs in a variety of a systematic ways (with some irregularities). Building up the language in this fashion was much more efficient than the word-by-word construction process I utilized with Kamakawi.

Initially, I'd also entertained the idea that I would be on set working with the actors and able to give feedback on all the lines as they were spoken. As it turned out, I never saw the set of *Game of Thrones*, and wasn't able to speak to any of the actors prior to shooting. This ended up having an impact on the language. For example, it's well known that Dothraki has a number of different words for horse (just as English or any other language that's spoken by a people who have horses does). Most of the terms refer to horses of different ages, gen-

Language	Root	Derived Words
Zhyler	*mat*	*matal* "to see," *madga* "eye," *matler* "horizon," *mattÿ* "judge," *matsha* "glasses," *madja* "telescope," *mattha* "wisdom"
Dothraki	*tih*	*tih* "eye," *tihat* "to see," *tihilat* "to look at," *tihak* "scout," *tiholat* "to understand," *tihikh* "view," *tihi* "glance," *attihat* "to show"

Table 3: An example of root derivation in Zhyler and Dothraki.

ders, breeds or colorings, e.g., *vado* "filly," *fansa* "dapple," *vezh* "stallion," *messhih* "perlino," etc. When a horse is referred to in the script, though, I had no way of knowing what color, gender, age or breed the horse would be, rendering all of this vocabulary unusable. Thus, even though there are a number of languages that lack basic level terms (for example, Yurok, a native language of California, has a number of words for different types of squirrels, but none that corresponds to the English word "squirrel"), Dothraki, of necessity, needed a basic level term for everything, so that it wouldn't matter which type of element was referred to on the screen.

Additionally, I also shied away from distinguishing number in too fine-grained a way. Inanimate nouns in Dothraki, for example, make no distinction between singular and plural, and the exponence for plurality on both nouns and verbs in Dothraki tends to be either optional or homophonous with some other category. And while many languages have a dedicated dual number, Dothraki makes no such distinction. The reasoning, again, was practical. Consider Arabic, which distinguishes singular from dual from plural in almost all levels of the grammar (nouns, verbs, pronouns and adjectives).[8] Were Dothraki to do the same, imagine a scene where the khal orders two others to go perform some task in Dothraki. At the last minute, the extras (or orderees) may be switched out, with one removed, or maybe one added. This would affect the grammar of the verb and any other elements referring to the orderees. Based on experience, it's likely I'd have no knowledge of the switch until the episode aired, which means that the resulting Dothraki phrase would be ungrammatical. Unless I wanted to be saddled with a host of ungrammatical utterances, then, agreement patterns like this one simply were not an option, however interesting and natural they might be.

Those concerns aside, though, my primary goal was to produce a naturalistic language. On demand translation is the main enemy to such an approach, which necessitated the large initial cache of vocabulary mentioned above. Even so, further problems can crop up simply as a result of miscommunication. For example, in episode 1.03 of *Game of Thrones* ("Lord Snow"), there's a line I completely mistranslated. I got an e-mail that simply asked for the translation of a new line for Jorah: "Stop the Horde!" Without context, I really didn't know what was intended, so I translated it as *Annakhas dozgosores! Annakhas* is the command form of *annakhat*, which means "to cause/force to stop." *Dozgosores* is the accusative of *dozgosor*, a collective of the word *dozgo* which means "enemy." Unfortunately, Jorah wasn't giving a command to stop the onslaught of an oncoming enemy horde: He was telling someone else to cause the Dothraki khalasar they were riding in to halt so that the khaleesi could get off her horse for a bit. As a result, I had to find a way to fold *dozgosor* into the vocabulary as a superlative term for one's own people, in addition to a word for an enemy—a not impossible, but nevertheless unpalatable task.

The challenges posed by the text itself were, in some ways, even more daunting. Returning to an earlier point, Martin toys with fantasy tropes throughout *A Song of Ice and Fire*. In treating the Dothraki as the Other, Martin must, of necessity, exoticize them—at least at the beginning. In order to subvert the trope, Martin must invoke it. As a result, the Dothraki come across as a bit barbaric, animalistic—stereotypical. Drogo acts the part of the silent savage, and the rest of the Dothraki act the part of the, well, *savage* savages. Acts such as two men fighting to the death over who will earn the right to rape a female dancer are intended not so much to shock the reader, but to bring to the reader's mind the stereotypical fear of the Other. In addition, though, this brutality is functional in terms of characterization. Like it or not, Daenerys is fated to start a new life as the khaleesi of the Dothraki. Initially, then, Martin has to put her through the wringer to see how she responds. The reader gets a third person limited perspective through Daenerys's eyes, so acts that shock the reader also serve to shock Daenerys. We see the Dothraki through Dany's eyes, and are intended to react to them in the same way she does: frightened, at first, but ultimately gaining a newfound respect and admiration for their ways.

But what of the Dothraki's perspective? We never see the Dothraki through the eyes of the Dothraki. Though Daenerys comes to admire and respect the Dothraki, what right has she to pass judgment on them at all—as if she were explaining the ways of God to men? These are questions a reader can entertain, but ultimately questions that aren't important for understanding and following the narrative. Indeed, the force of the narrative leads us away from the day-to-day lives of the Dothraki. First, in *A Game of Thrones*, we see Dany's struggle acclimating herself to not only a nomadic life, but to married life, to pregnancy, and to the tyranny of her older brother. Thereafter, Drogo and his Dothraki are basically in a state of war as they prepare to take back the Seven Kingdoms for Daenerys. Were there no foreigner among them at all, such events would be a time of great turmoil and change for the Dothraki. And then, of course, starting with *A Clash of Kings*, Dany takes her dwindling khalasar on a journey far beyond the realm of experience of even the most seasoned Dothraki. Dany never experiences a normal year as a Dothraki (or as normal as a khaleesi could experience)—and, as such, the reader likewise never experiences it.

When it comes to language, capturing the Dothraki people—describing their world—is quite difficult given the limited window we have into their culture. Language is entirely culture-dependent. The words that exist in a language exist precisely because some segment of its speakers has a need for those words to exist. In order to flesh out a lexicon, then, a language creator has to know everything about the culture of a people: where they live; what other peoples they encounter and have dealings with; what technology they have mastered (either on their own, or through contact with others); what their lives are like; what their belief structures are; what the outliers from their society are like—literally, everything that relates to a person or group's very existence.

But what do we know of the Dothraki? We know what their weddings are like. We know some facts about how they live (they're nomadic, they have one large city, they're adept at combat, their livelihood depends on the horse), and some anecdotes here and there, but mostly what we know is what Dany knows. What types of foods do they cook, and how? If rape is so commonplace in Dothraki society, how is parentage determined (after all, we're given to understand that the son of the khal plays an important role in their social structure)? Do the men really do nothing but gamble, fight, hunt, ride horses and take women by force? What do the women do when the men are out gallivanting about?

Stop for a moment and consider the English language. In English, we have a wealth of equestrian terminology: horse, mare, mustang, stallion, thoroughbred, filly, colt, perlino, mudder—and that's just horse types. Are English speakers primarily horse-based people? Of course not. Horses are certainly quite important to some English speakers, just as boats are to others. All we've described is the vocabulary associated with a certain subculture within the English language speaking community. But now consider another type of vocabulary. I won't list them, but think of all the insulting and derogatory terms that exist in English for women. It's possible to come up with a *sizable* list. Are English speakers, on the whole, misogynists? Now do the same with racial slurs. Are all English speakers racists?

A language is a product of *all* its speakers—even those with whom we disagree, and those who are generally disreputable. A natural language will contain all this vocabulary. A naturalistic language, then, must do the same. Due to the nature of the narrative, though, we get a very one-sided view of the Dothraki. Primarily we see the actions of men and warriors in extreme circumstances—and through the eyes of a foreigner to boot. Were Dothraki exclusively my creation, I would flesh out the rest of the culture and balance the vocabulary. The Dothraki people, though, are not a product of my imagination, and their story is not mine to tell.

Though George R.R. Martin isn't much interested in the development of the Dothraki language, I assume he would be interested if I suddenly developed a cache of vocabulary to describe the Dothraki practice of ritual mutilation. There's nothing about this in the books, so it's possible, but this isn't a decision that I should be making. At the same time, simply coining vocabulary forces these decisions to be made by the language creator. Early on, for example, I was asked to translate a sentence about the Dothraki gambling with money. Having read the books, I knew that the Dothraki didn't make use of money at all, and that such an activity would be unlikely, so ultimately we did something different. But what if I had simply translated that phrase? What would it mean for the Dothraki to have a native term for money? And what would that mean when it comes to sorting out canon?

Fans of the book series have already had to make their own choices when it comes to deciding how to handle the show when inconsistencies arise (for example, Irri and Rakharo, two characters still alive in the book series that are both now dead in the show), but I understand where my place is in the greater canon of the series: Martin's books will always trump what I come up with for the Dothraki language and people. This wouldn't be too much of a problem if Martin weren't still writing the book series. My greatest fear is that George R.R. Martin will come up with a new word of Dothraki for a future book that completely contradicts something I've come up with that's been used in the show. As a result, I've left the Dothraki language plenty of room to grow. There are certain aspects of Dothraki that have been left blank intentionally because I don't know what George R.R. Martin's answer will be. For example, though Dothraki are aware of the seasons (always wild and unpredictable), I have no answer to how they might keep track of the passage of time. Do they have months? If so, how many? What about days of the week? These are questions I could answer (and have some ideas about), but if George R.R. Martin would like to provide an answer in a future book, he must be allowed to do so. Perhaps when *A Song of Ice and Fire* has been completed and Martin has decided he's done adding to the universe, I may revisit the possibility of expansion, if there's still interest in the Dothraki language. At present, though, given the constraints I'm operating under, my hands are tied.

The future of the Dothraki language remains to be seen. Translation into Dothraki has declined in each season of *Game of Thrones*, with really only one line being thrown in for the third season. Part of the difficulty for the producers, a difficulty the novelist does not have, is managing their assets. Though, of course, there was no question of Ned Stark coming back in the future, as *Game of Thrones* gets to later points in the series (in particular *A Feast for Crows*), there's also no question of, for example, Emilia Clarke taking a season off while the show focuses exclusively on other point of view characters, as effectively happens in the book series. That said, it's my impression that Weiss and Benioff like Dothraki, and may try to shoehorn a line in here or there as the show progresses.

The fate of Dothraki amongst fans of the show and the book series has been interesting. From the very start, none of the fans of the books were particularly interested in there being a Dothraki language. Those fans who were interested in potential languages all wanted to see High Valyrian or Braavosi. The general consensus seemed to be that it was nice to have a Dothraki language, but few were very interested in learning anything about it. Further complicating matters, *Avatar* came out in theaters shortly after I got the job to create the Dothraki language, and there was a huge surge in interest in the Na'vi language. Those who were interested in learning a language in general flocked to Na'vi, and when Dothraki debuted along with *Game of Thrones* a year and a half later, the idea of learning a constructed language was no longer novel (and the fact that the potential viewership of *Avatar* was so much greater than that of the violent and sexually explicit *Game of Thrones* only exacerbated the disparity).

Despite the obstacles, Dothraki has achieved a modest but dedicated fan base. Centered around the forum at Dothraki.org, users will drop in for a few weeks and then drop out every couple months, with a core of eight or nine fans who have stuck with the language from the beginning. Of the professionally constructed languages in use in major productions over the past few decades, I'd wager that Dothraki's fan base is the smallest (unless *Land of the Lost's* Pakuni is included, though I'd wager that language's fanbase could give Dothraki's a run for its money). Of course defining what makes someone a fan of a constructed language is no simple matter. Generally I count those who have taken time to learn some of the grammar and made a sincere attempt to translate something into it (whether or not these criteria are fair is the subject of another essay). In addition, though, there are scores of Dothraki "well-wishers." If Twitter is any accurate measure, there are a hundred or so unique mentions of the Dothraki language (as opposed to the Dothraki people) per week.[9] The overwhelming majority of mentions are positive, but almost none of these users ever follow up (beyond perhaps an informal Google search). Consequently, Dothraki remains a very popular language to drop into conversation (cf. mentions on *The Simpsons* or *The Office*),[10] but it hasn't inspired a fanbase as fervent or as numerous as that of Na'vi or Klingon.

In the coming years, however, Dothraki will enjoy a benefit it's lacked in the past: the ability to borrow words. With the development of High Valyrian and a Low Valyrian variant for the third season of *Game of Thrones*—two languages spoken by peoples with whom the Dothraki have been in contact over the years—Dothraki can accept an influx of vocabulary for technology with which they are familiar but have no native term (for example, books), as well as items native to the Valyrian Empire or Slaver's Bay. It remains to be seen if Dothraki will survive beyond the show, or what impact High Valyrian will have as information about it starts to find its way onto the web. It's my hope, though, that Dothraki has at least helped to raise the level of linguistic awareness of the general public—both for conlangs and natural languages. The tremendous success of *Game of Thrones* (and also movies like *Avatar*, *The Lord of the Rings* and even *The Passion of the Christ*) has shown producers that audiences will accept long stretches of subtitled dialogue spoken in a language none of the audience knows. Even fifteen years ago, this is an eventuality no conlanger would ever have dreamed could be possible. And even though no one on the show has ever pronounced the word *khaleesi* correctly, I'm proud to have been able to lend a little authenticity to an aspect of the production that, in decades past, would have been completely overlooked.

Notes

1. Special thanks to Susan Johnston, Jes Battis, Erin Peterson and Jim Henry for their invaluable comments and assistance in helping me to prepare this essay.

2. A natural language is one that evolved naturally on Earth and whose creation was regional and spontaneous. Thus, English, Spanish and Russian are natural languages—as are creole languages like Tok Pisin and revived projects like Modern Hawaiian and Modern Hebrew—but not consciously constructed languages that are, nevertheless, spoken by a human community, like Esperanto, Ido or Interlingua.

3. For additional modern works that feature more realistic characters in unrealistic or fantastical settings, see the works of Guy Gavriel Kay (*The Lions of Al-Rassan*, *The Sarantine Mosaic*, *The Last Light of the Sun*) and Naomi Novik (*The Temeraire Series*).

4. Cf. Table 1.

5. In linguistic typology, the subject of the sentence is treated as an adjunct. Consequently, when it comes to headedness, the word orders SVO, VSO and VOS are all treated as head-initial.

6. Historically, the older consonants *$^*p$ and *$^*f$ merged to become modern *f*, and the older consonants *$^*b$ and *$^*v$ merged to become modern *v*. The latter change occurred in Spanish, with older *$^*b$ and *$^*v/w$ merging to become the voiced bilabial fricative [β] in most contexts.

7. Tamzin Merchant played the part of Daenerys in the unaired pilot of *Game of Thrones* produced for HBO executives. Schedule conflicts prevented Merchant from continuing as Daenerys once the pilot went to series.

8. Arabic doesn't distinguish dual from plural in the first person; it retains only a singular/plural distinction.

9. To do some informal research, use the "Dothraki" search term over at twitter.com.

10. *The Simpsons* 23.6 ("The Book Job"), 20 November 2011; *The Office* 9.3 ("Andy's Ancestry"), 4 October 2012.

Works Cited

"The Book Job." *The Simpsons*. FOX. KTTV, Los Angeles. 20 November 2011. Television.

Lewis, M. Paul, Gary F. Simons, and Charles D. Fennig, eds. *Ethnologue: Languages of the World*, 17th ed. Dallas: SIL International, 2013. Web. 26 March 2013.

Martin, George R.R. *A Game of Thrones*. New York: Bantam Books, 1997.

_____. "Klaatu Barada Nicto..." *Not a Blog*. LiveJournal, 12 April 2010. Web. 26 March 2013.

Roberson, Jennifer. *Shapechangers*. New York: Daw Books, 1984. Print.

Tolkien, J.R.R. *The Letters of J.R.R Tolkien*. Ed. Humphrey Carpenter and Christopher Tolkien. Boston: Houghton & Mifflin, 1981.

Vance, Jack. *The Languages of Pao*. New York: Ace Books, 1958. Print.

"Sing for your little life": Story, Discourse and Character

Marc Napolitano

Tyrion Lannister is perhaps the most well-read character in George R.R. Martin's *Song of Ice and Fire* series, and his first eponymous chapter in *A Game of Thrones* establishes his fundamental passion for reading. Still, Tyrion's love of books, along with his intellectual prowess as refined by this passion, cannot always be relied upon, particularly in a world filled with liars, traitors, and pretenders; reading a book and reading a person are two very different things. Notably, in the opening sentences of his first chapter in *A Clash of Kings*, Tyrion bemoans his inability to read the countenance of Ser Mandon Moore, an inscrutable knight in the service of King Joffrey: "Jaime had once told him that Moore was the most dangerous of the Kingsguard—excepting himself, always—because his face gave no hint as what he might do next. Tyrion would have welcomed a hint" (*CoK* 4 Tyrion 1: 39). The reader is similarly helpless in trying to "read" Ser Mandon, for the reader can only perceive Moore through Tyrion: Ser Mandon himself is not a "POV (point-of-view) character" and his thoughts remain unavailable. Later, when the knight attempts to murder Tyrion during the Battle of the Blackwater, we share Tyrion's mystification regarding Moore's motives.

In light of Ser Mandon's treachery, the passage quoted above proves an excellent example of foreshadowing, as Tyrion's failure to read Ser Mandon early on in the novel almost costs him his life in his penultimate POV chapter. In addition, the passage is a sharp reminder that becoming a POV character hardly guarantees that character's safety or survival, nor does it confer upon the character the clarity and clairvoyance of an omniscient narrator. Tyrion heavily influences the narrative's discourse, channeling the events of the story through his own unique perspective. However, he is simultaneously shaped and re-shaped by those same events.

It is easy to lose sight of the tension between observation and narration, for although Martin's texts are narrated in the third person, his anonymous narrator lacks distinct, individualized character traits. Commentary on the part of this storyteller is virtually nonexistent, allowing him to disappear behind the colorful personalities of the POV characters.[1] Thus, there is a strong temptation to misconstrue these characters as "narrators" despite the fact that they do not tell their own stories (ironically, though not surprisingly, many non–POV characters such as Old Nan, Meera Reed, Ser Jorah Mormont, and Maester Luwin display a narratorial tendency that eclipses the POV characters' storytelling sensibilities, though they must share their stories aloud and in the presence of a POV character if the account is to reach the reader). Still, whatever their limitations as "storytellers," the POV characters' ability to commandeer the narrative's discourse creates the illusion of narratorial power. The power of a POV character is strictly discursive, however. Often, these same characters are helpless in the face of cataclysmic events that take place outside of their control; memorable examples include Bran's inability to anticipate Jaime's throwing him from the Broken Tower (*GoT* 9 Bran 2), Daenerys's inability to thwart the brutal vengeance of Mirri Maz Duur (*GoT* 65 Daenerys 8), and Arya's inability to save her father's life (*GoT* 66 Arya 5).

This tension between event and discourse in *A Song of Ice and Fire* is immediately evocative of the tension that some critics perceive as a fundamental complication of the structuralist approach to narrative. Though the Russian formalist tradition of dividing a narrative in two—the *fabula* (story) and *sjuzet* (presentation of the story)—continues to influence the basic approach to narrative theory, the relationship between these two components is far more complex than traditional structuralist criticism implies. In the conflict between fabula and sjuzet, narrative theorists such as Jonathan Culler and Peter Brooks perceive something very like the contest between vulnerability to events and discursive authority that we see in the aforementioned *Song of Ice and Fire* examples. The two components frequently seem to clash rather than coalesce in the fight for narrative supremacy, a fitting metaphor given the power struggles that shape *A Song of Ice and Fire*.

Structuralist theory traditionally maintains that the events that constitute the fabula possess an independent power regardless of how they are revealed in the narrative, and the "primacy of events" (Culler 178) seems to hold true in Martin's narratives as well.[2] For example, the infamous "Red Wedding" is a defining event in *A Song of Ice and Fire*, marking the deaths of two major characters and the ostensible destruction of House Stark. Though the reader is only able to experience the event because Catelyn, a POV character, is present, Catelyn's centrality during this key point in the story does not give her any control over the event itself. Indeed, she is powerless in the face of a traumatic plot twist that will culminate in her madness—"Slow red worms crawled along her arms and under her clothes. *It tickles. That made her laugh until she screamed"* (*SoS* 52 Catelyn 7: 583)—and death—"Then the steel was at her throat, and its bite was red and cold" (*SoS* 52 Catelyn 7: 583). The former renders her discourse useless, while the latter ends it entirely, and yet the text goes on without her.[3]

However, this description belies just how vital Catelyn's discourse is to the overall meaning of the narrative. Were the reader to simply learn of the Red Wedding when Tyrion does, via a letter from Lord Frey, the significance of the event would be lost entirely. Even if the Red Wedding were experienced through another character who witnesses the massacre (an impossibility given that no other POV characters are inside the castle), the thematic importance of the event—and the very shape of the narrative—would change.[4] It is Catelyn's trauma, madness, and death that grant the occurrence true weight. The traditional primacy of the event must therefore be called into question, for just as the Red Wedding is meaningless without Catelyn, the event is meaningless without the discourse. Since Martin's discourse is placed squarely in the hands of his characters, the ostensibly "passive" ability of the POV characters to perceive and reveal events evolves toward a more significant power: the capacity to shape, and in fact, create meaning.

In this essay, I will examine the intricate relationship between character, story, and discourse in *A Song of Ice and Fire*, assessing Martin's book series from a structuralist perspective, while simultaneously addressing the post-structuralist narrative theories that complicate these definitions. I will likewise define the tension between narrative and discourse as one unique manifestation of the larger tension between the medieval and modern elements of Martin's narrative technique. Part of my analysis will focus heavily on the issue of "power." Though the true power of the POV characters may be debatable given the sheer number of events and situations that exist beyond the ken of these individuals, I contend that discursive power is in fact vital to the thematic meaning of *A Song of Ice and Fire*. Since Martin's narrative technique shifts in *A Feast for Crows* and *A Dance with Dragons*—with the division of a concurrent story into two separate texts based on specific groupings of characters, and the addition of POV characters who are designated by descriptive phrases—my analysis will focus mainly on examples from the first three books: *A Game of Thrones*, *A Clash of Kings*, and *A Storm of Swords*.

Interlaced Medieval Narrative vs. Invisible Modern Narrators

The first event in *A Song of Ice and Fire* is the haunting confrontation between three rangers of the Night's Watch and the Others. It is an event that continues to hold sway over the series' narrative despite the sheer multiplicity of storylines. If Martin's working titles for the final books—*The Winds of Winter* and *A Dream of Spring*—are any indication, the onset of winter will provide the climax for his epic by revealing the ultimate futility of the "game of thrones" in the face of the larger threat posed by the Others. Still, the progression toward this climax has been anything but continuous, and this lack of linearity is strongly reminiscent of traditional medieval narratives.

In his analysis of medieval narrative theory, William W. Ryding cites the writings of Torquato Tasso, noting the sixteenth-century writer's emphasis of the need to reconcile "unity of action with variety of incident" (14). Tasso outlines the desire to balance these two conflicting elements:

> I judge that by an excellent poet ... a poem can be formed in which, as in a microcosm, there would be read here arrays of armies, here battles on land and sea, here stormings of cities, skirmishes and joustings, here descriptions of hunger and of thirst, here storms, conflagrations, prodigies; there would be found seditions, discords, errors, adventures, magic spells; there deeds of cruelty, of audacity, of courtesy, of generosity; there experiences of love, sometimes happy, sometimes unhappy, sometimes joyous, sometimes pathetic; but may the poem that contains so great a variety of matter be one in form and soul, and may all its elements be put together in such a way that if one part is taken away, or its position changed, all is destroyed [qtd. in Ryding 15].

Tasso's list could serve as a virtual catalogue of the events that constitute Martin's epic, for there is no shortage of battles, jousts, seditions, audacious deeds, and adventures in *A Song of Ice and Fire*. Nevertheless, the tight coherence stressed by Tasso often seems to be lacking in Martin's narrative, partly due to the author's dividing the text between so many plotlines, locations, and characters.

Again, such divisions are suggestive of several celebrated medieval romances—narratives which David Quint describes as "interlaced" due to the juxtaposing and interweaving of multiple storylines (241–2). In the Prose *Lancelot* (aka the Vulgate Cycle), the unknown author "follows the careers of some eight or ten questing knights, telling a segment of one knight's story before turning to a segment of another's, and thus keeps multiple plots going at once" (Quint 242). Ludovico Ariosto took the process of interlacing narratives even further in his sweeping romance *Orlando Furioso*. Here, the sheer number of characters and events, along with the abrupt transitions between the various story arcs at climactic moments (Quint 243), creates a dislocated and at times disorienting plot that is strongly suggestive of Martin's narrative.

While Tasso disparages medieval narratives that feature the characteristic diversity of episodes but lack unity of action, Ryding asserts that the absence of overarching coherence does not justify the Italian critic's cursory dismissal of interlaced narratives. Though romances such as *Orlando Furioso* do not necessarily follow a coalescent pathway, "the various story threads tangle and untangle, cross and recross, in accordance with a carefully prearranged plan of narrative coincidences and interdependencies. This is not, obviously, a convergent pattern in which the various threads of the story move insistently toward a major knot … yet Ariosto has so arranged his story that the various parts are in fact structurally dependent on one another" (16).[5] Even more so than Tasso's description, this account is suggestive of *A Song of Ice and Fire*. As in *Orlando Furioso*, Martin's plotlines frequently intersect based on overlapping conflicts or reoccurring motifs; furthermore, just as Ariosto continuously draws the reader back to three central, overlapping story arcs (Charlemagne's war; Orlando's pursuit of Angelica; the love affair between Bradamante and Ruggiero), Martin does likewise (the "game of thrones"/War of the Five Kings; the conflict at the Wall; Daenerys's maturation in Essos).

Still, Martin's narrative is not convergent. Indeed, the principal movement, from *A Game of Thrones* onward, is one of continuing divergence: the divergence of the various storylines, and the divergence of the Stark family, whose fragmentation furthers the scope and size of the narrative. Though the final texts in the series will likely be directed toward a climactic convergence—as winter finally arrives and the Stark children fulfill their destinies—the slow buildup toward this unification can hardly be described as orderly, particularly according to Tasso's standards.[6] Nevertheless, there is a strong sense of interdependence permeating the series, and this interdependency comes through all the more forcefully in Martin's narrative techniques. POV characters constantly make decisions that influence the fates of other POV characters in spite of the fact that the paths of these two individuals may never actually cross.

The central discrepancy between Martin's narrative and the traditional medieval conventions that help to define his fabula clearly relates back to the discourse, and, more specifically, the narration. Due to the fact that medieval narratives emerged from an oral tradition of storytelling, narration tends to be extroverted, as the writer "think[s] in terms of speaking directly to the audience" (Davenport 43). Tony Davenport notes that third-person medieval narratives frequently feature overt and distinctive storytellers who take on a narrational role "somewhere in a spectrum ranging from the scholarly book-compiler to the popular entertainer" (43). In the prologues to his Arthurian romances, Chrétien de Troyes directly addresses the reader through an authorial/narratorial persona: "And now I shall begin the tale which will be remembered so long as Christendom endures. This is Chrétien's boast" (*Erec* 1). The Pearl Poet adopts a similar rhetorical strategy in *Sir Gawain and the Green Knight*; here, the oral dimensions are taken even further as he reveals that he is passing on a story that he once heard: "If you will listen to this lay but a little while now,/I will tell it at once as in town I have heard/it told" (25). In spite of his medievalist sensibilities and his paratextual framing of the narrative as a "song," Martin forsakes this oral approach to discourse for an internalized, psychological approach, and his determination to keep his narrator "invisible" is reminiscent of the narrative principles of the late nineteenth century. Roland Barthes once wrote that the notion of a limited narrator was an essentially modern development, claiming that "the ... most recent conception (Henry James, Sartre) decrees that the narrator must limit his narrative to what the characters can observe or know, everything proceeding as if each of the characters in turn were the sender of the narrative" (111). It is somewhat ironic to link Martin and Henry James considering that *A Song of Ice and Fire* seemingly epitomizes the "loose baggy monster" (x) that James condemned in his preface to *The Tragic Muse*. However, James's early rejection of the ostentatious, omniscient narratorial techniques of the Victorians in favor of interiority and unreliability creates a unique connection to Martin. Like James before him, Martin stresses character point-of-view; furthermore, both authors opt to "show" their stories rather than "tell" them.

Seeing and Sequencing: The Ambiguities of Perspective and Chronology

Martin's own prefatory words regarding the narrative principles of *A Song of Ice and Fire* establish this preference, as he asserts that his POV characters will provide a lens through which readers can view the story: "*A Song of Ice and Fire* is told *through the eyes of characters* who are sometimes hundreds or even thousands of miles apart from one another. Some chapters cover a day, some only an hour; others might span a fortnight, a month, half a year. With such a structure, the narrative cannot be strictly sequential; sometimes important things are happening simultaneously, a thousand leagues apart" (emphasis added, "A Note on Chronology"). Along with the emphasis on "showing," what is perhaps most noteworthy about this description is Martin's allusion to the traditional distinction between story and discourse, as he reveals that the division of the sjuzhet between the various POV characters necessitates that the events that make up the fabula occasionally be presented in a non-sequential fashion.

Of course, the author's rejection of sequential storytelling is hardly unique, as one of the chief discrepancies between story and discourse relates to the idea of chronology. In their structuralist definition of the fabula, Luc Herman and Bart Vervaeck boldly assert that a chronological order of events is rarely preserved by the discourse: "The story ... refers to the chronological sequence of events that are often no longer shown chronologically in the narrative" (46). As

Martin indicates in his "Note on Chronology," the geographic separation of his characters is partially responsible for the narrative's lack of chronological coherence, and even though *A Game of Thrones* begins with almost all of the POV characters congregating in the north, the author introduces his non-sequential discursive technique early on in the narrative.

A Game of Thrones' prologue, along with its first two chapters, initiates an ostensibly sequential narrative, as the confrontation between Royce and the Others (*GoT* Prologue) leads to Gared's execution and the discovery of the dire-wolf pups (*GoT* 2 Bran 1), and then to the conversation between Eddard and Catelyn regarding the death of Jon Arryn and the upcoming royal visit (*GoT* 3 Catelyn 1). However, the buildup toward the royal visit is disrupted by the abrupt "jump" from Winterfell to Pentos and the introduction of Daenerys and Viserys (*GoT* 4 Daenerys 1). There is no indication as to whether Daenerys's first appearance before Khal Drogo is taking place subsequent to Catelyn and Eddard's conversation, or whether the two events are occurring simultaneously. Moreover, at the end of Daenerys's first chapter—which unfolds over the course of one day—the narrative skips ahead to the king's arrival at Winterfell (*GoT* 5 Eddard 1).

Whether this chronological jump takes place between "Catelyn 1" and "Daenerys 1," or between "Daenerys 1" and "Eddard 1" does not significantly affect the narrative, though it establishes that the continuity between chapters is occasionally topical as opposed to chronological. Here, the chief link between Catelyn's chapter, Daenerys's chapter, and Eddard's chapter is Robert Baratheon himself, who is a prominent topic of discussion in "Catelyn 1" and "Daenerys 1" before his introduction in "Eddard 1."[7] Martin provides three different views of this character/subject over the course of the three chapters. In "Catelyn 1," Robert is established as the king and as a beloved friend to Eddard, while "Daenerys 1" presents the same man as the merciless "Usurper" who has deposed the Targaryens and hounded them throughout their exile. The king finally makes his first appearance in "Eddard 1," and though we perceive him only through Eddard, it is clear that he possesses qualities outlined in both of the previously established character portraits: Eddard's love for and loyalty toward Robert, and the Targaryens' fear and loathing of the same man, are immediately understandable. The ambiguity of sequence is thus matched by an even more significant ambiguity regarding perspective; however, both uncertainties are manifestations of the overarching tension between story and discourse given Martin's determination to present the story "through the eyes of characters" ("A Note on Chronology"). The non-chronological presentation of events and the uncertainty regarding the "proper" interpretation of these events both stem from the division of the narrative between diverse and distant individuals.

Though character and discourse are inextricably connected in *A Song of Ice and Fire* due to the influence of the POV characters on the sjuzhet, the traditional structuralist emphasis on the "primacy of events" implies that character and discourse are always subservient to the fabula. As Marvin Mudrick notes, the structuralist impulse is to perceive characters as existing solely "through an ordered sequence of events" (215):

> One of the recurring anxieties of literary critics concerns the way in which a character in drama or fiction may be said to exist. The "purist" argument—in the ascendancy nowadays among critics—points out that characters do not exist at all except insofar as they are a part of the images and events which bear and move them, that any effort to extract them from their context and to discuss them as if they are real human beings is a sentimental misunderstanding of the nature of literature [210–11].

The "subservience" of character to fabula goes back to the earliest roots of Western literary theory, as Jakob Lothe recounts Aristotle's belief that "characters are primarily important as performers of actions and are subordinate to the action itself.... Yet is it right to make characters subordinate to those fictional events which precisely *they* have initiated and constituted?" (Lothe's emphasis, 77). Lothe's skepticism is particularly applicable in the case of *A Song of Ice and Fire*, as the psychological complexities and forceful personalities of Martin's characters seem to grant them a power that transcends the "ordered sequences of events."

The Power of Perspective: Sansa vs. Robb

Perhaps more importantly, these events are revealed through the POV characters and would thus remain inaccessible to the reader without the presence of these individuals. In many ways, the power struggle between fabula and sjuzhet can be read as a larger struggle between event and character. These power dynamics are complex, even between POV characters and non–POV characters. For example, Sansa Stark seems a fundamentally passive character with virtually no control over her own destiny.[8] From her betrothal to Joffrey, to her mistreatment at the hands of the Lannisters, to her forced marriage to Tyrion, to her abduction by Littlefinger, the course of Sansa's story arc is shaped by those around her. Conversely, Robb Stark is an active character whose maturation, military victories, and marriage all unfold as a result of personal choices; as one of the five kings in the war of the same name, he obviously plays a prominent role in the story, and his decisions, both wise (governing Winterfell in the absence of his parents, adopting effective strategies on the battlefield) and imprudent (sending Theon Greyjoy to Pyke, marrying Jeyne Westerling), shape his fate. However, recalling Mudrick's critique of the "sentimental" tendency to read characters as "real human beings," it is essential to note that Robb, like Sansa, is a pawn; just as Sansa's course is shaped by the Lannisters and Littlefinger, Robb's course is delineated by a powerful force beyond his control.

Consider Martin's description of Robb's destiny: "I knew [Robb would die] almost from the beginning. Not the first day, but very soon.... I killed Ned because everybody thinks he's the hero.... The next predictable thing is to think his eldest son is going to rise up and avenge his father.... So immediately [killing Robb] became the next thing I had to do" (qtd. in Hibberd). However "active" Robb seems, he is ultimately subservient to the sequence of events as outlined by Martin. Sansa's fate (like Robb's) is predetermined by Martin's outline, but if POV characters and non–POV characters alike are at the mercy of the fabula, the only potential means of asserting real power in this narrative is through discourse. Fundamentally, Sansa's status as a POV character grants her the power to influence the way the reader experiences and interprets events, even if the reader disagrees with her perception—indeed, the temptation to disagree with her only enhances what Mudrick calls the "primal energy" (215) that allows literary characters to overcome the primacy of events. Granted, Sansa's discursive power may seem passive given that Sansa and the other POV characters do not actually narrate the text, but rather, "focalize" it. However, since first-person narration is traditionally retrospective, focalization allows Sansa to challenge the hegemony of pre-planned events: the fabula may be predetermined, but the immediacy of Sansa's internal perception of/reaction to events creates a direct and dynamic discourse. Conversely, Robb, who is never in control of the sjuzet and who is thus denied the discursive ability to perceive and react "in the moment," is constrained entirely by the fixed fabula.

Focalization simultaneously grants Sansa a psychological vitality that belies her passivity. Consider the following passage, which recounts Sansa and Joffrey's reconciliation the night of the Hand's Tournament:

> When Prince Joffrey seated himself to her right, she felt her throat tighten. He had not spoken a word to her since the awful thing had happened, and she had not dared to speak to him. At first she thought she hated him for what they'd done to Lady, but after Sansa had wept her eyes dry, she told herself that it had not been Joffrey's doing, not truly. The queen had done it; she was the one to hate, her and Arya. Nothing bad would have happened except for Arya.
> She could not hate Joffrey tonight. He was too beautiful to hate [*GoT* 30 Sansa 2: 250].

Here, Sansa's entire thought process unfolds spontaneously as she rationalizes her forgiveness of Joffrey, first by blaming Lady's death on Cersei, and then faulting Arya. In spite of her absurd logic, her thought process is clear: given her longstanding incompatibility with Arya, and her desire to keep Cersei and Joffrey on a pedestal, it is simply easier to criticize her younger sister. Obviously, the passage reveals Sansa's naiveté and vanity, but it simultaneously conveys her sensitivity and self-consciousness. In a few short sentences, Martin paints a psychologically complex and honest portrait of his character through the directness of focalization.

This psychological slant of Martin's series, as epitomized by his use of focalized discourse, is thus steeped heavily in Jamesian theory: "With Henry James, likewise, we witness the evolution of realism towards subjectivism and perspectivism, in part because of James's psychological bent. According to James, the novel (unlike drama) can reveal to us the inner life of characters, and this is the essence of the genre" (Onega and Landa 18).[9] As Roy Pascal observes, this approach grants James's characters "the 'feel of life' ... the feel of the choices open to them" (5), and indeed, the reader of *A Song of Ice and Fire* experiences these choices firsthand through the perspectives of the characters. Even the most illogical decisions on the parts of these characters—Catelyn's abducting Tyrion; Eddard's revealing his discovery to Cersei; Arya's "squandering" of Jaqen's gift— are understandable through the revelation of the character's thought process at the very moment that it takes place. Still, Martin simultaneously maintains a Jamesian objectivity; Mieke Bal describes variable focalization as an effective tool in creating "neutrality towards all the characters" (105), an observation which seems especially applicable in *A Song of Ice and Fire* given Martin's determination to preserve moral ambiguity.

"Sansa Stark, handsome, clever, and rich, with a comfortable home and happy disposition..."

Martin's ability to maintain sympathy for Sansa through his discursive technique, in spite of her narcissism, thoughtlessness, and misplaced priorities, seems strangely reminiscent of James's most noteworthy predecessor in the realm of free-indirect discourse, Jane Austen.[10] Certainly, when one considers the centrality of class-based prejudice to Sansa's negative qualities, the comparison seems all the more fitting, for Austen's supreme narrative achievement is built around a character who embodies similar prejudices. As Wayne C. Booth notes,

> Jane Austen never formulated any theory to cover her own practice; she invented no term like James's "central intelligence" or "lucid reflector" to describe her method of viewing the world of the book primarily through Emma's own eyes.... But whether she was inclined to speculate about her method scarcely matters; her solution was clearly a brilliant one. By showing most of the story through Emma's eyes, the author

insures that we shall travel with Emma rather than stand against her. It is not simply that Emma provides, in the unimpeachable evidence of her own conscience, proof that she has many redeeming qualities that do not appear on the surface; such evidence could be given with authorial commentary, though perhaps not with such force and conviction. Much more important, the sustained inside view leads the reader to hope for good fortune for the character with whom he travels, quite independently of the qualities revealed [245–6].

As in the case of Martin's series, "Austen's narrators and reflectors become virtually indistinguishable. When the narrator consistently places the narrative focus within a character's consciousness (it happens throughout *Emma*), readers may tend to see things from the character's visual, psychological, and ideological perspective" (Morini 31), and the effect on the reader's relationship with the character is significant. Austen's oft-quoted assertion that in writing *Emma*, she was creating a novel about a protagonist that no one would like (herself excluded) (Austen-Leigh 119), and the reality that readers have continued to gravitate toward Emma Woodhouse almost two-hundred years after the text's initial publication, has only served to reinforce the power of Austen's narrative technique.[11]

Reviewing the previously quoted passage from Sansa's second chapter in *A Game of Thrones*, one finds a smooth and logical transition from indirect discourse—"At first she thought she hated him for what they'd done to Lady" (*GoT* 30 Sansa 2: 250)—toward free-indirect discourse—"The queen had done it; she was the one to hate, her and Arya. Nothing bad would have happened except for Arya" (*GoT* 30 Sansa 2: 250). The following example from *Emma* follows a similar trajectory and provokes a comparable blend of frustration and sympathy toward the focalizing heroine:

> She was not struck by any thing remarkably clever in Miss Smith's conversation, but she found her altogether very engaging ... and so artlessly impressed by the appearance of every thing in so superior a style to what she had been used to, that she must have good sense and deserve encouragement. Encouragement should be given. Those soft blue eyes and all those natural graces should not be wasted on the inferior society of Highbury and its connections. The acquaintance she had already formed were unworthy of her [Austen 13].

As in the passage from *A Game of Thrones*, the narrator gradually "places himself ... directly into the experiential field of the character, and adopts the latter's perspective in regard to both time and place" (Pascal 9). The narrator thus forces the reader to do likewise, and though Emma's condescension toward Harriet and the Martins is just as exasperating as Sansa's worship of Joffrey, the discourse compels us to empathize with Emma and Sansa even as we disagree with them.

Though Sansa is the most obvious example for such a comparison, several of Martin's POV characters, if taken at the surface level or analyzed solely from the perspective of other POV characters, would seem highly disagreeable, whether due to crudeness and hedonism (in the case of Tyrion), haughtiness and intolerance (in the case of Catelyn), aloofness and corruption (in the case of Theon), or even unspeakable iniquity (in the case of Jaime). However, through his use of free-indirect discourse, Martin never allows the reader to take a fully judgmental position toward the POV character, as we experience their moments of self-consciousness, self-doubt, and even self-loathing: whether it is Sansa's depression following her father's execution, Tyrion's insecurity brought on by his deformities, Catelyn's guilt regarding her contempt for Jon, Theon's nightmares brought on by his crimes at Winterfell, or Jaime's realization of just how irreversibly he has degraded both himself and the Kingsguard. Jaime is a particularly striking example; Booth writes that "We have seen that inside views can build sympathy even for the most vicious character. When properly used, this effect can be of immeasurable value in forcing us to see the human worth of a character whose actions, objectively considered, we would deplore" (378). As in the case of Austen, Martin could allude to these complexities through the commentary of the third-person narrator, but it would not produce the same effect.

While Martin's technique allows for the cultivation of a complex Austenian relationship between reader, narrator, and character—however unsympathetic that character may be—it likewise facilitates his creation of an ambiguous universe in which monochromatic characters are given a chance to exist in shades of grey through discursive technique. Moreover, the ambiguity that defines Martin's narratorial perspectives can also be found in Austen, for as Massimiliano Morini has noted in his outstanding study of Austen's narrative techniques, the author's narrators "variously undermine their own authoritativeness and leave readers more or less stranded between the waves of conflicting interpretations" (19). Though Austen grants her narrators greater license and personality (occasionally allowing them to use the first person "I" even as she keeps their identities hidden) while Martin completely suppresses his narrator's personality behind the personalities of his POV characters, both authors shun the idea of an unquestionably authoritative narratorial voice. This technique prevents the reader from coming to a truly conclusive evaluation of the characters, their values, and the overarching "point" of the text.[12]

Still, the aforementioned comparisons belie the obvious fact that the fabulas of Austen and Martin are exceedingly incongruous. Pascal observes that

> Jane Austen's novels supply the preconditions one might consider necessary for the unhampered emergence of free indirect speech. They focus upon a small group of people who belong to one class and one cultural world, whose values, feelings, and thoughts, even if unknown, contain no mystery for them or for the narrator. They

do not lack plot, but the plot consists almost entirely of the changing attitudes of the characters to one another, so that their thoughts and feelings are the structural elements of the story [Pascal 45].

Comparing Austen's narrow view of society, her limited number of lead characters, and her subdued plots with Martin's sprawling social panoramic, his innumerable protagonists, and his convoluted medieval romance seems an exercise in absurdity. Yet, this disparity, when studied in the context of the discursive similarities between the two writers' narrational techniques, re-invokes the overarching issue of event vs. discourse. If, as Pascal notes, the sequence of events in Austen's novels is fundamentally conducive to the "emergence of free indirect speech," then why does Martin, whose fabula stands in such contrast to Austen's, utilize the same discursive technique?

Pascal's assessment of Austen belies the fact that in spite of the ostensible simplicity and straightforwardness of her plots, Austen is a master of suspense and secrecy; it is a talent she displays from early on in her career, as the "gothic" mystery of *Northanger Abbey* gives way to a more humorous domestic mystery regarding the scope of Catherine's misreading of the Tilney household. Similarly, in the case of *Emma*, the reader is so fully aligned with Emma's perspective that he or she misses vital clues regarding the true nature of Frank Churchill's relationship with Jane Fairfax. Though the scope and stakes of Martin's plots seem inestimably larger than Austen's courtships, his own understanding of how to build suspense within the preplanned events of the fabula is rooted in the same narrative principles of focalization and restriction.

Indirectness of Discourse, Incompleteness of Information

In his landmark texts on narrative discourse, Gérard Genette assesses focalization as a means of "restricting" the readers' vision and thus denying them access to vital plot information: "The variations in 'point of view' that occur in the course of a narrative … in such a case we can speak of variable focalization, of omniscience with partial restrictions of field, etc." (*Narrative Discourse* 194). He expands on this definition in *Narrative Discourse Revisited*, noting:

So by focalization I certainly mean a restriction of "field"—actually, that is, a selection of narrative information with respect to what was traditionally called *omniscience*. In pure fiction that term is, literally, absurd (the author has nothing to "know," since he invents everything), and we would be better off replacing it with *completeness of information*—which, when supplied to a reader, makes him "omniscient." The instrument of this possible selection is a *situated focus*, a sort of information-conveying pipe that allows passage only of information that is authorized by the situation [74, Genette's emphases].

Bal concurs that focalization is the ideal narrative strategy for achieving this effect, as "the focalizor's image can be incomplete. This is the case when the characters 'know' mor [sic] than the focalizor. That 'knowing more' must, of course, appear later. It is also possible for the focalizor to falsify an image by, for instance, leaving out certain elements, hiding them from the reader. In such a case, the characters also 'know more' than the reader" (114). The usefulness of both these narrative techniques in generating suspense is established early on in *A Game of Thrones*.

Tellingly, Bran, the youngest of all the major POV characters, is the first to take up the role of focalizor, and his youthfulness and innocence leave the reader uninformed about several important issues that unfold in the novel's very first chapter. When this chapter reaches its climax with the discovery of the dead direwolf, the event is imbued with a sense of mystery and foreboding, as Bran realizes that the other characters see something that he does not: "His father knelt and groped under the beast's head with his hand. He gave a yank and held it up for all to see. A foot of shattered antler, tines snapped off, all wet with blood. A sudden silence descended over the party. The men looked at the antler uneasily, and no one dared to speak. Even Bran could sense their fear, though he did not understand" (*GoT* 2 Bran 1: 15). Like Bran, the reader is confused by this unstated fear.

In the next chapter, "Catelyn 1," Bal's second scenario unfolds, as Catelyn, who clearly understands and shares the Winterfell residents' apprehension regarding the implications of the dead wolf, chooses not to reveal the foundations of this anxiety: "Catelyn wished she could share [Eddard's] joy. But she had heard the talk in the yards; a direwolf dead in the snow, a broken antler in its throat. Dread coiled within her like a snake, but she forced herself to smile at this man she loved, this man who put no faith in signs" (*GoT* 3 Catelyn 1: 21). Obviously, Catelyn is not purposefully withholding information from the reader, but the source of her anxiety remains hidden nevertheless. However, Catelyn reveals two important clues: (a) her apprehension regarding the dead direwolf is somehow connected with Robert Baratheon's looming visit to Winterfell, and (b) her fear relates to some sort of intangible, symbolic connotation of the animal.

Though the issue is dropped entirely in "Daenerys 1," and though no character ever actually reflects upon the full significance of the dead direwolf, the reader will find the necessary clue for solving this mystery in "Eddard 1," which begins with the following sentences: "The visitors poured through the castle gates in a river of gold and silver and polished steel, three hundred strong, a pride of bannermen and knights, of sworn swords and freeriders. Over their heads a dozen golden banners whipped back and forth in the northern wind, emblazoned with the crowned stag of Baratheon" (*GoT* 5 Eddard 1: 32). Eddard does not dwell on the banner and the revelation that House Baratheon uses a stag as its symbol is extremely subtle, yet it should now be obvious why Catelyn was so unnerved by the symbolism of the direwolf. Mystery thus gives way to portentous foreshadowing regarding Eddard's downfall, as initiated by his consenting to serve as Hand to King Robert Baratheon.[13]

Martin's gradual buildup toward the revelation of the direwolf's significance is just one example of the effectiveness of variable focalization in generating mystery. However, this same technique may likewise seem something of a "cheat," as Martin denies many characters the opportunity to serve as a focalizor so as to preserve a mystery. In reference to Austen, who utilized the same "trick," Booth claims "One objection to this selective dipping into whatever mind best serves our immediate purposes is that it suggests mere trickery and inevitably spoils the illusion of reality. If Jane Austen can tell us what Mrs. Weston is thinking, why not what Frank Churchill and Jane Fairfax are thinking? Obviously, because she chooses to build a mystery, and to do so she must refuse, arbitrarily and obtrusively, to grant the privilege of an inside view to characters whose minds would reveal too much" (254).[14] For Martin, it is imperative that not every major character take up the role of focalizor if the series' mysteries are to be preserved.

The most obvious example is Petyr "Littlefinger" Baelish, who, in the final chapter of *A Storm of Swords*, is revealed to be the ultimate mastermind behind the War of the Five Kings and the man responsible for initiating virtually all of the events that make up the fabula. One can take a more narrow view of the subject and simply point to *A Game of Thrones* itself, as Littlefinger's betrayal of Eddard is arguably the turning point of the novel; it would be folly to place Littlefinger in the role of focalizor as the sense of mystery surrounding his interactions with Eddard, along with the shock of his betrayal in "Eddard 14," would be lost. By allowing various characters who have conflicting views of Littlefinger to serve as focalizors, Martin can build a mystery around Littlefinger and raise the reader's suspicions regarding Baelish's true motives and loyalties even as Eddard and Catelyn begin to trust him.

In "Catelyn 4," Littlefinger's assertion that Tyrion tried to kill Bran is based entirely around the suggestion that Tyrion won the infamous dragon-bone dagger by betting on Ser Loras Tyrell to win a jousting tournament. However, in "Eddard 7," Renly Baratheon, who has won a significant amount of money by betting against Jaime Lannister, casually alludes to the fact that Tyrion always bets on his brother: "A pity the Imp is not here with us.... I should have won twice as much" (*GoT* 31 Eddard 7: 262). It is a throwaway line, much like the description of the Baratheon sigil in "Eddard I," and, as in the previous instance, Eddard ignores its implications. In the very next chapter, however—"Tyrion 4"—Tyrion himself insists that he never bets against Jaime. Obviously, having Littlefinger serve as focalizor and reflect on his deliberate misleading of Eddard and Catelyn would spoil the mystery, though the careful reader will note that his lie has been confirmed by two sources. Unfortunately, Catlyn only has Tyrion's word against Littlefinger's, and Eddard completely misses the significance of Renly's statement.

Here then is another benefit to "restriction" that Austen perceived and exploited in her own novels; as Booth notes, "On the one hand she cares about maintaining some sense of mystery as long as she can. On the other, she works at all points to heighten the reader's sense of dramatic irony, usually in the form of a contrast between what Emma knows and what the reader knows" (255). If one of the most enjoyable elements of rereading *Emma* is the opportunity to trace the title character's misreading of various situations (and reevaluate our own misreading as prompted by her faulty perspective), one of the most frustrating side-effects of rereading *A Game of Thrones* is watching Eddard and Catelyn stumble from one mistaken judgment to another due to their inability to perceive Littlefinger's villainy. Of course, it is impossible to truly fault them, for the reader is likewise unaware of the full extent of Littlefinger's plotting due to the absence of a Littlefinger POV chapter, and also to the marked subtlety of the aforementioned clues. Ultimately, Martin, like Austen before him, faces a balancing act in trying to alternate between mystery and dramatic irony:

> The sooner we see through Frank Churchill's secret plot, the greater our pleasure in observing Emma's innumerable misreadings of his behavior and the less interest we have in the mere mystery of the situation. And we all find that on second rereading we discover new intensities of dramatic irony resulting from the complete loss of mystery.... But it is obvious that these ironies could have been offered even on a first reading, if Jane Austen had been willing to sacrifice her mystery.... The author must, then, choose whether to purchase mystery at the expense of irony [Booth 255].

Martin, however, achieves both mystery and irony, intimating Littlefinger's villainy while keeping Littlefinger's perspective hidden. Similar situations unfold in the later books: in *A Storm of Swords*, Roose Bolton informs Robb and Catelyn that Robett Glover recklessly attacked Duskendale, and that his bastard son, Ramsay Snow, helped liberate Winterfell (*SoS* 50 Catelyn 6). Both of these statements are false: in *A Clash of Kings*, Arya observes Bolton ordering the attack on Duskendale (*CoK* 65 Arya 10), while Theon witnesses Ramsay sacking Winterfell (*CoK* 67 Theon 6). The wary reader thus knows that Bolton is deceiving the Starks, though the full extent of his villainy, along with his intentions, remains hidden. Consequently, the suspenseful buildup toward the novel's climax presents a fitting combination of mystery ("What is Bolton planning?") and dramatic irony ("I know Bolton is a villain, but Robb and Catelyn trust him.") As in the case of Littlefinger's betrayal of Eddard, the horrific shock of the Red Wedding is not diminished by either of these elements; though the mystery would be ruined and the dramatic irony greatly enhanced if Bolton were given a POV chapter, Martin opts to try and preserve both components through his meticulous varying of perspectives.

"That was when she saw her father": Discourse vs. Event, Round 2

Martin's successful use of focalized discourse as a means of generating mystery and suspense in his fabula inevitably returns us to the issue of discourse vs. event, and given that the Red Wedding factored prominently in the initial scrutiny of this conflict, this recapitulation seems all the more fitting. Focalization is obviously a discursive technique, and yet the way in which Martin applies it seemingly reinforces the primacy of events. By choosing not to turn the discourse over to characters like Littlefinger and Bolton, Martin ensures that the movement toward the solutions to the various mysteries will be gradual and climactic.[15] However, in light of the discursive power of POV characters, there is surely more to focalization than suspenseful plotting of events.

Jonathan Culler famously contested the traditional "primacy of events" argument by pointing out that events sometimes unfold due to a "convergence of discursive forces" (174) which produces meaning.[16] Still, though Culler promotes the power of discourse to shape meaning/signification (and thus, to justify events), he does not negate the importance of events in relation to discourse. Rather, the central target of the critic's ire is the traditionally "peaceful" reconciliation of story and discourse, a reconciliation that he rejects based on his own perception of an irreconcilable "double logic" that exists in all narratives (178): "every narrative operates according to this double logic, presenting its plot as a sequence of events which is prior to and independent of the given perspective on these events, and, at the same time, suggesting by its implicit claims to significance that these events are justified by their appropriateness to a thematic structure" (178). In the case of *A Song of Ice and Fire*, there is perhaps no better event to scrutinize through this lens than the most memorable event in *A Game of Thrones*: the death of Eddard Stark. It is an event that continues to reverberate throughout the series, though its reverberations outside of the texts and within the fan community that has embraced the books are perhaps more significant.

For certain, the universal and unwavering fan hatred for Joffrey is principally attributable to this event, though this is taking the first viewpoint outlined by Culler and accepting the independence/existence of events: Joffrey orders the execution of Eddard. The shock and bewilderment surrounding the death of the ostensible hero seemingly reinforces the primacy and forcefulness of the event. However, this view of the subject moves us closer to Culler's second perspective as we debate this plot twist: did Eddard have to die? Thematically speaking, the answer seems to be "yes." Not only does Eddard's death reinforce the harshness and complexity of Martin's universe—as a fundamentally good and honorable character is crushed out of existence by corrupt individuals who lack his integrity—but it likewise signifies the larger loss of the series' moral center. In many respects, the narrative demands that Eddard be sacrificed so as to prefigure the chaotic cruelty that will define the next two books in the series, a chaotic cruelty that seems all the more appropriate given that the one character who was fundamentally dedicated to order and morality was senselessly murdered.

However, the vital importance of focalization to Martin's discourse adds another dimension to Culler's theory. Staying on the current example, it is vital to note that Eddard's death unfolds through Arya's perspective, despite the fact that two other POV characters are present: Sansa and Eddard himself (and as Catelyn's final chapter in *A Storm of Swords* proves, a character is more than capable of focalizing his or her own death). However, Arya *must* serve as the focalizor at this moment in the narrative. Certainly, Arya's trauma as she watches her father pushed to his knees, along with her desperation as she tries to cut her way through the crowd in a hopeless attempt to save him, is wrenching and adds to the emotional resonance of the scene, but even more significant is the fact that Arya, the focalizor at this key turning point, loses her innocence at the very same moment that the series loses its innocence. The significance of this loss is perceptible because the discourse is placed in Arya's hands. Just as the series will now begin its descent into darkness and chaos with *A Clash of Kings* and *A Storm of Swords*, Arya will now begin her journey from a mischievous scamp attempting to find her place in the world, to a traumatized fugitive struggling against loneliness and terror, to a ruthless assassin plotting to avenge her family. Culler's assertion regarding the complex interrelationship between event, discourse, and meaning is thus taken to the next level by the use of a specific POV character at this moment in the narrative: Eddard's death is an event, but that event serves the "demands of signification" as set up by the narrative, and the use of Arya as a discursive POV character during this event underscores that signification given the thematic overlap between her perspective and the progression of the narrative.

Conclusion

In *The Rhetoric of Fiction*, Wayne C. Booth asserts that "narration is an art, not a science, but this does not mean that we are necessarily doomed to fail when we attempt to formulate principles about it" (164). In the case of *A Song of Ice and Fire*, articulating such principles can help to clarify misnomers (narrators vs. POV characters) and to define key tensions (story vs. discourse). Moreover, as I have tried to demonstrate, it is possible to resolve some of these tensions by analyzing how story and discourse work together; however helpless the POV characters may seem in the face of the fabula, their ability to define the reader's perception of events grants them a discursive power that profoundly shapes the text's meaning, ambiguous though that meaning may be. Still, as the narrative meanders toward its climax, and winter finally arrives, Martin may need to sacrifice those same ambiguities, both moral and narrative-based. In the same text, Booth ominously predicts that "there will come a time for many authors when there will be an open conflict between the obligation to seem dispassionate and objective and the obligation to heighten other effects by making the moral basis of the work unequivocally clear" (389). As *A Song of Ice and Fire* reaches its crescendo, and the series' characters find themselves in a fundamental struggle for survival, the moral ambiguity of characters like Tyrion, Jaime, Asha, Theon, Melisandre, and Stannis seems negligible; the division of the fabula and the discourse likewise seems counterintuitive given the necessity of unity and unanimity in the face of the apocalyptic threat posed by the Others. While the ultimate prospect of salvation appears to lie with Jon, Daenerys, or Bran, perhaps the true hope lies with an omniscient narratorial consciousness that can organize and unify the story, the discourse, and the characters in time for the coming winter.[17]

Notes

1. Martin makes certain exceptions when interpolating general accounts of Westerosi history; given the expository nature of these historical accounts, the personalities of the focalizors momentarily become less distinct.

2. Gérard Genette foregrounds the fabula by describing the story as "the totality of the narrated events" (*Revisited* 13), and placing the narrative in the subservient position of "the discourse, oral or written, that narrates them" (*Revisited* 13). Similarly, Mieke Bal's analysis of different versions of the same story establishes the story as a foundation that exists regardless of discourse: "Evidently, narrative texts differ from one another even if the related story is the same. It is therefore useful to examine the text separate from the story" (5). Scrutinizing this trend, Culler asserts that the story, as a "sequence of actions," is independent of the discourse (169–70).

3. I am glossing over Catelyn's return as Lady Stoneheart; whatever further influence Catelyn exerts on the narrative, it is doubtful that she will control the discourse again.

4. Granted, Arya is partially privy to the Red Wedding, as she arrives at the gate to the

castle just as the massacre begins (*SoS* 53 Arya 11). This marks one of the few instances in the series where the precise chronological relationship between sequential chapters is apparent; Catelyn and Arya react to the same sounds in their chapters ("Rains of Castamere," Grey Wind's howl), which creates an exact chronology and a rare instance of simultaneity. Still, it is essential that Catelyn's chapter be placed before Arya's. Placing Arya's chapter first would ruin the careful buildup toward the novel's climax by revealing the Freys' treason before it is executed on Robb and Catelyn. Moreover, presenting the Red Wedding solely through Arya's second-hand perspective would change the meaning of the text. The driving idea behind the scene is loss, as the Starks lose the war, their bannermen, and their lives in one fell swoop, and the only character who can effectively serve as focalizor in conveying the horror of that loss to the reader is Catelyn, who has already lost more than practically any other character in the series.

5. For example, the introduction of "fierce Ferrau" in Canto 1 initially establishes him as another warrior-suitor in pursuit of Angelica (4), though he becomes sidetracked by a quest to attain Orlando's helmet (8). Later, in Canto 12, the two quests intersect when Angelica steals Orlando's helmet; Ferrau ends up pursuing both the girl *and* the helmet, but only attains the latter (238).

6. It is perhaps fitting that the middle books in the series take the narrative in a divergent direction, for "in medieval narrative the middle is frequently a point of maximum logical discontinuity" (Ryding 40).

7. Martin employs a similar strategy in *A Clash of Kings*, using the red comet and the various characters' views of this heavenly body as a linking factor even as he jumps around geographically and chronologically.

8. Interestingly, when Sansa takes action in *A Game of Thrones*, her actions revolve around narration: lying to Robert when he asks her to recount Joffrey's behavior at the Trident (*GoT* 17 Eddard 3), and betraying Eddard's plans to Cersei (*GoT* 52 Sansa 4). This underscores the notion that Sansa's power is basically discursive.

9. Ora Segal notes that for James, "'seeing' ... could be an authentic rather than merely a vicarious form of 'being'—a form more intense and more valuable than any other" (xii). This description seems highly applicable to Martin, whose use of internal reflection as opposed to verbal narration reinforces the Jamesian elements of his narrative strategy: "First-person narrative is not adequate for [James's] purposes, because he is not looking for a conscious revelation of character, or for a novel based on recollection of past experience" (Onega and Landa 19).

10. I do not mean to imply that focalization and free-indirect discourse are interchangeable; focalization refers to a general discursive strategy, whilst free-indirect discourse is a specific form of narration. J. Hillis Miller—who disapproved of the terms "focalization" and "point of view" given narration's dependence on language (125)—describes the latter as a "genuinely linguistic term" while labeling the former a "figure of speech" (125).

11. Admittedly, I am evading the fact that the general fan reaction to Sansa—as conveyed through various *Song of Ice and Fire* blogs and message-boards—borders upon pure hatred. This fact seemingly negates my comparison between Sansa and Emma regarding the ability of discourse to facilitate sympathy for unsympathetic characters; still, the dichotomy between the events in their respective novels must be acknowledged: Emma's foolish actions threaten to *ruin* Harriet and Robert's lives, while Sansa's foolish actions *cost* people their lives.

12. In the case of Austen, Morini cites *Mansfield Park* as the most obvious example of this trend: "...Austen creates a narrator who questions his/her own authority by disseminating it in various ways and among various characters: and in the end, our reading of the novel is not double, but multiple, depending as it does on how much we identify with Fanny, Edmund, Mary, and even with such unattractive characters as the Bertram sisters, Sir Thomas, and Mrs. Norris.... The 'point' of [*Mansfield Park*] is so complicated that there almost seems to be no point to the novel" (53).

13. Catelyn's eventual insistence that Eddard agree to serve as Robert's Hand is curious given her insight into the symbolic significance of the dead direwolf, though it seems that her fears stem from Robert's potential anger were Ned to refuse the offer (*GoT* 7 Catelyn 2).

14. Granted, Martin repeatedly proves that a character can serve as a focalizor whilst keeping information hidden from the reader. Eddard himself serves as the focalizor more frequently than any other character in *A Game of Thrones*, and yet, vital questions regarding Jon Snow's parentage, the confrontation between the rebels and the Kingsguard in the Tower of Joy, and the death of Lyanna Stark remain unanswered despite the fact that Eddard possesses all of this information. Nevertheless, Martin is careful to deny certain characters (such as Littlefinger and Varys) focalization, for to put these characters in a POV role while simultaneously avoiding key bits of information that these characters possess would stretch the limits of Martin's narratorial credibility to the breaking point.

15. In spite of the essential moral ambiguity of *A Song of Ice and Fire*, the first three novels clearly favor the sympathetic/heroic characters over the antagonistic/villainous characters when it comes to focalization, primarily because these characters do not possess vital plot information; placing the narrative in the hands of Littlefinger, Cersei, Tywin, Joffrey, Pycelle, Varys, Bolton, Ramsay, or Lysa would undoubtedly hurt the mystery element, though, as Booth implies, it would simultaneously enhance the dramatic irony significantly.

16. Culler's citing of *Oedipus Rex* as a key example seems strangely applicable to *A Song of Ice and Fire*. In *Oedipus Rex*, all of the key events have taken place prior to the start of the play, and the tragedy is based on a series of discursive disclosures that reveal Oedipus as the murderer of Laius. However, Culler argues that "Instead of the revelation of a prior deed determining meaning, we could say that it is meaning, the convergence of meaning in the narrative discourse, that leads us to posit this deed as its appropriate manifestation" (174). As in the case of *Oedipus*, *A Song of Ice and Fire* opens with a murder mystery, and the key event—the death of Jon Arryn—occurs prior to the opening scene. The eventual revelation of Lysa Arryn as the murderer confirms that Lysa was the initiator of the novel's fabula on two different levels: her false letter to Catelyn in *A Game of Thrones* produces just as devastating an effect on the series' protagonists as her actual murder of her husband. The discovery of Lysa's guilt thus fulfills the "demands of signification" (174) as outlined by the narrative discourse in a way that would not be possible were Cersei, Jaime, Varys, or Pycelle exposed as Arryn's killer. Over the course of the first three novels, characters as diverse as Robert, Catelyn, Tyrion, Walder Frey, and Stannis have shaped the discourse in such a way that Lysa's dependability, morality, and basic sanity have been called into question long before the revelation of her treachery. Like Oedipus, she must "bow to the demands of narrative coherence" (Culler 174) and accept her role as murderer.

17. Like many fans, I believe the rumors of Jon's untimely death to be greatly exaggerated.

Works Cited

Ariosto, Ludovico. *Orlando Furioso*. Trans. David R. Slavitt. Cambridge: Harvard University Press, 2009. Print.

Austen, Jane. *Emma*, 3d ed. New York: W.W. Norton, 2000. Print.

Austen-Leigh, J.E. *A Memoir of Jane Austen and Other Family Recollections*. Ed. Kathryn Sutherland. New York: Oxford University Press, 2002. Print.

Bal, Mieke. *Narratology: Introduction to the Theory of Narrative*. Trans. Christine van Boheemen. Toronto: University of Toronto Press, 1985. Print.

Barthes, Roland. *Image, Music, Text*. Trans. Stephen Heath. New York: Hill and Wang, 1977. Print.

Booth, Wayne C. *The Rhetoric of Fiction*. Chicago: University of Chicago Press, 1961. Print.

Culler, Jonathan. *The Pursuit of Signs*. London: Routledge, 1981. Print.

de Troyes, Chrétien. *Erec Et Enide* in *Arthurian Romances*. Trans. W.W. Comfort. New York: Dutton, 1976. Print.

Davenport, Tony. *Medieval Narrative: An Introduction*. Oxford: Oxford University Press, 2004. Print.

Genette, Gérard. *Narrative Discourse: An Essay in Method*. Trans. Jane E. Lewin. Ithaca: Cornell University Press, 1980. Print.

____. *Narrative Discourse Revisited*. Trans. Jane E. Lewin. Ithaca: Cornell University Press, 1988. Print.

Herman, Luc, and Bart Vervaeck. *Handbook of Narrative Analysis*. Lincoln: University of Nebraska Press, 2005. Print.

Hibberd, James. "'Game of Thrones' author George R.R. Martin: Why he wrote The Red Wedding." *Entertainment Weekly*. 2 June 2013. Web. 3 June 2013.

James, Henry. *The Tragic Muse* in *The Novels and Tales of Henry James: New York Edition, Volume VII*. New York: Charles Scribner's Sons, 1908. Print.

Lothe, Jakob. *Narrative in Fiction and Film: An Introduction*. New York: Oxford University Press, 2000. Print.

Miller, J. Hillis. "Henry James and 'Focalization,' or Why James Loves Gyp" in *A Companion to Narrative Theory*. Ed. James Phelan and Peter J. Rabinowitz. Malden: Blackwell, 2005. 124–135. Print.

Morini, Massimiliano. *Jane Austen's Narrative Techniques*. Burlington: Ashgate, 2009. Print.

Mudrick, Marvin. "Character and Event in Fiction." *The Yale Review* 50 (1960): 202–218. Print.

Onega, Susana, and Jose Angel Garcia Landa. "Introduction" in *Narratology: An Introduction*. Ed. Susana Onega and Jose Angel Garcia Landa. New York: Longman, 1996. 1–41. Print.

Pascal, Roy. *The Dual Voice: Free Indirect Speech and Its Functioning in the Nineteenth-Century European Novel*. Manchester: Manchester University Press, 1977. Print.

Quint, David. "Narrative Interlace and Narrative Genres in *Don Quijote* and the *Orlando Furioso*." *Modern Language Quarterly* 58.3 (1997): 241–268.

Ryding, William W. *Structure in Medieval Narrative*. The Hague: Mouton, 1971. Print.

Segal, Ora. *The Lucid Reflector*. New Haven: Yale University Press, 1969. Print.

Sir Gawain and the Green Knight in *Sir Gawain and the Green Knight, Pearl, and Sir Orfeo*. Trans. J.R.R. Tolkien. Boston: Houghton Mifflin, 1975. 25–88. Print.

What Maesters Knew: Narrating Knowing

BRIAN COWLISHAW

"It is known"—Formulaic Dothraki response to various truth claims

"You know nothing, Jon Snow"—Frequent taunt from Ygritte the Wildling

Readers encounter these lines frequently in George R.R. Martin's *Song of Ice and Fire* books. Both lines generally prove wrong or misguided, though. "It is known"—that dragons are forever vanished from this world; that the Lamb Men "lay with sheep" (*GoT* 62 Daenerys 7: 557); that Qarth will be the death of Daenerys and her followers. Even as these truth claims are made they seem dubious not in spite but *because* of the "it is known" imprimatur,[1] and they do prove false in time. Ygritte's taunt has a bit more accuracy, relatively, but mostly its truth-value applies specifically only to Jon's virginal innocence. About sex and love he "knows nothing" until she shows him, yes, but he knows or figures out more than anyone else regarding the most pressing issues in his world: that the threat of the Others is real; how to fight them effectively; the necessity of joining forces with the Wildlings to save humanity. Thus, every time we read "It is known" or "You know nothing," it's a little bit funny because we know it's wrong. We can't help but hear the irony.

These lines serve as a Greek-chorus-like reminder of the central problem of *knowing* in this fantasy saga. In a word: no one knows anything. No one *can* know anything. This maxim holds true both for characters within Martin's fictional world and for us in the act of reading about it. Martin's maesters, designated professional knowers of numerous, widely varied bodies of information, ultimately know nothing of much importance. The level and value of their knowledge proves lacking at every turn. Maesters' epistemological shortcomings illustrate and mirror our own: as readers, we *really* know nothing. In this way, the experience of reading *A Song of Ice and Fire* provides an exaggerated exam-

ple—thus making the point powerfully—of the way all readers depend completely on authors for accurate information, and how authors may or may not,
at their whim, provide it.[2]

Maesters in Westeros are generalists in a world where most people are either
completely illiterate or just literate enough to manage their own circumscribed
business—account books, inventories, genealogies. Lords and ladies receive some
basic education due to their position, enough to send each other messages by
raven and check each other's family lineages. Few others learn much of anything
(aside from vocational skills; see below).[3] Maesters seem intellectual titans by
comparison, as signified tangibly in public by their chains of office. In Jon Snow's
words, "A maester forges his chain with study…. The different metals are each
a different kind of learning, gold for the study of money and accounts, silver for
healing, iron for warcraft" (*GoT* 42 Jon 5: 376). Bran adds: "Every time you learn
something you get another link. Black iron is for ravenry, silver for healing"
(*CoK* 29 Bran 4: 331). The oldest maesters have the longest, most varied, most
imposing chains. The chain of Grandmaester Pycelle, also the Small Council's
advisor to the Iron Throne, is an absolute wonder to behold:

> His maester's collar was no simple metal choker such as Luwin wore, but two dozen
> heavy chains wound together into a ponderous metal necklace that covered him from
> throat to breast. The links were forged of every metal known to man: black iron and
> red gold, bright copper and dull lead, steel and tin and pale silver, brass and bronze
> and platinum. Garnets and amethysts and black pearls adorned the metalwork, and
> here and there an emerald or ruby [*GoT* 21 Eddard 4: 162].

When *one* link requires uncountable hours of study to demonstrate mastery,
Pycelle's chain boggles the mind. Ensconced in the "wormways" of the Wall's
dark, dusty library, Samwell Tarly quails at the sheer scope of intellectual labor
ahead of him, despite his love for the work:

> [T]he dust was everywhere down here. Little puffs of it filled the air every time a
> page was turned, and it rose in grey clouds whenever he shifted a stack of books to
> see what might be hiding on the bottom.
>
> Sam did not know how long it had been since last he'd slept, but scarce an inch
> remained of the fat tallow candle he'd lit when starting on the ragged bundle of loose
> pages that he'd found tied up in twine. He was beastly tired, but it was hard to stop.
> *One more book*, he had told himself, *then I'll stop. One more folio, just one more. One
> more page, then I'll go up and rest and get a bite to eat.* But there was always another
> page after that one, and another after that, and another book waiting underneath the
> pile [*FfC* 6 Samwell 1: 78–79].

Sam knows from experience that a maester's chains take a lifetime to forge.

"In the kingdom of the blind, the one-eyed man is king," says an old proverb
in our world. In Martin's world filled with illiterates, even the barely-literate

wield some power. Literate-but-not-especially-widely-learned groups such as the Church's Septons and Septas maintain some limited power. For a time, they are able to imprison the disgraced Cersei, then force her to perform a naked, cross-town walk of shame, with complete impunity. The Silent Sisters, too, at least enjoy group autonomy, unlike most of the (living) people they assist with their work. An educated palace eunuch such as Varys may enjoy considerable power, too, relative to the laboring unlearned masses. Limited power corresponds directly to, and generally functions as, the perquisite of limited knowledge. Varys knows *more* than what he can glean from a few books, due to his vast network of "little birds"; thus, he has more power. As characters such as Varys and Littlefinger know very well, in Westeros, knowledge is power.

I'm distinguishing here between the kind of knowledge gained from education, and the "knowledge" Littlefinger and Varys gain from gossip and spies. My primary concern is with the former kind. Both of these characters' life trajectories suggest that education-based knowledge is the necessary precursor to power, and that dirty-laundry-type knowledge can only serve much of a purpose once the other kind has been achieved. After all, every illiterate chamber servant has volumes of dirt on her/his masters, but clearly they have little or no power. Gossip in itself does not lend power.

Maesters know much more than half-learned groups such as Church officials, as their chains remind the world every moment. Correspondingly, maesters have greater power. They advise kings and lords, and are actively sought after as symbols of power in themselves. As Lady Dustin observes to Theon Greyjoy, "Every great lord has his maester, every lesser lord aspires to one. If you do not have a maester, it is taken to mean that you are of little consequence" (*DwD* 38 The Prince of Winterfell 1: 495).

To say this is to say that maesters neatly embody Michel Foucault's concept of power/knowledge, which runs through all of that philosopher's work. As Foucault demonstrates, power and knowledge are intimately connected and mutually productive: they are not power *and* knowledge—separate phenomena—but rather, one, power/knowledge. They constitute and reaffirm each other. Those in power pronounce certain kinds of knowledge more valid and valuable than other kinds. Knowledge is not absolute; rather, it is contingent, relative, ever-changing. It has been different in different times and with different people in power; it will change again in the future, in new hands. Individuals and institutions possessing valued knowledge also possess greater power. They use that power in shaping knowledge. And so forth, in a constant, mutual, productive process: knowledge bestows power; power defines and validates knowledge. Hence, power/knowledge.[4]

In these Foucauldian terms, maesters are central to Westeros's edifices of power. Maesters are the individuals designated to *know*, when very few others know much of anything. Knowing is their raison d'être. They know more than the kings and lords they serve. By the authority of their state-approved knowledge, they define the ontology and status of nearly everything and everyone in the kingdom. For example, it's not officially autumn until they finally announce that it is, though by then it has become self-evident to all. Someone who knows that much surely can't truly be trusted, as Lady Dustin mutters to Theon Greyjoy:

> If I were queen, the first thing I would do would be to kill all those grey rats [maesters]. They scurry everywhere, living on the leavings of the lords, chittering to one another, whispering in the ears of their masters. But who are the masters and who are the servants, truly?... The grey rats read and write our letters, even for such lords as cannot read themselves, and who can say for a certainty that they are not twisting the words for their own ends?... Out of gratitude we give them a place beneath our roof and make them privy to all our shames and secrets, a part of every council. And before too long, the ruler has become the ruled [*DwD* 38 The Prince of Winterfell 1: 495–96].

But here's the rub: in Martin's saga, *that never happens*. For all that maesters probably ought to run the world, they simply don't. They serve—period. I've been building a case for the ways in which maesters *should* have power in Westeros, and/or *seem to* have power. But now I'll delineate how things truly stand with maesters and their power/knowledge.

In short: times are tough. More than anything else, age has caught up to the maesters. Blind Maester Aemon, long ago a Targaryen candidate for the Iron Throne, now long forgotten up at the Wall, is one hundred years old in *A Game of Thrones*. He dies of fever in *A Feast for Crows* at 102. Grandmaester Pycelle in *Feast* is 84; he's murdered by Varys, rather redundantly considering his ineffectuality, feebleness, and complete lack of influence on Regent Cersei and (the late) Prince Joffrey. Though on the Small Council, Pycelle was plainly nothing but a clueless pawn.[5] In the Prologue to *A Clash of Kings*, poor old Maester Cressen is too ancient and worn out to tend the ravens any longer. He suffers mightily when called to Stannis Baratheon's Round Room—all those stairs up to the tower pain his creaky old hips. Napping deep and long, he sleeps well into dinner time. He attempts to poison Melisandre, but succeeds only in poisoning himself and dying in agony. Archmaester Walgrave at the Citadel—Archmaester! the head man where maesters are educated!—is described in the saddest terms: "The old man remained an archmaester only by courtesy. As great a maester as once he'd been, now his robes concealed soiled small clothes oft as not, and half a year ago some acolytes found him weeping in the Library, unable to find his way back to [his] chambers" (*FfC* 1 Prologue: 3). Furthermore, "some days he seemed to think Pate was someone named Cressen" (*FfC* 1 Prologue: 10). The highest-ranking, most learned maesters—the ones most likely and qualified to wield real power—are the most ancient, feeble, doddering, ignored. Stannis, for one, has reached the end of his patience, telling Cressen, "Once you were young. Now you are old and sick, and need your sleep.... I have heard your counsel, Cressen. Now I will hear hers [Melisandre's]. You are dismissed" (*CoK* 1 Prologue: 14). During Tyrion's brief tenure as Hand of the King, he shears off Grandmaester Pycelle's beard and slams him into a black cell. Is there any reader anywhere who doesn't find that just and satisfying? After Maester Kerwin fails to cure Victarion Greyjoy's poisoned wound, but the wizard Moqorro *does* heal it, Victarion orders: "That one. Cut his throat and throw him in the sea, and winds will favor us all the way to Meereen" (*DwD* 57 The Iron Suitor 1: 753). Figuratively and literally, proceeding without maesters' dead old weight makes rulers' sailing smoother.

Now, it is true that although the maesters are most often and prominently described as old and worthless, there are a few young ones mentioned: Samwell Tarly and his acolyte companions in Oldtown's Citadel, primarily. (There is the ineffectual Kerwin, as well, who is described as a bit effeminate too.) These young ones are *so* young that they don't yet wear chains. Most haven't yet earned a single link. Thus, only two categories of maesters really exist: those too young to know or do much, and those too old to know or do much.[6] This speaks volumes for the kind of academically-grounded, systematic, disciplined, broad-based knowledge the maesters possess: ultimately, it doesn't matter or help much. Their knowledge is irrelevant to power, except perhaps—á la Lady Dustin—in the remotest, most vaguely symbolic way. They bear much the same reputation in Westeros that academics carry in our world: mildly respectable, and intelligent in obscure, impractical ways; full of "book-learning" that doesn't translate to the "real world"; useful for showing off how "advanced" a given house or kingdom is, but good for little else.

To return to the problems associated with becoming a maester: in addition to demonstrating infinite hours of study, the chain of office consistently communicates to us readers the other primary meaning of "chain"—tying down, binding, limiting, and above all *weighing down*. Remember Pycelle's "ponderous metal necklace" described earlier: that telling word "ponderous" comes up in connection with the chain multiple times. Talking to Regent Cersei, Pycelle "looked as if the weight of the huge maester's chain about his wattled neck was dragging him down to the floor" (*FfC* 37 Cersei 8: 542). Announcing King Robert's death, Pycelle's "shoulders slumped, as if the weight of the great maester's chain around his neck had become too great to bear" (*GoT* 50 Eddard 14: 438). Ancient Maester Aemon can barely support his chain's weight: "He was a tiny thing, wrinkled and hairless, shrunken beneath the weight of a hundred years so his maester's collar with its links of many metals hung loose about his throat" (*GoT* 22 Tyrion 3: 173). Before his own poison snuffs him out, Cressen notes that the "chain around his throat felt very heavy" (*CoK* 1 Prologue: 15). What energetic young person would choose to voluntarily chain himself thus? Samwell Tarly certainly doesn't relish the prospect. He loves to read—but those mountains of dry old books! The dust-choked wormways! Years upon years of (celibate!) slogging at the Citadel! Book-eating mice as his most constant companions! Dutiful and studious as he is, he "did not want to be a maester, with a heavy chain wrapped around his neck, cold against his skin" (*FfC* 16 Samwell 2: 216).

The other obvious candidate for maestership, the crippled but intelligent and nobly-born Bran Stark, has zero interest in that life path. Maester Luwin tries to redirect Bran's dreams of becoming a valiant knight by calling maesters "knights of the mind," and promising, "There is no limit to what you might learn" (*GoT* 54 Bran 6: 484). However, Bran insists, "I want to learn *magic*.... The crow promised that I would fly." In response,

> Maester Luwin sighed. "I can teach you history, healing, herblore. I can teach you the speech of ravens, and how to build a castle, and the way a sailor steers his ship by the stars. I can teach you to measure the days and mark the seasons, and at the Citadel in Oldtown they can teach you a thousand things more. But, Bran, no man can teach you magic."
> "The children could," Bran said. "The children of the forest" [*GoT* 54 Bran 6: 484–5].

This conversation gets at the heart of the way maesters simply "don't get it": Luwin is wrong, and Bran is right. Much of what the maesters "know" is wrong; much that is essential to know, they deny, ignore, or mistakenly consider a tale for children. Their standard for true knowledge does not incorporate anything which is at all magical or mystical, nor even that which is merely amazing. Maesters' knowledge is limited—"chained"—to that which is sanctioned by the Citadel as rational, scientific, empirical, and verifiable in person or by institutionally-approved expert witness. They are too skeptical. With their book-learning they have effectively reasoned out of the world everything magic, wondrous, and unusual; however, the central problem remains that these things nevertheless continue to exist. Maesters' "knowledge" has outstripped its subject, and thereby, its accuracy and worth.

Examples abound. Maester Luwin explains patiently to Bran that "there are no more giants. He says they're all dead, like the children of the forest. All that's left of them are old bones in the earth that men turn up with plows from time to time" (*GoT* 54 Bran 6: 483). The artifacts show that creatures—giants, or children of the forest—*once* existed; everyone can *see* that evidence and draw that conclusion.[7] So all right, maybe they *once* existed. But since the maesters haven't seen a living child of the forest or a giant any time recently, clearly (for them) they do not exist now. However, in the "real world," Jon Snow (not to mention the whole Wildling horde, plus many a "Crow") has traveled beyond the Wall and seen *scores* of living giants, so he knows from personal observation that they still exist.

Bran in *A Dance with Dragons* is learning incredibly powerful magic from the children of the forest. Inspired originally by dream-visions of the three-eyed crow, then guided and sustained by regularly-occurring mystical experiences (including the "wolf dreams," and the symbolic dream of the ocean overwhelming Winterfell), he travels under the wall and far north on mighty Hodor's back. By the time Bran reaches the Last Greenseer's dwelling, he has already gained considerable ability on his own. For example, he is able to order or "drive" Hodor from inside Hodor's mind. He then sets about learning from the Greenseer how to control the immeasurable power of the natural world. What he's learning clearly *works*. To use an example confirmed by another character's experience: Bran communicates with Theon Greyjoy, then hundreds of miles away, via weirwood. Yet the maesters deny the existence of magic in their world. If it ever existed, they proclaim, it surely doesn't now. Maester Luwin is a rare "expert" on magic, having earned the Valyrian steel link signifying mastery of that purely "academic" discipline: "Only one maester in a hundred wears such a link. This signifies that I have studied what the Citadel calls *the higher mysteries*—magic, for want of a better word. A fascinating pursuit, but of small use, which is why so few maesters trouble themselves with it.... Sad to say, magic does not work" (*CoK* 29 Bran 4: 331). So much more experience of life than Bran, so much more learning, so vast a store of "knowledge"—yet Bran knows so much better.

These examples are just the tip of a very large iceberg. Many kinds of creatures, magic, and mysticism "known" by maesters not to exist actually flourish in this world. To list some of the main examples: Daenerys's three dragons hatch, grow up to be huge and powerful, and begin wreaking havoc. The Others walk the land north (and south?) of the Wall, slaying the living and adding to their numbers. The children of the forest were mostly slaughtered in ages past, but a few still survive in the oldest woods. Melisandre, by Stannis's side, can conceive and give birth to murderous Shadows, and read the future and the present in the fire. Wargs (including Bran) really can inhabit the bodies and minds of animals (and in Bran's case, humans too). The warlocks of Qarth effectively use *some* mysterious kind of death- and illusion-related magic. Jaqen H'ghar has the ability to change his appearance completely and permanently through magic; something very similar or perhaps identical is being done to Arya Stark, a/k/a "Cat of the Canals" or "no one." Mirri Maz Duur consorts with mysterious ... demons? ancestral spirits? ... and raises Khal Drogo from the dead (physically). Assembled together like this, these examples add up to a wide world of ignorance, an incredible array of vital information that maesters do not possess—that they do not even *acknowledge*. Seeing all they don't know, you have to wonder: what *do* they know?

Here, then, is the point about maesters' knowledge: it's all wrong. What they "know" doesn't matter much, and what they *should* know, they don't. This is so despite the important fact that they are precisely the people *designated* in their world *to know things*. Thus they are singularly incompetent at what they do. After all, farmers know farming, blacksmiths smithing; septons know theology, soldiers warfare. Maesters fail spectacularly at their culturally designated specialty. Maesters, you know nothing.

But guess what: *neither do we*. To read *A Song of Ice and Fire* is to be dragged sequentially through all the possible ways of knowing nothing, as if through a field of cactus sprouts. Maesters' experience of life in Westeros mirrors and dramatizes our own as readers. If that sounds exaggerated: it *is* an exaggerated version of readers' relationship with any given author, but Martin's saga really does rub our noses in our not-knowing. Consider these ways in which even the most careful, photomnemonic readers *will* find themselves possessing incomplete, incorrect, or obstructed knowledge of the story. In increasing order of severity:

1. All information, all of the saga, is relayed through characters' necessarily limited points of view. The number and variety of these point-of-view characters accumulate over time. We're still encountering new ones at the end of *A Dance with Dragons*. Surely there will be more in future volumes.

This story-telling method pushes us to choose a reading strategy: we can remain skeptical of everyone, and everything they tell us, because after all we can't be sure which (if any) of this crowd we can trust; or we can try wherever possible to "read with the grain," to provisionally adopt the perspective and information of the current speaker. Samuel Coleridge famously termed this latter approach the "willing suspension of disbelief." As readers we tend to be willing to extend it, or else we wouldn't bother reading fiction at all. We can't be skeptical all the time; it's too much work and too much uncertainty. We *could* take the attitude that "Sure, that's what *Cersei* says—but you know how far you can trust her! I'm not buying it." But not only does there eventually come a point at which we have to trust what we're told, it's actually necessary most of the time.[8] Prudence might demand that for now we file some questions away in the back of our minds, but until we have reason to bring that file back out, we must work with the information we have.

As Steven Shapin points out in *A Social History of Truth*, we must extend a certain amount of basic trust just to get through life, let alone a book: "It is 'a basic fact of social life' [Georg Simmel's words] without which one could not get out of bed in the morning, still less function as a competent member of any conceivable social order. We take a necessary risk in reposing trust" (15). We would literally spend every waking hour verifying everything we're told. "You say you drove to Cleveland? Well, I won't believe Cleveland even exists until I see it for myself! See you in three days." Furthermore, "skepticism is always a possible move, but its possibility derives from a system in which we take other relevant knowledge on trust.... Distrust is something which takes place on the *margins* of trusting systems.... Both pragmatic and moral considerations weight against even considering such thoroughgoing skepticism" (18–19). There's no escaping the necessity of reposing trust; without it, we can't even really *know* anything. "Language alone, the very language knowledge is so heavily contingent upon, proves it" (Bal 301).

This is making the philosophical point in the most general, broadly applied terms. Specifically, as applied to Martin's saga, we have good reasons to suspend our disbelief. Most importantly, *all* of the point-of-view characters appear before us stripped and vulnerable. We have full access to their minds, in all their weakness and shame. Further, their versions of the story seem beyond skepticism because they're related not directly, by the characters themselves, but rather, in third person, with perspective limited to what the character would plausibly see and know. That third person—Martin (or the "implied" Martin, the author we infer from his text)—serves as an authoritative, unifying, witnessing presence for all point-of-view characters. And so, as readers we seem to get the best of both worlds in terms of believability. We get the multifaceted, mosaic quality of truth that arises only from multiple points of view. And we need not puzzle our way through the characteristic exaggerations, mistakes, and lies of an unreliable first-person narrator.[9] Or so it seems. Third-person realist narrative, with its "neutral, distant narrator," does impart a "false neutrality" (Bal 296). The narrator *seems* like a neutral, trustworthy source of information; however, please refer to points 3 and 4 below.

2. Different characters from competing political factions interpret the same information to mean fundamentally different things. For example, the red comet appearing in the sky at the beginning of *A Clash of Kings* "must surely mean," variously: Stannis is destined for the Iron Throne; Joffrey's kingship is favored by the Seven; "winter is coming"; Daenerys will regain the Seven Kingdoms; the corrupt Lannisters will soon be brought down; and Theon Greyjoy is destined for great power.

In a way, this is Martin performing a magical illusion while also showing us how he does it. That is, "right in front of us," as it were, he displays consecutive examples of how knowledge is contingent at best, or wish fulfillment at worst. To tell wildly differing versions of the same story, one after another in this fashion, calls attention to the potential untrustworthiness of any given narrator including himself. He virtually begs us to nurture doubt in him as a reliable storyteller. To put it another way: he effectively laughs in our face about how he can fool us.

3. Martin painstakingly sets up eventualities that ultimately don't happen the way they clearly "should." The most shocking of these is Eddard Stark's beheading. Everything we know about storytelling generally, and this story specifically, argues that he will escape to the Wall. There, Ned will recover his power, probably amass an avenging army, and return to put Joffrey, Cersei, and their corrupt ilk in their place. For the first three-fourths of *A Game of Thrones* Ned has been *the* central character. A large portion of the story is told (in third person) through his point of view, and when we're not seeing Westeros through his eyes, we're looking *at* him via other characters. This is a central character in what is explicitly marketed as the first book in a sprawling, multivolume fantasy saga. We "know" those characters don't die! That's true in most fiction,[10] but particularly so in fantasy. Brian Attebery observes in *Strategies of Fantasy* that most characters in fantasy fiction actually fulfill a *function* rather than comprise fully-realized characters in their own right: the Wise Old Wizard, the Young Damsel in Distress, and so forth. Ned bears all the marks of a Conquering Hero, a uniquely honorable, worthy man in a corrupt world. He "deserves" to live, so surely he will. He has to, in order to fulfill his assigned function. For him to actually die is as unexpected as, say, Frodo's suddenly being roasted and eaten by orcs in *The Two Towers*; or for Ged, savior of Earthsea, to drown alone, friendless, among uncharted desert islands. In addition to these meta-indications, the story's text also gives all kinds of specific indications of how and why Eddard Stark will live. Cersei wants Ned to live and instructs Joffrey accordingly; Varys brokers a compromise solution, a false but expedient confession and consequent banishment to the Wall; Ned chooses his daughter Sansa's life above his own reputation. Everything indicates that Ned will live—we "know" he must—then abruptly, he's killed.

Just as Ned's death begins to feel to us like an anomaly on Martin's part, and story events seem to be proceeding more predictably as they "should": the Red Wedding occurs.[11] It's almost literally unthinkable. We cannot conceive of so many carefully drawn, central characters being wiped out within a few pages— particularly not after two and a half books' worth of development. One popular Internet joke goes: "Why doesn't George R.R. Martin use Twitter? Because he killed all 140 characters." These huge surprises, plus the thousand smaller ones

Martin constantly unleashes upon us, demonstrate over and over again: "You know nothing, readers." We *think* we know how the story will proceed, how it "ought to" proceed, but we're as clueless as Martin's maesters.

4. Sometimes Martin outright lies to readers. To lie is to know one fact in private but to say something different in public. For example, telling readers explicitly that a key character is dead, while in fact knowing that he's alive: that's a lie. I need to spell out this point in order to distinguish Martin's lies from the kind of misdirection described in point 3 above. In several instances, Martin reveals, "Oh, you know that fact you learned hundreds of pages ago? That's actually false. Surprise!" For example, he tells us (via Theon's point of view, in third person) that Theon killed Bran and Rickon, cut off their heads, tarred them, and displayed them on Winterfell's wall. There they are, see? But a couple of chapters later Martin admits that those heads actually belonged to the local miller's children. Martin tells us that Mance Rayder was burned alive in front of Jon Snow and all the Night's Watch—a whole crowd of verifying witnesses; then a whole book later, we discover that it was instead the Lord of Bones killed, with a "glamor" cast by Melisandre lending him Rayder's appearance. Martin tells us in *A Game of Thrones* that the Mad King's infant scion was killed by having his head dashed against a wall; not until the end of *A Dance with Dragons*—four books later!—do we encounter the living prince. Surprise!

These strategies employed by Martin as a storyteller amount to a whole lot of deception. The potential for such deception is always there for authors of fiction; Martin's case just provides a particularly vivid example. We readers are in much the same position as the maesters: for all we "should" know, and think we know, we know nothing. The problem of knowing is central to this saga, in both Martin's world and our own. Central, and unconquerable.

Like Jon Snow, we readers of (any) fiction know nothing. We rely abjectly, totally, upon the author for what we (think we) know. Even texts whose interpretation requires that we read against the grain—ironic texts, for example, and works featuring untrustworthy storytellers—generally provide reliable signposts for our accurate navigation.[12] But what if the author really didn't want to lead us accurately? What if he wanted to lead us astray, lie to us, and generally play games (of thrones!) with our heads? Because this doesn't happen particularly blatantly or often—because we generally feel confident in the meanings we produce in collaboration with the author—we can forget this possibility even exists. George R.R. Martin's muddled maesters, and the huge, twisting narrative in which they act a key illustrative part, remind readers that no matter how often we reassure ourselves, "it is known": we *don't* know.

Notes

1. A professor of mine who was also a stickler for getting details correct used to say something similar, as a running joke: "It's a known fact, you can look it up." It may be significant, I'm not sure, that he eventually left academia to become a lawyer.

2. See, for example, the work of Guy Gavriel Kay, who frequently keeps readers guessing by offering competing perspectives.

3. There are a few notable exceptions, well-read people, who tend to come from noble families: Tyrion Lannister above all, and also the Stark children.

4. *Power/Knowledge* and *The Order of Things* delineate the general process. *Madness and Civilization* applies the concept to understandings of sanity and madness; *Discipline and Punish*, to constructions of prisons, obedience, and surveillance.

5. In the HBO series, actor Julian Glover strongly emphasizes Pycelle's doddering weariness and cluelessness even more than the books do. Glover plays Pycelle as the most egregious kind of out-of-touch, superannuated, placeholding academic.

6. It's hard to pin this down with any single quotation, but Martin implies that as with the Night's Watch at the Wall, there is a shortage of able young replacements for those now aging and dying off.

7. Unlike our world, Westeros has no group of people who would claim the bones were deliberately placed by an evil agency to mislead humanity from true religion.

8. This is a key point missed by old-school academics who dismiss out of hand the validity of poststructuralist literary theory. "Deniers" jump straight from the poststructuralist position that there is no such thing as absolute, permanent Truth, to, there's no meaning at all (and therefore, we must reject seeing knowledge as contingent). Not so. In Mieke Bal's words, this contingency "does not entail a facile rejection of all standards of objectivity" (300).

9. Even when the story comes to us via an unreliable narrator, we generally receive clear signals about how to read them. For example, when Huckleberry Finn fears he's "goin' to Hell" for illegally helping Jim escape, we have plenty of other indications that he's in fact doing the moral, just thing—that he's mistaken about his own morality. Similarly, no one reading Nabokov's *Pale Fire* can maintain for long the belief that Charles Kinbote is sane and trustworthy. Reconstructing what's really happening in that story is an easy, amusing task.

10. An obvious parallel from cinema is Janet Leigh's death in the shower in *Psycho*. She can't die half an hour into the feature—this movie is *about* her!

11. Reactions to this event in the HBO series have been intense. Any number of recorded freakouts by people who hadn't read the books and so didn't see it coming can be found online.

12. Wayne Booth's classic *A Rhetoric of Irony* explains the details of how this works. Basically, the actual words on the page present a "clash" of fact, value, or style; we reject what the text literally says and figure out what the author "really" means given broader contextual evidence. The point here is that this evidence does usually exist and generally proves reliable; in Martin, it's fraudulent or missing much of the time.

Works Cited

Attebery, Brian. *Strategies of Fantasy*. Bloomington: Indiana University Press, 1992. Print.

Bal, Mieke. "First Person, Second Person, Same Person: Narrative As Epistemology." *New Literary History* 24 (1993): 293–320. Print.

Booth, Wayne. *A Rhetoric of Irony*. Chicago: University of Chicago Press, 1975. Print.

Foucault, Michel. *Discipline and Punish: The Birth of the Prison*. Trans. Alan Sheridan. New York: Random House, 1977. Print.

____. *Madness and Civilization: A History of Insanity in the Age of Reason.* Trans. Richard Howard. New York: Vintage, 1988. Print.

____. *The Order of Things: An Archaeology of the Human Sciences.* New York: Vintage, 1994. Print.

____. *Power/Knowledge: Selected Interviews and Other Writings, 1972–1977.* Ed. Colin Gordon. Trans. Colin Gordon, Leo Marshall, John Mepham, and Kate Soper. New York: Pantheon, 1980. Print.

Le Guin, Ursula K. *A Wizard of Earthsea.* New York: Bantam, 1980. Print.

Nabokov, Vladimir. *Pale Fire.* New York: Vintage, 1989. Print.

Psycho. Dir. Alfred Hitchcock. Perf. Anthony Perkins, Vera Miles, Janet Leigh, John Gavin. Paramount, 1960. Film.

Shapin, Steven. *A Social History of Truth: Civility and Science in Seventeenth-Century England.* Chicago: University of Chicago Press, 1994. Print.

Tolkien, J.R.R. *The Two Towers.* New York: Houghton Mifflin, 1980. Print.

Twain, Mark. *Adventures of Huckleberry Finn.* New York: Dover, 1994. Print.

"Just songs in the end": Historical Discourses in Shakespeare and Martin

JESSICA WALKER

In Shakespeare's *Henry VI Part 2*, the Duke of Gloucester declares: "these days are dangerous: / Virtue is choked with foul ambition / And charity chased hence by rancour's hand: / Foul subordination is predominant / And equity exiled your highness' hand" (3.1.142–146). He is speaking of the fifteenth-century conflict known as the Wars of the Roses, in which two lines of the English royal family, the Yorks and the Lancasters, battled over the crown for the better part of a century. Shakespeare's dramatization of these events is a story of factions, backstabbing, and revenge: houses bound by blood and marriage fighting for the throne; multiple contenders backed by rich, powerful lords; broken engagements ending in bloodshed. His tale is very like the one George R.R. Martin tells in his epic fantasy series, *A Song of Ice and Fire*.

As a work of fantasy, Martin's series has no absolute correspondence to any one historical era. Instead, he draws from a wide range of periods: "[T]here's really no one-for-one character-for-character correspondence," he writes in a 1998 forum post on Westeros.org. "I like to use history to flavor my fantasy, to add texture and verisimilitude, but simply rewriting history with the names changed has no appeal for me" ("More Wars"). Nevertheless, his readers debate the parallels, with websites such as *The History Behind Game of Thrones* keeping track of such correspondences. We see much of ancient Egypt in Old Ghis and ancient Rome in Old Valyria; the Dothraki bear some resemblance to the Mongols, the Seven Kingdoms of Westeros to the early medieval Anglo-Saxon Heptarchy. Hints of Eleanor of Aquitaine emerge in Cersei Lannister, and shades of Joan of Arc in Brienne of Tarth. Of all possible influences, however, Martin has identified the Wars of the Roses as a particular inspiration for the series: "People have pointed out that probably the main influence on *Ice and Fire* is the War of the Roses, and that's certainly true," Martin told the *Austin Chronicle* in 2013. "[A]lthough I've drawn on many parts of history," Martin said elsewhere, "the War of the Roses is probably the one my story is closest to" ("George R.R. Martin Webchat").

Historical fiction based on the Wars of the Roses has always found an audience—from Phillipa Gregory's *The Cousins' War* series (adapted for television as *The White Queen*) and Sharon Kay Penman's *The Sunne in Splendour* in our own century to, perhaps most influentially, the series of plays usually known as Shakespeare's first or minor *Henriad*: *Henry VI* Parts 1, 2, and 3 and *Richard III*. Though Shakespeare purports to write about actual events, like Martin he picks and chooses from (and often distorts) the historical record. My purpose here is not to consider every possible parallel between history and Martin's series, but to look in particular at the events that Shakespeare highlights in his plays and their correspondence to Martin's work in order to understand them as works of *historiography*—as explorations of the process of remembering and reacting to the past.

Both series feature a rebel-turned-king, heroic and handsome in youth, who becomes a womanizing drunkard in later life (Edward IV and Robert Baratheon); a wealthy kingmaker unafraid to switch allegiances who strengthens his position through a daughter's marriage (Richard of Warwick and Tywin Lannister); a new dynasty under threat by the scion of the previous one (Henry of Richmond and Daenerys Targaryen). Striking similarities emerge not only between the events of these texts, but also between the ways in which characters recall and make sense of those events. Throughout both series, characters struggle with the burden of history and the trauma of past conflicts as they strive to move forward in a world torn apart by civil war. By examining these parallels in the context of medieval and early modern historiography, we may better understand how Martin's characters cope with the past and look to the future, the conception of time in Martin's universe, and the reader's relationship to his often demanding work.

The Problem of Interpretation

The multivocal nature of both texts complicates the characters' and the readers' ability to interpret the past. Through the use of multiple speaking parts, Shakespeare offers a wide range of perspectives on the events of the previous century, and their disagreement over the past—in particular, over which branch of Edward III's descendants has the right to rule England—drives the action of the tetralogy. The conflict itself takes its name from the symbols chosen to represent two sides that disagree over a matter of interpretation, with the red rose representing Somerset's party and the white the Duke of York's:

> YORK: Then say at once if I maintained the truth:
> Or else was wrangling Somerset in th'error? [....]
> The truth appears so naked on my side
> That any purblind eye may find it out.
> SOMERSET: And on my side it is so well apparelled,
> So clear, so shining, and so evident
> That it will glimmer through a blind man's eye [*Henry VI* 1 2.4.5–6, 20–24].

Over the course of the tetralogy, the house of York triumphs, then the house of Lancaster, then York again, then Lancaster again. While there is ultimately a clear victor, the question of which side has the moral and legal high ground is never satisfactorily answered, and audiences must contend with the historical record, their own previous knowledge of events, and the often opposing perspectives of the tetralogy's characters. The *Henriad* thus invites its audience to reach their own conclusions about history, even as the characters themselves struggle to make sense of the same events.

By assigning chapters to a wide range of point-of-view characters representing various sides of the conflict, Martin achieves a similar effect. Characters usually first appear in another point-of-view character's chapter; we see them through another's eyes and form assumptions based on other characters' beliefs. It may be thousands of pages later before new information surfaces and readers, discovering that their assumptions were mistaken, must reinterpret events in the light of this knowledge. These interpretive challenges emerge early: fifty-three of the seventy-two chapters in *A Game of Thrones* are from the perspective of the Starks; they make up six of the novel's eight POVs. Martin seems to establish the Starks, who bear the weight of the historical record and the role of interpretation, as the series' protagonists; readers are directed to remember Robert's Rebellion through Ned Stark's eyes and trust the decisions he makes based on his interpretation of those events. When Ned's interpretation runs counter to other characters', the text encourages us, through Ned's perceptions, to mistrust them: "Ned studied the eunuch's face, searching for truth beneath the mummer's scars and false stubble.... 'You want me to *serve* the woman who murdered my king, butchered my men, and crippled my son?' Ned's voice was thick with disbelief" (*GoT* 59 Eddard 15: 528, 530).

But the Starks, however sympathetic, are not always reliable narrators. Four of the six Stark POVs are children who do not fully understand the import of the events surrounding them, and the adults maintain loyalties and bear grudges that sometimes lead them to misread events. The emphasis on Ned and Catelyn's points of view in the first book of the series, for instance, leads us to misinterpret many events involving House Lannister throughout the series, because of the Starks' troubled relationship with the members of that house and subsequent bias against them. Ned's mistrust of the Lannisters stems in part from Jaime Lannister's own history; Ned feels he cannot trust a man who murdered the king he was sworn to protect. This mistrust makes it all too easy for Ned and Catelyn to believe Lysa Arryn's allegation that the Lannisters are responsible for Jon Arryn's death which, in turn, leads Catelyn to believe that the Lannisters ordered the assassination of her son Bran. Catelyn's subsequent arrest of Tyrion Lannister will be a major factor in the development of the war between the Lannisters and Starks. Yet the reader ultimately learns that these decisions are influenced by errors and false reports: Jaime Lannister saved King's Landing when he killed King Aerys; Lysa Arryn brought about her own husband's death (with the help of Petyr Baelish, who in turn pointed Catelyn's suspicions in Tyrion's direction); and while a Lannister may well have been responsible for the attempt on Bran's life, it was probably the young prince Joffrey, seeking to impress King Robert.

The closer one examines the series, the more apparent it becomes that none of the narrators are truly reliable and that what each character tells us must be weighed carefully against our overall knowledge of the series. Consequently, readers of *A Song of Ice and Fire* have found that the text requires rereading and reinterpretation. Online community has helped with the interpretive challenges presented by a series now several thousand pages long: the *Wiki of Ice and Fire* records and categorizes every known detail of the series, with pages devoted to puzzling out unsolved mysteries like Jon Snow's parentage or the identity of Azor Ahai; the Westeros.org forums offer thousands of topics for discussion; the blog *ASOIAF University* collects and shares posts from astute readers. The reader's experience mirrors that of the characters: just as Ned misinterprets the events of Robert's Rebellion and consequently misinterprets the Lannisters' motives in the first book, the readers run the risk of missing or misinterpreting information because it is related to us by unreliable narrators. But unlike the characters, who have limited information and must live or die by the choices they make based on their imperfect interpretations, the reader can piece together the "truth" about Martin's narrative as a whole. Given the complex nature of Martin's series, therefore, it may be beneficial to better understand how history and historiography—how events happen and how characters understand and respond to those events—operate in *A Song of Ice and Fire*. To that end, looking at the series through the lens of medieval and early modern historiography can prove useful.

Shakespeare's tetralogy reflects some of the predominant beliefs of his age about why events occur. Why, for example, do the Lancasters finally triumph over the Yorks? The tetralogy suggests that these events are set in motion by the hand of God, and that both sides are damned for the sin of usurpation until Henry Tudor unites them through marriage to Elizabeth of York: "O, now, let Richmond and Elizabeth, / The true succeeders of each royal house, / By God's fair ordinance conjoin together!" (*Richard III* 5.5.29–31). In addition to the hand of Providence, however, we see the power of Fortune, who raises the low and casts down the mighty without clear motive: "often up and down my sons were toss'd, / For me to joy and weep their gain and loss" (*Richard III* 2.4.58–59). This rise-and-fall pattern inevitably gives way to the ultimate equalizer, death, which reduces even the mightiest to forgotten bones:

> Methought I saw a thousand fearful wrecks;
> Ten thousand men that fishes gnaw'd upon;
> ... in the holes
> Where eyes did once inhabit, there were crept,
> As 'twere in scorn of eyes, reflecting gems,
> Which woo'd the slimy bottom of the deep,
> And mock'd the dead bones that lay scatter'd by
> [*Richard III* 1.4.24–25, 29–33].

While such methods of looking at cause and effect and consequently understanding the significance of historical events were common both in the medieval period in which the Henriad takes place and the early modern period in which it was written, the text also reflects a humanist perspective most strongly associated with the Renaissance—one that emphasizes the cyclical nature of history, urging readers to trace the patterns that link one generation of civil strife to the next and suggesting that not even Elizabeth's Golden Age is free of such conflicts and anxieties. By examining how Martin employs similar modes of interpretation, we can better understand the complicated relationship that his world has with its own past: what forces seem to control events, how characters interpret what has occurred, and how the reader must play an active role in making sense of events. The parallel historiographies in question include the role of Providence, which surfaces in *A Song of Ice and Fire* through the act of prophecies and portents; Fortune's Wheel, symbolized in Martin's work through the unusual passage of seasons in his world and his use of rise-and-fall imagery; the related but distinct concept of *memento mori* or *valar morghulis,* which reminds the reader of the inevitability of death; and the use of proto–Gothic imagery to underscore a cyclical interpretation of history, embodied here by the forces of ice and fire.

Premodern and Early Modern Historiographies:
Providence, Fortune's Wheel, and Memento Mori

As many scholars have noted, an increased "sense of national feeling" driven by the Reformation, the success of the Tudor dynasty, and the beginnings of English colonialism led to an upsurge in writing on the national past during the early modern period (Pearsall 15). Renaissance historiography suggests the study of history could "inspire the living, reveal the secrets of statecraft, teach the details of military tactics, expose the deceits of fortune, and illuminate the ways of providence" (Rackin 3). As the idea of English national identity developed and power became increasingly centralized around the monarch, public service became increasingly important: "the common weal," wrote sixteenth-century pedagogical scholar Richard Mulcaster, "is the measure of every man's being" (qtd. in Cressy 100). Texts meant to prepare young Englishmen for a life of public service, such as Thomas Elyot's *The Boke named the Governour,* promoted education as a means to successful participation in public life—particularly education in history:

> [H]istorie ... leaveth nothinge hydde from mannes knowlege, that unto hym may be eyther pleasaunt or necessarie. For it nat onely reporteth the giftes or actes of princes or Capitaynes: their counsayles and attemptates: entreprises, affaires, maners in lyvinge good and bad: descriptions of regions and cities with their inhabitauntes. But also it bringeth to our knowlege, the fourmes of sondry publike weales with their augmentations and decayes, and occasion therof. More over preceptes, exhortations, counsayles, and good persuasions comprehended in quicke sentences and eloquent orations. Finally so large is the compase of that whiche is named historie, that it comprehendeth all thynges that is necessary to be put in memorie [Elyot 228–9].

Shakespeare's chronicle plays reveal multiple historiographic modes, characteristic of medieval and Renaissance views, with distinct features but typically coexisting as part of a single worldview. The Renaissance was a pivotal time for historiography, a period during which shifting ideas about religion, nation, literature, and politics led to radical changes in ways of thinking and writing about the past, and frequently older and newer modes coexist in the same text. Premodern and early modern Christians commonly saw a providential impetus behind history—the hand of God guiding events from the creation of the world to the end times. In the *Henriad,* this ineffable plan often reveals itself through acts of prophecy that point to a predestined end. Warwick, for instance, foresees that the quarrel between York and Somerset in the Temple Garden will "send, between the red rose and white, / A thousand souls to death and deadly night" (*Henry VI 1* 2.4.126–127). Exeter recalls a prophecy that "Henry born at Monmouth should win all / And Henry born at Windsor should lose all"; a "cunning man" foretells that Suffolk will die "by water" (*Henry VI 1* 3.1.197–198, *Henry VI 2* 4.1.34–35). The future Edward IV interprets the appearance of three suns in the sky as a sign of victory for himself and his brothers, while Richard expresses concern that his new title of Duke of Gloucester is "too ominous" (*Henry VI 3* 2.1.25–40; 2.6.107). Henry VI proves much better at prophecy than he ever was at kingship, predicting that "many a thousand ... [s]hall rue the hour" of Richard's birth (*Henry VI 3* 5.6.37, 43).

A Song of Ice and Fire likewise features moments of forewarning. Shortly before receiving word of Robert's approach, Ned discovers a direwolf and a stag—his own sigil and Robert's—who have killed one another (*GoT* 2 Bran 1: 14–15). He feels "a terrible sense of foreboding" when Robert asks him to be his Hand; later, he takes his dream of the fight at the Tower of Joy to be a bad omen (*GoT* 5 Eddard 1: 40; 40 Eddard 10: 354–55). Jon, Bran, and Rickon all have dreams that presage their father's death (*GoT* 27 Jon 4: 224–25, 67 Bran 7: 612, 614). Cersei's marriage, children, and eventual downfall are foretold by Maggy the Frog (*FfC* 37 Cersei 8: 540–41). Unlike Shakespeare's prophecies, which are fairly straightforward, some of Martin's omens only make sense in retrospect: Daenerys' visions in the House of the Undying and Patchface's babbling, for instance, both foretell the Red Wedding (*CoK* 49 Daenerys 4: 526; *SoS* 11 Davos 2: 117). Other omens, like the images Melisandre views in her fires, have yet to be interpreted, leading to analysis and speculation among readers.

Providence, however, requires the hand of God. Multiple spiritualities emerge in *A Song of Ice and Fire*, including belief in the old gods of the north; the Seven, whose church functions as Westeros's mainstream religion; the Drowned God of the Iron Islands; and R'hllor, the fire god of Essos. It is unclear, however, which—if any—deity controls events within the world of the series. If Martin is the god of the text, he is not a benevolent deity seeking to punish the evil, reward the good, or console his faithful readers. His characters' lives are unpredictable, violent, and often brief, and beloved figures quickly fall from happiness and security to suffer betrayal, maiming, illness, and death. In the middle ages and Renaissance, such downfalls were often subscribed to Fortuna, whose wheel pulled men up to success and tossed them down again in failure. Fortune, like Providence, is a guiding force whose motion is inevitable. Her effects, however, were unpredictable; how quickly her wheel might turn or how high or low it threw those caught on it could not be foreseen. Unlike providence, Fortune does not seek to punish ill or reward good; her only motivation is movement, her only constant change itself.

In texts such as Boccaccio's *De casibus virorum illustrium* or the collection *Mirror for Magistrates,* those "beguiled by fame" were inevitably "cast off by the centrifugal force of Fortune's wheel, the victims of tragic falls" (Ziolkowski 892).

Ziolkowski traces the image of Fortune's Wheel to the ancient Greeks and to Roman worship of the goddess Fortuna; the concept reaches Renaissance Europe via Boethius's sixth-century *Consolation of Philosophy*, "whose impact on medieval thought in general, and on the development of the medieval concept of Fortuna and her wheel in particular, cannot be overestimated" (887–888). Popular works "invested her with greater power, making her supreme arbitress of human destiny. Nowhere was she more powerful than in the courts of kings, for she was jealous of prosperity and the highest place was most subject to her malice. Her ever-turning Wheel carried men from greatness to ruin in a moment" (Chapman 1–2).

Shakespeare frequently uses the image of the wheel's motion to convey the political rise and fall of his overreachers, such as the newly crowned Richard's "Thus high, and by thy advice / And thy assistance is King Richard seated" or Aaron's "Now climbeth Tamora Olympus' top, / Safe out of fortune's shot" (*Richard III* 4.2.3–4, *Titus Andronicus* 2.1.1–2). Martin's imagery also recalls the motion of Fortune's Wheel at key moments, such as Daenerys's triumphant rise on Drogon's back in *A Dance with Dragons* or Lysa Arryn's fatal fall through the Moon Door in *A Storm of Swords*. The unpredictability of Fortune's motions coupled with the up-and-down movement of her wheel is echoed in Petyr Baelish's speech in HBO's *Game of Thrones*, the television adaptation: "Chaos isn't a pit. Chaos is a ladder. Many who try to climb it fail and never get to try again. The fall breaks them. When some are given a chance to climb, they cling to the realm or the gods or love. Only the ladder is real. The climb is all there is" (*Thrones* S3: Ep. 6, "The Climb").

The seasons that play such a significant role in Martin's series act as a powerful symbol of Fortuna. Just as the Wheel of Fortune will surely rise and fall, the wheel of nature turns and summer, as House Stark's words tell us, will give way to winter. However, seasons in Martin's world do not fit a predictable pattern; they may last for years at a time, with no way of knowing when the seasons will change, how intense they will be, or how long they will last. Just as the players in the game of thrones must prepare for a winter that may last a decade or more, they also act from a desire to maintain the "glorious summer" (to borrow Richard III's phrase) of their success a little longer despite the inevitability of the winter of their discontent.

The approach of downfall and death likewise emerges in the medieval and early modern concept of *memento mori*, or "remember you will die." Most famously used by Shakespeare in the figure of Hamlet contemplating Yorick's skull, the tradition relied upon images of skulls, skeletons, and tombs to "remind a sinner of the latter end of his body" and urge the viewer to "prepare for salvation by giving over evil ways" (Morris 1035). The concept of *memento mori* is closely related to that of Fortuna; but while the constant motion of Fortune's Wheel reminds us to prepare for change, *memento mori* discourses remind us that the only significant movement is the linear progression toward death that renders the up-and-down motion of Fortune's Wheel ultimately meaningless, since the high and low alike meet the same end. As Talbot declares in *Henry VI 1,* "kings and mightiest potentates must die, / For that's the end of human misery" (3.2.136–137). The most consistently powerful figure throughout the first *Henriad* is not any of the contenders for the crown but, rather, the wealthy, influential nobleman who controls them: the original Kingmaker, Richard Neville, Earl of Warwick. Yet even he is not invulnerable:

> For who lived king, but I could dig his grave?
> And who durst smile when Warwick bent his brow?
> Lo, now my glory smeared in dust and blood.
> My parks, my walks, my manors that I had,
> Even now forsake me; and of all my lands
> Is nothing left me but my body's length.
> Why, what is pomp, rule, reign, but earth and dust?
> And live we how we can, yet die we must [*Henry VI 3* 5.2.21–28].

A Song of Ice and Fire likewise features a powerful kingmaker who, like Warwick, wields authority not through a claim to the throne but through wealth, opportunism, and beneficial arrangement of marriages: Tywin Lannister, who "looms as eternal as Casterly Rock" at the opening of the series only to suffer an undignified fate when he is shot by a crossbow while on the privy. Of his fate, Martin is more succinct: "Lord Tywin Lannister, in the end, did not shit gold" (*SoS* 78 Tyrion 11: 880). *A Song of Ice and Fire* even has its own Valyrian version of *memento mori: valar morghulis,* or "all men must die."[1] A particularly compelling image in *A Storm of Swords* invokes both *memento mori* and Fortune's Wheel, symbolizing the fates of all the characters. Watching the stairs burn beneath the Wilding assault, Jon Snow observes: "Some continued upward, and died. Some went downward, and died. Some stayed where they were. They died as well" (*SoS* 56 Jon 7:753).

Cyclical Time and (Proto-)Gothic Anxieties

Although Providence continued to be considered a powerful force behind events into the Renaissance period, early modern English historiography increasingly emphasized man's role in events: "second causes," the "effects of political situations and the impact of human will and capabilities" (Rackin 6). We find in such texts a concern about inevitable repetitions of human behavior, the tendency for events to recur as men (particularly men in power) failed to learn from their mistakes; instead of simply moving inexorably toward God's planned end, humanity was doomed to repeat its errors. This "cyclical time" of early modern humanism is not to be confused with the circular motion of Fortune's Wheel; while Fortuna governs the individual's rise and fall, cyclical time looks for patterns across the course of history. However, such a viewpoint is the inevitable product of the *de casibus* tradition: these tales of political rise and fall are read so the reader can avoid making the same errors and suffering the same fate. These narratives were particularly directed toward politicians; Castiglione's *Il Cortegiano* and Elyot's *Book of the Governor* both urge those in public service to learn from history, and in the popular collection *A Mirror for Magistrates*, the ghosts of dead political figures (including many who appear as characters in the *Henriad*) come back to warn the living against making the same mistakes.

The Renaissance felt an acute need for such lessons in a time during which the Protestant Reformation, the development of English-language literature, and political successes such as the defeat of the Spanish Armada and the birth of English colonialism contributed to a rapidly developing idea of the national self. As the sixteenth-century English started to develop a new sense of Englishness, they hoped to learn from the past, and medieval historiography and historical fiction, including Edmund Spenser's *The Faerie Queene*, Richard Hooker's *Of the Lawes of Ecclesiastical Politie*, William Camden's *Britannia*, Shakespeare's *Henriad* cycles, Marlowe's *Edward II*, Michael Drayton's *England's Heroical Epistles* and *Poly-Olbion*, and Sir Walter Ralegh's *History of the World* became wildly popular among audiences worried about the forthcoming end of the Tudor dynasty as the childless Elizabeth I aged. Shakespeare underscores this theme in his history plays by echoing key words and actions: for instance, the unseated Henry VI asks, "Why? Am I dead? Do I not breathe a man?" while Richard III, his own reign threatened by Richmond's approach, asks, "Is the chair empty? Is the sword unsway'd?" (*Henry VI 3* 3.1.82; *Richard III* 4.4.469). Richard's own soliloquies echo the speeches that first alerted the audience to his father's ambition. The Duke of York ends his first soliloquy thus: "And force perforce I'll make him yield the crown, / Whose bookish rule hath pulled fair England down" (*Henry VI 2* 1.1.258–259). Richard's first soliloquy concludes with a similar couplet: "Can I do this, and cannot get a crown? / Tut, were it further off, I'll pluck it down" (*Henry VI 3* 3.2.194–195).

Such reminders and repetitions are characteristic of *A Song of Ice and Fire*, as the dangerous politics of its narrative make the same demands of its players— with the same risks, rewards, and consequences—time and time again. When Ned first sees Renly Baratheon, he observes, "it was as if the years had slipped away and Robert stood before him, fresh from his victory on the Trident" (*GoT*

21 Eddard 4: 161). Renly, like his elder brother, will rebel, be declared king, and die of a stab wound. Robb Stark, like his father, will make an honorable but politically unwise choice in his marriage to Jeyne Westerling, and that choice will lead to his betrayal and beheading. Jaime recounts to Brienne how he was faced with the choice of sacrificing either his father or his king; later, Brienne will be forced to choose between her own life and Jaime's (*SoS* 38 Jaime 5: 419; *FfC* 43 Brienne 8: 640). Ned Stark expresses anxiety about these repetitions: "My father went south once, to answer the summons of a king. He never came home again." Maester Luwin reassures him, "A different time.... A different king" (*GoT* 7 Catelyn 2: 53). In fact, times have changed very little, and Ned, too, will be executed on a mad king's orders.

Cyclical history is perhaps the most powerful force in Martin's series, as the greatest tensions in the narrative rely on the threat of returning forces that once held power. Indeed, the entire work could be said to be the tale of such returns. The forces of ice are the White Walkers, driven back years ago but threatening to return and wreak havoc as winter looms. Fire symbolizes House Targaryen, the dynasty that once brought Westeros to heel with fire-breathing dragons and, after a brief interval of Baratheon rule, threatens to do so once more. The imagery underscoring these two forces—dead people reborn as ice zombies, dead eggs reborn as dragons—places *A Song of Ice and Fire* within a Gothic tradition in which anxieties about the return of the past are embodied by the resurrected dead. In texts dealing with the traumas of history, anxieties about the past often surface in the form of creatures that come back from the dead, such as zombies, vampires, mummies, and ghosts. As a tradition, the Gothic is often associated with the eighteenth century, with Horace Walpole's 1764 novel *The Castle of Otranto* frequently cited as the first "Gothic" text. The use of supernatural elements to express cultural anxieties, however, predates that period; witness the tension between paganism and Christianity, for instance, symbolized by Grendel in *Beowulf* or the eponymous figure of *Sir Gawain and the Green Knight*. In the work of Shakespeare and his contemporaries, proto–Gothic images of ghosts or unburied bodies often symbolize the challenges of making peace with a past that refuses to stay dead. Old Hamlet's ghost rises to spur his son to an act of revenge, while Banquo's spirit haunts Macbeth with his misdeeds. In Thomas Middleton's *The Revenger's Tragedy*, Vindice carries around his dead wife's skull and ultimately uses it as a tool to exact revenge on her murderer; in John Webster's *The Duchess of Malfi*, Duke Ferdinand's imaginary lycanthropy leads him to dig up graves much as he fears his sister's grave will be dug up and her murder revealed.

Gothic imagery has long been associated with anxieties about familial and national pasts in particular:

The ghosts—whether real or imaginary—derive from the past passions, past deeds, past crimes of the family identified with [the haunted house]. The psychic as well as the physical space of the castle bears its marks.... That the house embodies the family history reminds us that the word "house" has two meanings relevant to Gothic fictions—it refers both to the building itself and to the family line [Williams 45].

In *Richard III*, Shakespeare frequently employs Gothic imagery to underscore Richard's use of paranoia about the past to stir up discord at court; the play opens with Henry VI's paranormally bleeding corpse and closes with the ghosts of Richard's victims. As I have argued elsewhere, the Gothic plot developments and imagery of *Richard III* serve to underscore Richard's use of historical anxiety as a weapon to manipulate his victims (Walker 181). The play's characters only wish to move forward from "foul annoy" to "lasting joy," from a "winter of discontent" to "glorious summer," yet are doomed to repeat the factionalism and backstabbing that led to civil war in the first place (*Henry VI 3* 5.7.45, 46; *Richard III* 1.1.1, 2). They are pulled back into the quarrel by Richard, who constantly reminds them of these wrongs and mistrust of the past in order to promote his own interests. His physical monstrosity symbolizes such disruptions of linear time; he characterizes his breech birth as a desire to "make haste" in destroying his enemies, yet as a premature birth he also lags behind, "unfinished, sent before my time" (*Henry VI 3* 5.6.72, *Richard III* 1.1.20). The fear he engenders of history repeating itself echoes the fears of the play's audience, for whom "enough had happened in the 1580s to evidence the fragility of the Tudor myth and cracks in its ideology" (Watson 22). The same flattery and factionalism that drives the action of *Richard III* was well-known at Elizabeth's court, and with the elderly queen past childbearing age and refusing to name an heir, her subjects were left as uncertain of their future as those in Shakespeare's play:

[N]owhere, perhaps, is the conjunction between past and present more unsettling. For however central the story of Richmond's triumph at Bosworth field was to the Tudors' own legitimating myth of history, to retell the story at the close of the century is to offer a perplexing tribute to the last Tudor monarch, the Virgin Queen who had no hope of continuing Richmond's line [Levine 99–100].

The only figure of the tetralogy more consumed with the past is former queen Margaret of Anjou, who first appears as a young French princess not long before her compatriot Joan La Pucelle is taken away to be burned at the stake. As Joan exits, the Duke of York declares, "Take her away; for she hath lived too long, / To fill the world with vicious qualities" (*Henry VI 1* 5.4.34–35). Reenforcing the parallels both between Joan and Margaret and between Richard of York and Richard of Gloucester, York's statement presages his son's threat against Margaret: "Why should she live, to fill the world with words?" (*Henry VI 3* 5.5.43). Margaret, as a woman warrior in her own right, therefore enters the scene as Joan reborn, another representation of the relentless cycle of repeating history. By the end of the tetralogy, having lost her husband, son, and status, Margaret is a witchlike, ghostlike figure haunting the stage to remind other characters of their wartime crimes and curse them with the same torment she has suffered:

> Can curses pierce the clouds and enter heaven?
> Why then, give way, dull clouds, to my quick curses:
> Though not by war, by surfeit die your King,
> As ours by murder, to make him a king.
> Edward thy son, that now is Prince of Wales,
> For Edward our son, that was Prince of Wales,
> Die in his youth, by like untimely violence.
> Thyself, a queen, for me that was a queen,
> Outlive thy glory like my wretched self ... [*Richard III* 1.3.194–202].

A Song of Ice and Fire likewise features a vengeful witch-woman born out of fire. Lady Stoneheart, known in life as Catelyn Stark, is brought back from the dead by Beric Dondarrion, whose own regenerative talents originate from the powers of Thoros of Myr, a priest of R'hllor, the fire god of Essos. Like Margaret, Stoneheart has lost her husband and son to civil war, and her primary function is to recall and revenge the wrongs she and her family have suffered; though, unlike Margaret, she does not rely on the power of language: "She don't speak.... But she remembers" (*SoS* 82 Epilogue: 924). She uses the act of memory as an impetus to renew violence; if she cannot bring back the remembered dead, she will revive and recreate the trauma that haunts her: "She wants her son alive, or the men who killed him dead.... She wants to feed the crows, like they did at the Red Wedding" (*FfC* 43 Brienne 8: 640). Like Margaret, Stoneheart is unconcerned with truth in her pursuit of revenge, dismissing Brienne's truthful assertion that Jaime Lannister was uninvolved in the Red Wedding (*FfC* 43 Brienne 8: 640). A symbol of memory in its most harmful form, Stoneheart exhibits no contextualization of events, no interpretation, no ability to move forward from the past. Like the White Walkers, she cannot grow or change, only repeat the same cycles of violence.

Such Gothic monsters play a vital role in the overall narrative of the series. *A Game of Thrones* opens with: "'Dead is dead. We have no business with the dead'" (*GoT* 1 Prologue: 1). It closes with: "and for the first time in hundreds of years, the night came alive with the music of dragons" (*GoT* 73 Daenerys 10: 674). Of the many threats facing the characters of the series, these two forces loom the largest—the forces of ice and fire, the White Walkers from beyond the Wall and Daenerys's dragons from across the Narrow Sea. As creatures assumed dead who come back to life and bring with them the threat of returning violence, both these forces act as monstrous representations of the cyclical nature of history. Even before the reader learns of the returning civil strife that will consume the narrative, the first threat that we learn of is White Walkers that ravaged the land thousands of years before, creatures that embody the mercilessness of the forest in winter: "Tall, it was, and gaunt and hard as old bones, with flesh pale as milk. Its armor seemed to change color as it moved; here it was white as new-fallen snow, there black as shadow, everywhere dappled with the deep grey-green of the trees. The patterns ran like moonlight on water with every step it took" (*GoT* 1 Prologue 7). Though summer may return temporarily, winter's return is inevitable; and just as ice keeps objects locked in stasis, the White Walkers represent a nation unable to move forward permanently from the traumas of the past.

If Gothic images of the resurrected dead represent the inescapable repetitions of violence in Martin's series, another set of resurrected creatures—the dragons of House Targaryen—show how the dead may be reborn. Both Shakespeare's *Henriad* and *A Song of Ice and Fire* demonstrate cyclical history in the form of heroic figures who die and are "reborn" to complete the work of their forebears. Shakespeare's tetralogy opens with a dead march as the court laments Henry V's passing, encouraging the viewer to compare the more glorious era of Henry V's victories in France with his son's failures as a ruler. The recently departed king is compared to a dragon:

> His arms spread wider than a dragon's wings:
> His sparkling eyes, replete with wrathful fire,
> More dazzled and drove back his enemies
> Than midday sun, fierce against their faces [*Henry VI 1* 1.1.11–14].

Throughout the series, Henry V stands as an idealized reminder of a victorious past and a symbol of what England could have been if Henry VI had proved to have been more like his warlike father. When Henry VI proves an unimpressive king, his subjects transfer their expectations to the next generation in hope that "Henry, son unto a conqueror, / Is likely to beget more conquerors" (*Henry VI 1* 5.5.73–74). Oxford declares of Edward of Lancaster, "O, brave young prince, thy famous grandfather / Doth live again in thee: long mayst thou live / To bear his image and renew his glories!" (*Henry VI 3* 5.4.52–55). This hope proves to be misplaced, however; the young prince will soon fall in battle. Ultimately, England's lost glory is revived in the form of the young Earl of Richmond, whom Henry VI identifies as "England's hope": "Suggest but truth to my divining thoughts, / This pretty lad will prove our country's bliss" (*Henry VI 3* 4.6.67–74). Richard III recalls this prophecy, as well as another that foreshadows his defeat: "a bard of Ireland told me once / I should not live long after I saw

'Richmond'" (*Richard III* 4.2.106–107). While Richard wishes to associate himself with the imagery of the dragon as conquering hero—"Our ancient word of courage, fair Saint George, / Inspire us with the spleen of fiery dragons!" he declares as he rides into his final battle (*Richard III* 5.3.349–350)—the role of dragon belongs to his opponent, Henry Tudor, Henry V's true heir, a Welshman who marched into battle under a dragon standard. Crowned as Henry VII, Richmond represents the return of Lancaster power, strengthened by Yorkist alliance through marriage.

Just as the loss of Henry V haunts the *Henriad*, so is *A Song of Ice and Fire* haunted by Rhaegar Targaryen, "the last dragon" (*GoT* 24 Daenerys 3: 195). Those who recall the Targaryen prince remember him with admiration and lament the loss of the king he could have been. His life is cut short before he can rule: "Rhaegar fought valiantly, Rhaegar fought nobly, Rhaegar fought honorably. And Rhaegar *died*" (*SoS* 24 Daenerys 2: 273). Despite his defeat, however, an unlooked-for restorer of Targaryen glory comes in the form of his sister, Daenerys. The Targaryen sigil, the dragon, frequently appears throughout the series to remind readers of the power of history and memory to revive old conflicts. Just as *Henry VI* opens with a comet that foreshadows civil strife returning after the death of the heroic Henry V, *A Clash of Kings* opens with the appearance of a comet that fortells "[b]lood and fire" (*CoK* 5 Bran 1: 53), echoing the Targaryen words, *Fire and Blood*, and so suggesting the return of dragons seen at the end of the previous book.[2] Martin's dragons likewise represent military power, but their dead skulls indicate the Targaryen dynasty's defeat. Even dead, however, the dragons evoke a horror and fascination that observers immediately associate with violence and loss. Recounting how he found Jaime Lannister in the throne room standing over the body of the slain king Aerys Targaryen, Ned recalls feeling that the dragon skulls "were watching me, somehow" (*GoT* 13 Eddard 2: 97). When Tyrion recalls seeing the skulls in the cellars of the Red Keep as a child, he remembers how his own ancestor, King Loren of the Rock, escaped the flames of these very dragons and survived to swear fealty to the Targaryens (*GoT* 14 Tyrion 2: 102–3). When Arya discovers them, she immediately associates them with the crypts beneath Winterfell (*GoT* 33 Arya 3: 286–87).

Viserys Targaryen, King Aerys's son, draws a direct link between his family's sigil and preoccupation with the past, warning, "You do not steal from the dragon, oh, no. The dragon remembers" (GoT 4 Daenerys 1: 24). The deposed heir to a fallen dynasty, Viserys lives only to revive the past: "When they write the history of my reign, sweet sister, they will say that it began tonight" (*GoT* 4 Daenerys 1: 24). His obsessive fixation on the return of Targaryen triumph recalls the ambitious Duke of York, whose desire to regain his birthright drives the action of the *Henry VI* plays: "A day will come when York shall claim his own.... And, when I spy advantage, claim the crown" (*Henry VI* 2 1.1. 239, 242). Viserys, however, cannot truly conceive of a future, only wait for the return of a glorious past that he is barely old enough to remember. When he threatens to kill King Robert, his sister Daenerys "knew he was fighting the Battle of the Trident once again"—a battle that occurred when Viserys was only a child and in which he played no part (*GoT* 4 Daenerys 1: 28). Daenerys, on the other hand, wishes for "no past and no future" (*GoT* 4 Daenerys: 24). As the last Targaryen, she is constantly reminded of her family home and history; as an exile, however, she is cut off from them, recalling only the house with the red door where she briefly knew childhood happiness: "perhaps the dragon did remember, but Dany could not" (*GoT* 4 Daenerys 1: 26, 24).

Over the course of *A Game of Thrones*, Daenerys begins to think of herself not as a Targaryen princess but as *khaleesi* of the Dothraki, a nomadic people who live by pillaging "the trash of dead cities" rather than being bound to the past (*GoT* 37 Daenerys 4: 324). She hopes to bring her family's past glory into the future through her son Rhaego, who, as the prophesied "Stallion who mounts the world," will reestablish Targaryen rule (*GoT* 47 Daenerys 5: 415; 55 Daenerys 6: 495–96). But for all his promise, Rhaego is born a decayed image of House Targaryen's past glory, a dead dragonlike creature "full of graveworms and the stink of corruption." Like the Targaryen's hopes, "[h]e had been dead for years" (*GoT* 69 Daenerys 9: 632). As Daenerys miscarries, however, she begins to hallucinate, hearing the echo of "you don't want to wake the dragon," Viserys's threat in times of anger. As the vision progresses, "waking the dragon" turns from a fear into a desire: she sees her brother Rhaegar in armor but, looking beneath his helm, sees her own face (*GoT* 69 Daenerys 9: 628–29). Rather than the inescapable, cyclical return to the traumas of the past symbolized by Stoneheart and the White Walkers, Daenerys sees a triumphant return to Targaryen power—not through her brothers or son, but through herself. In order to claim this power, she must discard her personal past—"*If I look back I am lost*"—but reclaim her family identity: "I am Daenerys Stormborn, Daenerys of House Targaryen, of the blood of Aegon the Conqueror and Maegor the Cruel and old Valyria before them. I am the dragon's daughter, and I swear to you, these men will die screaming" (*GoT* 69 Daenerys 9: 634, 636).

When the dragon eggs first appear, Illyrio warns Daenerys that "[t]he eons have turned them to stone" (*GoT* 12 Daenerys 2: 86). But like the White Walkers of the north or Ned's persistent memories of Lyanna, the dead still have power. By the end of the novel, those dragons have returned to life, suggesting that Robert's reign is just a brief interlude before the Targaryens reclaim power— just as the Wars of the Roses were an intense but temporary state of Yorkist power bookended by Lancastrian rule. And just as the direwolf puppies are born from their mother's death in the novel's opening, so Daenerys's dragons are born from the ashes of the life she has known as an exile and child bride. Rather than perishing, the mother triumphs, claiming an identity as ruler in her own right rather than one of sister or wife. Dany's transformation therefore echoes cyclical history, but it also transcends it. While the frozen undead of the north can only go through the motions of life, much as those who have not learned from the past can only repeat their mistakes, fire transforms. Just as the phoenix must destroy its adult form to re-emerge as an egg, Daenerys must destroy her old self to emerge—naked and hairless, reborn—to reclaim her birthright.

The Problem of Interpretation Revisited, or the Case of Ned Stark

Political power in the *Henriad* frequently stems from interpretative power over past events: Richard of York wins allies by tracing his line back to Edward III while his son, Richard III, manipulates his victims by controlling the historical narrative. He turns the court against the king's wife and her family by reminding everyone of their previous alliance to the enemy:

> In all which time you and your husband Grey
> Were factious for the house of Lancaster;
> And, Rivers, so were you. Was not your husband
> In Margaret's battle at Saint Alban's slain?
> Let me put in your minds, if you forget,
> What you have been ere now, and what you are;
> Withal, what I have been, and what I am [*Richard III* 1.3.126–132].

Richard manipulates Anne into feeling sympathy for him by comparing his sorrow over his love for her with that over losing his father:

> [T]hy warlike father, like a child,
> Told the sad story of my father's death,
> And twenty times made pause to sob and weep,
> That all the standers-by had wet their cheeks
> Like trees bedash'd with rain: in that sad time
> My manly eyes did scorn an humble tear;
> And what these sorrows could not thence exhale,
> Thy beauty hath, and made them blind with weeping [*Richard III* 1.2.159–166].

Richard is deliberately misrepresenting events here; he had refused to weep at his father's death not out of masculine pride, but out of violent anger: "I cannot weep; for all my body's moisture / Scarce serves to quench my furnace-burning heart.... / Tears then for babes; blows and revenge for me" (*Henry VI* 3 2.1.79–

80, 86). Interpreting the past and using that interpretation to your advantage, as the popularity of the *de casibus* tradition demonstrates, is an indispensable tool for anyone seeking political power. Martin likewise foregrounds the importance of interpreting history in order to access political power and safety throughout his series, particularly through the narrative that drives the action of *A Game of Thrones*. In the ominous scene that greets Ned and his sons at the opening of the series, a lion is not responsible for the animals' deaths, even though Cersei will engineer Robert's death and Joffrey will order Ned's. Rather, the direwolf and the stag kill one another, just as Ned and Robert contribute to each other's—and their own—demises. The fundamental difference between Ned and Robert, we find, is in their interpretation of events—a conflict that emerges in their very first scene together.

On Robert's arrival at Winterfell, Robert and Ned pay their respects at the grave of Ned's sister, Lyanna. Robert, who idealizes Lyanna as the lost love he barely knew, thinks she belongs "on a hill somewhere, under a fruit tree, with the sun and clouds above her and the rain to wash her clean" (*GoT* 5 Eddard 1: 35). To Ned, Lyanna represents the terrible losses the Starks suffered in the war and the unnamed vow that continues to haunt him: "the promises he'd made Lyanna as she lay dying, and the price he'd paid to keep them" (*GoT* 36 Eddard 9: 318). Ned insists that it was Lyanna's wish to remain in the family crypt below Winterfell.

These respective stances represent two distinct attitudes towards the past that emerge in the series. The postwar generation, having grown up without the threat of violence, understandably idealizes the glorious exploits of their forebears: Jon admires Daeren Targaryen, the Young Dragon, even though his uncle reminds Jon that his hero died young; Arya names her direwolf after Nymeria, the "warrior queen of the Rhoyne," and searches the banks of the Trident for the rubies that scattered when Rhaegar fell in combat; the names of the knights of the Kingsguard are "like music" to Bran, and Sansa sees the world in terms of the heroes and monsters of the songs (*GoT* 6 Jon 1: 45; 8 Arya 1: 59; 16 Sansa 1: 117; 9 Bran 2: 65; 45 Sansa 3: 394). Those who know the fierceness of combat are excited by the prospect of becoming part of history: "Winter will never come for the likes of us," says the warrior maiden Brienne of Tarth. "Should we die in battle, they will surely sing of us, and it's always summer in the songs. In the songs all knights are gallant, all maids are beautiful, and the sun is always shining" (*CoK* 23 Catelyn 2: 264). Even those who have been through the horrors of war idealize the past as a time when they were younger, stronger, more admirable. This is particularly true of Robert, who declares he "was never so alive as when I was winning this throne, or so dead as now that I've won it." Asking Ned to be his Hand, he says:

You helped me win this damnable throne, now help me hold it. We were meant to rule together. If Lyanna had lived, we should have been brothers, bound by blood as well as affection. Well, it is not too late. I have a son. You have a daughter. My Joff and your Sansa shall join our houses, as Lyanna and I might once have done [*GoT* 5 Eddard 1: 39].

Robert sees the past in terms of lost opportunities and believes he could correct his mistakes by repeating that past; instead, he will only revive the violence that accompanied it. His desire for revenge can never be fulfilled; he laments that he could only kill Rhaegar Targaryen once and resolves to "kill every Targaryen I can get my hands on, until they are as dead as their dragons, and then I will piss on their graves" (*GoT* 5 Eddard 1: 36; 13 Eddard 2: 94). When he calls the threat of Daenerys bearing a child "the shadow of an axe" hanging over him, Ned calls it "a shadow of a shadow," urging Robert to learn from the past rather than repeating it (*GoT* 34 Eddard 8: 294). Instead, Robert's paranoia leads him to order Daenerys's assassination which, in turn, only encourages her desire to claim the Iron Throne. As the series progresses, events continue to be driven by cycles of revenge with roots in the crimes of Robert's Rebellion, such as when Oberyn Martell seeks revenge on Tywin Lannister and Gregor Clegane for the deaths of his sister Elia and her children. When Oberyn falls to Clegane in single combat, his brother plots to pick up the cycle of retribution where Oberyn left off: *"Vengeance.... Justice.... Fire and blood"* (*FfC* 41 The Princess in the Tower 2: 604).

In *Henry VI 1*, Exeter observes of such conflicts:

> no simple man that sees
> This jarring discord of nobility,
> This shouldering of each other in the course,
> This factious bandying of their favourites,
> But that it doth presage some ill event [4.1.187–191].

This is no prophecy; rather, as brother of the rebel-turned-king Henry IV, Exeter speaks from experience. Of more than twenty point-of-view characters in *A Song of Ice and Fire*, only about half are old enough to even remember Robert's Rebellion, and only two veterans of it—Ned and Jaime—have a substantial number of point-of-view chapters. In the first installment of the series, we see events chiefly through Ned's perspective as one who has been through the war and wants to learn from the past rather than recreating it. The Starks are an ancient family and, as such, Ned is acutely aware of the presence of the past. Just as the lands of the north are spotted with ancient burial sites, Ned's thoughts are riddled with memories of the dead. He is particularly fixated on his sister Lyanna, whose abduction by Rhaegar Targaryen started the war; he is also haunted by Rhaegar's death and those of his children. Unlike those who idealize the past, Ned seeks to learn from it; for instance, he tries to dissuade Robert from repeating the cycle of violence by ordering the young Daenerys's death as he once ordered that of her young aunt and uncle.

In order to learn from the past, however, we must first understand it. A major turning point in *A Game of Thrones* relies on correct interpretation of a historical text: *The Lineages and Histories of the Great Houses of the Seven Kingdoms, With Descriptions of Many High Lords and Noble Ladies and Their Children*. Ned turns again and again to this book in hopes of uncovering its significance to Jon Arryn's murder, but only when Sansa points out the discrepancy between Robert's appearance and Joff's does Ned realize the truth of the prince's parentage. She says that she and Joff will "be ever so happy, just like in the songs" (*GoT* 45 Sansa 3: 399), idealizing their future in terms of Joff's beautiful golden hair. Ned realizes, however, that her comment is the key to how the past is being misrepresented: the lovely story in which Robert Baratheon and Cersei Lannister bore a golden-haired, legitimate child must be a lie, and the past must be reinterpreted in light of that knowledge. Ned's actions reflect those of the readers themselves: a long text filled with genealogies and the intricacies of politics must be visited and revisited until the truth begins to reveal itself. Just as Ned dresses in "black and white and grey, all the shades of truth," he encounters a wide spectrum of historical truth (*GoT* 44 Eddard 11: 387). On one end of this spectrum is the objective truth offered by the book of lineages, factually accurate but so dry and distanced as to render the information in it meaningless without context. On the other end lies an idealization of the past which, like Sansa's childlike belief in heroes and monsters, offers much psychological comfort but is dangerously inaccurate. Only by integrating these two types of truth can he interpret the past correctly, and evade the weight of the past.

Notes

1. The series' trend towards character death has become a running joke among readers, who have created *memento mori* images of their own: internet memes featuring Martin's picture with captions such as "Makes you love characters; kills them all"; mock book covers entitled "Don't Get Too Attached"; and copies of "All My Friends Are Still Dead" placed near displays of the *Song of Ice and Fire* series. Just as memento mori images "[dwell] with insistent horror upon the corruption of the body, the terrors of the grave, and the punishments of that greater pit into which an unprepared soul might fall," these memes serve as warnings to potential readers not to become emotionally invested in Martin's characters (Morris 1035).

2. The connection is made more overt in the HBO series, where Osha interprets the comet as a sign that dragons have returned to the world (*Thrones* S2: Ep. 1, "The North Remembers").

Works Cited

ASOIAF University. No date. Web. 19 May 2014.
Baldwin, William. *The Mirror for Magistrates*. Cambridge: Cambridge University Press, 1938. Print.

Benioff, David, and D.B. Weiss, prods. *Game of Thrones*. HBO. 2011–2014. Television.

Castiglione, Baldesar. *The Book of the Courtier*. New York: Doubleday, 1959. Print.

Chapman, Raymond. "The Wheel of Fortune in Shakespeare's Historical Plays." *The Review of English Studies* 1.1 (1950): 1–7.

Cressy, David. *Education in Tudor and Stuart England*. New York: St. Martin's, 1976.

Elyot, Thomas. *The Boke Named the Governour*. Ed. S.E. Lehmberg. New York: Dutton, 1962. Print.

The History Behind the Game of Thrones. No date. Web. 19 May 2014.

Levine, Nina. *Women's Matters: Polics, Gender, and Nation in Shakespeare's Early History Plays*. Newark: University of Delaware Press, 1998. Print.

Martin, George R.R. "George R.R. Martin Webchat Transcript." *Empire Online*. 23 April 2012. Web. 27 June 2014.

_____. "LoneStarCon 3: The George R.R. Martin Interview." *The Austin Chronicle*. 29 August 2013. Web. 15 December 2014.

_____. "More Wars of the Roses." *The Citadel: The A Song of Ice and Fire Archive*. 27 November 1998. Web. 15 December 2014.

Morris, Harry. "*Hamlet* as 'Memento Mori' Poem." *PMLA* 85.5 (1970): 1035–1040. Print.

Pearsall, Derek. "The Idea of Englishness in the Fifteenth Century." *Nation, Court and Culture: New Essays on Fifteenth-Century English Poetry*. Ed. Helen Cooney. Dublin: Four Courts Press, 2001. Print.

Rackin, Phyllis. *Stages of History: Shakespeare's English Chronicles*. Ithaca: Cornell University Press, 1990. Print.

Shakespeare, William. *1 Henry VI*. *The Riverside Shakespeare*. Ed. G. Blakemore Evans. Boston: Houghton Mifflin, 1997. Print.

_____. *2 Henry VI*. *The Riverside Shakespeare*. Ed. G. Blakemore Evans. Boston: Houghton Mifflin, 1997. Print.

_____. *3 Henry VI*. *The Riverside Shakespeare*. Ed. G. Blakemore Evans. Boston: Houghton Mifflin, 1997. Print.

_____. *Richard III*. *The Riverside Shakespeare*. Ed. G. Blakemore Evans. Boston: Houghton Mifflin, 1997. Print.

_____. *Titus Andronicus*. *The Riverside Shakespeare*. Ed. G. Blakemore Evans. Boston: Houghton Mifflin, 1997. Print.

Walker, Jessica. "'We are not safe': History, Fear, and the Gothic in *Richard III*." *Shakespearean Gothic*. Ed. Christy Desmet and Anne Williams. Cardiff: University of Wales Press, 2009. 181–197. Print.

Watson, Donald G. *Shakespeare's Early History Plays: Politics at Play on the Elizabethan Stage*. Athens: University of Georgia Press, 1990. Print.

Westeros: The Song of Ice and Fire Domain. No date. Web. 19 May 2014.

A Wiki of Ice and Fire. No date. Web. 19 May 2014.

Williams, Anne. *Art of Darkness: A Poetics of Gothic*. Chicago: University of Chicago Press, 1995.

Ziolkowski, Eric J. "Don Quijote's Windmill and Fortune's Wheel." *The Modern Language Review* 86.4 (1991): 885–97. Print.

Dividing Lines: Frederick Jackson Turner's Western Frontier and George R.R. Martin's Northern Wall

Michail Zontos

"When he had donned his glove again, Jon Snow turned abruptly and walked to the low, icy northern parapet. Beyond him the Wall fell away sharply, beyond him there was only the darkness and the wild. Tyrion followed him, and side by side they stood upon the edge of the world"—*A Game of Thrones*

Among the several impressive constructions that the reader discovers throughout the pages of *A Song of Ice and Fire,* the Wall separating the Seven Kingdoms of Westeros from the frozen lands of the far North stands out for its grandeur. An immense fortification made of ice, the Wall represents a frontier line that separates the civilized part of George R.R. Martin's fictional world from the wilderness of the North. It marks the end of the settlement, it protects the realm from the barbaric inhabitants of the uncharted territories that lie beyond its protective veil, and it is a point where different cultures meet.

Martin himself feels proud of his Wall because "it's unique in fantasy" ("Patrick"). Nevertheless, it has its equivalents in history. From Hadrian's Wall and the Great Wall of China, immense fortifications constructed to protect powerful empires from "barbaric" invasions, to the Berlin Wall, the wall of the West Bank and the Mexico–United States barrier dividing lines have separated communities with different religions, languages or political systems.

Martin conceived the Wall while walking around the remnants of Hadrian's Wall in Scotland, a once magnificent fortification that marked the borders of the Roman Empire in Britannia and protected its territory from the various tribes that lived beyond its protective veil. He wondered "what it would be like to be a Roman soldier ... to stand here, to gaze off into the distance, not knowing what might emerge from the forest" (MacLaurin).

This link underscores how heavily influenced by European history is *A Song of Ice and Fire*. Several commentators have connected events from European history with Martin's world. Besides Hadrian's Wall, the War of the Roses has influenced the game of thrones described in the books while the Black Dinner that took place at Edinburgh Castle in 1440 has been referred as a major influence for the infamous Red Wedding. The author himself has verified these sources and the Europeanness of Martin's series has become somewhat of a commonplace.

While such connections are extremely interesting, the lack of any analysis of his work from the perspective of American history is at least striking. This essay will remedy this absence by pursuing an innovative reading of Martin's work from an Americanist's perspective, focusing on the Wall itself. While frontiers have existed in almost every country in the form either of unoccupied lands or borders, no other country's historiographical narrative has been based so much on a frontier explanation. This has been largely the legacy of Turner, the most important American historian of the late nineteenth century.

In 1893, Frederick Jackson Turner, a young historian at the University of Wisconsin, presented his essay "The Significance of the Frontier in American History" at a meeting of the American Historical Association that took place in Chicago. Turner argues that "up to our own day American history has been in a large degree the history of the colonization of the Great West. The existence of an area of free land, its continuous recession, and the advance of American settlement westward, explain American development" (Turner, *Frontier* 1). According to Turner, European settlers had to move westwards with each successive generation. As they created their settlements the frontier line which divided their communities from the wilderness moved from the Atlantic coast towards the Pacific, so that, moving westwards, they found themselves constantly on a moving frontier line, at the "outer edge of the wave"—the meeting point between "savagery" and "civilization" (Turner, *Frontier* 3). The harsh American environment transformed them, for as they entered the primitive life of the frontier they abandoned the traits of European civilization, thus becoming something new: Americans. Like the Wall in *A Song of Ice and Fire*, which separates the civilized Seven Kingdoms from the Wildlings and the creatures that dwell in the North, Turner's frontier separates Euro-American civilization from the lands inhabited by Native Americans.

This essay will show that while the relationship between Martin's Wall and Hadrian's is obvious, it is the American rather than the Scottish frontier which most fully captures the trope of the borderland in Martin's world. It will reveal the inherent, and so far neglected, Americanness of *A Song of Ice and Fire* and it will engage in a broader discussion concerning cultural encounters upon the American frontier and the Wall.

Frederick Jackson Turner and George R.R. Martin

Turner's thesis dominated the field of American history from the time of its proclamation until at least the 1930s. Although many of its basic elements have since been refuted, it remains influential due to its solid impact on American culture. As Martin Ridge underlines, almost a century after the 1893 conference,

> Its themes regarding American society and character as depicted in fiction, art, drama, and film have so effectively captured the American public's imagination and are now so deeply woven into the American consciousness that it may still be a part of the American mentality a century from now [4].

The Western as an American form of art has been essentially influenced by Turner's perception of the West. Although its origins can be traced back to the journals of the Lewis and Clarke expedition and James Fenimore Cooper's *Leatherstocking Tales,* the genre acquired its definite characteristics at the beginning of the twentieth century, influenced both by Turner's thesis and by popular spectacles such as Buffalo Bill's Wild West Show (McVeigh 39).

In his introduction to the short story collection *Warriors,* Martin mentions that during his childhood he discovered literature by getting paperbacks from the spinner track. There he became acquainted with several literature genres, the western among them. Jack Schaefer's *Shane* was the novel that introduced him to the western (Martin, *Warriors* 13). Steve McVeigh argues that "Schaefer pared the popular Western story down to its essential mythology" (McVeigh 50), and indeed the book reveals how basic tenets of the frontier thesis have influenced American popular culture. *Shane*'s plot is an archetype. Set in the nineteenth century Wyoming, the novel concerns a mysterious gunman, Shane, who arrives at an established frontier town and helps the Starretts, a family of homesteaders, to keep their farms by confronting a greedy cattle baron who wants to force them off the land. The story, much like Turner's thesis, reveals the distinction between the "customary way," the established frontier family, and the "primitive condition," the lonely gunman who comes from the far west (Work 315), and neglects the Native Americans who remain almost absent in the story.

Martin also mentions Robert A. Heinlein and Robert E. Howard as influences. Heinlein in particular projected the concept of the American frontier into space, especially in his novel *Farmer in the Sky* (1953), while Howard, the creator of Conan the Barbarian, once declared, "I'm seriously contemplating devoting all my time and efforts to western writing, abandoning all other forms of work entirely" (Howard ix). What is obvious in Martin's account is that the concept of the frontier was apparent in the readings of his childhood. It is no surprise that the image of black-dressed members of the Night's Watch walking into the wilderness of dark forests covered with snow and holding their swords in order to fight the creatures of the wilderness is so much like the image of a gunman who rides through the plains fighting villains. In the end, as Jack Schaefer mentions, "the man with a gun using it to right wrongs" is "in a sense the American version of a knight on horseback" (qtd. in McVeigh 50).

The western is not the only thing that links the historian Turner with the author Martin. The two share a perception of history. Martin stresses that "history is full of stories, full of triumph and tragedy and battles won and lost. It is the people who speak to me, the men and women who once lived and loved and dreamed and grieved, just as we do" (Gevers). Compare this with Frederick Jackson Turner's perception of history:

> The intrigues of courts, knightly valor, palaces and pyramids, the loves of ladies, the songs of minstrels, and the chants from cathedrals pass like a pageant, or linger like a strain of music as we turn the pages. But history has its tragedy as well, which tells of the degraded tillers of the soil, toiling that others might dream, the slavery that rendered possible the "glory that was Greece," the serfdom into which decayed the "grandeur that was Rome" [Turner, *Early Writings*, 48].

Both Turner and Martin emphasize the role of ordinary people in history and it is the story of those very people who lived in their borderlands that is the focus of this comparative study. It is the story of those who linger in the "civilized" part of the frontier line and of those who dwell on the side of "savagery."

Last but not least, the comparison between a real and a fictional frontier should not puzzle the reader. Martin justifies the relation by mentioning that while he grew up in New Jersey, books were the only way of escape for him: "As soon as I opened a book, suddenly I was in some imaginary world; the Mines of Moria are more real to me than some of the things that actually happened to me while I was reading about them" (Salter). Or, as André Breton would have it, "what is admirable about the fantastic is that there is no longer anything fantastic; there is only the real" (Breton 15).

Moving Frontiers, Static Frontiers: Democracy and Monarchy

When Jon Snow left Winterfell, the last northern capital of the Seven Kingdoms and seat of his father and Warden of the North Eddard Stark, in order to arrive at the Wall and become a member of the Night's Watch, who defend it, he encountered a harsh environment of ice and snow. As "the North went on forever ... it had grown colder ... and far more quiet" (*GoT* 14 Tyrion 2: 99). As with the American pioneers when they moved westward, Snow senses with each step northward that he is leaving civilization behind.

> Three days ride from Winterfell, however, the farmland gave way to dense wood, and the kingsroad grew lonely.... Farms and holdfasts grew scarcer and smaller as they pressed northward, ever deeper into the darkness of the wolfswood, until finally there were no more roofs to shelter under, and they were thrown back on their own resources [*GoT* 14 Tyrion 2: 99–101].

When Jon Snow sees the Wall, he is impressed by its magnitude: "To the North loomed the Wall. Almost seven hundred feet high it stood, three times the height of the tallest tower in the stronghold it sheltered.... He could feel the great weight of all that ice pressing down on him, as if it were about to topple, and somehow Jon knew that if it fell, the world fell with it" (*GoT* 20 Jon 3: 154–155). What was a moving line of settlement in the case of the West, here, in the deep North, was an immense fortification, titanic in size and solid as the ice from which it was built.

There is an interesting, almost poetic, distinction between the nature of the American frontier and the nature of the Wall. The first was a moving line of settlement, a harsh but vibrant environment full of life and adventure which led to the advance of civilization. In Turner's idealistic perception, which down-played the strong relation between the frontiering experience and imperialism, it was an inherently progressive force, manned by pioneers who decided to struggle for survival. On the contrary, there is an implied conservatism in the essence of the Wall. For more than eight thousand years it stood there, older than the Seven Kingdoms themselves, constructed in the Age of Heroes, according to the tales of Westeros, protecting the lands from the long winters. There was no promise of progress or advance beyond the Wall and defense was its primary goal. It literally represented the end of the world (*GoT* 20 Jon 3: 154).

Turner mentions that the first official frontier in America was established in 1690 when "a committee of the General Court of Massachusetts recommended the Court to order what shall be the frontier and to maintain a committee to settle garrisons on the frontier" (Turner, *Frontier* 39). During the first major conflict between Native Americans and New England colonists (with their Native American allies), King Phillip's War (1675–1678), the idea of the construction of a static wall, like the one that stands north of Winterfell, had been suggested: "In the session of 1675–1676 it had been proposed to build a fence of stockades or stone eight feet high" in order to protect the lives and property of the frontier inhabitants from enemy attacks (Turner, *Frontier* 40). This proposal reminds us that New England, which in Turner's frontier thesis tended to be the bastion of civilization, was itself once a wilderness (and, in reality, homeland of Native Americans, a fact almost insignificant in Turner's thought). The frontiering experience began on the Atlantic coast, which was the very frontier of Europe (Turner, *Frontier* 4).

Turner could have added that this was not the only time the idea of a static wall had been proposed in America. In 1717, a Scottish baronet called Sir Robert Mountgomery argued for the creation of what he called the Margravate of Azilia, a British colony on the southeastern frontier, in South Carolina (Nobles 57):

> Our meaning here relates to what immediate Measures will be taken for Security against the Insults of the Natives, during the Infancy of our Affairs. To which End we shall not satisfie [sic] ourselves with building here and there a Fort, the fatal Practice of America, but so dispose the Habitations and Divisions of the Land, that not alone our Houses but whatever we possess, will be enclos'd by *Military Lines*, impregnable against the *Savages*, and which will make our whole Plantation one continued Fortress.... As the Inhabitants encrease [sic] New Lines will be made to enclose them also, so that all the People will be always safe within a well-defended Line of Circumvallation [Mountgomery 13].

Both plans took place when the settlements of the country were still new and outposts of the British Empire: the frontier was still a monarchical institution. Both failed. Turner, commenting on the first of these projects, mentions that "this project, however, of a kind of Roman Wall did not appeal to the frontiersmen of the time. It was a part of the antiquated ideas of defense.... In this era the frontier fighter adapted himself to a more open order, and lighter equipment suggested by the Indian warrior's practice" (Turner, *Frontier* 40). Even from that early time, Turner thought, the American reality rejected the notion of a static frontier on the American soil. Movement has been the dominant fact in American life and Turner's frontier was, accordingly, a democratic moving line.

Turner seems familiar with these failed efforts to construct static walls in America, efforts that validate his theory of a moving frontier, but he fails to mention that moving frontiers that conquered wildernesses and established freer societies had also existed in Medieval Europe. Bryce Lyon has shown that land reclamation in the eleventh and twentieth century, led by pioneers who "cleared the forests, drained the marshes, and won land from the sea" (47) with the support of "counts and ecclesiastical establishments" converted "Maritime Flanders from a desolate waste into a fertile, revenue producing land peopled with free farmers living in an economically, socially, and legally privileged area" (55). Martin refrains from hinting at these aspects of the medieval world. The Westeros society rejects mobility and is based on rigid class distinctions. There is scarcely movement in a world in which the high lords play their game of thrones and the smallfolk suffer accordingly. The static northern frontier has never been moved since its construction in a mythical past.

Men of the Frontier, Men of the Metropolis

Despite the static nature of Martin's Wall and the dynamism of Turner's frontier, they impact the frontiersmen in much the same way. Frederick Jackson Turner described the social and cultural transformation pushed by the frontier.

> The wilderness masters the colonist. It finds him a European in dress, industries, tools, modes of travel, and thought. It takes him from the railroad car and puts him in the birch canoe. It strips off the garments of civilization and arrays him in the hunting shirt and the moccasin. It puts him in the log cabin of the Cherokee and Iroquois and runs an Indian palisade around him.... In short, at the frontier the environment is at first too strong for the man. He must accept the conditions which it furnishes, or perish, and so he fits himself into the Indian clearings and follows the Indian trails. Little by little he transforms the wilderness, but the outcome is not the old Europe.... The fact is, that here is a new product that is American [Turner, *Frontier* 4].

This process, which has been described as deculturation or de–Europeanization (Bassin 504), implies that American democracy was not based on a society of highly cultivated men with a democratic vision but rather that it was the outcome of harsh environmental conditions. As the European colonists approached the frontier, they had to cope with hard environmental conditions, different from those of their homelands, and to enter into complicated relations with the Native Americans, which varied from friendship to open hostility. In order to survive their ordeal, Turner believed, they became more egalitarian, individualistic, and they developed a sense of resentment towards authoritarian government, traits which created a democratic society of survivors. This "deculturation" makes more sense when we realize that when Turner writes about the impact of the environment on the settlers, he almost means it literally. Richard Hofstadter underlines the social Darwinism that dominated the intellectual environment of the late nineteenth century (Hofstadter, *Social Darwinism* 4–5), a view which explains, for example, Turner's belief that the new American democracy "came, stark and strong and full of life, from the American forest" (Turner, *Frontier* 216).

Among others, Turner was influenced by the French naturalist Jean Baptiste de Lamarck who contended that "the environment generated in sensate organisms, among them man, a need or mental desire, either conscious or unconscious, to adjust structure and behavior to new and presumably more appropriate conditions" (Coleman 32–33). From such a perspective, Turner mistakenly deemphasized the Native American contribution to the formation of the American character. He believed that it was the American forest itself that generated American democracy in the sense that the extreme conditions of the frontier developed hard individualistic survivors who rejected the notion of authoritarianism:

> That coarseness and strength combined with acuteness and inquisitiveness; that practical, inventive turn of mind, quick to find expedients; that masterful grasp of material things, lacking in the artistic but powerful to effect great ends; that restless, nervous energy; that dominant individualism ... and withal that buoyancy and exuberance which comes with freedom [Turner, *Frontier* 37].

It would be an exaggeration to say that Lamarck inspired Martin; nevertheless the impact of the environmental conditions on the psychology of his characters is apparent, especially in the frontier conditions of the North. During his first days at Castle Black, the main stronghold of the Night's Watch at the Wall, Jon Snow reflects on the place: "*So cold*, he thought, remembering the warm halls of Winterfell, where the hot waters ran through the walls like blood through a man's body. There was scant warmth to be found in Castle Black; the walls were cold here, and the people colder" (*GoT* 20 Jon 3: 149). Even his beloved uncle, Benjen Stark, had changed. "Even his uncle had abandoned him in this cold place at the end of the world. Up here, the genial Benjen Stark he had known became a different person" (*GoT* 20 Jon 3: 150); as Donal Noye, the armorer of the Night's Watch, says: "Yes. Cold and hard and mean, that's the Wall, and the men who walk it" (*GoT* 20 Jon 3: 153).

In the American setting, this process of de-culturation reveals Turner's nationalistic intentions, as it promoted the idea of a unique American identity, though in Westeros this nationalism is absent. According to Martin, the medievals "didn't have our current sense of nationalism. They weren't English; they were citizens of a town or members of their family. They didn't have the sense of country that we do" (MacLaurin). Nevertheless, even as Europeans abandoned their old traits and allegiances and became Americans, the members of the Night's Watch also abandoned their old allegiances in order to become sworn members of the brotherhood. The words of the Lord Commander, Jeor Mormont, to the newcomers are revealing.

> Some of you bear the names of proud houses. Others have only bastards' names, or no names at all. It makes no matter. All that is past now. On the Wall, we are all one house....
>
> At evenfall, as the sun sets ... you shall take your vows. From that moment, you will be a Sworn Brother of the Night's Watch. Your crimes will be washed away, your debts forgiven. So too you must wash away your former loyalties, put aside your grudges, forget old wrongs and old loves alike. Here you begin anew [*GoT* 49 Jon 6: 431].

In leaving the traits of civilization behind, as the American pioneers did, the black brothers enter one of the few places in the Seven Kingdoms where feudal class stratifications recede in favor of a slightly more egalitarian society. The members of the Night's Watch were brothers amongst themselves. Their duty was to the realm. Aspiring monarchs could rebel and overthrow kings in order to sit on the Iron Throne but the "the black brothers were sworn to take no part in the quarrels of the realm" (*GoT* 32 Tyrion 4: 273). Its focus was always towards the North, beyond the frontier. Moreover, this ancient order is a meritocracy. Every member of the Night's Watch could be nominated as Lord Commander and the decision was based on elections. Thus, in this far corner of a world in which birth determined the life and career of everyone and advancement from one social class to another was almost impossible, the frontier was the exception. Jon Snow's father, Ned Stark, reflects, "even a bastard may rise high in the Night's Watch" (*GoT* 7 Catelyn 2: 56).

The Night's Watch is not a democratic society like that of the American pioneers, but in Martin's work, like in Turner's, the idea that "savagery" leads to more democratic institutions is apparent. The Night's Watch chooses its leader, as both the wildlings and the Dothraki do, while Tyrion's allies among the primitive mountain clans have "an absurd notion that every man's voice should be heard in council, so they argued about *everything*, endlessly. Even their women were allowed to speak" (*GoT* 57 Tyrion 7: 508).

If the frontier is a place of opportunity, it is also a safety valve. Turner believes that the frontier offered an escape from the more stratified East: "Whenever social conditions tended to crystallize in the East, whenever capital tended to press upon labor or political restraints to impede the freedom of the mass, there was this gate of escape to the free conditions of the frontier" (Turner, *Frontier* 259). Martin's Wall functions likewise, "a midden heap for all the misfits of the realm ... sullen peasants, debtors, poachers, rapers, thieves, and bastards like you," as Tyrion Lannister once said to Jon Snow. "All wind up on the Wall" (*GoT* 14 Tyrion 2: 104). For most of them life on the Wall offered escape from an even harsher reality. In this way, the northern frontier offered a second chance to prisoners, exiles and misfits, while also protecting the realm by manning the Wall and by removing those hideous criminals and outcasts that could stir trouble in the South just as the Western frontier diminished social conflict in the American East.

Tyrion's disdain for the members of the Night's Watch also reminds us of how the American frontiersman was often perceived before Turner's mythmaking revision of them as a hero. A century before Turner, Crévecoeur, the French-American writer who in his book *Letters from an American Farmer* (1782) anticipated the frontier thesis, called frontiersmen "no beter [*sic*] than carnivorous animals of a superior rank, living on the flesh of wild animals when they can catch them, and when they are not, they subsist on grain" (59). Indeed Crève-coeur was distressed to find that "thus are our first steps trodden, thus are our first trees felled, in general, by the most vicious of our people" (72).

This characteristic perception of the pioneers, Nobles argues, started changing only in 1829 when the election of Andrew Jackson to the presidency of the United States brought to prominence a person who was perceived by his fellow Americans as a frontier hero himself (Nobles 103,125). By the end of that century Turner's thesis had "recast these ruffians and their role in history entirely. Far from being the 'worst sort,' these trappers and traders constituted the very vanguard of American civilization" (Conn 225).

The Night's Watch reverses the pattern. Once a noble brotherhood, it has somehow degenerated. It no longer has the luxury of choosing the quality of its members as it has a severe problem of lack of men. Lord Commander Mormont's requests to the king and the noble houses of the realm for reinforcements are revealing: "The Night's Watch is dying. Our strength is less than a thousand now.... Should an attack come, I have three men to defend each mile of wall.... Winter *is* coming, and when the Long Night falls, only the Night's Watch will stand between the realm and the darkness that sweeps from the North. The gods help us all if we are not ready" (*GoT* 22 Tyrion 3: 174–175).

The appeals of the frontier towns of New England for garrison sound like the Lord Commander's pleas. The towns of Lacaster, Dunstable, and Deer-field were particularly eloquent: "As God has made you father over us so you will have a father's pity to us" ... "unless you will be pleased to take us (out of your fatherlike pitty) and Cherish us in yo' Bosomes we are like Suddainly to breath out o' Last Breath" (Turner, *Frontier* 48). As was the case in the Night's Watch, the settlers of the frontier towns in New England were not allowed to abandon them, and if they did without proper leave from the authorities they had to face severe punishment: "An act of March 12, 1694–95, by the General Court of Massachusetts enumerated the 'Frontier Towns' which the inhabitants were forbidden to desert on pain of loss of their lands (if landholders) or of imprisonment (if not landholders), unless permission to remove were first obtained" (Turner, *Frontier* 42). This early period restriction on movement meshes poorly with our myths of the western frontier in particular, but the monarchical frontier, it is clear from Turner's description, was much more static, like the Wall.

The Night's Watch is located at the most extreme edge of the northern set-tlements, but the northerners in general are different from the southerners. King Robert Baratheon contrasts the "vast emptiness" (*GoT* 5 Eddard 1:33) of the north with the abundance of the south:

In Highgarden there are fields of golden roses that stretch away as far as the eye can see. The fruits are so ripe they explode in your mouth—melons, peaches, fireplums, you've never tasted such sweetness.... And you ought to see the towns, Ned! Flowers everywhere, the markets bursting with food, the summerwines so cheap and so good that you can get drunk just breathing the air. Everyone is fat and drunk and rich [*GoT* 5 Eddard 1: 34].

Needless to say, when Eddard Stark eventually arrives in King's Landing, he sees more complicated reality. For a straightforward frontiersman like him, the complexity and intrigue of the Court are striking and unwelcome. After his first meeting with the Small Council, the king's cabinet, Stark felt that he did not belong there. "He had no patience with this game they played, this dueling with words" (*GoT* 21 Eddard 4: 162). There was nothing pleasant for Eddard Stark in the South: "For a moment Eddard Stark wanted nothing so much as to return to Winterfell, to the clean simplicity of the north, where the enemies were winter and the wildlings beyond the Wall" (*GoT* 31 Eddard 7: 269). This contrast between simplicity and complexity marks northern and southern characters.

Frederick Jackson Turner, a westerner himself, faced similar experiences in the East. As a young historian he was aware that many easterners tended to look with disdain on westerners. Richard Hofstadter recalls the attitudes of some of Turner's contemporaries: "I do not like the western type of man," E.L. Godkin sneered, saying that "no scenery or climate I had to share with western people would charm me," while George Edward Woodberry, the literary critic and poet from Massachusetts who taught for a while at the University of Nebraska, wrote, "This life requires a hardihood of the senses ... I doubt very much whether the hardihood I gain will not be a deterioration into barbarism, not sinew for civilization" (Hofstadter, *Progressive Historians* 54–55). Hofstadter argues that Turner tried to "be on his guard and looking for trouble when a New England resident explains things to him" (Hofstadter, *Progressive Historians* 55), an attitude he preserved all his life: "I love my Middle West," Turner once wrote. "I am still a Western man in all but my residence" (Billington 385). Nevertheless, simplicity of lifestyle does not mean simplicity of mind. After all, it is Lord Eddard Stark who discovered the mystery of Joffrey's parentage.

Wildness

Most of the inhabitants of the Seven Kingdoms have not seen the people who live beyond the Wall. The knowledge of them comes either from the knowledge of the maesters, the scholars of Westeros, or from legends and myths like the ones told by Old Nan, whose stories are the sum of popular cultural beliefs of the realm. What is known about them comes from the people of Westeros. For a long time the same situation applied to Native Americans: due to their oral culture, what was known about them came from "the pens of Europeans" (Nobles 29).

In the world of Westeros, the maesters are attached to the dominant elite, their "official" knowledge serving the several noble families that rule the Kingdoms. By contrast, the popular narratives, as expressed for example in the stories of the Old Nan, do not necessarily convey the same principles and ideas as the narratives of the maesters. But they do have their own power. As Gregory Nobles mentions, "repeated over and over, the images and stories that permeate popular culture come together to form a more enduring American myth, what some historians call a 'master narrative,' which provides both an explanation for the past and a justification for the present" (Nobles x–xii). In a way, popular culture comes from the stories and narratives of the society itself, while at the same time it helps to inform the popular beliefs and narratives.

The people who live beyond the Wall are known in the South as the wildlings. According to Old Nan's tales "the wildlings were cruel men ... slavers and slayers and thieves. They consorted with giants and ghouls, stole girl children in the dead of night, and drank blood from polished horns" (*GoT* 1 Bran 1: 11). In Old Nan's tales the wildings are depicted as degenerate, uncivilized, cruel and savage, an abomination to civilization, but others, south of the Wall, tend to underestimate them. "Mance Rayder is nothing for us to fear," Eddard Stark says, considering a pre-emptive strike on the leader of the wildlings (*GoT* 3 Catelyn 1: 20). Lord Tywin disbelieves news that the wildlings are moving south in vast numbers: "The lands beyond the Wall cannot support vast numbers" (*SoS* 33 Tyrion 4: 363). Only the rangers of the Night's Watch, who stand as the first line of defense against the wildlings and who share the same harsh environmental conditions, tend to view them in a more realistic light: "They are as brave as we are, Jon. As strong, as quick, as clever.... They name themselves the free folk, and each one thinks himself as good as a king and wiser than a maester," Qhorin Halfhand says to Jon Snow (*CoK* 54 Jon 7: 574).

Underestimating or ignoring the "uncivilized" other has been a common tactic for placing certain people outside the master narrative. In the United States of the late nineteenth century, during Turner's lifetime, this was almost the norm concerning Native Americans. Steven Conn argues that Native Americans had become almost invisible during this period, the result of systematic genocide, which culminated in the massacre at Wounded Knee, on December 29, 1890 (1–2). He also mentions that in many period textbooks, the Indian appeared as something vanished forever. A few years before Turner's proclamation, in

1885, Francis S. Drake wrote in his *Indian History for Young Folks*: "With the exception of a few roving bands of Apaches and other wild tribes of the plains, the Indian pictured in these pages no longer exists.... Civilization has taken hold of him, and one by one his old superstitions and savage customs will disappear" (Drake 6). Among the few popular shows that portrayed Native Americans differently, Buffalo Bill Cody's Wild West Show depicted the "savage" as "worthy adversaries" and William Cody, a frontiersman himself who had fought against the western tribes, much like the Halfhand, argued that they should "be admired and understood" (Moses 8). Cody, a frontiersman himself who had fought against Indians, managed to see them with a more sympathetic eye, like the Halfhand did with the wildlings. But whether as a mere savage or a noble savage, the Native American was absent from the scene, and Cody's shows presented nostalgic images from a waning world.

If the Native American was absent in popular culture, he was also absent in the work of the nineteenth century historian. Already from the beginning of the nineteenth century, Conn argues, the generation of "romantic historians"— Jared Sparks, George Bancroft, Francis Parkman, John Lothrop Motley, and William Prescott—had articulated a narrative of American history "as the progressive fulfillment of an almost providential mandate" in which Native Americans "could not register as actors or even as sympathetic figures" (Conn 201). Frederick Jackson Turner's approach was similar. According to David Nichols, "Turner believed the Indian was important only insofar as he contributed to the 'environment' of the frontier—the pioneer's environment." More or less, the Indian "was part of the landscape" (386). Turner believed the Native Americans were disappearing, because "failure to use resources will submit people to subordination of a superior type which *does*. An inevitable process" (Bogue 378).

By neglecting those who lived behind the frontier as a "vanishing race," Turner justified the dominance of "civilization" over "savagery." The "savage" had no have place in the story of the development of the United States. Native Americans just happened to be there, mere obstacles to the expansion of civilization. House Stark expresses a similar view: "Winter is Coming." Winter of course, like Turner's frontier, includes all the dangers that the Wall was erected to keep at bay, and the people who live behind the frontier line are part of those dangers. As Jon Snow will discover, it is winter that men should fear, not the wildlings in particular.

If Native Americans had disappeared from the American master narrative, the wildling culture had disappeared from the narrative of the maesters. When Osha, a captured wildling, tries to warn the Starks about the dangers of the North, she realizes that she is not taken seriously. Maester Luwin reacts to her stories of children of the forest, giants, magic and white walkers, by saying that "the wildling woman could give Old Nan lessons in telling tales" (*GoT* 54 Bran 6: 485). Her stories and beliefs are dismissed as fairytales. Initially, young Bran Stark shares this dismissive view: "Maester Luwin says there are no more giants. He says they're all dead, like the children of the forest" (*GoT* 54 Bran 6: 483), but eventually they become friends and when Bran passes beyond the Wall, he realizes that magic, children of the forests and other supernatural creatures actually exist (*DwD* 14 Bran 2: 168–178).

Osha's story recalls the story of Ishi, the last survivor of the Yanna people in Sierra Nevada. Like Osha, Ishi came out of a forest. He was adopted by white people and was treated as a specimen to be studied. Like Osha, Ishi became friends with the man who adopted him, the anthropologist Alfred Kroeber. Like Osha, he won the sympathy of the academics who studied him. But as Gerald Vizenor argues, "these college men ... were the same men who discovered and then invented an outsider, the last of his tribe, with their considerable influence and power of communication. They were not insensitive, to be sure, but their studies and museums would contribute to the simulations of savagism" (Vizenor 131). Osha was not exhibited in any museums, as Ishi was, but she realized the power of the dominant narrative when she encountered the indifference of Maester Luwin.

The connection of the wildlings to a supernatural perception of nature increases the indifference towards them. There was a similar case in the American experience. As Tom Holm argues, "by the early nineteenth century, many white Americans ... adhered to the idea that American Indians were mystically in tune with the wonders of the natural world." For this reason they used to call them "children of the forest." This connection was for many Americans the reason that Native Americans, "along with the forests and streams, would be crushed under the advance of a 'civilized' society" (Holm 54). Yet these perceptions contrasted what those beyond the border thought about themselves. The wildlings collectively call themselves the free folk and they resent the southerners whom they call "kneelers." Like the term wildlings, which was imposed and accepted by the dominant elite of the South, the term Indian, in the American case, is a "colonial enactment, not a loan word, and the dominance is sustained by the simulation that has superseded the real tribal names" (Vizenor 11).

Misperceptions about the "other" are enhanced by the notion of the frontier as the end of the settlement. Nevertheless, as Maier argues, "no matter how physically demarcated, the edges of empire and the edges of the unmeasured 'barbarian' realms outside mesh in many ways, and the walls are osmotic membranes establishing a flow of influences and interaction" (Maier 81). This perspective sees the frontier not only as a line of separation, but as a line of communication. Nobles argues that the traditional definition of the frontier as the end of the settlement can be replaced by terms such as "cultural contact zone" or "inter-group contact situation." In his own definition, the frontier "is a region in which no culture, group, or government can claim effective control or hegemony over others. In this regard, contact often involves conflict, a sometimes multisided struggle with an undetermined outcome" (Nobles xii).

Jon Snow's adventures beyond the Wall indicate this side of the frontier. His captivity recalls stories of Euro-American captives at the hands of Native Americans. June Namias argues that the stories of white captives reveal the simplicity of the representations of frontiers as places dominated by "Indian fighters and war whoops" and verify "the coexistence of men, women, and children of a variety of cultures as the norm in American frontier life" (Namias 1). She distinguishes between male captives of the "heroic mode," a term which refers to frontiersmen who defended "civilization" and fought "savagery" in the name of God, the empire or the country (53–54), and male captives as "white Indians," namely those who were eventually adopted and assimilated into the tribal culture, temporarily or permanently (70–83). In the "heroic mode," the captive experiences "amusement, disdain or contempt [for his captors] ... little appreciation or understanding of the other resulted" (53–54). By contrast, "white Indians" expressed "sympathy for Indian ways and, even when they were not adopted as young children," had the ability to "see the group in which they found themselves, not as monsters but as people like themselves" (71).

Snow's case portrays a transition from the "heroic" to the "white Indian" model, but like the famous frontier hero Daniel Boone, who was held by Indians from February 7 to July 15, 1778 (Namias 63), Snow only pretends to assimilate. In this narrative, Boone pretended to become a "white Indian" while in captivity. He participated in tribal life, and even befriended Chief Blackfish, the leader of the tribe, who trusted him deeply. In the end, Boone escaped and returned to his compatriots at Boonsborough in order to inform them about an ensuing Indian attack (Filson 63–67). Jon Snow likewise becomes a wildling hostage in order to discover their strategy and their secrets. They accept him in as long as he proves that he has abandoned his old allegiances. But when the time comes, before the wildling attack on Castle Black, he betrays them and, like Daniel Boone, he returns to his people in order to fight against them.

Nevertheless, Snow experiences a tension between the things that he knows and the things that he sees beyond the Wall. By getting "adopted" by Ygritte, the wildling woman who protects him and with whom he falls in love, he enters the role of a "white Indian" who eventually comes to understand the wildling culture. At first, when Snow arrives in front of Mance Rayder, the King-beyond-the-Wall, he kneels, something that makes Mance and his companions laugh at him. Snow realizes that Rayder is not the southerner kind of king that he was used to: "The King-beyond-the-Wall looked nothing like a king.... There was no crown on his head, no gold rings on his arms, no jewels at his throat, not even a gleam of silver" (*SoS* 8 Jon 1: 80).

Snow also realizes that the wildlings are not just one folk, but several tribes and clans with different cultures. Like different Native American tribes, they occasionally collaborated and occasionally they had their own wars. At the time of Jon Snow's capture, Mance Rayder had unified them in order to lead them beyond the Wall.

> Mance had spent years assembling this vast plodding host, talking to this clan mother and that magnar, winning one village with sweet words and another with a song and a third with the edge of his sword, making peace between Harma Dogshead and the Lord o' Bones, between the Hornfoots and the Nightrunners, between the walrus men of the Frozen Shore and the cannibal clans of the great ice rivers, hammering a hundred different daggers into one great spear, aimed at the heart of the Seven Kingdoms [*SoS* 16 Jon 2: 172].

The wildlings chose Mance as their leader and his leadership recalls that of a sachem or sagamore, a tribal village leader, whose authority "was by no means absolute ... it had to be maintained through consent" (Nobles 35). In the history of Native Americans, several of these leaders had united many different tribes like Mance did. The sachem Tatobem had united several Pequot tribes in a confederacy while the legendary sachem Hiawatha was the one who created the powerful Iroquois Confederacy (Nobles 38).

Mance tells Snow that "there is more commerce between the black brothers and the free folk than you know" (*SoS* 8 Jon 1: 83). The possibility of commerce between the northerners and the wildlings points to the fact that these two clashing sides of the frontier may establish communication and eventually cooperate when pressing common interests or common threats appear. They can even reach military agreements. As we know, again from the tales of the Old Nan, as recalled by Bran, that once the thirteenth leader of the Night's Watch collaborated with dark forces and proclaimed himself the Night's King. Against this threat "the Stark of Winterfell and Joramun of the wildlings had joined to free the Watch from bondage" (*SoS* 57 Bran 4: 629).

In North America, trade and collaboration was always apparent in the relations between Native Americans and Euro-Americans. Even Turner, who never had a special role for Native Americans in his work, acknowledged that. His dissertation, published in 1891, was a study on the Native American trade in Wisconsin. In this work, Turner describes several intercultural contacts between Native Americans and Euro-Americans and reveals the complex relations that existed between them: "The French had accepted the alliance of the Algonquins and the Hurons, as the Dutch, and afterward the English, had that of the

Iroquois" (Turner, *Character* 13). He recognized the intercultural aspects of diplomacy in America but he could not use it for a more inclusive historical approach. His conclusion was filled with the prejudices of his time: "The stage of civilization that could make a gun and gun powder was too far above the bow and arrow stage to be reached by the Indian. Instead of elevating him the trade exploited him" (Turner, *Character* 68). But the relation was far more complicated than Turner thought. As Nobles mentions, "Indians and Europeans seldom engaged in a simple, two-sided relationship ... it is important to understand at the outset that neither 'Indian' nor 'European' has meaning as a monolithic, cohesive culture with a sense of unity and a single-minded strategy" (Nobles 23).

Finally, Snow realizes that the wildlings are human beings capable of feeling emotions as much as he does. During the time that he spends with them he retains some of his prejudices: "*They have no laws, no honor, not even simple decency. They steal endlessly from each other, breed like beasts, prefer rape to marriage, and fill the world with baseborn children*" (*SoS* 16 Jon 2: 171). Yet, he falls in love with Ygritte. Their romance is strong, dramatic and, eventually, doomed. "You know nothing, Jon Snow," Ygritte keeps telling him, underlining Snow's ignorance of her culture. But during their romance, Snow realizes that the wildlings are like the people of Westeros, capable of both beauty and atrocities, with their own perception of the world. "*We look up at the same stars,*" he reflects, "*and see such different things*" (*SoS* 27 Jon 3: 294). Eventually Snow abandons her but in the end he has redefined his perceptions of the freefolk. He comes to see the black brothers' jest about "savages" as "*pig ignorance.... The free folk were no different than the men of the Night's Watch; some were clean, some dirty, but most were clean at times and dirty at other times*" (*DwD* 22 Jon 5: 271).

The defeat of the wildling force at Castle Black, and Stannis Baratheon's decision to allow them to come across the Wall in order to support the Night's Watch against the threat of the White Walkers leads us to the last point to be made here: the question of assimilation. The deal with Stannis had a tremendous impact on their identity, for the free folk had to kneel in front of a king, like the despised southerners. Despite the fact that the wildlings are not so different from the northerners—after all, they share the same gods—the question of how they are going to experience their life after the deal with Stannis is important. Questioned if the wildlings will leave the villages of the North intact, Martin replied: "They would see this as a question of choosing between their freedoms and their lives. Raiding is part of their culture ... on the other hand, they also value a man keeping to his sworn word" ("Lannister," ellipsis in original). In the American case, it was the Euro-Americans who, in most of the cases, did not keep their word. After a long time of struggle, the Native Americans who once were considered independent nations had to walk on the Trail of Tears, encounter massacres such the one at the Wounded Knee and, during Turner's lifetime, experienced a policy of forced assimilation into American (and Canadian) society through the reservation system. Yet, as Holms argues in his work on Native American affairs at the end of the nineteenth century, "they would survive and eventually bring a reformation of American Indian policy" (Holm 22). Today, the essential Native American contribution to American identity is apparent in literature, arts and culture. The "Indian" never disappeared, as Turner thought. The impact of the wildlings at the "civilized" part of the frontier remains to be seen, but, as this essay has shown, the people of the borderlands and their relations have always been far more complicated than an exponent of a dominant idea, like Turner, would have imagined.

Both Martin's Wall and Turner's frontier represent dividing lines of separation, meeting points between "savagery" and "civilization." For the peoples of Westeros, as for Turner's Americans, the frontier line was the end of the world—a line on the map that separates "us" from "them."

But the simplicity of the "savagery" and "civilization" dividing line, as this essay has shown, is refuted by the reality of the frontiers themselves. Cultural encounters are never simple and the outcome of contact between different cultures cannot be seen as a zero sum game. The relations among different frontiersmen are characterized by complexity and diversity and for this very reason they cannot be divided just by a simple line of separation. On the contrary, cultural exchanges, conflict, cooperation, alliances and differentiated interests are only some of the elements that underline the dynamic nature of the frontier—which appears in the end to be not only a dividing line but also a line of contact.

For many years, the identity of the United States was linked with Turner's frontier thesis—the idea that what was important in America was born upon a frontier line of separation. But the perception of the frontier has changed throughout time. What once was a strict dividing line has been now seen in a different light. Where Turner once saw a frontier, recent historians have seen "cultural contact zones." The same transformation has taken place in American popular culture. From Buffalo Bill's Wild West Show to Jack Schaefer's *Shane* and from there to Martin's *A Song of Ice and Fire,* the notion has endured "stark and strong," as Turner himself would have frame it. But it has been also transformed at any given time. Martin may have been inspired by Hadrian's Wall, but his Wall has a unique American identity. It is the same old frontier line that Turner first mentioned. But it has changed into is a multisided frontier, a frontier as a setting of conflict as well as of contact. Its complexity and transformation reveal the changes that have been wrought upon American identity itself. From such a perspective, the Americanness of Martin's story is not only obvious, but it can be read as a work which reveals the transitions of Americanness itself.

Works Cited

Bassin, Mark. "Turner, Solov'ev, and the 'Frontier Hypothesis': The Nationalist Signification of Open Spaces." *The Journal of Modern History* 65.3 (1993): 473–511.

Billington, Ray Allen. *Frederick Jackson Turner: Historian, Scholar, Teacher.* New York: Oxford University Press, 1973. Print.

Bogue, Allan G. *Frederick Jackson Turner: Strange Roads Going Down.* Norman: University of Oklahoma Press, 1998. Print.

Breton, André, *Manifestoes of Surrealism.* Trans. Richard Seaver and Helen R. Lane. Ann Arbor: University of Michigan Press, 1997. Print.

Coleman, William. "Science and Symbol in the Turner Frontier Hypothesis." *The American Historical Review* 72.1 (1966): 22–49.

Conn, Steven. *History's Shadow: Native Americans and Historical Consciousness in the Nineteenth Century.* Chicago: University of Chicago Press, 2004. Print.

Crèvecoeur, J. Hector St. John. *Letters from an American Farmer.* New York: Fox, Duffield, 1904. *Internet Archive.* 22 August 2013.

Drake, Francis S. *Indian History for Young Folks.* New York: Harper and Brothers, 1885. *Internet Archive.* 19 August 2013.

Filson, John. "The Adventures of Col. Daniel Boon." *The Discovery, Settlement and Present State of Kentucke.* Wilmington: James Adams, 1784. 49–82. *Internet Archive.* 22 July 2013.

Gevers, Nick. "Sunsets of High Renown: An Interview with George R.R. Martin." *Infinity Plus: SF, Fantasy, Horror.* 3 February 2001. Web. 6 March 2013.

Hofstadter, Richard. *The Progressive Historians: Turner, Beard, Parrington.* New York: Vintage, 1970. Print.

____. *Social Darwinism in American Thought.* Rev. ed. Boston: Beacon Press, 1955. Print.

Holm, Tom. *The Great Confusion in Indian Affairs: Native Americans and Whites in the Progressive Era.* Austin: University of Texas Press, 2005. Print.

Howard, Robert E. *The End of the Trail: Western Stories.* Ed. Rusty Burke. Lincoln: University of Nebraska Press, 2005. Print.

"Lannister." "The Wildlings in the North." *The Citadel: So Spake Martin.* Correspondence with Fans. 23 April 2009. Web. 12 August 2013.

Lyon, Bryce. "Medieval Real Estate Developments and Freedom." *The American Historical Review* 63.1 (1957): 47–61.

MacLaurin, Wayne. "An Interview with George R.R. Martin." *SF Site.* November 2000. Web. 6 March 2013.

Maier, Charles S. *Among Empires: American Ascendancy and Its Predecessors.* Cambridge: Harvard University Press, 2006. Print.

Martin, George R.R., and Gardner Dozois, eds. *Warriors.* New York: Tor Books, 2010. Print.

McVeigh, Stephen. *The American Western.* Edinburgh: Edinburgh University Press, 2007. Print.

Moses, L.G. *Wild West Shows and the Images of American Indians, 1883–1933.* Albuquerque: University of New Mexico Press, 1996.

Mountgomery, Sir Robert. *A Discourse Concerning the Design'd Establishment of a New Colony to the South of Carolina in the Most Delightful Country of the Universe.* London, 1717. *Internet Archive.* 8 July 2013.

Namias, June. *White Captives: Gender and Ethnicity on the American Frontier*. Chapel Hill: University of North Carolina Press, 1993.

Nichols, David A. "Civilization over Savage: Frederick Jackson Turner and the Indian." *South Dakota History* 2.4 (1972): 383–406

Nobles, Gregory H. *American Frontiers: Cultural Encounters and Continental Conquest*. London: Penguin, 1998. Print.

"Patrick." "Interview with George R.R. Martin." *Sffworld.com*. 17 May 2006. Web. 8 August 2013.

Ridge, Martin. "The Life of an Idea: The Significance of Frederick Jackson Turner's Frontier Thesis." *Montana: The Magazine of Western History* 41.1 (1991): 2–13. Print.

Salter, Jessica. "Game of Thrones: Interview with George R.R. Martin." *The Telegraph*. 25 March 2013. Web. 25 March 2013.

Schaefer, Jack. *Shane*. New York: Laurel-Leaf, 1949.

Turner, Frederick Jackson. *The Character and Influence of the Indian Trade in Wisconsin: A Study of the Trading Post as an Institution*. Baltimore: Johns Hopkins University Press, 1891. Print.

_____. *The Early Writings of Frederick Jackson Turner*. Ed. Everett E. Edwards. Madison: University of Wisconsin Press, 1938. *HathiTrust Digital Library*. Web. 4 March 2013.

_____. *The Frontier in American History*. New York: Holt, Rinehart and Winston, 1962. Print.

Vizenor, Gerald. *Manifest Manners: Postindian Warriors of Survivance*. Hanover: Wesleyan University Press, 1994. Print.

Work, James C. "Settlement Waves and Coordinate Forces in Shane." *Shane: The Critical Edition*. Ed. James C. Work. Lincoln: University of Nebraska Press, 1984. Print.

PHILOSOPHIES

"All men must serve": Religion and Free Will from the Seven to the Faceless Men

RYAN MITCHELL WITTINGSLOW

Given its epic scope—not merely in narrative and cast, but also its conceptual concerns—it is both inevitable and somewhat natural that George R.R. Martin's *A Song of Ice and Fire* finds itself compared to the Lord of the Rings. Although one might dispute the usefulness of such a comparison, it does seem unavoidable given the great debt that Martin, like all writers of contemporary fantasy, owes to J.R.R. Tolkien. And certainly, these comparisons vary in their legitimacy: grand adventures, magical beasts, dark artifacts and darker politics, all anchored by the richness and ambiguity of what it means to be a human being, as we register our befuddlement and dismay in the midst of such incomprehensible events as the death of Ned Stark and the birth of the dragons. However, regardless of one's view of these comparisons, there is one crucial and significant difference between Tolkien and Martin. Tolkien's Middle-Earth has its own structure and its peoples agree on its origin; the respective myths of the sentient races are mutually coherent, and there exists an unbroken oral history from the transcendent origins of Eru Ilúvatar to the destruction of the One Ring in the fires of Mount Doom. However, the same can certainly not be said of Martin's world. Instead of the totalizing mythology of Tolkien's account, we find in Martin a vision of the world that is fractured. For unlike Tolkien, there is no grand narrative, and certainly no single coherent oral history; whereas the main dispute in Tolkien is fundamentally a difference of opinion about how to order a commonly agreed-upon universe, the denizens of Westeros and beyond are incapable of even agreeing upon the boundary conditions of the debate.

This essay is my attempt to clarify some of these disputes. I begin with an analysis of the four most narratively significant religions in Westeros and Essos—

the Faith of the Seven, the old gods, R'hllor and the Many-Faced God of the Braavosi—including their internal structure, and any extant magical rites. Thereafter, having established these facts, I will attempt to render an account which will not only serve to demonstrate what I believe to be the metaphysical assumptions that underpin Martin's universe, but will also answer some narratively significant questions regarding the truth or falsity of certain kinds of in-universe religious belief, as well as examining the roles and ramifications of prophecy in Westeros and beyond.

The Faith of the Seven

I want to begin this discussion with the most visible of all the respective religious traditions: the Faith of the Seven. With the Seven worshipped by most Westerosi, it seems clear that the Faith functions in much the same way as the Roman Catholic Church did during the High Middle Ages and the Renaissance, as an indelible and unavoidable part of the lifeworlds of Westerosi, whether by virtue of its undeniable influence upon social and cultural mores, its political clout or its metaphysical content—and indeed, Martin himself has made this relationship quite clear (see Hodgman). Although technically a monotheistic religion (*CoK* 34 Catelyn 4: 372), seven aspects of this core deity are the objects of worship: three male (Father, Warrior, Smith), three female (Mother, Maiden, Crone), and one androgynous (Stranger). Like the Catholic Church, the Faith— governed by a papal figure known as the High Septon—operates a number of organizations throughout the Seven Kingdoms, including nunneries and monasteries known as septries dedicated to each of the Seven, as well as militant organizations (the Warrior's Sons and the Poor Fellows) in echo of the Knights Templar,[1] the Hospitallers and the Teutonic Knights. Since Westeros' laws and secular virtues are themselves also derived from the teachings of the Faith (disapproval of gambling, prostitution and bastardy; denouncing kinslaying and incest), a person in the Seven Kingdoms—regardless of the depths of their own personal religiosity—would nonetheless find the Faith accompanying them from birth to death, and all of the significant life events in between: from naming ceremonies, to marriage, to the funerary rites of loved ones. Much like the historical Roman Catholic Church, one quite easily imagines the Faith of the Seven—at least until the theological shift that occurs with the promotion of the new High Septon in *Dance with Dragons*—accompanying even religiously unobservant Westerosi as an inert, silent partner throughout their lives.

In addition to occupying the social niche that the medieval Catholic and Orthodox churches filled,[2] certain metaphysical beliefs are ostensibly similar as well. Despite the belief that the Seven once roamed the earth in corporeal form prior to the Andals' invasion of Westeros, they are nonetheless something like Martin's understanding of the Trinity—that is, manifestations or aspects of the same hitherto nameless deity (again, see Hodgman).[3] However, I do say "ostensibly similar" for a reason: despite the apparent similarity of the two entities, the beliefs of the Roman Catholic Church and the Faith of the Seven are not perfect metaphysical analogues. There are two points of difference in particular. The first and most obvious difference is that rather than observing the inseparable Trinity of Father, Son and Holy Spirit—the Father being the unseen progenitor of divinity, the Son being the divine revelation and the Holy Spirit its articulation in the world—the Seven are instead a cluster of separate entities that have a common source but do not appear to be mutually contingent: the character or qualities of the Mother are seemingly not premised upon the character or qualities of the Father, for instance. Indeed, the seven figures—the Father, Mother, Warrior, Maiden, Smith, Crone and Stranger—seem far more akin to primordial images or character archetypes such as one would find in the work of Carl Jung or, more strikingly, Joseph Campbell in his landmark analysis *The Hero with a Thousand Faces*. The second point of difference is that whereas the Trinity can be seen as constituting God both individually and as a collective (thus, for Christians, it is theologically sound to claim that "Jesus is God" in the same way that "The Trinity is God"), the Seven are but abstracted facets of a central unifying deity.

However, consider the following: the septuple-faced god of the Faith is, as previously noted, divided into two triune gods—Mother, Maiden, Crone (redolent of triple-faced Hecate [Betz 89–92]) and Father, Warrior, Smith—and a single, solitary, sexless figure known as the Stranger. Jung notes that "Triads of gods appear very early, at a primitive level. ... Arrangement in triads is an archetype in the history of religion" (Jung 113)—a fact, Georges Dumézil claimed, that is characteristic of certain conceptual structures that are then articulated in the social realm in the form of social classes or roles (148–51). If this is so, the two sexed triads in the Seven may be reflective of mankind's relationship with itself, as each triad preserves the gendered aspect of social rules apparent in Martin's universe. I will not belabor this point, leaving analyses of gender roles in *A Song of Ice and Fire* to those in a better position to comment, but it nonetheless seems clear that the two triads—Smith, Warrior, Father and Crone, Maiden, Mother— reflect the respective spheres of influence of men and women in Martin's universe. Moreover, these norms are sufficiently pervasive that any perceived threat to those norms is treated with confusion, if not outright hostility.[4] These roles are both socially informative and world-constituting; informing a petitioner's good and proper engagement with the social by observing those gender roles, mankind (understood more broadly) becomes aware of the needs of other beings and thus his obligations towards them: in short, man individuates as a social creature.

However, this does seem to leave the problem of the Stranger: a figure who is "neither male nor female, yet both, ever the outcast, the wanderer from far places, less and more than human, unknown and unknowable ... the face ... a black oval, a shadow with stars for eyes" (*CoK* 34 Catelyn 4: 372). It seems clear that the Stranger, although not evil in the sense that we would think, is certainly not a force for good. Indeed, as something approaching a god of death, it is almost as if the concerns of the Stranger are utterly beyond the possibility of human understanding; death and the infinite are such things that our minds reel in the face of them. Indeed, following Kant's cues in the *Critique of Judgement*, it seems that the Stranger is representative of another source of individuation.[5] Kant writes that our inability to conceive of the size or power of a thing or event (the mathematical and dynamical sublimes, respectively) means that such a thing or event is capable of being an object of the senses. However, despite the fact that we cannot grasp the enormity of sublime events—for instance, the Lisbon earthquake of 1755—with our sensible faculties, we are still nonetheless capable of identifying the Lisbon earthquake as a singular event. Our imagination strives "to advance to the infinite, while in our reason there lies a claim of absolute totality," meaning that in the face of the sublime we realize our own power to render supersensible judgments: "That is sublime which even to be able to think of demonstrates a faculty of the mind that surpasses every measure of the senses" (Kant 134). We might even want to say, invoking Plotinus, that the sublime is something like the phenomenal aspect of the infinite, from which all actualities spring forth: "The Supreme is not a particular form but the form of all ... it follows that The First must be without form, and if without form, then it is no Being; Being must have some definition and therefore be limited; but the First cannot be thought of as having definition and limit" (qtd. in Burns 60; ellipses in original). Without the sublime—without the feeling of insignificance and powerlessness instigated by everything the Stranger represents—we would not be aware of our own capacity for abstract thought. Struck with the ineffability of infinity ("We are in agony for a true expression ... this name, The One, contains really no more than a negation of plurality" [qtd. in Burns 60; ellipses in original]), we appreciate the limits of our capacity for inquiry; we are made radically aware of our own powerlessness in the face of the vastness and muteness of the world. Accordingly, we can say that much as man individuates as a social being in his relationship with other like beings—as signified by the other six deities—so too does man individuate existentially in the face of the unimaginable void.

Moreover, if the Seven anchor meaning by symbolizing man's phenomenological encounters with the world, it seems to follow that the unidentified central figure at the heart of the Seven is the religious petitioner him- or herself: the locus of an ongoing synthesis of a spiritually conscious content (the perceiving ego) with its worldly opposites (the universe and the people it contains). In simultaneously individuating in the presence of and serving to constitute those seven figures in some kind of elaborate psychoanalytic process, the transcendental Hero-Self thus becomes both deity and petitioner; the gods are both products of and reactions to our social and existential anxieties. Furthermore, if we buy this account—that the Seven are best understood as being some kind of formalized morality tale prescribing our processes of *self-individuation*—it may explain the unusual fact that, as of *A Dance with Dragons*, no devotee of the Seven has been seen to possess anything in the way of supernatural ability, unlike petitioners of the old gods, R'hllor and the Many-Faced God. Although, as we will discover later, the Stranger is something of an exception by virtue of his association with the Many-Faced God, the lack of supernatural powers invested in devotees of the Seven is likely explained by the fact that they are little more than projections of their worshippers.

The Old Gods

Until the invasion of the Andals some four to six thousand years prior to Aegon's Landing—thus catalyzing the cultural and religious dominance of the Faith of the Seven—the predominant faith across Westeros was that of the old gods. Although the faith remains viable in certain regions of Westeros, particularly among the Northmen, Free Folk and the Crannogmen (all descended from the First Men), it has all but died out in the heavily-populated southern half of the continent: "In the south the last weirwoods had been cut down or burned out a thousand years ago, except on the Isle of Faces" (*GoT* 3: Catelyn 1: 19). This narrative of cultural displacement seems to have real-world analogues; just as the Faith is broadly analogous to the medieval Catholic Church, so too do the old gods seem reminiscent of Druidism as practiced across Celtic Europe. A religion with no liturgies, holy texts, priests or songs of worship, the old gods appear to provide little and promise little in return; what passes for religious observation seems largely restricted to the practice of certain rites performed in front of a "weirwood" tree—a tree with bone-white smooth bark, five-pointed leaves not dissimilar to the sweetgum or redgum, and thick sap the color and consistency of blood. At least insofar as we have observed or have had reported, these rites appear largely restricted to the performance of public commitments, such as marriage or the swearing of oaths.

However, beyond these meager hints, the belief structure observed by the devotees of the old gods is so far deeply inscrutable. Although I previously described them as either animistic or totemistic, it is unclear whether the worship of the old gods falls neatly into either category, despite apparently sharing qualities with both. Certainly, the worship of the old gods seems to suggest a kind of group totemism, wherein certain groups—in this case the First Men and the children of the forest—are mystically associated with the weirwoods, the weirwoods then becoming a kind of totemic entity and thus the object of ritual and spiritual veneration. Of course, it is not readily apparent if this is itself reflective of a kind of deeper animism—an assumption that the world and the things within it each have "souls" or some other unique spiritual content—or it is simply the fact that only the weirwoods themselves have spiritual power.

Regardless of what the case may be, it is tempting to understand the old gods as a kind of analogue for pre–Roman Celtic religious observances practiced in Gaul and the British Isles: although syncretic Gallo-Roman religious practices invoked deities in anthropomorphic terms (i.e., the most famous of which, Cernunnos or the Horned God, became identified with the Roman Bacchus), pre–Roman Celts did not understand or envisage their gods as having human properties (Wood 3–4). Indeed, the explicit focus on groves of sacred trees appears to owe a direct debt to Celtic *nemeta*, or sacred spaces in Celtic pagan practices named after such spaces dedicated to the goddess Nemetona. Already we see an evocation of the old gods, knowing that *nemeta* served as a place of worship for pre–Roman Celts. However, the connections grow even more obvious when we read the lurid Roman depictions of these exotic locations:

> An old inviolated facred Wood
> Whofe gloomy Boughs, thick interwoven, made
> A chilly chearlefs everlafting Shade:
> There, nor the ruftick Gods, not Satyrs fport,
> Nor Fawns and Sylvans with the Nymphs refort:
> But barb'rous Priefts fome dreadful Pow'r adore,
> And luftrate every Tree with human Gore [Lucan III.i. 591–98].

The brutal, savage imagery of Lucan's *nemeton* seems to support the observation that pseudo–Celtic religious practices inform Martin's characterization of the old gods. The gloom, the quiet and even the blood sacrifices are present; when learning to be a greenseer and looking through the eyes of a heart tree, Bran Stark watches a man get his throat slashed with a sacrificial sickle: "through the mist of centuries the broken boy could only watch as the man's feet drummed against the earth ... but as his life flowed out of him in a red tide, Brandon Stark could taste the blood" (*DwD* 35 Bran 3: 460). If nothing else, there is certainly an appeal to Roman intuitions about the Celtic powers: like the purported gods of the Celts, the power of the old gods is seemingly premised upon the oldest kind of magic—the magic of life and blood.

Although common wisdom has it that the weirwoods have a profound relationship with the old gods, it is not until *A Dance with Dragons* that the truth of the matter is revealed: the weirwood trees, at least according to the children of the forest, *are* the old gods (*DwD* 35 Bran 3: 452). Although the old gods might be understood to be "nature" in some kind of broadly pantheistic sense, it is only after the children of the forest carve faces into their trunks that they are awakened and able to see (*DwD* 35 Bran 3: 458–59)—and thus, presumably, to act upon the world. Moreover, it seems that by carving the faces in the trees and awakening the wisdom contained therein, the children of the forest thus guarantee their own longevity: when the children of the forest die, they "become part of that godhood" that is the land, a land which was given voice and vision by carving the faces in the heart trees (*DwD* 35 Bran 3: 452). It seems likely that this awareness of land and nature is what prevents the children of the forest from pursuing the arts and crafts of men. Maester Luwin tells Bran: "The children worked no metal. In place of mail, they wore long shirts of woven leaves and bound their legs in bark, so they seemed to melt into the wood. In place of swords, they carried blades of obsidian" (*GoT* 67 Bran 7: 616). Given the historical taboo against the use of iron in magical rites due to its industrial tenor (Luck 35), this kind of behavior certainly seems in keeping with the implication that the children are, in some fundamental way, both more inherently magical and more attuned to the land than the Andals or the First Men.

The Red God

Endorsing a kind of Manichaeistic dualism, worshippers of R'hllor, Lord of the Light and God of Flame and Shadow, believe that the universe is a battleground between R'hllor and his evil opposite: a god whose name must not be spoken, and is only ever described as The Great Other. Equally matched, R'hllor and the Great Other are compelled to do battle until the fabled return of the Azor Ahai: a messianic figure capable of defeating the darkness that the Great Other will hang over the world.

However, beyond these observations, we know little about the Red God, though his power is by no means as limited as that of the old gods, nor as abstract as the Seven. Although it is likely that worshippers of R'hllor believe him to have created the world, being the divine aspect of order—it seems unlikely that

R'hllor is responsible for the creation of the Great Other. Equally necessary, equal in might and manifesting contrary substances, both R'hllor and his counterpart seem like inalienable properties of the universe itself. However, whether or not the property of being understood as necessary means that his followers believe him to possess other properties, such as omniscience or omnipotence, that remain as-yet unaddressed in the series.

> "*There are two*, Onion Knight. Not seven, not one, not a hundred or a thousand. *Two!* Do you think I crossed half the world to put yet another vain king on yet another empty throne? The war has been waged since time began, and before it is done, all men must choose where they will stand. On one side is R'hllor, the Lord of Light, the Heart of Fire, the God of Flame and Shadow. Against him stands the Great Other whose name may not be spoken, the Lord of Darkness, the Soul of Ice, the God of Night and Terror. ... It is death we choose, or life. Darkness, or light" [*SoS* 26 Davos 3: 288].

In addition to this cosmology, there are a couple of other interesting things to note. The first concerns the nature of R'hllor's enemy, the Great Other—a figure about whom we know very little. Although we can surmise that just as R'hllor is the god of flame, light and warmth, and the Great Other is the god of cold, death and absence, there is otherwise very little upon which to draw (indeed, as far as I can tell, the phrase "Great Other" appears exactly once in the entire series, namely the excerpt above). Nonetheless, Martin deigns to leave us some tantalizing clues. For though Melisandre does not speak of the Great Other again, she does speak of his champions, just as Melisandre believes herself to be a champion of R'hllor: "*A wooden face, corpse white*. Was this the enemy? A thousand red eyes floated in the rising flames. *He sees me.* Beside him, a boy with a wolf's face threw back his head and howled" (*DwD* 32 Melisandre 1: 408). The reference seems clear: a wooden face with a thousand red eyes can only refer to the Three-Eyed Crow, who has partially melded with the weirwood and observes the world only through the eyes carved in heart trees; similarly, the boy with the head of a wolf can only be his greenseer apprentice, Brandon Stark.

The significance of this revelation could easily serve to endorse one of two positions (excluding the possibility that Melisandre's visions are mistaken).[6] The first position is that, unbeknownst to Bran and possibly the Three-Eyed Crow, they are but luckless pawns in a greater game that is being played between two inscrutable cosmic powers. Although they may believe they are communing with the weirwoods, all of their actions are in service to the dark power of ice, absence and death. The second position is the more radical proposal: namely, that Bran and the Three Eyed Crow are both servants of the Great Other, and indeed they are both serving of their own volition. If course, this is not to suggest that, unbeknownst to readers they have sworn a dark pact with a malevolent deity; rather that what Melisandre calls the "Great Other" is what the other characters in the book have hitherto called the "old gods."

> [The dwarf woman] cackled again. ... "Look in your fires, pink priest, and you will see. Not now, though, not here, you'll see nothing here. This place belongs to the old gods still ... they linger here as I do, shrunken and feeble but not yet dead. Nor do they love the flames. For the oak recalls the acorn, the acorn dreams the oak, the stump lives in them both. And they remember when the First Men came with fire in their fists" [*SoS* 44 Arya 8: 492].

Faced with these options, which position makes sense? Both are problematic. The first position—that Bran and the Three-Eyed Crow are pawns of the Great Other—is difficult because it forces us to assume that the Bran, the Three-Eyed Crow and the children of the forest have been co-opted into the service of the inhuman evil responsible for the White Walkers. This account, having no clear textual basis, seems both narratively unsatisfying and suspiciously *ex post facto* and should probably be avoided. However, to endorse the second position poses any number of other problems, not least of which being that it flies in the face of certain facts that we already have in our possession: namely, that the children of the forest were historically the enemies of the White Walkers, and indeed reached an alliance with the First Men against the Walkers in the Pact of the Isle of Faces.

There are further complications. The first is that the Pact that historically united the children of the forest and the First Men is clearly longer being observed by the latter party—according to the original terms of the agreement between the two peoples, the children were awarded the forested regions of Westeros and the First Men the open plains. However, the intervening millennia have seen Men intrude upon the territory of the children; as noted earlier, the weirwoods in the south of the continent long ago fell to axes and fires as local economies became more agrarian. Although reneging upon the disagreement was clearly not a product of malice—the commitments of Men are venal and our memories are short—the terms of the agreement have clearly not been observed. And indeed, the children of the forest no longer observe their responsibilities either; under the Pact, during the Age of Heroes the children would deliver 900 obsidian daggers to the Night's Watch every year; this has clearly not occurred for some millennia (*FfC* 6 Samwell 1: 80). Meanwhile, the second thing we should recall is what the children call themselves in the True Tongue: *those who sing the song of the earth* (*DwD* 35 Bran 3: 448). Their habits, technology and culture is mystical and broadly Paleolithic; the children of the forest are more explicitly attuned with the rhythms of the natural world by virtue of utilizing the raw materials offered by nature. The children are not artisans, like the First Men; though they have magical techniques, they have no industry. Of course, this is in sharp distinction to Men more broadly and the followers of the Red God specifically: in R'hllor's myth of the Azor Ahai, the hero spends 180 days smithing a sword before tempering the steel with the heart-blood of his beloved, Nissa Nissa (*SoS* 55 Davos 5: 609). Steel in the worship of the Red God is rendered a venerative substance; shaped for human purposes using the power of flames, iron and industry can then be understood as earthly instantiations of the transformative power of fire—a fire that enables us, through its heat and its light and through our tools, to ward off nights that are dark and full of terror: "We thank you for our hearths and for our torches, that keep the savage dark at bay" (*SoS* 64 Davos 6: 706).

So what have these observations to do with the battle between R'hllor and the Great Other? If we endorse the more radical view—that the old gods and the Great Other are one and the same—then it seems to suggest that the White Walkers are, at least in this instance, acting in the service of the old gods, of the inexorable and inevitable rhythms of nature. If the children are those who sing the song of the earth, are the White Walkers part of that song? Should R'hllor be understood as the dispassionate justice constituting the civilizing force of firelight, with the narrative of the Azor Ahai nothing less than a symbolic rendering of man's struggle against the chaotic, senseless givens of the natural world, and his eventual triumph over it? Is the god of darkness also a god of nature, the motions of which are those of the world without the impediment of human action? In *A Game of Thrones,* Bran's first vision of the "heart of winter" fills him with terror; he sees below him "the bones of a thousand other dreamers impaled upon ... points" (*GoT* 18 Bran 3: 136–37); given his terror, it certainly seems unlikely that Bran would willingly ally himself with the White Walkers.

Amidst all of this conjecture is a worrying dearth of clear answers. Relationships, commitments and alliances remain shady and ambiguous; one cannot help but wonder who is playing, and on behalf of whom. At least in the case of the Red God, we require more information to proceed.

The Many-Faced God

Bleak, windowless and sea-swept, the House of Black and White sits upon the Braavosi Isle of the Gods, offering succor and dreamless finality to any petitioners who seek it. Inside, the walls are lined with the figures of exotic gods and goddess, each representing the grim specter of death: the Stranger of the Seven, the Lion of Night, the Hooded Wayfarer, Bakkalon, the Moon-Pale Maiden, the Merling King. And yet, despite hailing from different lands and serving different petitioners, to the Faceless Men each of these gods is but an aspect of the true god: Him of Many Faces, he who grants the gift of death. Devotees may present themselves to the house at any time, and those who drink of the black pool in the center of the temple will find themselves sink into a warm blackness from which they will never awaken, their bodies lying inert in the stone beds that line the walls. Eventually their bodies will be removed by acolytes and subject to various ablutions before they are laid to eternal rest in the sanctum below. Others—those with darker motives perhaps—can approach the temple for another reason: to request the demise of another human being by engaging the services of the Faceless Men. Mute, velveteen and mysterious, the Faceless Men and their services are available to all: regardless of the person who asks, the price that is charged for a person's demise will be very great indeed, but not beyond their ability to pay.

> [The] waif replied. "My mother died when I was little, I have no memory of her. When I was six my father wed again. His new wife treated me kindly until she gave birth to a daughter of her own. Then it was her wish that I should die, so her own blood might inherit my father's wealth. ... When the healers in the House of the Red Hands told my father what she had done, he came here and made sacrifice, offering up all his wealth and me. Him of Many Faces heard his prayer. I was brought to the temple to serve, and my father's wife received the gift" [*FfC* 35 Cat of the Canals: 517].

The Faceless Men trace their origins to the Valyrian Freehold, where the worship of the Many-Faced God began as a folk religion practiced by slaves: according to the legend told to Arya in the House of Black and White, the first Faceless Man realized that all of the gods to whom slaves prayed to deliver them from their misery were but aspects of the one, unified deity: Him of Many Faces. Believing himself to be the instrument of this god, the first Faceless Man defied the Valyrians and their dragons and began freeing the slaves from their bondage (*FfC* 23 Arya 2: 321–22). Not by releasing them into the world—"Revolts were common in the mines, but few accomplished much"—but by introducing them to the angels who would lead them to the nightlands "where the stars burn ever bright" (*FfC* 23 Arya 2: 321, 316). But there is more to this story: although at first simply acting in service to the slaves by relieving them of the burden of living, it is heavily implied by the Kindly Man that it was in fact the Faceless Men who were eventually responsible for the Doom of Valyria: "[The first Faceless Man] would bring the gift to [the Dragonlords] as well ... but that is a tale for another day, one best shared with no one" (*FfC* 23 Arya 2: 322)—an event which saw lakes boil away, volcanoes erupt and much of the land collapse into the sea. Most significantly, the Many-Faced God is a syncretistic combination of the deities of other religions, and thus serves as the key to unlocking some of the metaphysical problems inherent to *A Song of Ice and Fire*. It is quite clear that the Many-Faced God is understood to be a stand-in for the many gods of death in the various pantheons in Martin's world, as the Kindly Man tells Arya: "Men of a hundred different nations labored in the mines, and each prayed to his own god in his own tongue, yet all were praying for the same thing. ... The slaves were not crying out to a hundred different gods, as it seemed, but to one god with a hundred different faces" (*FfC* 23 Arya 2: 322).

However, this comment is also to a degree ambiguous: although it is obvious that the hundred different faces of the one god would be at least partially constituted by gods of death such as the Merling King, the Moon-Pale Maiden and the Stranger, it is by no means clear whether those faces are entirely comprised of gods of death. Complicating things further is the fact that Jaqen H'ghar, despite being a Faceless Man, happily invokes the powers of other gods when engaging in the serious business of swearing his service to Arya, even those who are not deities of death: "By all the gods of sea and air, and even him of fire, I swear it. ... By the seven new gods and the old gods beyond count, I swear it" (*CoK* 48 Arya 9: 514). And, even more curiously, he invokes R'hllor—a god of life, by the admission of his clergy—very explicitly: "The Red God has his due, sweet girl, and only death may pay for life" (*CoK* 31 Arya 7: 348). Although this may be merely a figure of speech—a reference to his near-death by flame—I suspect he is referring to R'hllor, just like the gods of sea and air, as constituent aspects of the Many-Faced God. However, one might reasonably ask how the devotees of the Many-Faced God are able to reconcile the respective attributes of these gods with one another; certainly, these conflicting mythoi seem mutually incompatible, at least according to their own proponents.

One could approach this problem in one of two ways. For instance, I think it telling that attempts to reconcile each of the religious traditions, both with each other and with the Many-Faced God, could well succeed. We could say, for instance, that the Many-Faced God is indeed all gods at once, being something like a kind of "reality substrate" from which all points of difference emerge. Being many-faced, the god is polysemous and indeterminate; although it has no properties of its own, the dynamic processes that at least partially constitute the character of the deity might be argued to produce things with determinate properties, understood as instantiations of opposites: hot/cold, wet/dry, good/evil, etcetera.[7] Everything appears as an opposite of something else, and all things that come to pass are due to these opposites acting in according with a kind of cosmic "justice" or "vengeance"—the process by which opposites are reconciled and once again subsumed within the dynamical and indeterminate godhead: "Into that from which things take their rise they pass away once more, as is ordained; for they make reparation and satisfaction to one another for the injustice according to the appointed time" (Anaximander, qtd. in Russell 116). Following such a model, one could argue that all of the gods—whether Seven, old gods, Red God or Great Other—may simply be examples of such opposites, whilst the grand panoply of history is reduced to a mere process by which opposites are re-absorbed into the generative substrate that is the Many-Faced God.

Yet this theory seems totalizing in a way that doesn't quite accord with Martin's interest in multiple narratives, multiple views. Rather than assuming that He of Many Faces is comprised of all of the gods, including their accidental features, what if the Many-Faced God were only comprised of their shared, necessary features—such as sublimity, inexorability and judgment? That is to say: what if the Many-Faced God is intended to capture the possibility that all gods—regardless of the contingent details underpinning their cosmology, ethics or given worldview—are instead the imperfect reflections or readings of a coextensive teleological force active in Martin's universe? A force that extends into the physical facts of the matter whilst providing some kind of momentum and direction to causal proceedings? What if, in fact, there is a god?

Consider that when Jaqen H'ghar invokes the Red God, he renders in no uncertain terms the importance of Arya giving him three names: "This girl took three that were his. This girl must give three in their places. Speak the names, and a man will do the rest" (*CoK* 31 Arya 7: 348) Moreover, when Arya asks Jaqen to instead take her to Riverrun, he refuses outright: "Three lives you shall have of me. No more, no less. Three and we are done. So a girl must ponder" (*CoK* 31 Arya 7: 348). Why is Jaqen H'ghar so insistent? It is certainly not due to fear of contravening convention, or otherwise infringing upon his social obligations. Moreover, he is by no means opting for the less dangerous path; even despite his skill and expertise, offering to quietly assassinate anybody in the entire world is likely to be more taxing than stealing a horse and chaperoning a girl to Riverrun. Indeed, his choice seems entirely inscrutable until we realize an important fact: that Jaqen H'ghar's insistence essentially constitutes a form of religious observance. He seems convinced that the deaths of himself and his two companions were a certain kind of necessary event: part of the well-ordered unfolding of the universe. However, Arya's intervention jeopardized the proper outcome of events and so Jaqen H'ghar is forced to make amends by offering Him of Many Faces three more lives in recompense. Who dies and who lives is largely immaterial; what is important is that three men who were expected to die did not, and it is up to Jaqen H'ghar to balance the books. Moreover, Jaqen himself cannot make the decision himself, because he is not able to render these judgments: as a faceless device of his god (thus a "Faceless Man") he is but a passive tool acting in the service of fate or some other profound teleological force. This is why he refuses to help her—not out of cruelty, but because he does not wish to sin in the eyes of his deity.

Metaphysical Implications for Free Will

And so we reach what is, to me, the crux of the matter: the question of fate and free will. Whether or not free will is an element of the doctrinal teachings of the various religious traditions is not a particularly easy question to answer, but I think we can certainly make educated guesses in that direction. Moreover, as I will establish, testing for the presence or absence of free will in Martin's universe via textual examples provides a means by which we find ourselves able to judge which metaphysical system most closely cleaves to the perceived facts of the matter.

In the cases of the Faith of the Seven and the worship of R'hllor, I strongly suspect that free will is taken as doctrine by their devotees. With regards to the former, the moral character of religious observance coupled with a collection of seemingly non-interventionist deities seems to strongly suggest that people are responsible for their own decisions, and thus have been granted freedom of will; without freedom of will, it seems difficult to account for the moral significance of human action. A similar argument serves for the worship of the Red God: given the hearts and minds of men and women partially constitute the metaphysical battleground between R'hllor and his nameless counterpart, we can assume they are moral agents—and indeed, freedom of will in Zoroastrianism is defended on similar grounds. I would also argue that followers of the old gods tacitly endorse the concept of freedom of will, even if it cannot be considered an item of faith by virtue of the lack of an organized church and clergy. However, the entrenched libertarian disposition of those in the North and those beyond the Wall seemingly provide a far better endorsement of that position; it is surely evidence of something that the wildlings refer to themselves as the "Free Folk" whilst disdainfully branding southrons as "kneelers." Given their politics, I find it incredibly hard to believe that the Free Folk would believe themselves shackled to a determined universe.

However, despite what appears to be a commonly-held belief in free will, I believe the position held on the subject of free will by devotees of the Many-Faced God is contrary to these claims. Indeed, if my argument is correct, it almost seems as if free will is fundamentally incompatible with belief in Him of Many Faces. We have already seen that devotees of the Many-Faced God grant credence to the idea of necessary events, presumably as articulations or instantiations of the afore-mentioned teleological force that they have chosen to deify—that is to say, as gods. Although this may not result in a complete absence of free will—one imagines, for instance, that what Jaqen H'ghar chose to have for breakfast was a mere accidental or contingent fact, and the breakfast itself a contingent event—but that necessary events are both insurmountable and unavoidable. Moreover, these fundamental assumptions are an integral part of the rites and rituals of the religion itself: one must not forget that that correct answer to the phrase *Valar Morghulis* ("all men must die") is *Valar Dohaeris* ("all men must serve" [*FfC* 23 Arya 2: 316]). Death and service are thus rendered as relevantly similar concepts (or even overlapping concepts, in the case of the Faceless Men): both are utterly inescapable, and in both cases a person must do their duty.

But what of whether free will exists in Martin's universe? Given that we appear to have three sets of beliefs that endorse free will and one that denies it, if we can render a metric by which the presence of freedom of will can be detected in Martin's universe, then we can neatly discard either three or one of those sets of belief in a single act. Although one might be dubious of the possibility of isolating such a test case, there is, I believe, one reasonably unambiguous example. Consider the following: when apprenticed to the Three-Eyed Crow and subject to the feeding regimen of the children of the forest (the red ichor from weirwood trees), Bran is granted two visions of the past: one an image of his father, Eddard, praying in front of Winterfell's heart tree, asking that Jon Snow and Robb grow up "close as brothers"; the other an image of Eddard as an older man, polishing his Valyrian steel greatsword. In awe of what he is seeing, Bran whispers to himself, at which point Eddard looks up and demands, "Who's there?" (*DwD* 35 Bran 3: 457). Bran is understandably shocked, and asks of the Three-Eyed Crow whether he would be able to warn his father of what is to come. The Three-Eyed Crow responds: "You cannot speak to him, try as you might. I know. ... The past remains the past. We can learn from it, but we cannot change it" (*DwD* 35 Bran 3: 458).

There is a subtle point, here. Bran not only has been afforded knowledge of the past, but his whisper causes Eddard to start and enquire: "Who is there?" And yet the past is inviolable—that is, unable to be changed by those in the present—per the expert testimony of the Three-Eyed Crow. This seems like an obvious contradiction, but not one that is intractable. Let us consider: Bran's precognition or foreknowledge adopts the phenomenal character of lived experience; he does not read the events as if in a book, but rather he experiences them as if he were there, in all their plenary richness. Now, to have this kind of phenomenal or experiential knowledge of events to which you are not present means that your experience carries a heavy epistemic burden: there can be no more doubt as to their veracity than there is to the veracity of any other kind of phenomenal experience. This is what it means when I say that Bran has knowledge of those events; otherwise, it would be more accurate to ascribe Bran's visions to careful extrapolation, an overactive imagination, or perhaps a series of wild hunches. To know what is in the future means that that future must necessarily occur; to know what has occurred in the past means that you were there, in some important sense. This precognition is experiential, and thus as factive as any other kind of sense data.

Subsequently, we can posit a kind of necessity relation between Bran's precognitive experience and the facts of the matter, just as we can do so for lived experience. The perception of p necessarily entails a certain state of affairs p; it is necessarily connected to p in a way that is not contingent upon human understanding. Bran's experience of those events, being naive and pre-theoretic, is such an experience, just as, say, my experience of my office entails that my office have certain properties. For Bran to have experienced Eddard polishing Ice in the weirwood, it entails that Eddard at one point polished Ice in the weirwood; it is necessarily true that it is the case. Now, it is also true that Eddard, at some point in the past, asked after a noise that caused him to start. We know that Eddard necessarily performed this action, per Bran's experience of the event. We also know that Bran could not have changed the past, as the past is, per the Three-Eyed Crow, inviolable.

Furthermore, this seems to imply that Bran must mutter "Winterfell" to himself in a way that attracts Eddard's attention; it is in fact obligatory for Bran to do so. For if Eddard's reaction is necessary and the past is inviolable, it is also necessary for Bran to have performed an action that captures Eddard's attention; had he not performed an action that attracted Eddard's attention, Eddard would not have enquired as to who was there. Accordingly, if Eddard's action in the past is necessary, then so too was Bran's action in the *present*. Although Bran cannot save his father, the implications of this interaction seem to suggest that Bran is caught in a tight causal loop with Eddard at that instance. Given that Bran is required by necessity to perform an action that will materially constitute an inviolable past, it seems plausible to think that Bran's *present,* at least at that time, is equally inviolable; certainly, at least in this instance, human agency does not bear relevantly upon the kind of actions and events that occur. Although Bran cannot save his father, the implications of this interaction seem to suggest that Bran is caught in a tight causal loop with Eddard at that instance; the interaction seemingly necessary, unavoidable, and scripted by fate.

It follows, then, that if the present is as inviolable as the past, so too is the future; Bran's capacity for precognition necessarily guarantees that predestination or fate is an integral and constituent aspect of the metaphysical quality of Martin's universe. Accordingly, I argue that this kind of event—Bran forced to exclaim, Eddard forced to inquire—has the possibility of problematizing free will in Martin's universe, though it by no means settles the problem. In that case, it is possibly helpful to look at the question of prophecy more broadly, and see to what extent acts of prophecy can co-exist with free will. Martin's universe, as is readily apparent, is absolutely filthy with prophecy. Many of the main characters—particularly Daenerys, Bran, Jojen Reed, Jon and Melisandre—are confronted with prophetic visions at various points throughout the series. Moreover, although many of these prophecies are ambiguous or have yet to come true, there are others that have unambiguously come to pass: Daenerys foreseeing the birth of her dragons (*GoT* 12 Daenerys 2: 83); the Ghost of High Heart predicting both the slaughter of Renly by Melisandre's shadow creature and Catelyn's death at the Red Wedding (*SoS* 23 Arya 4: 249); or Jojen Reed prophesying the demise of Winterfell at the hands of Theon Greyjoy (*CoK* 36 Bran 5: 392). Even despite ambiguities or claims to the effect that prophecy is "like a treacherous woman" and will "bite your prick off every time" (*FfC* 46 Samwell 5: 682–683), prophecy in Martin's universe is actually extremely reliable as a source of information; even though prophecies may be misunderstood or may go unheeded (Melisandre is particularly guilty of this), never to my knowledge has a prophecy in *A Song of Ice and Fire* been unequivocally incorrect. Rather, the outcome seems almost guaranteed by the act of prophesying itself; all that is left is to await with bated breath the doubtless gory manner in which the prophecy comes into effect.

As we await the fulfillment of these prophecies, we are struck with the lack of ontological privilege afforded to human beings in Martin's universe—despite our conceits that we are in possession of free will and that our actions bear relevantly upon the universe, our actions—as in the case of Bran and Eddard above—are just as subject to the inexorabilities of fate and circumstance as falling leaves or thrown rocks. We are not distinct from the universe by virtue of the fact that we are free; rather, our freedom is an illusion to which we subscribe, and that only serves to mask our ontological identity with rain and castles and dirt. Despite our desires to the contrary, our actions are just as guaranteed and unremarkable as any other kind of causal relation; in being guaranteed in some sense, our actions are no longer accidental, no longer *contingent*. Instead, the power of prophecy reveals that we are instead slaves to *necessity* regardless of the size or banality of what we do: instead, all actions are revealed to be invariant features of the temporal and causal topography of Martin's universe.

Given the available evidence, then, this reasoning leads to the conclusion that, despite any intuitions we may hold to the contrary, it is the belief of the Many-Faced God that most closely cleaves to the metaphysics of Martin's universe. Given the if-then conditional posed at the beginning of this section—*if* free will exists, *then* x—it seems obvious that it is the worshippers of the Many-Faced God that have the most accurate articulation of the facts inherent to the world of *A Song of Ice and Fire*. Although it may still be possible to speak sensically of R'hllor or the Seven or the old gods, it must nonetheless be acknowledged that Him of Many Faces—or at least, something relevantly like him, at least in the sense of there being a coextensive teleological force—functions as the unifying principle in the world of *A Song of Ice and Fire*. Indeed, this kind of grand teleological principle or entity seems like a necessary property of Martin's universe, for without it prophecy would merely be sound and fury, signifying nothing. *Valar Dohaeris.*

Notes

1. The full name of which was "The Poor Fellow-Soldiers of Christ and of the Temple of Solomon" (*Pauperes commilitones Christi Templique Salomonici*).

2. At least, insofar as these organizations are depicted in the public imagination. The historical realities, however, were rather more complex, and exceed the purview of this work.

3. Of course, the Seven do not map seamlessly upon any world religion; one could just as easily argue that the Faith shares certain common properties with the public aspects of Greco-Roman religious observance. Nonetheless, it seems appropriate to defer to Martin's obvious intentions in this regard.

4. Arya's story arc proves perhaps the most sustained example of this trope.

5. It might seem anachronistic to reference Kant, given the broadly Renaissance tenor of Martin's universe. Although the concept of sublimity has antecedents in both the Christian and Greek traditions (the earliest arguably being the work of Pseudo-Longinus in *On the Sublime*, dating from the first century CE), it is nonetheless Kant's work on individuating in the face of vastness that seems to resonate most closely with Martin's description of the Stranger.

6. Although it might seem glib to ignore the possibility that Melisandre is incorrect, particularly given what appears to be her clearly mistaken view that Stannis is the Azor Ahai (*CoK* 11 Davos 1: 113–14; *SoS* 26 Davos 3: 289)—consider Maester Aemon's observation that Stannis' sword cannot truly be Lightbringer as it does not exude heat (*SoS* 79 Samwell 5: 886)—it seems that although the contents of Melisandre's visions are truly prophetic, it is her exegesis of these visions that are actually problematic. It is not so much that her visions are unreliable or incorrect, but more that she herself doesn't understand them.

7. For more information see Heidel on Anaximander: 212–213; 233–234.

Works Cited

Betz, Hans Dieter, ed. *The Greek Magical Papyri in Translation: Including the Demotic Spells*. Chicago: University of Chicago Press, 1989. Print.

Boyce, Mary. "Ardwashišt." *Encyclopaedia Iranica*. Vol. 2. New York: Routledge & Kegan Paul, 1986. Print.

Burns, Robert M. "Divine Infinity in Thomas Aquinas: I. Philosophica-Theological Background." *The Heythrop Journal* 39.1 (2002): 57–69.

Hansen, William. *Classical Mythology: A Guide to the Mythical World of the Greeks and Romans*. New York: Oxford University Press, 2005. Print.

Heidel, W.A. "On Anaximander." *Classical Philology* 7.2 (1912): 212–234. Print.

Jung, Carl. "A Psychological Approach to the Trinity." *The Collected Works of C.G. Jung, Vol. 11: Psychology and Religion, West and East*. Princeton: Princeton University Press, 1973. Print.

Kant, Immanuel. *Critique of the Power of Judgement*. Ed. Paul Guyer. Trans. Paul Guyer and Eric Matthews. Cambridge: Cambridge University Press, 2000. Print.

Lucan. *Pharsalia*. Trans. Nicholas Rowe. London: J. Tonſon, 1722. Print.

Luck, Georg. *Arcana Mundi: Magic and the Occult in the Greek and Roman World*, 2d ed. Baltimore: Johns Hopkins University Press, 2006. Print.

Russell, Bertrand. *History of Western Philosophy*. London: Routledge, 2012. Print.

Wood, Juliette. "Introduction." *The Mythology of the British Islands: An Introduction to Celtic Myth, Legend, Poetry and Romance*. Rpt. *Juliettewood.com*. Web. 25 June 2014.

"Silk ribbons tied around a sword": Knighthood and the Chivalric Virtues in Westeros

CHARLES H. HACKNEY

> "It is chivalry that makes a true knight, not a sword.... Without honor, a knight is no more than a common killer. It is better to die with honor than to live without it"—Ser Barristan Selmy (*DwD* 68 The Kingbreaker: 878)

> "A knight's a sword with a horse. The rest, the vows and the sacred oils and the lady's favors, they're silk ribbons tied round the sword. Maybe the sword's prettier with ribbons hanging off it, but it will kill you just as dead"—Sandor Clegane (*SoS* 35 Arya 6: 385)

In *A Song of Ice and Fire*, George R.R. Martin drew inspiration from a wide swath of European history, primarily from the English High and Late Middle Ages, including the Albigensian Crusade and the War of the Roses, to create the Seven Kingdoms, a country that dominates the continent of Westeros. Westerosi history and culture are not meant to be direct analogues of a specific time in English history. Using arms and armor as an example, the presence of full plate armor would indicate a time after 1450 (Bull 57), but the absence of cannons in warfare would indicate a time before 1327 (Rogers 229). Direct comparisons between actual historical eras and Westeros should therefore be handled with a light touch.

One strong connection between the Seven Kingdoms and the medieval Europe of the real world, however, involves Martin's handling of chivalry. Chivalry is presented in the novels as a clash between high idealism and grim reality. Septons and singers speak of Westerosi knights as shining armour-clad beacons of moral excellence, heroically defending women, the poor, and the Faith of the Seven. One must search high and low, however, to find knights who genuinely embody such ideals. The majority of Westerosi knights are often brutal, often uncouth, often dishonest, often impious, often lecherous, and certainly no friend to the smallfolk. Daenerys (although her view is coloured by having received her information from her brother) contemplates that "in the songs, the white knights of the Kingsguard were ever noble, valiant, and true, and yet King Aerys had been murdered by one of them, the handsome boy they now called the Kingslayer, and a second, Ser Barristan the Bold, had gone over to the Usurper. She wondered if all men were as false in the Seven Kingdoms" (*GoT* 37 Daenerys 4: 391). When Sansa expressed disappointment that Ser Loras, who appeared to her as a hero from the songs, was not sent on a quest to slay the monster Ser Gregor, Petyr Baelish sadly must inform her that "life is not a song" (*GoT* 45 Sansa 3: 473), a lesson that Sansa learns throughout the series of novels, much to her sorrow.

In the ninth and tenth centuries, the knights of Europe were amoral terrors. By this time in history, the word "knight" referred to a mounted warrior of the lesser landowning class who fought under the banner of a feudal lord. Knights were expected to use the income of their land to provide their own weapons, armor, supplies, and support crew, and to dedicate at least forty days of each year to service in the field. Knights had a reputation for ferocity and savagery, as well as for impiety and bestial moral character. They were brutal, greedy and merciless, qualities that were useful when directed against Saracens and Magyars, but far too often were directed against their own folk. Knights of that time were known for plundering churches, killing nuns, and cruelly oppressing commoners. Historian F.J.C. Hearnshaw said of such a knight that he was psychologically "no more interesting than a modern machine-gun, or any other engine of indiscriminate slaughter" (6). Ser Gregor Clegane would have fit perfectly in this era.

Knights of Clegane's mold may have been tolerated in times of invasion, but in the eleventh century, when most of the foreign invaders had been successfully repelled, king and cleric combined forces to reshape knighthood into a moral, as well as martial, force. In medieval Europe, the ethic of chivalry was an attempt to "tame murderous instincts by providing a Christian ideal of the warrior" (Seward 12) by fusing aristocratic, martial, and religious values. So could brutality in war be curbed, military power directed toward defending the weak rather than self-centered ambition, and the individual warrior could find a way of personal spiritual growth that was coherent with his role in battle.

In *A Song of Ice and Fire*, Westeros has its own version of the code of chivalry. Instead of devotion to the Catholic Church, the vows, symbols, rituals, and moral codes of Westerosi knights are oriented toward the worship of the Seven. There are numerous examples of warriors in George R.R. Martin's world that live by a code of honor, but are not technically knights. For example, Northerners are more likely to follow the old gods and so do not take knightly vows, making Lord Eddard Stark a viable exemplar of honorable character, but not specifically a representative of chivalry as an ethical or social system. A broader consideration of ethics, or of warriorhood, in *A Song of Ice and Fire* would be beyond the scope of this essay, and so this examination of martial virtue will be restricted to those specifically designated as "knights" in the novels, with certain non-knights brought in for the purposes of comparison and contrast.

For some, the temptation exists to look back at the age of chivalry as a better age than our own, when moral excellence and martial prowess went hand in hand. Tennyson saw King Arthur as "ideal manhood closed in real man" in his *Idylls of the King* (159). Sir Walter Scott, through works of fiction such as *Ivanhoe*, and nonfiction such as his *Essays on Chivalry*, sparked a romantic fascination with medieval ideals in nineteenth-century English-speaking culture (a phenomenon greatly lamented by Mark Twain in his *Life on the Mississippi* [347], in which he accuses Scott of being responsible for the American Civil War). Victorian polymath Sir Richard Burton argued in *The Book of the Sword* that the decline of knighthood (and especially swordsmanship) in favor of firearms and artillery had cast Western civilization back to the moral level of rock-throwing savages (xviii), contributing to the steady eradication of courtesy and respect in contemporary society, which he described as being "a waste[land] of bald utilitarianism" (xx).

A similar, possibly-misplaced, nostalgia exists among some of Martin's characters. On more than one occasion, characters lament that knighthood is not what it used to be. Considering the Kingsguard, for example, Varys laments that "the days when men like Ryam Redwine and Prince Aemon the Dragonknight wore the white cloak are gone to dust and song" (*GoT* 31 Eddard 7: 322). However, when we are given the opportunity to see the chivalry of an earlier day in *The Hedge Knight* (set two generations after the time of Aemon the Dragonknight and ninety years before *Game of Thrones*), knighthood is in no better condition. Prince Aerion is vain and monstrous, and Daeron is a coward and a drunkard. Ser Steffon Fossoway is a traitor. And when Ser Duncan confronts Aerion to protect the puppeteer that he is assaulting, this virtuous act is so atypical of contemporary knighthood that hundreds of smallfolk flock to his trial to bless and honor him. "A knight who remembered his vows" (*THK* 515) is apparently a rare thing.

As it was in Westeros, the ideal of chivalry was seldom truly achieved in Europe, even in its thirteenth-century "Golden Age." In her analysis of medieval popular ballads, Gwendolyn Morgan points to their common use in criticizing those who violated chivalric values more often than upheld them (83), and Richard Kaeuper describes the chivalric literature as "a range of ideologies with high praise for an ideal knighthood at one end, bitter denunciation of the evils of knighthood at the other" (64). Maurice Keen describes chivalry as "an ideal vision, more useful to contemporaries who wished to measure and impugn the actual shortcomings of society than to the historian who wishes to know things as they once were" (4). Such a use of chivalry as a moral yardstick can be seen in *A Clash of Kings*, when Tyrion walks in on Ser Boros beating Sansa at King Joffrey's command. "Is this your notion of chivalry, Ser Boros?" shouts Tyrion, "What sort of knight beats helpless maids?" (*CoK* 33 Sansa 3: 366).

On the other hand, historians note that chivalry was more than a mere exercise in hypocrisy or empty posturing. Knights conceived of chivalry "as a practiced form of religion, not merely as knighthood with a little pious and restraining overlay" (Kaeuper 50). Chivalry inspired many to pursue a life of continuous self-improvement (Keen 15), and the example set by the great 14th-century knight Geoffroi de Charny inspired the creation of an order of knight-hood dedicated to his moral ideals (Kaeuper & Kennedy 14). Similarly, chivalry in Westeros does have a positive effect on the residents of the Seven Kingdoms. There are those, such as Barristan Selmy and Brienne of Tarth, whose devotion to the chivalric vision serves to craft them into persons of impressive moral char-acter. Their examples inspire others; Barristan is seen in *A Dance with Dragons* passing on his teachings to the next generation of knights, and Brienne's true heart is one of the primary factors that sparks Jaime Lannister's ongoing efforts toward redemption. So Martin's portrayal of chivalry is neither an exercise in sentimental nostalgia nor in bare cynicism, but is a relatively accurate handling of the contrasts found in the Age of Chivalry, as well as a reflection of the struggle in every age to be a good person in a corrupt world.

Chivalric Virtues

In every society that has had a warrior tradition, there has existed the idea that a warrior of excellence is more than just someone who is good at hurting people, and that the crucial difference is the warrior's moral character. In Book II of *The Republic*, for example, the ancient Greek philosopher Plato discusses the ideal virtues of the guardian class of his hypothetical perfect society. In 7th-century Korea, the *hwarang* were an aristocratic society dedicated to ideals such as mercy, indifference to material temptations, and a calm acceptance of death (Tikhonov 334). Samurai of the Tokugawa period in Japan were taught to value virtues such as benevolence, filial piety, and loyalty (Dore 36). European chivalry was no exception to this pattern.

Central to the chivalric ethic was the idea of knightly virtues, personality characteristics that empower the knight to achieve both pragmatic effectiveness as a soldier and moral excellence as a human. Knights were encouraged to study the lives of excellent warriors such as Judas Maccabeus and Charlemagne, holding them up as exemplars worthy of emulation. Scholars, clerics, and elder knights wrote treatises and instruction manuals on the ideals of chivalry, and lists were generated of the virtues that knights should cultivate. The content of these virtue lists varied considerably. Medieval historian Sidney Painter lists prowess, loyalty, generosity, and courtesy as the core knightly virtues (29). F.J.C. Hearnshaw lists courage, loyalty, generosity, fidelity, obedience, chastity, courtesy, humility, and beneficence (32), while Gwendolyn Morgan lists the virtues of honor, hospitality, loyalty, courage, and piety (83), and Maurice Keen lists prowess, loyalty, generosity, courtesy, and frankness as the virtues of good knighthood (2). Guided by my earlier work on the warrior virtues (*Martial Virtues* 2010), I will discuss seven core chivalric virtues and their relation to Martin's text: prowess, courage, justice, temperance, wisdom, benevolence, and courtesy.

Prowess, defined by Sidney Painter as "the ability to defeat the other man in battle" (29), is a catch-all term for traits, such as strength, speed, cunning, and skill at arms, that make knights effective in battle. Philosopher Alasdair MacIntyre describes such "qualities of effectiveness" as distinct from the "qualities of excellence" (32). The qualities of effectiveness are what empower one to achieve rewards such as status, riches, prestige, and power, but are not enough to make one a *good* practitioner of an activity. An athlete who cheats may win medals. An attorney who hides evidence may win cases. A scientist who falsifies data may receive a prestigious research grant. But by no means would we call such an individual a *good* athlete or attorney or scientist. Mere victory is not enough. The practitioner must also possess the qualities of excellence. In the examples above, the quality of excellence that is missing is honesty.

Loyalty serves as a good example of a quality of excellence in the *Song of Ice and Fire* novels. Bronn the sellsword (later Ser Bronn of the Blackwater and later still Lord Stokeworth) possesses prowess in abundance, succeeding in battle against the mountain clans and defeating Ser Vardis Egen in single combat. He also saw success in the Battle of the Blackwater, and slew Ser Balman Byrch in a duel. But by no means would we call Bronn a *good* knight, and loyalty is one of the qualities of excellence which Bronn utterly lacks. A knight who serves only himself can never be trusted, a lesson that Tyrion learned, to his regret. It is Ser Gregor Clegane, though, who serves as the ultimate example of a knight of enormous prowess and utter lack of excellence. Ser Gregor is a man with no compassion, no self-control, and not the slightest conception of justice; his own people lack respect for him, seeing him as nothing more than a useful monster, reminiscent of Hearnshaw's description of a tenth-century knight as the moral equivalent of a walking machine gun.

Where prowess is a quality of effectiveness, courage, justice, temperance, wisdom, benevolence, and courtesy are all qualities of excellence. These virtues occasionally impair effectiveness in the short term (for example, a loyal knight might be betrayed by an unscrupulous lord, just as an honest attorney might lose a particular case against a dishonest attorney), but in the long run these virtues empower both success and moral praiseworthiness. Though this does not directly connect to knighthood, I will illustrate this principle by referring to the Red Wedding. Lord Frey's betrayal of hospitality served him and his house in the short term, winning the good will of House Lannister and adding Riverrun to their territory. However, this act destroyed the last remnant of Frey honor, and on multiple occasions it is made clear that now no-one will trust the word of a Frey. Without trust, it becomes impossible to enter into negotiations or make agreements, so the influence and effectiveness of House Frey is sent into a steep decline through lack of virtue.

It should be noted, however, that this seeming devaluation of the qualities of effectiveness does not render them optional or irrelevant. The qualities of excellence are not sufficient by themselves without the qualities of effectiveness. Sansa Stark, for example, is courteous, gentle, perceptive, and (thanks to a series of very unpleasant experiences) is growing in wisdom. At the time of this writing, however, she remains a pawn in others' games. She is unable to exert her own will or bring about her own goals due to her weakness and lack of strategic competence. And her belief that "a lady's armor is courtesy" (*CoK* 3 Sansa 1: 37) offers her no genuine protection from the abuse she suffers at the hands of Joffrey's Kingsguard. Individuals must possess high degrees of both the qualities of effectiveness and the qualities of excellence, to which we now turn.

The virtue of *courage* is grounded in our awareness of our vulnerability to injury and death, and the necessity of overcoming the fear that this awareness generates (Foot 8). The centrality of fear and vulnerability to the nature of courage forms the basis of the often-heard statement that courage is never to be understood as the absence of fear, but as doing the right thing in the face of fear (Goud 111). In *A Game of Thrones*, Bran asks his father, "Can a man still be brave if he's afraid?" to which Lord Stark replies, "That is the only time a man can be brave" (*GoT* 2 Bran 1: 13).

As fear can take many forms, courage can take many forms. Many scholars distinguish between "active" forms of courage, involving heroically acting in the face of fear, and "static" forms of courage, involving heroically standing firm in the face of fear. Defense master Fiore dei Liberi provides one treatment of an "attack" aspect of courage in his 1410 treatise *Flos Duellatorum* ("Flower of Battle"). In the prologue to the Pisani-Dossi version of *Flos Duellatorum*, Liberi writes: "*Audatia et virtus talis consistit in arte*," which is translated as "Audacity is the virtue that makes this art" (Hackney, "Reflections"). The use of the term "audacity" may strike readers as odd. In common use, "audacity" carries with it the connotation of thoughtlessly trampling standards of polite behavior, which contradicts frequent references to courtesy as necessary for a knight. However, audacity as a martial virtue may be seen as a form of courage in which the warrior overcomes fear and decisively acts in the face of danger.

Both forms of courage (but especially the static) are on display in the prologue to *A Game of Thrones*. A team of Rangers, led by Ser Waymar Royce, goes looking for wildlings but instead finds Others. Ser Waymar is shown to be a spoiled child of wealth and privilege, arrogant and inexperienced. And yet, facing the terrible inhuman, he holds his ground, saying, "Dance with me then," at that time truly becoming "a man of the Night's Watch" (*GoT* 1 Prologue: 7) through his act of bravery. Ser Waymar meet and parries blow after blow from the Other's unearthly blade, holding firm but not launching any attacks of his own, ceasing his defense only once he has been cut down and killed. This passage also provides another example of the complexity of Martin's treatment of the knightly virtues in these novels, as chivalry is simultaneously shown to be false (Ser Waymar is a knight in name but a green boy in reality) and true (Waymar shows genuine chivalry at the end).

Medieval European thought on *justice*, which was derived primarily from Plato, was grounded in the belief that "the universe is the manifestation of a single pervading law, and that human life is good so far as it obeys that law" (Nettleship 10). Justice is defined in this tradition as a life lived in harmony with the structure and functioning of the universe. To be a just person within this definition is to be someone whose life "fits" in the order of the universe. When interacting with others, the others are treated in a manner which fits their place in the universe. Whether dealing with oneself or with others, an unjust act is "an unfitting act; it is an act which fails to accord with the status of the person treated" (Cupit 2). If a person deserves a reward, justice is ensuring that the person gets that reward; if a person deserves punishment, justice is ensuring that the person is punished.

When dealing with oneself, justice takes the form of honor. Honor is a troublesome concept, at once inherently social and transcending society. To say that something is honored requires a social group to highly esteem that thing, but that which is esteemed by society is not always worthy of esteem, and many of the highest examples of honorable behavior are found in those who have defied popular opinion and placed their personal moral convictions above the dictates of the social group. Throughout Western history, conceptions of honor have maintained this tension between its individualistic and social natures.

In medieval thought, it is common to see issues of honor linked to issues of social prestige and reputation. Geoffroi de Charny, in his 14th-century *Book of Chivalry*, connects the honor of a knight to the public performance of feats which are valued by other knights. Whether honor is won by participating in jousts and tournaments, by fighting in local or foreign wars, or by undertaking long journeys and pilgrimages, "whoever does best is worth most" (Kaeuper & Kennedy 95). Historian Richard Kaeuper considers knightly honor to be intimately connected to prowess, as honor is the result of military victory. He claims that "the assumption, almost without exception, is that honour originates, is merited, proved, and increased sword in hand by those whose lineage leads them to such deeds" (130). Henri de Laon, writing in the 13th century about those who fight strenuously in tournaments, said, "To be soaked in one's own sweat and blood, that I call the true bath of honour" (Keen 88).

The notion that chivalric honour is a matter of social status (lineage and deeds) exists in an often-uneasy balance with the idea that nobility is owed more to virtue and personal integrity than status and reputation (Keen 162). When Chaucer introduces his fourteenth-century knight in the *Canterbury Tales*, he places a history of the knight's military exploits alongside a list of moral qualities such as his love of truth, his meekness, and his prudence (5). Geoffroi de Charny describes certain categories of knights to be praiseworthy if they fight well, but still less than perfectly honorable. These include knights who spend so much time jousting or competing in tournaments that they neglect to take part in actual military endeavors (Kaeuper & Kennedy 87), those who are too fond of profit (93) and plunder (99), and those who waste so much money on unnecessary displays of wealth and status that they cannot afford to sustain themselves in the field (97). Further, those who perform deeds that are noble, but not noticed or spoken of, are still honorable (97). The anonymous 16th-century treatise *Institucion of a Gentleman,* written in the twilight of medieval chivalry (Kaeuper 302), distinguishes between honour derived from social strata (high birth) and honour derived from character, advancing the claim that only those with integrity of character are true gentlemen, regardless of high or low birth (Mason 37). Integrity may be a considered a form of justice-turned-inward in which, rather than the honorable one demanding to be treated in a manner that is true to one's social status, the honorable one behaves in a manner that is true to oneself. Rather than honour being preserved by conforming to others' expectations, honour is preserved by adhering to one's own beliefs and internalized standards of right conduct.

One example of such honour in the *Song of Ice and Fire* novels is Brienne of Tarth. Although she is never anointed as a knight due to her sex, in every other sense she lives according to the chivalric code, and is a far better exemplar of honour than most of her male counterparts. She is repulsed by the dishonorable conduct of other knights, even if they are considered "normal" deviations from true morality. She does not conform to the expectations of others (almost all of whom would wish her to give up battle, go home, and get married), so she is held in dishonor by many. But her behavior is governed by a strong adherence to her ideals, to such a degree that her vow to Catelyn Stark holds her even after Lady Stark's death. Even though she is mocked, insulted, betrayed, rejected, and assaulted, she displays perhaps the truest heart in all of Westeros.

While the application of justice to oneself produces honour, the application of justice beyond the self produces piety and loyalty. Working from the perspective that justice involves giving to people that which they are due, piety takes this idea and applies it to social units such as family, country, and religion. While most forms of justice between persons involve the satisfaction of obligations, piety involves obligations that can never be satisfied. Can any act of service really "pay back" our parents, canceling out the debt that we owe them for giving us our lives? While social contract theory maintains that it is possible for the State to behave so unjustly that it violates its side of the agreement, what act of patriotic service finishes our obligations toward the nation under whose protection we live? For those who operate within a theistic worldview, at what point can creature and creator be "even"? When does a resident of Westeros get to say to the Seven: "What I have just done for you balances your act of creating the universe and letting me live in it"? The answer is clear: we are never freed from pious duties, nor can we ever be without ceasing to be human. Piety, whether it is oriented toward family, country, or the divine, sets in the warrior's mind the idea that there is something out there that is of greater value than the self. The impious fighter is willing to risk injury and death, but only because that is the price for glory (or, in the case of sellswords, for payment). The pious fighter goes beyond that, and is willing to sacrifice his or her life for a greater cause than self-interest. As Carol Andreini puts it, "It is only when the heroism of the warrior combines with [piety] and works for a goal other than individual glory—be it for the country, the family, or the gods—that anything is truly won" (86).

Piety toward the Seven as a knightly virtue gets little respect in George R.R. Martin's writings. The majority of knights are either portrayed as godless (e.g., Jaime Lannister's mockery when Catelyn Stark tells him that he is destined for one of the seven hells), or their religious devotion is superficial and ill-defined (e.g., Barristan Selmy participates in rituals and tells the Green Grace that he worships the Seven, but when we finally are shown his point of view in *A Dance with Dragons*, the closest thing to sincere belief we see is that he recalled thanking the seven gods that King Joffrey had stripped him of his white cloak so that he would play no part in the dishonor of Eddard Stark's beheading). The Saltpans monk known only as Elder Brother is revealed to be a former knight, and his devotion to the Seven involves a complete rejection of his previous profession. Active knights who demonstrate religious piety are bemusedly derided or dismissed. Lancel Lannister's turn to the Faith is accompanied by a degradation in his physical and psychological functioning (or might be seen as a symptom of psychological dysfunction following his severe wounding in the Battle of the Blackwater). His cousin Jaime thinks of him as a "pious fool" (*FfC* 17 Jaime 2: 229) with "milk in his veins" (*FfC* 17 Jaime 2: 228).

Another pious knight found in *A Feast for Crows* is Ser Bonnifer Hasty, described as a withered "solemn stork of a man" (*FfC* 28 Jaime 3: 405) who leads the Holy Hundred. Jaime's impression of the Hundred is that they are thoroughly mediocre knights, neither disgracing nor distinguishing themselves, except by their spotless record of committing no atrocities. Littlefinger had once joked that such knights, who committed no rapes, must have been gelded. Religious piety, it seems, is antithetical to masculinity as well as prowess. Further, Jaime recalls that Ser Bonnifer had a traumatic incident of some sort early in his career that turned him from a "promising knight" (*FfC* 28 Jaime 3: 406) toward what he has become. Between Lancel and Bonnifer, the message appears to be that piety is for lesser knights who are not quite psychologically intact. The book series, however, is not complete. With the recent resurrection of the Faith Militant (which Lancel has now joined), it is possible that we may see more pious knights, perhaps even some who are admirable.

Piety is closely linked with loyalty, so much so that Royce's definition of loyalty ("the willing and practical and thoroughgoing devotion of a person to a cause" [16]) seems indistinguishable from Andreini's description of heroic piety. Loyalty might be thought of in terms of integrity and piety working together. The person of honour commits to the support and defense of someone or something beyond the self, and demonstrates the personal integrity to remain true to that commitment.

Ser Davos Seaworth, the Onion Knight, demonstrates an extreme loyalty toward Stannis Baratheon that serves well as an example of the admixture of piety and integrity. Davos' devotion to King Stannis is plainly shown to have reached the level of religious devotion, with Davos declaring to Salladhor Saan: "King Stannis is my god. He made me and blessed me with his trust" (*CoK* 11 Davos 1: 119). Davos is true to his king, regardless of consequence. He will not break faith with Stannis or act against Stannis' interest, even to the point of risking his own life to give true advice to his king. It is fortunate for Davos that Stannis recognizes and rewards his devotion; a less just or temperate lord might have the head of someone who conspired to assassinate his sorceress, called his battle plans folly and cowardice, and all but accused him of treason for siding with his brother against King Aerys.

Temperance is the virtue that empowers individuals to align their lives with the principles of reason, such that a healthy balance between "too much" and "too little" is attained. Temperance is a quiet virtue, in which strength is directed inward, and relatively few stories exist that provide exemplars of temperance in the warrior's life. If I was to point to a modern exemplar of temperance, I might point to the Canadian UFC fighter Georges St-Pierre ("GSP" to his fans). GSP has spent several years ranked as the #1 Welterweight fighter in the world, with a stellar win-loss record. The secret of GSP's success is, however, also the reason that some UFC fans dislike him. GSP is calm and collected, indulging in little trash talk outside the octagon, and winning fights inside the octagon through methodical application of strategy rather than all-out aggressiveness or high-risk techniques.

The major form of temperance to be considered here is self-control. In the scholarly literature, the terms "self-control" and "self-regulation" are often used interchangeably, and are defined as "the exercise of control over oneself, especially with regard to bringing the self into line with preferred (thus, regular) standards" (Vohs & Baumeister 2). This control over oneself extends to patterns of thought, emotions, and behavior, and is centered around the achievement of some purpose. When self-regulation is functioning as it should, the person notices when there is a discrepancy between their current state and preferred standards, and discrepancy-reducing corrective adjustments are made in order to "stay on track" and achieve that goal, whether that change involves alteration of one's thought processes (such as staying focused on a topic of study), emotional reactions (such as staying calm during a confrontation), or overt behaviors (such as sticking to an exercise regimen).

Self-control is valuable for a knight, as battle is emotionally-intense, and uncontrolled emotions can be a warrior's undoing. Self-control is also necessary for the performance of precise techniques. In the Tourney of the Hand in *A Game of Thrones*, temperance is on display in the joust between Loras Tyrell and Gregor Clegane. Ser Loras has deliberately chosen a mare in heat, a cunning trick meant to distract Gregor's stallion. The trick succeeds; Gregor finds himself unable to control his horse, and Loras calmly lands a perfectly-placed strike that unseats Clegane. Ser Gregor then further demonstrates his lack of temperance by losing control of his emotions, furiously killing his own horse and attempting to unlawfully kill Ser Loras (and then attempting to kill his brother Sandor when Sandor intervenes).

Wisdom is often thought of as having two major forms: transcendent wisdom and practical wisdom (Wink and Helson 2). Transcendent wisdom involves the contemplation of the "big questions" of human existence, and the transcendently-wise person tends to show inner self-awareness, the ability to reconcile seemingly-opposed intellectual concepts, and the search for answers to the meaning of life. Transcendently-wise people tend to demonstrate elevated levels of cognitive openness, intuition, and creativity. This form of wisdom is in short supply among Westerosi knights, as the higher questions about life, the universe, and everything are typically left to maesters and septons. One exception would be Rhaegar Targaryen, who demonstrated intellectual complexity even at a very early age, greatly impressing the maesters, though it made him an object of grumbling among the household knights, is itself a sign of the relative lack of this virtue among the knights of Westeros.

Practical wisdom involves an understanding of how to achieve goals and solve problems in real-world scenarios, and the practically-wise person tends to show good interpersonal skills, superior decision-making ability, and expertise in giving useful advice. Jeor Mormont, Lord Commander of the Night's Watch, shows this form of wisdom. He counsels Jon Snow in the wake of his father's execution, sets watch over Jon because he knows that Jon will run, and allows Jon's friends to persuade him to return, but has others ready to arrest him if that failed. "Do you think," he asks Jon, "they chose me to be Lord Commander of the Night's Watch because I'm dumb as a stump, Snow?... I know my men" (*GoT* 71 Jon 9: 653).

An example of practical wisdom among warriors in our world is the work of the English swordmaster George Silver. In his *Brief Instructions*, Silver discusses the application of good judgment in the fight. "Judgment" is Silver's term for the ability to quickly perceive the distance between oneself and the opponent, the amount of time it takes to traverse that distance, what possible attacks are available from any position, and how best to make use of that information to attack and defend. A wise fighter can quickly perceive the essential elements of a situation, the goal to be attained, and the best method for the pursuit of those goals. Bronn the sellsword displays precisely this kind of practical wisdom in his fight with Ser Vardis Egen (*GoT* 40 Catelyn 7). Bronn fights in ways that are derided by others as cowardly and unfair, but are the best methods for pursuing victory.

A *benevolent* act is one that is motivated by a feeling of caring for the target of the action, intending to alleviate the suffering or promote the welfare of the target, and a benevolent person is "a person who tends to care about other human beings, is generally concerned about other people's well-being, and is motivated to perform acts which are aimed at doing good" (Livnat 304). Virginia Held, a central figure in care-based ethical theory, claims that "the central focus of the ethics of care is on the compelling moral salience of attending to and meeting the needs of the particular others for whom we take responsibility" (10). In the case of knighthood, one is adopting the responsibility to protect relevant others (the King, the Church, women, commoners), meeting their needs for safety and security.

A benevolent knight is one who acts out of a desire to alleviate the suffering of others, or to spare others from the suffering that would result from victimization. Ser Duncan demonstrates this virtue in *The Hedge Knight* when he comes to the rescue of the puppeteer. Later, when Raymun Fossoway receives his knighthood from Ser Lyonel Baratheon, the oath includes the charge to protect the young, the innocent, and all women.

In medieval chivalric literature, Alexander the Great was listed among the "Nine Worthies," historical and literary warriors held up as examples of virtuous character for knights to study and emulate. In 333 BC, Alexander the Great routed the army of Darius III, Emperor of Persia. Darius fled, abandoning his mother, his wife, and his children. Alexander promised to treat these royal captives with the *courtesy* due their station, and they remained well-treated "guests" of his for two years. Alexander's handling of his enemy's family was so considerate that, when Alexander died eight years later, Darius' mother wept for him (some versions of the story describe her as so distraught that she starved herself to death out of grief). In addition to creating a favorable impression on Darius' mother, Alexander's actions created a favorable impression in many biographers, and this person who lived well before the development of knighthood was long held to be a paragon of chivalry.

Scholars disagree about whether or not traits such as "courtesy" or "politeness" may be properly considered virtues in themselves, or if they should be treated as subsidiaries of higher-order virtues such as justice or benevolence. I have taken the position elsewhere (Hackney, *Martial Virtues* 189) that courtesy is not a virtue in and of itself, but is instead a venue for the cultivation and display of the other five virtues. Given courtesy's low reputation among the virtues, it is interesting that courtesy, especially in the form of being "sporting" toward opponents, is the virtue most strongly associated with chivalry in the *Song of Ice and Fire* novels. Leo Tyrell is described as chivalrous in *The Hedge Knight* for respectfully refusing to aim his lance at Ser Robyn Rhysling's unprotected head, while Aerion is unchivalrous for deliberately aiming his lance at Ser Humphry horse, and Baelor Breakspear is described as the "soul of chivalry" for returning Ser Arlan's horse and armor after defeating him in a tourney. Renly refused to advance his army against his brothers too early, because that would have been an unchivalrous attack. At the Tourney of the Hand, Sansa is overwhelmed by the gallantry of Ser Loras Tyrell and describes him as a "true knight" after he gives her a rose and a well-crafted compliment (the fact that Loras quickly and completely forgot all about Sansa and the rose speaks to the superficiality of his courtesy, as does his private arrogance toward Jaime in *A Storm of Swords*).

In addition to its role in facilitating virtue, courtesy also has practical advantages in a warrior society. In a dangerous world, the fewer people one antagonizes, the safer one is. This is especially important in societies in which dueling and/or an armed citizenry is common, and the ability to move and operate in society without creating enemies is of great usefulness. From the opposite perspective, warriors can be frightening people at times, which makes the ability to make others feel at ease especially useful while functioning in society. There is a tactical advantage to politeness in the fight, involving the degree of emotional self-control involved. By cultivating the ability to follow the rules of etiquette in all circumstances, the result is an imperturbability that reveals nothing to one's opponent. An opponent whose overall behavioral style is exactly the same while fighting as it is during everyday activities is an opponent who is very difficult to read. Cultivate courtesy, and you can deprive your enemy of a potential advantage.

Effectiveness and Excellence Interacting

Several knights in the *Song of Ice and Fire* novels display complex relationships between the qualities of effectiveness and the qualities of excellence. As was mentioned earlier, Ser Gregor Clegane serves as the best example of a knight who possesses all the qualities of effectiveness but none of the qualities of excellence.

A knight who possesses high degrees of both the qualities of effectiveness and the qualities of excellence, who best displays how the two can exist in a state of mutual reinforcement, is Ser Barristan Selmy. Described by Bran as "the greatest living knight" (*GoT* 9 Bran 2: 65), and by Varys as the only remaining "true steel" of the Kingsguard (*GoT* 31 Eddard 7: 270), Ser Barristan is legendary for his prowess, proving his effectiveness in battle against Maelys the Monstrous, and in tourneys against opponents ten and twenty years younger than himself. When dismissed by King Joffrey, Ser Barristan (despite having no sword) slew half a dozen Gold Cloaks on his way out of King's Landing. During the siege of Meereen, Selmy (still using the alias "Arstan Whitebeard," and again without a sword) defeated the Titan's Bastard, and after Meereen was taken, he slew the formidable pit fighter Khrazz (who was two stone heavier and forty years younger).

Barristan's effectiveness as a warrior is only enhanced by his high levels of the remaining virtues. His courage is undeniable, facing opponents younger and stronger and more numerous than he. He displays his temperance by maintaining a simple lifestyle as Arstan, humbly submitting to the blustering Strong Belwas and keeping his emotions in check during and after the fight with Khrazz. Facing Hizdahr, whom Selmy believes to have betrayed Danaerys and who had just ordered Khrazz to kill him, Selmy shows no sign of bloodlust or vengefulness and calmly arrests Hizdahr. He shows compassion for fallen comrades, standing vigil for Ser Hugh of the Vale and grieving over Quentyn Martell. Although he considers himself insufficient in matters associated with transcendent wisdom, his scheme of approaching Danaerys in disguise to assess her mental state shows considerable practical wisdom, and he is able to offer her sound advice. Ser Barristans excels at the virtue of justice, especially in terms of loyalty. His loyalty to King Aerys was tested by the king's madness, but Ser Barristan remained true to his vow. After he was defeated and captured during Robert's Rebellion, he experienced inner conflict about accepting the new king's pardon, but once he chose to accept the new king's rule, he stayed loyal to the Baratheons until his dismissal by King Joffrey. Loyalty is so deeply ingrained in Selmy's character that he found himself lost without someone to defend, and saw his dismissal as an opportunity to redeem his acceptance of Robert by seeking out Viserys and serving him loyally. He now follows this path by loyally serving Danaerys as Hand of the Queen, even during the time when it seemed that she had been killed by one of her dragons. Selmy is also notable for courtesy, speaking politely to Sansa while others rudely jested, to the Green Grace even as he refused her request to release Hizdahr, and even to Khrazz as the pit fighter was preparing to kill him. This habit of courteous speech pays very practical dividends when his explanation to Danaerys of his deception earns him her pardon.

While Barristan may represent the convergence of effectiveness and excellence at every level, Ser Jaime Lannister demonstrates a curious pattern in which a loss of effectiveness occurs alongside an increase in excellence. At the beginning of the series, Jaime is a knight of outstanding skill and social standing, and is admired by Jon Snow, who thought that Jaime was "what a king should look like" (*GoT* 6 Jon 1: 42), with his stunning appearance and golden armor. His skill with a sword is on display in *A Storm of Swords,* when he faces Brienne and, even weakened and chained, proves himself to be a terrifying opponent. Despite his extreme prowess and courage, though, Jaime is utterly lacking in honour. He is mistrusted by all, and unable to escape the nickname "kingslayer." Ser Barristan Selmy describes him as "the false knight who profaned his blade with the blood of the king he had sworn to defend" (*GoT* 58 Sansa 5: 520) and had argued (along with Eddard Stark) that Jaime should have been stripped of his white cloak and sent to the Wall for his killing of King Aerys.

Jaime's maiming at the hands of the Bloody Mummers causes him to sink into self-doubt and wander through previously-unexplored territories of introspection. The first time Jaime says that he "may indeed have shit for honor" (*CoK*

56 Catelyn 7: 597), it was a riposte to an insult from Catelyn Stark. However, the phrase became a recurring theme in his thoughts after losing his sword hand, as he came to realize the truth of it. It had only been his prowess that caused people to treat him with even a façade of respect, and now the prowess was gone. Jaime now faces the uphill battle of learning the virtues that might make him truly honorable, and though he finds it a hard road, we do see progress by *A Dance with Dragons*. He determines that, having given his word to Catelyn Stark to return her daughters, he will in fact carry out the oath by supporting Brienne in her quest to find Sansa. He begins to find satisfaction in justice. He begins to provide the Kingsguard with true leadership. He opposes his father, and finds himself repulsed by his sister's lack of morality. Jaime transforms from a knight who possessed effectiveness but not excellence into one who has lost effectiveness but is slowly growing in excellence. It remains to be seen whether or not this redemption trajectory will be allowed to continue its work, or if circumstances will cut his arc short before he can become truly excellent.

The Hound of the King or the Hand of the Queen

This essay began with a set of contradictory quotes, one from Barristan Selmy, and the other from Sandor Clegane. Sandor rejects chivalry and knighthood in all its forms throughout the novels, going so far as to snap at anyone who mistakenly assumes him to be a knight and calls him *ser*. He tells Sansa, "there are no true knights, no more than there are gods" (*CoK* 53 Sansa 4: 569), and lectures her that "knights are for *killing*" (*CoK* 53 Sansa 4: 568) and nothing more. Sandor sees the institution of knighthood as an exercise in hypocrisy, pointing out to Sansa that his monstrous brother is an anointed knight, and delivering the following diatribe to the Brotherhood Without Banners:

> A knight's a sword with a horse. The rest, the vows and the sacred oils and the lady's favors, they're silk ribbons tied round the sword. Maybe the sword's prettier with ribbons hanging off it, but it will kill you just as dead. Well, bugger your ribbons, and shove your swords up your arses. I'm the same as you. The only difference is, I don't lie about what I am. So kill me, but don't call me a murderer while you stand there telling each other that your shit don't stink [*SoS* 35 Arya 6: 385–386].

Given the sorry state of chivalry in Westeros, his attitude is understandable, and there are many in our world who share his view when it comes to the knights of European history.

But does widespread failure to live up to an ideal invalidate the ideal? Looking at our own times, whether the topic is military ethics, business ethics, religious ethics, or academic ethics, those who are truly paragons of virtue are no less rare in our world. When Hearnshaw spoke of chivalry, he pulled no punches in describing the atrocities of the crusaders, the corruption of the Templars, and the libidinousness of the gallants, but points out that, even among such hypocrites and brutes, "there were knights in whom piety and courage were mingled in the true chivalric blend" (10) whose example raised the moral tone of a society trying to emerge from post–Roman chaos:

> Perhaps nowhere outside of the realm of fiction could quite so perfect a paragon as Sir Parsifal be found. But it is enough to mention Godfrey of Bouillon, Tancred of Sicily, William Marshall, Saint Louis, the Cid, Sir Walter Manny, Sir John Chandos, Bertrand du Guesclin, the Black Prince, and the Chevalier Bayard, to recall to all who are familiar with the history of the later Middle Ages the careers of a noble company of illustrious men who in bravery, courtesy, integrity, devotion, piety, and chastity, will well stand comparison with the representative men of any age; men whose lives did much to redeem the reputation of the chivalry to which they owed their education and their inspiration [21].

And widespread failure to live up to the chivalric ideal was not due to moral myopia or ingroup bias on the part of knights themselves. Maurice Keen points out that "chivalry had always been aware that it was at war with a distorted image of itself. That indeed was part and parcel of its ideal" (234). There were no rose-colored glasses when it came to the difference between idealism and reality. Perhaps Ser Barristan Selmy had the right of it when he examined the lives of the knights recorded in the White Book:

> Some had been heroes, some weaklings, knaves, or cowards. Most were only men— quicker and stronger than most, more skilled with sword and shield, but still prey to pride, ambition, lust, love, anger, jealousy, greed for gold, hunger for power, and all the other failings that afflicted lesser mortals. The best of them overcame their flaws, did their duty, and died with their swords in their hands [DwD 56 The Queensguard: 735].

Works Cited

Andreini, Carol. "*Arete* to *Virtus*: Virgil's Redefinition of the Epic Hero." *Human Virtue and Human Excellence*. Ed. A.W.H. Adkins, J.K. Lowrence, and C.K. Ihara. New York: Peter Lang, 1991. 73–94. Print.

Bull, Stephen. *An Historical Guide to Arms and Armor*. New York: Facts on File, 1991. Print.

Burton, Richard F. *The Book of the Sword*. 1884; Toronto: General, 1987. Print.

Chaucer, Geoffrey. *The Canterbury Tales*. 1400; Ed. A.K. Hieatt and C. Hieatt. New York: Bantam Books, 1964. Print.

Cupit, Geoffrey. *Justice as Fittingness*. Oxford: Clarendon Press, 1996. Print.

Dore, R.P. *Education in Tokugawa Japan*. London: Routledge, 1965. Print.

Foot, Philippa. *Natural Goodness*. Oxford: Clarendon Press, 2001. Print.

Goud, Nelson H. "Courage: Its Nature and Development." *Journal of Humanistic Counseling, Education and Development* 44 (2005): 102–116. Print.

Hackney, Charles H. *Martial Virtues*. North Clarendon, VT: Tuttle, 2010. Print.

_____. "Reflections on *Audatia* as a Martial Virtue." *Journal of Western Martial Art* (2006). Web. 17 September 2006.

Hearnshaw, F.J.C. "Chivalry and Its Place in History." *Chivalry.* Ed. Edgar Prestage. New York: Alfred A. Knopf, 1928. 1–36. Print.

Held, Virginia. *The Ethics of Care: Personal, Political, and Global.* New York: Oxford University Press, 2001. Print.

Kaeuper, Richard W. *Chivalry and Violence in Medieval Europe.* New York: Oxford University Press, 1999. Print.

Kaeuper, Richard W., and Elspeth Kennedy, eds. *The Book of Chivalry of Geoffroi de Charny: Text, Context, and Translation.* Philadelphia: University of Pennsylvania Press, 1996. Print.

Keen, Maurice. *Chivalry.* New Haven: Yale University Press, 1984. Print.

Livnat, Yuval. "On the Nature of Benevolence." *Journal of Social Philosophy* 35 (2004): 304–317. Print.

MacIntyre, Alasdair. *Whose Justice? Which Rationality?* Notre Dame: University of Notre Dame Press, 1988. Print.

Martin, George R.R. "The Hedge Knight." *Legends.* Ed. Robert Silverberg. New York: Voyager, 1998.

Mason, John E. *Gentlefolk in the Making: Studies in the History of English Courtesy Literature and Related Topics from 1531 to 1774.* Philadelphia: University of Pennsylvania Press, 1935. Print.

Menache, Sophia. "The Templar Order: A Failed Ideal?" *Catholic Historical Review* 79 (1993): 1–21. Print.

Morgan, Gwendolyn A. *Medieval Ballads: Chivalry, Romance, and Everyday Life.* New York: Peter Lang, 1996. Print.

Nettleship, Richard L. *Lectures on the Republic of Plato,* 2d ed. 1901; New York: St. Martin's Press, 1961. Print.

Painter, Sidney. *French Chivalry: Chivalric Ideas and Practices in Medieval France.* Baltimore: Johns Hopkins University Press, 1940. Print.

Rogers, Clifford J., ed. *The Oxford Encyclopedia of Medieval Warfare and Military Technology,* Vol. One. New York: Oxford University Press, 2010. Print.

Royce, Josiah. *The Philosophy of Loyalty.* New York: Macmillan, 1924. Print.

Scott, Sir Walter. *Essays on Chivalry, Romance, and the Drama.* London: Frederick Warne, 1887. Print.

_____. *Ivanhoe.* 1830; Oxford: Oxford University Press, 1996. Print.

Seward, Desmond. *The Monks of War: The Military Religious Orders.* London: Eyre Methuen, 1972. Print.

Tennyson, Alfred Lord. *Idylls of the King.* Cambridge: Houghton Mifflin, 1896. Print.

Tikhonov, Vladimir. "Hwarang Organization: Its Function and Ethics." *Korea Journal* 38 (1998): 318–338. Print.

Twain, Mark. *Life on the Mississippi.* New York: Harper and Brothers, 1874. Print.

Vohs, Kathleen, and Roy Baumeister. "Understanding Self-Regulation: An Introduction." *Handbook of Self-Regulation: Research, Theory, and Applications.* Ed. Roy Baumeister and Kathleen Vohs. New York: Guilford Press, 2004. 1–12. Print.

Wink, Paul, and Ravenna Helson. "Practical and Transcendent Wisdom: Their Nature and Some Longitudinal Findings." *Journal of Adult Development* 4 (1997): 1–15. Print.

Cursed Womb, Bulging Thighs and Bald Scalp: George R.R. Martin's Grotesque Queen

KARIN GRESHAM

In the final chapter of *A Dance with Dragons*, Daenerys, exhausted by a series of physical challenges that has depleted her almost totally, is approached by a Dothraki rider, who, should he see her, will take her to the crones and thus put an end to her pursuit of the Iron Throne. However, Drogon, her strongest dragon, puts the rider to flight and eliminates the threat. Daenerys is hardly a vision of feminine beauty at this moment. She is clothed in a dirty, ragged undergarment that is covered in menstrual blood, absent once again her hair, unwashed, her hands smeared with offal. Except for her bloodied thighs, she appears not only unfeminine, but beyond the social. Nevertheless, Martin grants Dany, the name she is affectionately called throughout the series, her greatest strength when she appears in these liminal states that embrace in combining imagery from the empowering aspects of the feminine, masculine, and bestial. Presenting her as the embodiment of all life in this final point of view (POV) section just before the epilogue, Martin showcases her potential to win the throne and become an ideal leader of the people.

Bakhtin's theory of grotesque realism provides an effective lens through which to consider how the depiction of Dany redefines the heroic, transforming her into a character who integrates and expands gender, culture, sexuality, and even humanity, who accepts and absorbs all sources of strength and power, so that she emerges as a likely candidate for the throne of Westeros. While Martin's treatment of a character like Sansa Stark suggests the negative representations of women in the high Middle Ages, his treatment of Dany reflects the more positive attitudes towards femininity that Bakhtin claims for the late Middle Ages and early Renaissance. The positive interpretations of the grotesque that Bakhtin identifies—the recognition of value in variety and otherness, the intellectual power of the contrary, the saving graces of the macabre and gross—likewise correlate to postmodern interpretations of medieval monsters as both more and less than the traditional view would have them. Both lenses clarify Dany's growth from pliable marriage commodity to heroine, especially with reference to her monstrous and grotesque emotional and physical transformations. By employing traditionally negative narrative materials for positive purposes and allowing his heroine to challenge and redefine order, Martin persistently empowers her.[1]

Bakhtin's understanding of grotesque realism has also gained acceptance in some postmodern interpretations of the medieval. In *The Monstrous Middle Ages,* for example, Bettina Bildhauer and Robert Mills suggest that monstrosity is not only a way for medieval and modern citizens alike to understand themselves, but that it can even be alluring and desirable (Bildhauer and Mills 8–9). St. Augustine opens that door when he denies the devil the generative power necessary to create monsters and refuses to allow that God, the author of all, would create anything monstrous. Thus he recognizes "monstrous" forms born among us as part of the divine plan and that they call on our charity. Bildhauer and Mills also identify how seemingly negative representations of the monstrous may be viewed as positive from the perspective of political and social transformation. A radically re-gendered creature could be perceived as horrifically monstrous "when the binary categories by which it was perceived broke down," but in such a state of being it also becomes a living site on which traditional notions of gender can be challenged (12).

In a similar move, Jeffrey Cohen deftly aligns the monstrous with the queer to make a related point in his study of medieval monstrosity, *Of Giants:* "the queer designates a supposedly 'unlivable' space, and yet the production of this impossible realm marks a foundational moment for the identities that attempt to exclude it. The queer can thus become a contestatory point of resistance to systemization, as well as a powerful site from which to deconstruct dominant ideologies" (Cohen 180, qtd. in Bildhauer and Mills 21). Supporting Cohen's argument, Bildhauer and Mills claim that monsters can perform a powerful social function, precisely because they resist categorization: "There is something in the monster that cannot be subsumed into the categories of identity that the monster is perceived to disrupt, a queerness that potentially opens itself out to the possibility of affirmative resignification" (21).

Bakhtin is among the first to maintain that grotesque and monstrous forms were a means to challenge dominant ideologies. In *Rabelais and His World* and "Problems of Dostoyevsky's Politics," he studies the tradition of carnival grotesquerie from the Middle Ages through the sixteenth-century, exploring how it provides a way for common people to escape oppressive authority by celebrating "reversal, parody, song, and laughter" (Vice 150). Moreover, carnival is present in literature as well as life, "its traces ... detected, for instance, in representations of legends and unofficial history" that present alternative and subversive texts to give the lie to official versions of reality and events (Bakhtin, *PoDP* 132). The imagined histories and myths within a given text, as well as their contexts and the subversive laughter they may generate, function additionally as temporary, compartmentalized escapes from social oppression when they reject the actual to envision modes of life not otherwise or elsewhere attested. Even though the outward effects of carnival are temporary, the radical ideas they instill are lasting.

Because carnival is aligned with the values of the common man, Bakhtin claims that it esteems folk art and rejects high art and literature. His understanding of grotesque realism is most clearly understood through his interpretation of the Kerch terracotta collection of laughing, pregnant hags: "There is nothing completed, nothing calm and stable in the bodies of these old hags. They combine the senile, decaying and deformed flesh with the flesh of new life, conceived but yet unformed. Life is shown in its two-fold contradictory process; it is the epitome of incompleteness. And such is precisely the grotesque concept of the body" (*RaHW* 25–6). Bakhtin perceives the grotesque body as one that is deeply positive and life affirming, because it represents the communal body's relationship to the lifecycle and social regeneration. Sex is basically irrelevant; Bakhtin addresses this ideal grotesque as an ambivalent form that signifies the renewal of all beings.[2]

Like the hag, Daenerys embodies the biological and social contradictions that reinforce Bakhtin's understanding of grotesque realism, a concept that abandons individualism to embrace the totality of the community. At a young age, Dany has experienced all stages of femininity, and in her most empowered moments she represents the strongest qualities of both genders. She accepts fully her femininity while acquiring physical strengths, recognizing and accepting sexualities of all sorts. She thus fulfills her human potential. But she also takes strength from the animal world, from the rough, almost bestial life of the steppe world and the horses it venerates. To these she adds the general power of the mythic, of the imagination, when she organizes her quest around the protection of her dragon eggs and the nurturing of the young hatchlings against all those who want to take them from her.

Bakhtin's generalist view of grotesque realism likewise accounts for bestial representations of the body. The body's ambivalent and unfinished qualities suggest not only its relationship to the lifecycle but also its open, borderless relationship to the universe: "The unfinished and open body (dying, bringing forth and being born) is not separated from the world by clearly defined boundaries;

it is blended with the world, with animals, with objects. It is cosmic, it represents the entire material bodily world in all its elements" (Bakhtin, *RaHW* 26–27). This grotesque acceptance of existence in all its forms on all the levels of its possibilities from the most conceptual to the most physical becomes Daenery's strength and the core of her claim to the throne. While other characters like the Stark children are able to see through the eyes of animals, Dany is able to connect with them on a much more integrated and visceral level: she does not have to abandon her own body to experience another's. This is a celebration of physical connection and community rather than corporeal transience and transcendence.

Modern studies on heroics connect the positive attitudes towards social regeneration located in Bakhtin specifically to acts of female heroism. Through Dany, Martin likewise establishes a brand of heroism rooted in the power of a woman who comes to represent the idyllic regeneration of the community. In the course of discussing Lee Edwards' theories about similar representations of female heroism and "communitas," Elizabeth Ordoñez observes, "the heroine, simultaneously inside and outside the dominant culture, is instrumental in uncovering 'gaps in its social ideology.' By revealing the gaps in patriarchal culture, she points to an alternative cultural synthesis, toward the restructuring of human society, toward the values of cooperation and the serving of human needs" (Ordoñez 53).[3] As Daenerys learns her powers and those of the communities dependent upon her, she slowly evolves from a mistreated subject, one who was subsumed into a network of exchange by her brother Viserys, into a heroine ruler who knows how to consider the needs of others, especially the marginalized and mistreated, and rises accordingly to power as a positive representative of the people.

Traces of the grotesque are apparent from the moment of Dany's conception. When readers first meet Dany, they are told that "her mother had died birthing her," that the new life had taken the old (*GoT* 4 Daenerys 1: 26). This scenario clearly correlates with Bakhtin's description of the birth of Gargantua and the death of Gargamelle, in which the mother dies to give way to new life. As Bakhtin describes it, the birth is unusual, because Gargantua is conceived through Gargamelle's gluttony and birthed through her ear (Bakhtin, *RaHW* 220–21). Bakhtin does not see the relationship between food and inception as strange, because "the image of tripe, life and death, birth, excrement, and food are all drawn together and tied in one grotesque knot" (163). This process of consumption, birth, and death represents the "ever-regenerated body of the people" (226). Martin crafts a similar moment, albeit a less comic one, as he describes Dany's origins. Viewed within the context of Gargantua and Gargamelle, the death of Dany's mother at her birth is not a harbinger of doom but instead simply a life-affirming representation of regeneration. That we meet Dany during her betrothal to Khal Drogo further affirms this connection: death feeds life, which in turn marries and gives birth again.

Through her marriage to Khal Drogo, Dany's absorption into Dothraki horse culture further contributes to the development of both her heroic potential and respective culture, and the auspices of her period convey this potential. Dany's menstrual cycle is a positive rite of passage to marriageability: "'She has had her blood. She is old enough for the khal,' Illyrio told him, not for the first time. 'Look at her. That silver hair, those purple eyes ... she is the blood of old Valyria, no doubt, no doubt ... and highborn, daughter of the old king, sister to the new, she cannot fail to entrance our Drogo'" (*GoT* 4 Daenerys 1: 27). Here, her first blood is conflated with her desirability and rich ancestry. By way of contrast, Martin's depiction of the first blood of Ned Stark's eldest daughter, Sansa, also highlights her potential for marriage, but hers is not depicted so positively. The night before Sansa wakes to discover her period, she dreams that she is being attacked by a mob of women. The final image before she wakes up is "the bright glimmer of steel. The knife plunged into her belly and tore and tore and tore, until there was nothing left of her down there but shiny wet ribbons" (*CoK* 53 Sansa 4: 570). After the dream, she feels the sticky blood between her legs and reacts in horror, attempting to burn all evidence of her bleeding, which is the final stage of her maturation that the Lannisters require before she weds Joffrey. The appearance of blood is presented not only as violent and vile but also as a betrayal of the girl's safe status by the advent of uncontrollable femininity represented as a rampage of violence. It shows that Sansa cannot control her own circumstances, is without borders, cannot be rationally contained, and in this capacity it reflects traditional medieval representations of menstruation.

Pliny the Elder's *Historia Naturalis*, a text widely respected by medieval medical practitioners, remarks, "nothing could be found that is more remarkable/monstrous [*monstrificium*] than the monthly flux of women" (Pliny qtd. in Miller 4). Interpreting these lines through a medieval lens, Sarah Miller claims that "menstrual fluid is a medium that violates boundaries and disorders bodies" (Miller 4). In its most negative representation, menstrual fluid highlights the instability of corporeal integrity, as it merges the once "stable and attractive [i.e., the virgin body] into something loose and leaky (i.e., the multiparous body) before the final dissolution into old age and eventual decay" (3). Julia Kristeva engages similar perspectives of the leaky, decaying female body through her theories on abjection, which are often viewed alongside Bakhtin's insights into the grotesque and various other theories on medieval monstrosity.[4] Put simply, Bakhtin's understanding venerates the loss of individual boundaries, while Kristeva's problematizes it. That Sansa's menstruation, which signifies a connection to those around her, is depicted in such a problematic way highlights how Martin does not treat women uniformly. Dany's period, by contrast, is associated with promise, and we may therefore look to Bakhtin for a more positive representation of reproductive power. While menstruation is often represented as a source of shame, Bakhtin sees it in his discussion of degradation as life-affirming, because it is related to the lower stratum of the body, "the life of the belly and the reproductive organs; it therefore relates to acts of defecation and copulation, conception, pregnancy, and birth. Degradation digs a bodily grave for a new birth; it has not only a destructive, negative aspect, but also a regenerating one" (Bakhtin, *RaHW* 21).[5] Unlike Sansa's, Dany's first blood is not an embarrassing and threatening function of femininity but instead is connected to both her rich ancestry and ability to continue, and perhaps re-envision through a previously marginalized perspective, that rich, ancestral line.

Additionally, Dany's wedding spectacle contains overt representations of the grotesque. Without judgment, Martin describes a scene in which men kill one another to conquer a particular woman, and copulation occurs openly and without shame. Ilyrio reminds her, "A Dothraki wedding without at least three deaths is deemed a dull affair," and the event-goers (aside from Dany) are neither surprised nor upset by the sex and violence (*GoT* 12 Daenerys 2: 85). Despite the deaths, the scene celebrates a Bakhtinian cycle of death, marriage, and birth, and seats Dany firmly within it. To be sure, each of her major life events, including birth and marriage, is characterized by death and sacrifice (Ibid), from which she nevertheless acquires significant bounty, especially the dragon eggs that will later prove to be her primary source of military power and the horse, Silver, who gives her status among the Dothrakis and understanding of bestial power.

Dany's first ride upon Silver celebrates their oneness: "A daring she had never known filled Daenerys then, and she gave the filly her head. The silver horse leapt the flames as if she had wings. When she pulled up before Magister Illyrio, she said, 'Tell Khal Drogo that he has given me the wind'" (88). The horse has granted her both power and autonomy. While her newfound freedom may be customary for indigenous Dothraki women, for Dany it is a new and exciting mode of freedom, a source of her budding social belonging and strength, as her new husband, who smiles at her remark, clearly approves of her ride. Dany will continue to be connected to the grotesque not only through the human life cycle but also through her intimate relationship to animals, a relationship that Bakhtin claims is a central quality of the grotesque, because it embraces the totality of all beings (Bakhtin, *RaHW* 26–7). When Dany couples with her husband under the open sky (*GoT* 12 Daenerys 2: 90), she explores her newfound social strength in an outdoor setting with an act that emblematizes theirs as a social rather than a private union. Their copulation promotes the social regeneration of the Dothraki and potentially also the Targaryen clan. Martin promotes a clear connection between the lower extremities and the social growth that is the wished-for consequence of the sex act. Aligning her experience with grotesque celebration, Martin gives readers a hopeful picture of Dany's future.

Dany thrives in the khalasar and continues to develop into a queer figure that defies category. Her body, once easily bruised by lovemaking and tired by the long rides, is forged into something strong and supple: "From that hour onward, each day was easier than the one before it. Her legs grew stronger; her blisters burst and hands grew callused; her soft thighs toughened, supple as leather" (*GoT* 24 Daenerys 3: 192). Furthermore, she and her horse grow to share "a single mind" (Ibid). While her body absorbs a new strength, one that is customary for Dothraki women but considered masculine for Westerosi women, her mind at the same time learns to transcend the limitations of human thinking. She is now woman, man, and beast. Certainly Martin privileges this transformation, for it improves the life of his protagonist in connecting her to everything around her. Her body having transformed, she is consequently better able to appreciate life and integrate herself into all its forms, signified by her newfound capacity to "notice the beauties of the land around her" (Ibid).

To be sure, the men in the khalasar do not perceive her physical hardening as a threat. Instead, it grants her varying degrees of power over her brother and husband. For the first time, she stands up to her brother after he threatens her with physical harm. This scene is placed in context by their opposing dress: "She was barefoot, with oiled hair, wearing Dothraki riding leathers and a painted vest given her as a bride gift. She looked as though she belonged here. Viserys was soiled and stained in city silks and ringmail" (193). Her gender-neutral attire highlights her strength and adaptability, while his traditional Western attire represents his stubborn and inflexible nature. This scene is followed by his subsequent belittling for having attempted to harm her. She proclaims he will walk behind the khalasar in their travels, because "the man who does not ride was no man at all" (194). That she rides and he walks symbolizes the absolute shift in their power dynamic. Soon thereafter, she seduces her husband outside in front of the khalasar. Instead of being a shameful moment, it is life-affirming, for in this moment she becomes pregnant. Moreover, she "tops" her husband in a public display of a shifting power dynamic that anticipates her rise to dominance (198). Again, we are met with deeply positive and socially regenerative allusions to the grotesque each time Dany achieves a degree of upward social mobility. Her power is inextricably tied to the collective body of the grotesque, which celebrates societies rather than individuals. In making this connection, Martin favors her as a ruler, one whose development is innately tied to social development and renewal.

Yet Dany's strength does not come solely from her ability to adapt to her new culture but from her connection to the grotesque in all of its associations. While she may look like the Dothraki women, she does not always behave as they do. In one instance, Dany rescues Mirri Maz Duur, one of the conquered lamb people, from a group of Dothraki riders who are raping her, and in doing so challenges Dothraki culture and the subordinate role of women therein (*GoT* 62 Daenerys 7: 557). While the Dothraki women experience the same physical hardening as Dany, they are still subservient to men, who view the rape of women, especially when they are spoils of war, as a basic right of manhood. Khal Drogo allows her intervention and rationalizes her peculiar behavior by attributing it to maternity (559). His remark once again establishes a connection between the grotesque female body, one that is "bringing forth" (Bakhtin, *RaHW* 26–7), and Dany's redefinition of heroics. Duur's rescue has devastating consequences for Dany's life, but these later prove to have been necessary. The loss of those who are most special to her and closely tied to her development proves to be an essential part of her heroic journey. Initially, Dany's potential seems to wane as she suffers a series of tragic losses, including the death of her husband and child and the loss of the strongest members of her khalasar. However, as the Maegi Mirri Maz Duur implies, individual loss is a necessary part of development. After she has orchestrated the deaths of Dany's family, the maegi claims, "The stallion who mounts the world will burn no cities now. His khalasar shall trample no nations into dust" (*GoT* 69 Daenerys 9: 635). The maegi believes that Dany's dead son would have been a tyrant and his death was necessary to ensure a peaceful future, and Dany learns from her that his live birth would have produced more untimely deaths—the deaths of all those who lay in the path of his khalasar—than his stillbirth did.

After this revelation, Dany further realizes her heroic potential, which embraces the egalitarian, reproductive, and communal values of the grotesque. Now cursed by the Maegi Duur, who made her son monstrous and her womb barren, Dany finds solace and strength in her dragon eggs, a symbol of her earlier identity as Daenerys Stormborn, heir to the Targaryen Dynasty, the blood of the dragon (*GoT* 69 Daenerys 9: 630). At the same time she feels the power of her restored identity, she begins to make difficult decisions that underscore a new sense of empowerment: she smothers her comatose husband Khal Drogo, not wishing him to suffer in the twilight state to which Duur has condemned him, and then commits to burning her eggs and Duur in the funeral pyre alongside him (*GoT* 73 Daenerys 10: 672). She likewise promises the members of the khalasar, freemen and slaves, that she will find a place for each of them if they choose to remain with her (668). In making these decisions, she clearly embraces the egalitarian and communal values of the grotesque. In grotesque realism, the body is a universal form that represents the renewal of the common people, rather than the elite (Bakhtin, *RaHW* 19). In the grotesque spectacle that follows, death makes possible the birth of a new community.

Sacrificing the maegi to the fire, Dany burns the woman who threatens the life of her community and simultaneously displays a new sense of power and understanding of the world. The maegi is made to show fear for the first time (*GoT* 73 Daenerys 10: 671), and Dany walks fearlessly into the fire. Here the grotesque is positive, aligned with the maternal and animal: "The painted leather burst into sudden flame as she skipped closer to the fire, her breasts bare to the blaze, streams of milk flowing from her red and swollen nipples" (673). Out of the life-promoting fire that causes the flow of her mother's milk, she is reborn: "[I am] Daenerys Stormborn, daughter of dragons, bride of dragons, mother of dragons" (Ibid), linked to the bestial and the community that provide strength and life-affirming power. She emerges live from the fire, naked and covered in ash with two dragons sucking on her breasts and a third on her shoulder (Ibid). The events that kill her human son, the maegi, and her husband also bring forth her three dragon children. An even stronger life has been forged in the fire.

Even though Martin stages events such as this one in a medieval setting, his values are decidedly more progressive. For instance, the popular medieval series of images depicting St. George's defeat of the dragon represents femininity in a far more sinister light. In these images, medieval artists frequently depict the dragon with female breasts and genitalia as a way of emphasizing the saint's chastity. The feminized, bestial body symbolizes the sins of the flesh, which St. George must defeat in order for righteous order to prevail (Bildhauer and Mills 12). By contrast, Martin inverts the meaning of these iconic representations by venerating Dany's transformation into the dragon mother, which is aligned with the empowering elements of reproduction.

After the fire spectacle, the blood riders, who refused to serve her because she is a woman, now swear her allegiance. Again, we see Bakhtin's understanding of grotesque realism as a form of art that treats gender in an ambivalent way: the grotesque, liminal body represents all people (Bakhtin, *RaHW* 24–6). Clearly, Dany's transformation into a more masculine figure illustrates her emergence as the true representative and leader of her people. The absence of her beautiful hair, which was burned off in the fire, coupled by the display of her lactating nipples illustrates her embodiment of the masculine and feminine: the upper stratum is represented by a masculine, western appearance, while the lower stratum is represented by the feminine universal of fertility. Sue Vice reminds us, "Bakhtin points out that the terms 'upward' and 'downward' in grotesque realism do not have simply relative meanings, but 'strictly topographical' ones— and, one might add, what look like gender-related ones" (Vice 155). While the upper and lower strata appear gender-related, Bakhtin would have us believe that each domain is an aspect of the community rather than the individual. Certainly, her connection to masculine, feminine, and bestial elements earns her strength, as well as love and respect, from her community.

As Dany leads the khalasar in her first POV section in *A Clash of Kings*, she embraces her communal nature, which is central to her strength as khaleesi. In grotesque fashion, she makes that which is unrecognizable in terms of socially constructed sex and gender the ambivalent representation of all people. In the absence of her long hair, she wears her husband's lion's head cape, absorbing bestiality alongside gender and humanity: "[The white lion's] fearsome head made a hood to cover her naked scalp, its pelt a cloak that flowed across her shoulders and down her back. The cream-colored dragon sunk sharp black claws into the lion's mane and coiled its tail around her arm, while Ser Jorah took his accustomed place by her side" (*CoK* 13 Daenerys 1: 143). Bakhtin aligns the positive change that this image promotes with a transformation of culture that in part venerates the marginalized and disempowered. Wearing the lion's head and carrying the dragon wrapped firmly around her arm, Dany has become a challenging symbol of transformation.[6]

While she continues to lead her people through the desert wasteland, her body and behaviors continue to transform. She takes on attributes considered masculine by her parent culture, a hardness that signifies the strength and endurance necessary to keeping up with a mobile culture and, as the dragons wean themselves, her milk dries up (144). When Dany begins to grow her hair back, she regards its length as a function of Dothraki masculinity rather than femininity and considers wearing it like a blood rider (143). Nevertheless, she is still a beautiful woman, which is evident by Ser Jorah's desire. For her part, having transformed beyond the purely feminine and no longer fertile, she does not desire him (151). In any case, she can maintain sole power of the khalasar only by distancing herself from traditional heterosexual practice since she would forfeit rule through marriage. As I will show, her later decision to take a husband consolidates her rule of Meereen, which forsakes this transformative path, ultimately compromising her power rather than fortifying it.

In *A Storm of Swords*, Dany allows her beautiful handmaiden, Irri, to sexually pleasure her when earlier she had rejected Ser Jorah's sexual advances. Irri wakes to find Dany masturbating in bed, and she wordlessly "put a hand on [Dany's] breast, then bent to take a nipple in her mouth.... It was no more than a few moments until [Dany's] legs twisted and her breasts heaved and her whole body shuddered. She screamed then. Or perhaps that was Drogon. Irri never said a thing, only curled back up and went to sleep the instant the thing was done" (*SoS* 24 Daenerys 2: 268). This moment of sexuality, involving queen, mythical beast, and slave, falls far outside typical practice. It furthermore evades definition: we cannot truly assert that the encounter includes all three figures, as the dragon's participation is merely assumed. Drogon's potential, yet unde-fined, involvement transforms a homosexual moment into a queer one and brings to mind Cohen's notion that desire is queered by being "caught up in, and dis-persed throughout, a mobile network of bodies, objects, temporalities, and sub-jectivities" (Cohen 179). Most importantly, Dany's unorthodox experience of pleasure allows her to challenge dominant order and pursue the heroic path in a way that marriage to Ser Jorah would deny. The monstrous, queer sex act thus "potentially opens itself out to the possibility of affirmative resignification" (Bild-hauer and Mills 21). Dany's queer sexuality allows her to chart her own unique course and can be best perceived by Cohen's understanding of the queer monster and Bakhtin's representation of body politics.

Carol Adlam observes how Bakhtin addresses the body as a site upon which power is disputed: "Clearly Bakhtin does not discuss the sexed body, or even less, sexual orientation, but he stresses that 'the body' is an effect of its social, positional interactions" (Adlam 146). Martin, too, also seems to suggest that Dany's choice of sexual partners has much more to do with her position of power and social options than it does with her desire for either men or women, because she chooses to have sexual experiences with both. She later takes a male lover, Daario Naharis, who, like Irri, does not change the power dynamic, because "she was a queen, and Daario Naharis was not the stuff of kings" (*DwD* 12 Daenerys 2: 152). Jorah, a nobleman with some status, differs from Irri and Daario as a lover and potential mate, because he would usurp some or all of her power. Irri, by contrast, is a bed slave who Dany can use for physical gratification without worry about her power and influence, and Daario is a sell sword driven by his lust for women and battle rather than authority. The threat Jorah poses is made plain at the end of this section when he attempts to call Dany by her first name, an act of clear insubordination. His desire for her causes him to forget his place as a knight subservient to his queen (*SoS* 28 Daenerys 3: 308). By keeping him at a distance, she maintains power and order, and as a consequence explores alternative modes of sexuality.

Her acceptance and adoption of the objects, animals, and people around her also leads Dany to acquire a powerful eunuch army whose sexuality likewise stands beyond the normal reproductive cycle. Its castrated warriors dwell in a distinct gender category that was used for the better part of a thousand years to represent and uphold social order (Ringrose 4). As Kathryn Ringrose notes in *The Perfect Servant: Eunuchs and the Social Construction of Gender in Byzantium*, eunuchs were created to stand outside of family obligations and the reproductive cycle in order to function as ideal servants: "This made them ideally suited to serve as servants, agents, and proxies for their masters or employers, male or female. They moved freely across social and gender barriers and were not pre-cluded from a wide range of roles often deemed unsuitable for the persons whom they served" (Ringrose 5). While Varys, the utterly inscrutable member of the Lannister court, frequently undermines those he serves in order to achieve his own opaque aims, the Unsullied are model representations of orderly Byzantine servants. Even in the chaos of war, they maintain their extreme discipline. Ser Jorah remarks, "There is a savage beast in every man, and when you hand that man a sword or spear and send him forth to war, the beast stirs.... Yet I have never heard of these Unsullied raping, nor putting a city to the sword, nor even plun-dering, save at the express command of those who lead them" (*SoS* 24 Daenerys 2: 271). If Dany's intent is to restore order to Westeros, then the type of precise and orderly warfare that the Unsullied soldiers conduct will promote her aims.

The service of the Unsullied also reflects Dany's own movement into a new category of gender. During the considerations that lead up to the acquisition of this army, Ser Jorah tells the story of how the Unsullied bested the hyper-masculine Dothraki: "The Dothraki charged. The Unsullied locked their shields, lowered their spears, and stood firm. Against twenty thousand screamers with bells in their hair, they stood firm" (*SoS* 9 Daenerys 1: 97). The Dothraki are depicted as undisciplined, the Unsullied, by contrast, patient and calculating. The battle favors the Unsullied and demonstrates a privileging of self-mastery. We may take this analysis further by aligning these liminal figures with Bakhtin's celebration of the ambivalent crone. As ambivalent figures, the eunuchs, like the female hero, transcend "the polarization and dualism" of social disarray and instead contribute to order (Ordoñez 53). By acquiring this army, Dany is better able to promote the heroic, grotesque change she now embodies.

The manner in which Dany first attains this slave army and then gains its loyalty epitomizes her unique approach to heroism. She steals it from the slavers by sharing a single mind with her dragon, and she maintains control of it by earning the soldiers' loyalty, a task she accomplishes by granting each eunuch an individual voice and identity. Even though her most valued advisor warns her not to surrender Drogon, the dragon she will trade for the slaves, Dany ignores his words of caution (*SoS* 28 Daenerys 3: 308). Initially, this plan seems to contradict her values, as she appears to sell one of her children off to slavery, but she soon reveals that it supports them. After she has taken "the harpy's fin-gers," the whip that commands the Unsullied, she shouts, "IT IS DONE ... YOU ARE MINE!" (314). Making this open proclamation assures that the Unsullied will follow her commands, not the slavers'. After her assertion, one of the slavers notes that Drogon "will not come" (Ibid). To this she replies, "There is a reason. A dragon is no slave" (Ibid). Dany teaches the slavers that harnessing another's power is both unnatural and can have horrific consequences.

Even though Dany claims the slaves in order to slaughter and defeat the slavers, she soon offers her new soldiers positions of power and identity. One of her first decisions upon leaving Astapor is to command them to elect their own leaders. While the eunuchs occupy an accepted gender category, they are accepted, largely because they do not threaten order and are not considered deserving of power (Ringrose 2). Dany makes a unique, egalitarian change in their status by promoting these men and allowing them a voice in her army. Overwhelmingly, they elect as their highest ranking official Grey Worm, who soon becomes Dany's close advisor and confidant. She furthermore abolishes "the custom of giving the Unsullied new slave names every day" (*SoS* 44 Daenerys 7: 474). As part of their methods of subordinating these soldiers, some of whom were born free, the Astapori slavers denied the Unsullied names, which suggest both individuality and autonomy. In order to grant them an elevated place in her khalasar, Dany returns this privilege of individuality.

Dany continues to liberate slaves as she conquers new cities, an act that suggests she is concerned with the interests of the common people rather than the well-born. The way in which the slaves address her, and the manner in which she conquers and liberates cities, relates once more to Bakhtin's grotesque. In her fourth POV section, Dany again reminds us of the grotesque crone. Even though she can no longer physically reproduce, Dany becomes the "mother" to the slaves she has liberated, a name they chant to her when she greets them after Daario brings her victory. The role of mother represents one who both leads and protects (488). Here, the role is not uniquely aligned with a stage of femininity but instead with one who nurtures, cares for, and protects a community, an ambivalent figure who promotes social regeneration.

Dany further aids in social regeneration by liberating slaves when she conquers Meereen in sections six and seven and promotes the grotesque celebration of defecation, which relates and contributes to this regeneration. Just as King David in the Old Testament uses the subterranean water pipes to invade Jerusalem, Dany uses the sewers as a point of entry to take the city of Meereen "with sewer rats and a wooden cock" (*SoS* 72 Daenerys 6: 804), reminiscent of Bakhtin's positive representations of the lower stratum, specifically sexuality and defecation. For Bakhtin, humor is an important aspect of grotesque realism, because "laughter degrades and materializes" (Bakhtin, *RaHW* 20). Bakhtin connects degradation to the body's lower stratum, which represents defecation. While he admits that defecation has a negative connotation, he also acknowledges that it is an essential component of the life cycle and is therefore a central topic in grotesque humor (20–1). Clearly, this base entry, like humor, brings the stalwart conquerors back to earth. It forces them to recognize that they are a part of rather than above or apart from the community. These knights of the

Queen's Guard refer to themselves now as "sewer rats" (810). Furthering this sense of coming down to earth, Dany too aligns herself with the community after sacking the city. She destroys the harpy throne to sit atop a more modest bench. She aligns herself with the common people here as she abandons class signifiers and destroys abject symbols. Once again, the slaves of Meereen call her "mother" instead of "queen" (804). Clearly, the lowest of subjects, the kind Bakhtin venerates, believe that their queen represents them in a communal fashion. Bakhtin insists that grotesque realism represents the renewal and growth of the common people, not the social elite (Bakhtin, *RaHW* 19). Dany is not an aloof, status-conscious leader, and her ability to align herself with grotesque degradation provides her with strength and support.

In the final, climactic moments of *A Dance with Dragons*, Dany's connection to the universe around her—the universe of slaves, beasts, fertility, masculinity, and defecation—enables her to escape death and reengage her quest for the Iron Throne with the enduring strength provided by her bestial nature. To overcome difficulty and oppression in Meereen, Dany reestablishes her relationship with her mythic aspect, with Drogon, the strongest of her dragons, concerning whom a crisis arose when he was accused of having eaten a small child after the city's conquest. To pacify her subjects, Dany locks two of her dragons in a pit, but Drogon disappears and remains at large (*DwD* 3 Daenerys 1: 44) until the novel reaches a climax in the fighting pit when Barsena, a strong female fighter, is impaled upon a boar's tusk (*DwD* 53 Daenerys 9: 695). The death of this fighter, killed by a phallic object that assaults her inner thigh and crotch before "rooting out her entrails" (696), can be read as a metaphor for Dany's marriage to Hizdahr, which she thought would grant her strength and improve her position. Instead, Hizdahr has subjugated her and is, unknown to her, attempting to feed her poisoned locusts. Recognizing in Barsena's fate her own danger, Dany subconsciously summons Drogon, who flies into the pit and consumes both boar and woman as Dany echoes his cries. "Dany and Drogon scream as one" (697), Martin remarks, affirming their connectedness.

Drogon is the physical manifestation of Dany's strength, which defies oppressive order and exerts itself against a corrupt society. Re-mastering Drogon, her source of strength and power, Dany subdues him with a whip and rides him out of the pit in a moment that appears almost rapturously sexual (698). After ripping a spear out of Drogon's back that was hurled at her in a phallic attack against her feminine strength, Dany mounts the dragon: "Drogon's wide black wings beat the air. Dany could feel the heat of him between her thighs. Her heart felt as if it were about to burst. Yes, she thought, yes, now, now, do it, take me, take me, Fly" (699). This carnivalistic spectacle celebrates a queer, sexual moment, both masturbatory and bestial, in an indefinable act such as those which in medieval art signify the "affirmative resignification" of undesirable and oppressive cultural traits (Bildhauer and Mills 21). Here the image serves to illustrate a union of strength separate from Dany's experience in Meereen, since Drogon does not return her to the city but instead takes her to a remote location that she calls Dragonstone, "name of the ancient citadel where she'd been born" (*DwD* 72 Daenerys 10: 929). Connecting this barren spot to her own beginnings, Dany identifies Drogon and her current state with a key aspect of her identity and prepares to begin the most crucial phase of her development, the potential final rise to power.

Understanding that she cannot survive there, she searches for the river that will take her back to Meereen, to her husband and her lover. However, as she follows the moving water, symbol of life and progression, her journey reminds her of her original pursuit of the Iron Throne, and she recognizes she must revise her course. As she travels, earth, beast, excrement, and blood all function as symbols of hope, cleansing, and rejuvenation. She laughs over the open sores on her feet and her staggering stride, not abject signs of death and disease but symbols of movement and development. In this revisionary state, she acquires clarity about Hizdahr's true nature (935) as she pursues a course, characterized by earthly degradation, which leads her to physical, intellectual, and emotional clarity.

Other negatives also combine to bring about grotesque revelations that grant Dany insight and clarity. Nearly starved, she eats berries that prove to be poisonous and cause her to retch up "green slime" and defecate "brown water." The moment is so painful that she thinks, "I will die. I may be dying now" (937). However, she does not die but instead has feverish hallucinations that both empower and enlighten her. For one, she has a dream about her brother in which she finally understands that he was a monster who would have damaged the kingdom of Westeros. The vomit and defecation in this scene again link Dany's experience and source of power to grotesque realism: physical debasement, or lowering, is directly tied to mental enlightenment. The upper and lower strata work in harmony.

Her insight into her brother's true nature is followed by a vision of Quaithe, the seer who appeared in her garden and warned her at length and opaquely in her first POV section: "The glass candles are burning. Soon comes the pale mare, and after her the others. Kraken and dark flame, lion and griffin, the son's son and the mummer's dragon. Trust none of them. Remember the Undying. Beware the perfumed seneschal" (*DwD* 12 Daenerys 2: 153). Hidden behind a red mask that suggests powerful regenerative menstrual blood, Quaithe is a frightening vision of female strength. She has, moreover, the power to project herself as an illusion that visits Dany in this moment. Yet while she appears to be a frightening figure, she provides strength in the form of knowledge. Not only does she warn of the coming plague, but she also warns against those who threaten Dany's crown in distant lands and those close to her who wish to deceive her. Because of the insight she provides, Quaithe proves to be a celebration of social rejuvenation that helps Dany pursue her proper course to Westeros. Whereas Dany had appeared confused by Quaithe's prophesies initially, she begins to remember and learn from the seer's foresight as *A Dance with Dragons* progresses, for instance when she dreams about Hizdahr's impotence (*DwD* 44 Daenerys 7: 573).

Even though Dany does not follow Quaithe's guidance at first, she calls to her in her tenth and last POV section as the poison leaves her body, and she learns that the seeress is aligned with the dragons, her primary source of strength: "'Quaithe?' Dany called. 'Where are you Quaithe?' Then she saw. Her mask is made of starlight. 'Remember who you are, Daenerys,' the stars whispered in a woman's voice. 'The dragons know. Do you?'" (*DwD* 72 Daenerys 10: 936). This connection clearly suggests a Bakhtinian celebration, a union between the bestial and the feminine, two aspects of the "cosmic," the "unfinished and open body" of humanity that are "blended with the world, with animals, with objects" (Bakhtin, *RaHW* 27). Quaithe's mask, made up of stars, connects her to the celestial bodies that commonly signify cosmic order, insight, and direction. As she regains her strength, Dany embraces the wisdom and vision of this powerful woman and regains simultaneously a connection that suggests the text's veneration of the feminine and its relation to social order and rejuvenation.

When she wakes the next day, she has blood on her thighs, not a threatening blood that signifies her death to come but rather her "moon blood" (*DwD* 72 Daenerys 10: 938). While it frightens her at first, her period shows itself a symbol of strength and fertility. That she does not understand the reason for her heavy flow—perhaps a symbol of the return of her reproductive powers—suggests that she is still working on self-discovery. Nevertheless, her period is a promising sign, if not for another child then for her own rebirth and renewal as queen. Certainly, when she speaks with the grass in her hallucinatory state, it connects her moon blood to her having "turned against [her] children" (939). If this is the case, then her period has returned to remind her of her status as a mother. The blood, under the auspices of the crescent moon, represents the maternal, generative strength that Dany has recently ignored. Because she can no longer birth human children, we can tie this generative allusion to the growth of her relationship with the only children she will know, her dragons, which will help her fulfill her destiny.

As she moves forward, she follows the water, which "flows downhill" (939). The description of the stream she is following parallels that of the fluid running down her thighs. Here, a prophetic hallucination of Ser Jorah visits her to tell her that she has abandoned her true purpose. He reminds her that she is "the blood of the dragon" and not a "young girl" as a means of reminding her that she has strayed from her path to Westeros (941). Martin connects these images and functions of the lower extremities to Dany's renewal as a leader, and in doing so implies that these functions have the same life-giving power as Bakhtin claims they do. Soon after this point, Dany reconnects with Drogon and her blood-riders in the final moments of *A Dance with Dragons,* where her heroic potential is reasserted (942).

Even though Dany is represented as a heroine with great potential for power, Martin is not always kind in how he represents her. She is an empowered figure who attains mythical status, but Martin also represents her as a young girl who makes foolish and impulsive mistakes, and he colors these choices and experiences in a negative light. Additionally, she is perceived as a threat by those like the well-born citizens of the slave cities whose power she threatens. Dany's ability to overcome her shortfalls and defeat those who reject her aligns her with the grotesque, monstrous celebration of a new, all encompassing order. To illustrate her struggle in pursuing this new order, Martin presents Dany as not only empowered and grotesque, but also as one who is inexperienced, dependent upon others, and flawed. Martin himself admits, "All of the characters should be flawed; they should all have good and bad, because that's what I see. Yes, it's fantasy, but the characters still need to be real" (Martin qtd. in Salter). In Dany's experience and person, these flaws and imperfections, just as grotesque imagery suggests, are a key component of even her most positive moments. Dany would never have had the potential to achieve power had she not married Drogo and received her dragon eggs as a wedding gift, yet she would never have been able to realize that power if he had survived and their son had lived. Therefore, the situation is both disparaging and hopeful. In making connections between frightening visions of looming death and hopeful illustrations of social renewal, the text suggests the complexity of human life in general and the pursuit of power in particular.

To be queen of Westeros, Dany must shed certain fairytale illusions about her life as a woman, but in doing so she acquires the potential to unite and save a kingdom. Certainly, Sansa Stark, whose first blood also holds great significance in the series, likewise rejects fairytale illusions about knights and chivalry, which are most notably destroyed for her through her exposure to Joffrey's cruelties, as she matures and is forced to take responsibility for her own survival. Regardless, Sansa has little autonomy by the end of *A Feast for Crows,* at which point she is contained in the Eyrie under the guise of Alayne Stone and very much at the whim of Petyr Baelish and his ambitions. Thus far, Dany is the one who has been able to transform Martin's disillusionment into true heroic potential. The final images in *A Dance with Dragons* suggest such a potential is possible, yet Martin is known for undermining goodness in order to highlight humanity's devious nature. Even if Dany does perish prematurely, Elizabeth Ordoñez claims that such female heroism, even on the smallest scale, makes an impact: "Though perhaps never actually achieving radical and widespread transformation, [the heroine] nevertheless incarnates new beginnings, encodes the potential for renewed cultural values" (53). If Dany is not successful in achieving the Iron Throne, then she at least succeeds at liberating minds, and in many instances lives, from oppression in her world within the novel through her connection to the monstrous and grotesque.

Notes

1. In a recent interview with Jessica Salter from *The Telegraph,* Martin, whose fan base is at least fifty percent women, claims that he once considered himself to be a feminist but no longer does because "in the 80s and 90s I read some pieces by women saying that no man can ever be a feminist and you shouldn't call yourself that because it's hypocritical, so I backed off." In response to a follow-up question about how he feels now, he replies, "To me being a feminist is about treating men and women the same" (Martin qtd. in Salter).

2. Sue Vice notes that "Bakhtin suggests that the bodily element of carnival and grotesque realism concerns bodies in general and not bodies as distinguished by gender, which some see as transcending, and others as succumbing to, the usual gender stereotypes" (Vice 155–56). In this latter capacity, many feminist scholars find that Bakhtin's interpretation of the grotesque female body, specifically the hag, is limited and even negative. Mary Russo notes that "for the feminist reader, the pregnant hag is more than ambivalent. It is loaded with the connotations of fear and loathing associated with the biological processes of reproduction and aging" (Russo 219). More positively, Stephen Brown, Lorna Stevens, and Pauline Maclaren assert, "The carnivaleque has attracted feminist theorists because it provides a conceptual space where marginalized voices can theorize about the possibilities of resistance and, consequently, where established assumptions about gender ... may be renounced, rescinded, and reversed, albeit temporarily" (Brown, Stevens, and Maclaren 12). But Martin need not be a modern feminist to use these novels, space readers temporarily occupy and within which they can be therefore challenged, to oppose and reject an elitist world order and to embrace communal values.

3. Ordoñez is treating Dolores Medio's heroine, Irene, as heroic in this sense. Irene's aims appear to be more modest than Dany's, but she achieves significant goals that are also aligned with the improvement of a large community. Through her work as an educator, Irene succeeds at infusing the pre–civil war Spanish educational system with those liberal ideas that "would later flourish into the democracy of post–Franco Spain" (54). Even though Martin places his texts in a medieval context, he is still a contemporary writer who has potentially been influenced by similar modern ideas of heroism.

4. In *Powers of Horror: An Essay on Abjection*, Kristeva asserts that the abject is a lens through which we may interpret the female and decaying body. She claims that the abject is tied to all that is unclean—the menstrual and excremental—and it therefore undermines social order by highlighting its fragility. The abject also signifies the potential breakdown between self and other as well as the infringement upon personal autonomy. She notes that maternal power is strong and threatening because menstrual blood signifies the power of birth and life, which undermines a male-dominated social order. Therefore, fear of women,

more specifically mothers, is the fear of "generative power," and its potential threat to individual autonomy (77).

5. Julian of Norwich, a medieval Christian mystic, connects the menstruating woman to her vision of a woundlessly bleeding Christ, seeing both as signs of "redemptive suffering" (McAvoy 59). If Christ's abject bloodied form can be transformed into something positive, then the monstrous menstruation of women is a "potential source of salvation" (59). Her interpretation is clearly aligned with Bakhtin's understanding of the lower stratum, because it is connected with growth and development.

6. Her image, specifically through its associations to the lion, reflects the affirmative interpretations of the medieval monster that Bildhauer and Mills identify. Addressing the "man-monster," the creature that contains the body parts of man and beast, they note that such creatures in medieval art are an attempt by medieval people to understand change and transformation (Bildhauer and Mills 15). Like Bakhtin's, their analysis identifies this mode of representation as a reactionary tool against the regulatory severity of medieval culture. Like the raucous social inversions that occur during carnival, the hybrid creature becomes emblematic of the urge to express repressed desires and thus challenges the strictness of medieval order (19).

Works Cited

Adlam, Carol. "Ethics of Difference: Bakhtin's Early Writings and Feminist Theories." *Face to Face: Bakhtin in Russia and the West*. Eds. Carol Adlam, Vitalii Makhlin, and Alastair Renfew. Sheffield: Sheffield AP, 1997. Print.

Bakhtin, Mikhail. *Problems of Dostoyevsky's Poetics*. Ed. and trans. Caryl Emerson. Minneapolis: University of Minnesota Press, 1983. Print.

____. *Rabelais and His World*. Trans. Helene Iswolsky. Bloomington: Indiana University Press, 1984. Print.

Bildhauer, Bettina, and Robert Mills. "Introduction." *The Monstrous Middle Ages*. Ed. Bettina Bildhauer and Robert Mills. Toronto: University of Toronto Press, 2003. Print.

Brown, Stephen, Lorna Stevens, and Pauline Maclaran. "I Can't Believe It's not Bakhtin! Literary Theory, Postmodern Advertising, and the Gender Agenda." *Journal of Advertising* 28.1 (1999): 11–24.

Cohen, Jeffrey Jerome. *Of Giants: Sex, Monsters, and the Middle Ages*. Minneapolis: University of Minnesota Press, 1999. Print.

Kristeva, Julia. *Powers of Horror: An Essay on Abjection*. Trans. Leon Roudiez. New York: Columbia University Press, 1982. Print.

McAvoy, Liz Herbert. "Monstrous Masculinities." *The Monstrous Middle Ages*. Ed. Bettina Bildhauer and Robert Mills. Toronto: University of Toronto Press, 2003.

Miller, Sarah A. *Medieval Monstrosity and the Female Body*. New York: Routledge, 2010. Print.

Ordoñez, Elizabeth. "'Diario de una maestra': Female Heroism and the Context of War. *Letras Femeninas* 12.1 (1986): 52–9. Print.

Ringrose, Kathryn. *The Perfect Servant: Eunuchs and the Social Construction of Gender in Byzantium*. Chicago: University of Chicago Press, 2003.

Russo, Mary. "Female Grotesques: Carnival and Theory." Ed. Teresa de Lauretis. *Feminist Studies/Critical Studies*. Bloomington: Indiana University Press, 1986: 213–39. Print.

Salter, Jessica. "Game of Throne's George RR Martin: 'I'm a feminist at heart.'" *The Telegraph*. 1 April 2013. Web. 15 May 2013.

Vice, Sue. *Introducing Bakhtin*. Manchester: Manchester University Press, 1997. Print.

"A thousand bloodstained hands": The Malleability of Flesh and Identity

BETH KOZINSKY

Like most heroic fantasy, George R.R. Martin's *A Song of Ice and Fire* recreates the medieval world for his purposes. Though fantastic elements abound, Martin's series juxtaposes the constraints of chivalry, the distinct lines and loyalties in a coat of arms, with the corporeal realities, and often grotesqueries, that result from this game of thrones. Martin describes in grisly detail all that flesh is heir to. But before we dismiss such butchery as mere sensationalism, we must recognize the way in which these physical bodies illustrate, often in contrast to their heraldry, our characters' identities. Martin's focus on the material nature of bodies brings to the forefront the medieval notion that "the body somehow reflects the status of the soul" (Westerhof 38). For a medieval reader, a misshapen exterior reveals the corruption of the interior, and Martin certainly seems to play upon such expectations with characters like the dwarf, Tyrion. More often, though, the series depicts bodies that are injured or maimed rather than those born with a disability. When, for example, the Greatjon threatens Robb Stark, he loses two fingers to Robb's direwolf Grey Wind. The Greatjon accepts this loss nonchalantly and then becomes Robb's strongest supporter (*GoT* 54 Bran 6: 480). Part of the hand is taken forcibly into Robb's service while the injury signals a shift in loyalty to Ned Stark's heir. Through such injuries Martin embraces the connection between interior and exterior, yet he resists the long tradition of using injury as a mark of moral corruption. Despite the gritty realism of Martin's medieval world, the texts betray a more contemporary approach to both disability and identity. Though we encounter some congenital disabilities within this world, this essay will investigate amputation, principally of the hand, to better understand the conception of self throughout the series and its connection to the body.

Tracing heroic fantasy's lineage back to William Morris' reimagining of the Middle Ages, Raymond Thompson reminds us that fantasy has always illustrated another period's vision of medieval romance (212). As Mendlesohn explains in her discussion of immersive fantasy, readers are positioned between the fictional world and their own reality. The text "invites [them] to share not merely a world, but a set of assumptions" even while the readers retain one foot in their own world's beliefs (Introduction xx). In this way Martin presents an "authentic" medieval world while indirectly commenting upon it. For example, the inhabitants of the Seven Kingdoms accept Tyrion's monstrous shape as physical proof of his debauched character even while his chapters reveal a far more complex person. Martin disputes the immorality assigned to the disabled, in both medieval and modern texts without avoiding the connection between interior and exterior.[1] In cases of change to the body, as in amputation, physical changes signal shifts in identity without assigning value to one form or the other. Martin manages to avoid such moral weight by presenting a world in which its characters are further and further removed from any permanence of self, and thus from an idea of lost self. Granted, fantasy often considers questions of the self through "magical operations such as shape shifting, transfer of personalities, or reduplication of characters" (Attebery 74). However, like the medieval tales that heroic fantasy often imitates, such texts usually conceive of physical change as obscuring or revealing the "true" self (Bynum, *Metamorphosis and Identity* 23). According to Thompson, fantasy is continually tasked with "self-realization" for its characters, but such fantasy assumes there is a constant self to discover or lose (222). By resisting the concept of a constant self, Martin recasts the meaning of disability for his characters.

Perhaps because of heroic fantasy's lineage, disabled characters are rare, but where they do surface, often a "burden of symbolism" accompanies them (Stemp 9). The rarity of a damaged body sets it up as Other, signaling moral or mental corruption. In the *Sword of Shanara*, by Terry Brooks, Panamon Creel is a con-man, and though the loss of his hand is an accident, the pike that replaces it signals a less-than-trustworthy character. Defying the pity his weakness illicits, Raistlin (*Dragonlance Chronicles*, Margaret Weis and Tracy Hickman) seems to act villainously because of his disability. Disabled characters tend to foil, as villains or sidekicks, the more able-bodied protagonists; even damaged heroes, though, mirror their moral corruption through the burden of the body. For example, Roland Deschain (King's *The Gunslinger* series) loses two fingers after sacrificing the boy Jake. As a gunslinger, Roland's morality is already questionable, but the guilt he attaches to this act suggests that it contributes to his fragmentation. And Moorcock's Elric (The Elric Saga) is a "neurasthenic albino" who gives souls to a god of chaos. Though Moorcock created him as "a deliberate anti-thesis of earlier fantasy heroes," the dramatic swing away from tradition still holds to a conservative view of the body in which physical frailty signals moral ambiguity (Mendlesohn and James 78). A fruitful comparison can be made between Martin and J.R.R. Tolkien in their treatment of disability. Though much has been said of how these two authors diverge and converge, their differing treatment of bodies helps to understand their texts' assumptions. Despite innumerable battles, Tolkien's characters in *The Lord of the Rings*, with few exceptions, remain whole. Some die, but it is rare to see a surviving injury. Where there is loss, in the case of Frodo's finger, the amputation signals Frodo's loss of innocence. While the reader understands that Frodo's mind is affected by the one ring long before this moment, it is the body that fully reveals this change. That he is later referred to as Frodo of the Nine Fingers reinforces the change of body and substance. Tolkien recognizes the malleability of the self, but such changes are the regrettable result of evil forces, as in Frodo and Gollum's exposure to the ring's influence. Tolkien's world imagines fractures and shifts in identity as the exception to the rule and favors those original identities as "true." By contrast, Martin's world is littered with scarred and maimed characters to show the consequences of such a brutal world. Physical change here is commonplace and does signal a shift in identity. Yet Martin complicates situations that would otherwise appear to be judgments upon characters. Jaime Lannister might deserve punishment for his crimes, but he loses his hand through a series of unrelated circumstances and political maneuvering. Moreover, Jaime is a flawed and conflicted character to begin with, but the loss of his hand does not represent the cutting away of his corruption. Therefore, the amputation is not the destiny of a character becoming himself; it is simply the beginning of a new role for the character. Martin himself has said he hopes to illustrate a more complex world than the good and evil that Tolkien depicts. In an interview with *The Detroit Free Press* he said that "the battle between good and evil is waged every day within the individual human heart," and Martin resists writing that battle upon the flesh (Lacob).

Yet the importance of the body is not diminished. Jaime Lannister's entire identity is shaped around what his hand can do with a sword. This link between identity and hands crops up again and again. Keep in mind that Davos Seaworth is identified by his missing fingers, and in order to pass off Reek as Theon Greyjoy, his former self, Roose Bolton gives him gloves with stuffing where his missing fingers should have been. Even Cersei Lannister, whose agency comes from her beauty, fears a loss of power and self in terms of her hands. In a nightmare where she is naked and vulnerable she cuts her hand on the Iron Throne. Upon waking she must check to see if her hand is injured as a way of knowing how she herself fares (*FfC* 4 Cersei 1: 46–47). Though Martin scars his inhabitants in other ways, the hand on some level becomes the seat of self. In a study of the medieval view of the body, Katherine Rowe in "God's Handy Worke" explains the metaphoric significance long attributed to hands. In discussing how hand clasps and pledged hands solidify contracts and claims of fealty, she explains "the hand represents and effects a point of contact between collective notions of person and the world of interiority, intentions, and will" (286). In other words, the hand functions as the most clear representation of who a person is through its actions and connections to others. Still, Rowe imagines whole and able hands in someone's service. But what might an injured hand represent? After illustrating how identity is wrapped up in these hands, Martin then rends them apart, in some instances, piece by piece. We might then expect characters to demonstrate similarly scarred or fragmented identities, shadows of the former self. However, while the wounded do undergo changes to identity, the text resists the idea that they are crippled, psychically or physically. Though the people of the Seven Kingdoms often view those injured as broken, these characters continue to function within the story. Therefore, rather than viewing the shift in identity as a diminishment, Martin's text proposes a redirection of the self. This view of a newly adapted self echoes the notion in disability studies of a shift in the horizon for a body that undergoes trauma. The horizon orients our perception of the world, and as Miho Iwakuma explains in "The Body as Embodiment: Investigation of the Body by Merleau-Ponty," acclimating to a newly disabled body causes a new horizon to "[open] from a different angle" (80). One horizon or view of the world is not privileged over another. Iwakuma uses this idea to explain how newly disabled persons come to terms with their physical realities.[2] Eyes are a tool just as a cane is, but someone who becomes blind must embody the cane, as he once did his eyes. Iwakuma notes the marked difference between those newly impaired and those born with impairment to explain that much of the issue lies in changing one's view of the self. The analogy illustrates that an amputee is not conceived as a lesser person or as the "true" self realized through physical form. Because the self is tied to the body, each shift in identity is "true." Though Martin has created a medieval world that believes in a permanent and determined self, the text betrays this more complex understanding of self and body.

In his effort to collapse the divide between mind and body, the interior and exterior, Merleau-Ponty wrote that "the body is also what fleshes out a world for us: it is the living interpreter of the world" (qtd. in Glendinning 106). Thus the self is shaped by its environment through the body. And Martin's use of changing point-of-view chapters allows us to see how each self/body interprets its world. However, the society that Martin presents also interprets the bodies it sees, and its view is often in keeping with the medieval notion of moral corruption written upon the body. Nor has this idea entirely disappeared from contemporary literature. As Mitchell and Snyder argue in their work *Narrative Prosthesis*, disability most often "serves as a metaphorical signifier of social and individual collapse" (47). While this practice is not unique to heroic fantasy, critics have noted a dearth of positive portrayals of the disabled in the genre.[3] Such scarcity means those few exceptions are burdened with significance beyond the character, for "disability inaugurates the act of interpretation" (6). Still, representations of disability can also be used to subvert expectations. By aligning the reader with particular characters/bodies, Martin highlights the way in which these bodies are so often misinterpreted. By denying the body's role as moral sign, Martin invites new interpretations on the malleable form and substance of his characters. In a series centered upon changing loyalties, these losses of flesh often signal the creation and shifting of social connections which make up the self.

Injury and amputation of the hand in *A Song of Ice and Fire* often assign such change as proof of loyalty. In Martin's world, loyalty can make you a lion or a wolf, so the question of alliance is central to identity. In a discussion of how hands mark fealty, the most obvious example would be the Hand of the King. However, this hand is metaphoric and given in exchange for wealth and power. Certainly, Martin's text is interested in the body as commodity, but here a whole body becomes a piece of the king. The title brings to mind other metaphors of the body politic that are in keeping with a medieval world view, for example the king's health as an indicator of the country's health.[4] But Martin distinguishes between the public post of Hand and physical *marks upon* the hand. Westeros may have its customs, but the texts themselves value the body over empty gestures. Rather than physically changing one's form or identity, the advisor post functions like other cultural signs of allegiance. Giving Ned Stark the silver hand is a mark of the service Robert asks of him, like the cloak given at marriage or the banners raised to proclaim feudal loyalties. These cultural markers, in a sense, cover the body in one loyalty or another. But cloaks and banners are easily exchanged. In exchange for the power of this silver hand, Ned pledges his service to Robert. When Ned returns the hand, he loses position without affecting his identity. And, in fact, it is Ned's inability to adapt that leads to his death. Rather than the outward signs of power, Martin allows us to see shifts in character through the markings of the flesh. This emphasis on materiality helps to illustrate the "permanence" of self in Martin's world. Consider for a moment the way in which a tattoo is permanent, but anyone with a tattoo knows that *permanent* isn't exactly the right word. In the same way Martin's characters are stable but mutable. Such mutable power further distances Martin's texts from the medieval world he imitates, by illustrating a post-modern conception of self, one shaped by a collection of social ties that are ever-changing.

Martin introduces characters with physical markers to help keep them straight. This is a practical move on the author's part, but it also invites questions about the body's role in identity, because he is always cutting off pieces, particularly hands. If there is indeed such a strong psychosomatic connection, we must ask ourselves how the change in form will affect so many characters whose hands are injured. Davos serves as our model for change, introduced to the reader as a smuggler turned knight. Stannis cuts off his fingers for his crimes but rewards him with a title for bringing stolen food to the starving. Davos' dramatic change in status is signaled with the loss of his fingers even though Stannis is clear about the separate causes for his judgment. The reader only has the report of this transformation since Davos is introduced after the fact, but Martin allows readers to witness the ongoing transformations of characters like Jaime Lannister and Theon Greyjoy. By grounding these transformations in the form of the hand, Martin illustrates the strange relationship between body and self. This is not an issue unknown to medieval writers, but the conclusions Martin's series draws out makes clear the way postmodern conceptions of identity are placed within a medieval world.

As Caroline Bynum notes in *Metamorphosis and Identity*, European writers in the twelfth-century also grappled with questions of how physical change affects someone.[5] The increase in stories of werewolves and other shape-shifters at that time suggests an anxiety over change that may have been the result of larger societal changes of the period.[6] However, while a change to one's form might threaten one's substance, most characters reveal their true selves through such change or are returned to their true forms by the end. Bynum uses Marie de France's story of a werewolf with human eyes to illustrate the idea that one's substance remains in spite of physical change (170). Though stuck in this form for many years, the creature still pays homage before his king, and for that deference is later able to transform back into a man. Therefore, the wolf form is simply a covering over the true man. By contrast, the man's wife, who wickedly keeps the man a wolf, loses her nose when her husband, in wolf form, attacks her. Thus, both characters show what they really are through their actions and later their appearance. Characters, at this time, "tend to display an essential self" even when disguised (23). By returning characters to their "true" forms in the end, medieval writers avoid acknowledging any change in identity.

This insistence on stability also surfaces in the developing notion of the noble body, the physical form of virtue. As Danielle Westerhof explains, nobility as a concept in the twelfth-century was increasingly considered "*interior* and *innate* to the members of the aristocratic elite, rather than something which could be acquired as easily as money or political influence" (34). In response to the threat of lower classes' social mobility, the aristocracy developed the myth of an inherently virtuous class in both soul and body. Therefore the best men, by blood, will reveal themselves by form and manner. The people of Westeros seem to embrace such an idea when describing certain men, again through the use of hands. When Ser Alliser Thorne barks, "Your hands were made for manure shovels, not for swords" (*GoT* 42 Jon 5: 371) at the new recruits to Castle Black, we are confronted by the assumption that heredity will dictate both form and expectations, neither of which will change throughout these men's lives. Yet Martin also thumbs his nose at such ideas in the story of Duck. In *A Dance with Dragons*, Ser Rolly Duckfield explains an altercation with a nobleman's son. Rolly recounts, "He told me my hand was made to hold a hammer, not a sword. So I went and got a hammer and beat him with it" (*DwD* 9 Tyrion 3: 116). Here physical strength trumps the abstract idea of heredity and problematizes the world's assumptions about the signification of the body. Though immersed within this fantasy world, the reader is continually confronted by evidence that refutes the idea of innate nobility even while all of Westeros holds to it. Much more than medieval writers who only hinted at a difference between form and substance, Martin's characters complicate the idea of the noble body. However, they cannot overturn it. Rolly runs away to become a sellsword after this incident, and his violence toward a superior is seen by the world as proof of his baseborn instincts. Thus we see the reverse of the noble body. Bad blood will out; interior corruption will eventually reveal itself upon the body. But when nature doesn't cooperate, medieval authorities used amputation to make this corruption apparent.

As David King notes, legal documents from the twelfth and thirteenth century in northern France "indicate amputation as punishment for several infractions" (40). Henry II in the Assize of Northampton called for amputating the limbs of felons (Westerhof 118). William I of England ordered traitors to lose their eyes as well as their hands or feet, but to be kept alive so that their mutilated forms could tell the story of their crimes (King 39). It's unclear how often these laws were enacted, or if anyone could survive such trauma, but the audience of the 12th-century poems King investigates were clearly familiar with the idea of amputation as punishment. This idea of crimes written upon the body is interesting when applied to Martin's work. King argues that while the heroes suffer injury, only villains ever lose their hands. Suffering is part of a hero's work, but amputation of the hand implies a corrupt character, which would dispute the idea of the noble body. Westerhof also notes increasingly harsh punishments for traitorous aristocrats in the thirteenth century, which included cutting off the person's hands and hanging them about his neck (118–20). Aristocrats were formerly given the option of exile, but it would seem that alongside the developing philosophy of nobility, traitors were dealt with to advance the idea of the noble body. Rather than noting a change in the person's substance, such punishments only revealed the non-noble's "true" form through amputation.[7] The corrupt body reveals the moral corruption of the traitor. Martin, however, gives us a wealth of characters with varying degrees of corruption while using amputation and injury of the hand to different effect. He repeatedly presents situations in which theft and treason are answered with amputation of the offending limb. Randyll Tarly orders that a man cheating at dice lose a finger while the man who stabs the first receives a nail through his palm (*FfC* 15 Brienne 3: 207). Ser Jorah threatens to cut off Viserys' hand if he steals a dragon egg (*GoT* 47 Daenerys 5: 414). And Erik Anvil-Breaker of the Iron Islands sets his worth by how many thieves' "hands [he's] smashed to pulp with [his] hammer" (*FfC* 20 The Drowned Man: 272). Such punishments physically reference the crime, and while other body parts are equally vulnerable, as in the case of Illyn Payne, who loses his tongue for speaking words against King Aerys (*FfC* 28 Jaime 3: 394), Martin returns to hands again and again. Yet we never get the sense that evil men fail in body and thereby lose limbs. Amputation for thieves forms part of the set dressing to this world without hinting at the question of fairness or the amount of corruption a thief may have. Though Davos Seaworth receives punishment for his crimes in a clear manner, he seems an exception to the rule. Characters like Jaime Lannister and Theon Greyjoy are injured without even the pretense of justice. Jaime's loss is a result of political maneuvering, and Theon might deserve punishment, but he only receives it because his jailer is a sadist. Noble or not, these bodies are divorced from moral representation. Rather than reveal the substance that was always there, these marks upon the flesh signal shifts in identity.

Now certainly there are examples of corrupt bodies. We can logically understand the smell emanating from Tywin Lannister's corpse after being disemboweled by a quarrel (*FfC* 8 Cersei 2: 103, 107), but the rotten nature of the man seems to be on display here. Similarly, Victarion's wounded hand festers in *A Dance with Dragons* (*DwD* 57 The Iron Suitor 1: 746–47). Though he suffered the injury in an unrelated battle, he nurses the hand alongside his desire to kill his brother. Here it would seem that the body is reflecting moral corruption of the sort David King mentions. For a medieval audience, both disease and disfigurement were linked to moral corruption; illness "was considered the result of an internal imbalance of the humours and … could be taken as a physical manifestation of a lack of moral control over one's flesh" (Westerhof 39–40).[8] But a distinction needs to be made between disfigurement and disease for Martin. Though a wealth of his characters are cut, their wounds rarely suffer from infection. In fact, most characters who don't die immediately from injuries tend to recuperate so they can tell the tale of their dismemberment. Such resilience supports the notion that Martin's use of amputation functions separately from those physical signs of corruption. While injuries signal the effect of outside forces upon one's form, and thus upon his identity, the decay of flesh is internal, even if a modern audience understands disease as an outside influence. Used sparingly, the presence of decay seems to hint at the flesh's talent for self-destruction.[9] Rather than transforming and adapting to outside influences, the flesh dissolves. With so many fluid identities within the series, dissolution would seem to be a constant threat against identity, but the men and women of the Seven Kingdoms seem to accept such malleability without hazard. At least in cases of amputation, Martin does not write a man's sins upon his flesh. Even where we might see redemption, such change is secondary to the shifts in identity and loyalty.

Both Davos Seaworth and Jaime Lannister admit to wrongs in their past and recognize that the loss of their fingers and hand respectively has changed their lives forever. For Davos, his life as a smuggler ends when he brings supplies to the besieged forces at Storm's End under Stannis Baratheon's command. While we never know Davos before this transformation, the fact that his smuggling saved people from starving opposes shaping his story as a tale of redemption. We cannot know Davos' character from before, but what seems clear is the complete shift in loyalties that accompanies Davos' loss of fingers. Davos' identity as a smuggler is cut away at the same time he is raised to a knight. This trajectory runs counter to the concept of the noble body, for it is as an unwhole body and a loyal and honest supporter of Stannis that Davos enters the aristocracy. As part of a conversion narrative, Davos' fingers might be read as the corrupt part of him cut away, much as John of Salisbury, writing in the twelfth century, saw traitors as "corrupt matter which had to be expelled from society in the way a surgeon would cut away diseased limbs" (Westerhof 106). Yet Davos carries his fingertips in a pouch around his neck, and even holds them as a lucky charm in times of trouble. The stumps Stannis left him identify Davos as the Onion Knight when storms beach him at Sisterton on his way to White Harbor to see Wyman Manderly (*DwD* 10 Davos 1: 124). Therefore, any sense of corruption in flesh is dispelled even if characters continue to read the world this way.

Though Jaime bemoans the name that Westeros has given him, he explicitly refers to his lost hand as *the hand that made me Kingslayer* (*SoS* 38 Jaime 5: 419). He insists to Brienne of Tarth that she should be pleased; the hand he used to commit regicide and incest is gone. Displacing his own agency onto the hand, Jaime distances himself from his own sins as if his corruption was but one piece of him. And the rotting hand about his neck reinforces this idea. We might then expect a reformed Jaime to emerge; however, Salisbury's metaphor is problematized when Jaime reveals the crimes of King Aerys and his choice to kill the king for the sake of the country. In presenting a corrupt and mad king, Martin upends the image of a stable government "body" from which corruption must be cut away, and the clear boundaries between loyal subjects and traitors Salisbury's view entails. In his explanation to Brienne, Jaime mockingly ascribes to the notion of embodied sin and then exposes the shortcomings of such a view. As Jaime puts it, "The goat [Vargo Hoat] had robbed him of his glory and his shame, both at once," but the question that now follows Jaime is who will he be, not will he be good (*SoS* 38 Jaime 5: 419). In this way Martin resists the tendency to morally situate the flesh itself. The rotting hand hanging around Jaime's neck seems to recall those aristocratic traitors in the 12th century, sentenced to death and dismemberment, so that their sins are clearly displayed. Yet his "sentence" comes from a man trying to save his own skin.

David King also responds to the reading of injury as redemption in a discussion of Pope Leo I. Recounted in Jacobus' *The Golden Legend* from the 15th century, the story of Leo's lost hand would seem to affirm the view that injuries can illustrate one's virtue. Taking literally Jesus' words in Matthew 5:30, Leo cut off his own hand when tempted by the flesh of a woman. He hid himself from view, but the Virgin Mary appeared to him and restored his hand to him (I: 339). This miracle illustrates both Leo's commitment to his faith and his redemption. However, as King notes, Leo hides himself because the "missing member imposes shame and suspicion on the amputee" (39). Though Leo obeys the word of God in avoiding sin, even he recognizes the way wounds are read. Unwhole bodies signal sin, not newfound grace. He is only redeemed when his body is whole once again. Similarly, King Nuada in the Irish saga *The Second Battle of Mag Tuired,* is deemed unfit to rule when he loses his hand in battle. His brother constructs for him a hand of silver that later transforms into a hand of flesh; once he is whole, he retrieves his throne. In Nuada's case, no crime or sin is committed, yet injury to the body is not read as proof of bravery or virtue. The physical proof of an internal deficiency is more important than the circumstances surrounding one's injury. And while Jaime is neither a saint nor a king, his story remarks upon this medieval tradition of regeneration and return.

Unlike Leo, Jaime is ashamed both of his stump and the golden hand he receives later; he will never return to his former wholeness. The gaudiness of the gold hand makes this clear even while it highlights society's need to hide disfigurements. Made from the gold of Casterly Rock, the hand stamps Jaime as a true Lannister. This material sign of heredity is similar to other marks of loyalty, and could signal the "true" hero emerging. However, Martin makes a distinction between the story written upon the flesh and the trappings used to hide it. By entering Jaime's thoughts after the amputation, we know his old loyalties are shifted, if not severed all together along with his hand. Jaime's hand does not function as sacrifice to a master, as Davos' does, yet Jaime's loyalties are so closely aligned to his self-image that this change in body immediately registers as a change in identity and social ties. Consider for a moment Jaime and Cersei's relationship as twins and lovers. As children they were indistinguishable from each other, and their devotion to one another stems from this interchangeableness of identity and form. Cersei even says that when they make love she feels "whole" (*GoT* 46 Eddard 12: 405). But Jaime's disfigurement marks him now as separate and alien. The erosion of their relationship on his return to King's Landing reveals the degree to which he has changed internally, a change that the golden hand attempts to mask. Moreover, Jaime's inability to relate to the whole and unblemished Cersei coincides with his growing concern for the "ill-favored" Brienne of Tarth. Though not impaired, Brienne's strength and lack of feminine grace has earned her the name "freak" on several occasions. While whole she is in a sense as disfigured as Jaime, and their friendship may signal that like Tyrion he is now an advocate for "cripples, and bastards, and broken things" (*GoT* 25 Bran 4: 206).

Jaime's hand becomes first a rotten, then a golden, reminder of his loss. By contrast, Davos' finger pouch serves as proof of his good fortune (*CoK* 11 Davos 1: 113). Though the flesh itself functions differently, both Davos and Jaime experience shifts in loyalty, and thus identity. And since so much of *A Song of Ice and Fire* revolves around such loyalties, it makes sense that exterior changes mirror interior changes of alliance rather than virtues and vices. Martin has peopled his world with a multitude of mangled and unwhole bodies. If such shapes display moral corruption, it is only because his texts seem to resist the idea that any bodies are truly noble. Moreover, the series does not depict these injured bodies as disabled. Davos still sails and is of great value to Stannis as a loyal subject with a smuggler's abilities. Jaime views himself as disabled, but without losing a man he is able to open the gates of Riverrun. It seems unlikely that the old Jaime would have fared so well, if we consider Loras Tyrell as a younger version of Jaime. Also facing a siege, Loras rushes in with full faith in his body's ability, and is wounded (*DwD* 55 Cersei 1: 717). Jaime bemoans his loss of identity as a swordsman even while he explores his abilities as a diplomat. Thus, the mark upon the flesh anchors these characters in a world of fluid identity.

Martin's emphasis on hidden identities and alliances illustrates what Vitz and Felch term a post-modern conception of self: multi-faceted, adaptable to changing environments, and created through social connections. Such opportunity for change further complicates the game of thrones. Neither the amorphous nature of identity nor the connection to post-modernism is new to fantasy criticism. As Jim Casey explains, "fantasy by its very nature, challenges the dominant political and conceptual ideologies in a manner similar to that of post-modernism" (115). And each new permutation of the medieval in heroic fantasy comments on what has come before. Yet a truly post-modern conception of self seems scarce in the genre, as is the presence of disabled bodies. Brian Attebury describes character within fantasy as a tension between the individual and his or her archetypal function in the text.[10] An ordinary boy comes to accept his role as hero. Change takes place; characters struggle with identity. Still this construction limits characters to a function they are destined to fulfill, much like the "true" revealed identity at the end of medieval texts. "No character is complete until she has encountered her own mythic narrative" (85). Thus heroic fantasy mimics the medieval culture that inspires it. However, in Martin's world a shift in identity does not suggest loss or gain for a character, merely change. Both the body and self are malleable, and such malleability comes to represent the very essence of humanity. While the people of the Seven Kingdoms still perceive injured bodies as other, the real threat to humanity rests with the White Walkers. As a mysterious species from the North, the White Walkers function as the series' Other, but it is with an army of the human dead that they lead their assault. The Others and their undead servants threaten not just lives, but the malleability of identity. For the dead may walk, but they cannot change.

Even here the body creates an understanding of self, or lack thereof. Martin takes some care in describing the hands of wights. Osha fears their cold black hands, and Bran's guide Coldhands explains that blood congealing in the body's extremities causes the change in color while the rest of the body becomes ghostly white (*DwD* 5 Bran 1: 69). Even these supernatural figures are anchored to their own corporeality. And in case there were any doubt whether hands are of significance, let's remember that Lord Commander Mormont's stand against the wights is on an outpost known as "the Fist of the First Men" (*SoS* 19 Samwell 1: 199–202). But because wights are created after death almost by happenstance of where they fall, the text does not use becoming a wight as a moral judgment on individual characters. Instead the struggle for identity is highlighted here. The wights are rarely named as individuals, and even one distinct from the others, Coldhands, if he is in fact another wight, only bears a name of description. Perhaps this too can be read as a mark of loyalty to the White Walkers, who only come when it is very cold. But the dead flesh here also reflects the absence of self. They are known by their hands, but only in the way that the flesh is othered, not by way of the work and experience imprinted on the hands.

The Stone Men who live on the banks of the Rhoyne present a variation on this theme. For while they are yet alive, the greyscale that takes over their bodies also takes over their minds (*DwD* 19 Tyrion 5: 237). The physical transformation of flesh to stone deprives the body of its ability to go on changing. The Stone Men's madness comes from a kind of stasis in which they await their own deaths and try to take others with them. Thus in both cases the petrification of flesh is what causes this loss of self. Granted, greyscale is a slow, degenerative disease. We might consider this another example of decaying flesh and dissolution, a sin that slowly eats to the heart of a person. But the material body of someone with greyscale remains. In fact, they become like stone. Illyrio Mopatis keeps the preserved hands of his wife, who succumbed to greyscale, in his bedroom (*DwD* 6 Tyrion 2: 80). The flesh becomes its own monument. But ironically, what Illyrio remembers most about his wife is the softness of her hands. Here, the literal malleability of her flesh identified her as a person. Once the ability to change is lost so is the self.

We may go on in later books to watch this slow petrification of self in the character Griff. Having saved Tyrion from the water, he hides from the others the greyscale spreading along his hand in *A Dance with Dragons* (*DwD* 25 The Lost Lord: 319). Functioning as a memento mori, the affliction motivates Griff to finish his tasks before he is no more. Instead of bearing the mark of his master, Aegon Targaryen, who he hopes to return to the throne, Griff's flesh illustrates the paradox of one's dissolving substance in a stabilized form. In this way Martin's world argues for the interdependency between body and self. One is not undone by change, but by its absence. Rather than portray characters on quests of "self-realization," Martin illustrates the malleable nature of identity while recognizing that it requires an equally malleable form. Therefore, the greyscale functions differently than a wound. The shape of the body remains the same even while the skin greys and becomes like stone. The self-exam that both Tyrion and Griff go through to watch for the disease is the pricking of their fingers (*DwD* 25 The Lost Lord: 319; *DwD* 23 Tyrion 6: 277). The vulnerability of the flesh, the ability to feel pain, is used to prove one's humanity. By contrast, greyscale mocks the idea of a stable self while representing the threat to a malleable self. Rather than fear mental fragmentation or diminishment when a character changes, the fluid and de-centered post-modern self is threatened by stasis. The reader struggles to define and decode so many changing characters by identifying them with the archetypes common to heroic fantasy. But this is a doomed quest. The postmodern self can never be fully defined. To do so is to end it. And thus we see creeping into Martin's world of medieval assumptions a contemporary view of identity.

Ironically it is the most ignoble character who seems to hint at the perseverance of a "true" self in spite of changes to form. We are never given Theon Greyjoy's perspective as a ward of the Starks, but it's later made clear that he has always struggled with conflicting loyalties (*CoK* 12 Theon 1: 135–36). Theon is from the Iron Islands but was raised in the North. He follows Rob Stark into battle but then betrays him by the command of his father. Theon attempts to prove whose side he's on through his actions, but it is physical change instead that decides his loyalties. Captured by the bastard Lord Ramsay, Theon is tortured with flaying until he asks that the flayed parts of his body be cut off. When we meet Reek, the identity Ramsay gives Theon, he has already given up three fingers and two toes (*A DwD* 13 Reek 1: 167). And such an active role in his physical transformation makes Reek's sacrifice of flesh all the more clearly a mark of his loyalty, even if that loyalty comes out of pain and fear. When asked why he's still alive, Reek answers, "The gods are not done with me ... Lord Ramsay is not done with me" (*DwD* 47 A Ghost in Winterfell: 612). The parallel structures of this statement suggest that on some level they are the same, and Theon has become a kind of blood sacrifice. The pieces Ramsey takes from him transform Theon into Reek, and this shift in identity is all the more dramatic because his chapter heading bears his new name.

However, Theon/Reek continually practices his identity by guarding his thoughts. He knows who he is by his body and outward show—smell, clothes, and missing appendages. However, the ghost of his past self still nags at him the way that his phantom pains do. Iwakuma explains that amongst amputees "a phantom limb signifies that the person's body image has not matched the actual body situation" (81). Theon's physical and mental struggle reminds us that the transformation is not instantaneous, yet the interior and exterior still mirror each other since in both cases there exists some ambiguity. He remembers the day *"Theon Greyjoy died, to be reborn as Reek"* (*DwD* 38 The Prince of Winterfell: 489), yet thoughts belonging to Theon continue to emerge, causing a good deal of anguish for the creature Reek. His attempt to save Jeyne Poole, betraying his master, in contrast, suggests a more constant self lurking within. Perhaps the "real" Theon is only lying in wait under a false form like the wolf of Marie de France's story. Certainly Martin is playing here with questions of self, but this conflict only arises because Reek is asked to dress like Theon again. In order to give away Jeyne Poole as the bride Arya Stark, lending credibility to her union with Lord Ramsay, Theon Greyjoy must play-act his old identity (485–86). He's given fine clothes and stuffed gloves to hide his missing fingers. And surrounded by the walls in which he was raised, Theon does recover some of his old self. When he dresses for the part, the text refers to him as Theon. Still these are merely the trapping of what he was. The flesh remains malleable, but it cannot regenerate.

Theon's escape and subsequent abandonment of the identity Reek might be read as proof of a constant self, but it is unlikely that after such tortures Theon will ever be the same. Moreover, the change of reference to multiple characters in chapter titles suggests that no one identity is true. Chapters titled "Theon" are not privileged over those bearing Reek's name. Instead they are all true for their moment. Therefore, Martin does not illustrate permanent change through physical forms but the continuation of change over form and substance. Lasting change only comes with the petrification of the flesh, and the resulting "stable" self is actually the end of self. By flipping the script on the interior/exterior connection that readers expect, Martin refigures the way in which injury "reveals" a character without denying the body's connection to the self. In Martin's world the ability to adapt is paramount to survival. Therefore, the disability from the loss of a hand, a tongue, a nose signals a change in self rather than its fragmentation or destruction.

Yet, the threat of further fragmentation is there. With the help of the Lord of Light, Thoros of Myr brings Beric Dondarrion back to life after a number of mortal wounds (*SoS* 40 Arya 7: 443–44). But with each return, he becomes less and less himself. The self is made finite in its connection to the pieces of the body, and while Martin's text suggests that there is always the possibility of change while the flesh lives, we are left to wonder how fragmented one can be before the self is annihilated. This danger is especially relevant for a character like Arya. Her survival has depended on her ability to adapt and trade one alias for another. She remains physically whole, yet the text repeatedly amputates her from the families she joins. And in the House of Black and White, the Kindly Man explains the end result of an identity disconnected from others. In explaining the cost for her education, he says,

> Stay, and the Many-Faced God will take your ears, your nose, your tongue. He will take your sad grey eyes that have seen so much. He will take your hands, your feet, your arms and legs, your private parts. He will take your hopes and dreams, your loves and hates. Those who enter His service must give up all that makes them who they are [*FfC* 23 Arya 2: 320].

Even in our own world, taking on a new persona in order to serve in a religious house is not so strange an idea. But this man describes the self in terms of physical pieces and experiences. Hands are only a fraction of what she will lose, but the list acknowledges the role of the body in creating identity. We later learn that this description is not mere metaphor. In order to carry out the work of the temple, Arya is literally given a new face. This process causes her great pain, but the greater danger is losing her past and forgetting her family. The House of Black and White requires the erasure of self so that personal prejudices are never involved in the many-faced god's work to give certain people death. Here, identity is understood as a series of affiliations, but they are erased through the flesh. And an ever-changing body makes it harder to remember who one is.

However, the Kindly Man also recognizes identity in physical objects outside the body. Before her training can begin in the House of Black and White,

Arya must give up all of her possessions. Though not a sacrifice of flesh, throwing her belongings into the canal still represents a shift in identity. Arya relinquishes her possessions, but hides her sword "Needle" under a stone (*FfC* 23 Arya 2: 320). Rather than emphasize the hand itself, the sword becomes an extension of Arya's self, defining her much the way Jaime Lannister's sword hand defined him. Needle serves as her link to Jon, who gave it to her; Mikken, who made it in the forge at Winterfell; Syrio Florel, who taught her to use it; and to her own ability as a sword-fighter. It is worth noting here that while Arya has lost over the course of five books most of her family, she has not lost her affiliation with them. Her nightly prayer for revenge is in answer to wrongs against the Starks. This is the aspect of identity that Arya doesn't understand, for she seems sincere in her attempts to "rid herself" of Arya (*FfC* 35 Cat of the Canals: 505). She even separates her thoughts from those of her former self. *"I should not be dreaming wolf dreams....* The wolf dreams belonged to Arya of House Stark" (505). But while she might not understand the makeup of the self, the text does. As part of her identity is moved outside of her body, it remains material, and therefore vulnerable to change or destruction, but it also represents the separation of her Arya thoughts from the rest of her. Much of her training focuses on controlling the mind as much as the physical form, but even when she succeeds at this, a piece of her remains hidden under a stone. Interestingly, this understanding of identity resembles the close relationship many disabled develop with prosthetics or other aids. Miho Iwakuma explains that "[a]s a process of embodiment, an object becomes a part of the identity of the person to whom it belongs" (79). Though certainly Needle differs from a cane, Arya has clearly embodied the object, and as the rest of her self is erased it serves as a prosthetic of memory. Moreover, as an object to be held it resembles the talismanic finger pouch Davos wears around his neck. Yet while Davos' fingers remind him of how he's changed, Needle functions as a connection to past affiliations when all the rest is given up to the many-faced god. By inscribing her memories of Winterfell on the sword, Arya creates a physical piece of self, not so different from the other stories written in flesh.

The Kindly Man's price for protection in the House of Black and White is just one example of flesh as offering in Martin's texts. Even when separated from the body, the pieces of these characters remain valuable in locating identity and affiliation. Martin's series muses on the idea of the body as commodity in Slaver's Bay and the brothels, but more often fragments of flesh and identity are offered up or taken rather than exchanged. The Greatjon asks for nothing in return for his fingers (*GoT* 54 Bran 6: 480). Theon/Reek wants only to be spared his god's wrath. The sacrifice of flesh is not even limited to the hand, for the office of *blood*rider amongst the Dothraki suggests a sacrifice of blood for one's khal (*GoT* 65 Daenerys 8: 591), and the Burned Men customarily burn off a nipple or finger to prove their bravery and commitment (*GoT* 57 Tyrion 7: 508). Both groups are identified by the kind of sacrifice they make. Though Martin presents variations between cultures, the assumption seems consistent that through physical sacrifice or change one makes commitments that shape the self.

Moreover, the gods of this world seem to draw power from the flesh that is sacrificed. The gods of the North were once powerful, and the rumors persist that followers offered "blood sacrifice to their heart trees" (*DwD* 30 Davos 4: 385). Thus, we can surmise that this power was a result of the blood. The trees themselves, with "leaves dark red, like a thousand bloodstained hands" (*GoT* 3 Catelyn 1: 19) reinforce this connection to the body. Followers of the Seven see this as proof of the North's barbarity, yet the new Lord of Light, who seems to control at least some of the pieces on the board, asks his servant Melisandre to sacrifice unbelievers to his fire (*SoS* 11 Davos 2: 115). And Jaqen H'gar is tasked with repaying the many-faced god the three deaths that were stolen from him (*CoK* 31 Arya 7: 348). The texts avoid any clear answer for these warring theologies, but what all of these examples make clear is the power that resides in flesh, and by extension the power of an individual, who may volunteer pieces of himself to a cause.

Heroic fantasy has always been interested in this power of the individual, but it is most often represented as a constant self living in a whole body. By illustrating both self and body as a collection of pieces, flesh and affiliations, Martin's texts recognize the fluid relationship of a self/body within society. Moreover, fragmented or damaged bodies do not dissolve; they survive because of their malleability. In this way Martin's text reconsiders representations of disability. Mitchell and Snyder note that disability can often create subversive innovation within a medium or genre, but at the expense of the disabled, who must represent all that is "alien to the normal course of human affairs" (5). Martin's innovation, however, is throwing off the moral weight so often attached to the disfigured body within heroic fantasy.

The fear of disintegration still emerges in the form of rotten flesh, but these instances only hint at a much larger issue, the dissolution of the very world Martin has created. As Farah Mendlesohn explains in *Rhetorics of Fantasy*, immersive fantasies describe themselves in terms of loss (61). Loss of dragons, of real magic, but also the old laws. When Arya Stark strikes Joffrey on their journey to King's Landing, Cersei demands that the girl lose a hand, "[t]he old penalty, for striking one of the blood royal" (*FfC* 31 Jaime 4: 459). This incident not only reminds us of how debts are paid in flesh, but that the old law is making room for a new one. Because King Robert shows mercy to the girl and disregards the old law, we understand that Martin's world is moving away from its relationship to the material body. Thus the power of the flesh is equated with other fantastical elements that are disappearing. Servants of the king will only wear the *representation* of a hand rather than give their own. And while the dwindling of this older culture might signal a more merciful world, it also denies the body's power to speak for the self.

Notes

1. Leonard Kriegel refers to this type of villainous, disabled character as the Demonic Cripple, deserving of and defined by his impairment (34–35).

2. Iwakuma explains the concept of *umwelt* as a person's perceived environment. With new impairments, patients must reconceive their world and how they manoeuver in that world. Once they've successfully embodied aids or prosthetics, their *umwelt* becomes transparent. That is, the work of a wheelchair becomes taken for granted in the same way one takes his legs for granted.

3. See, for example, Stemp and Cristea.

4. Kantorowicz's *The King's Two Bodies: A Study in Mediaeval Political Theology* explains the perceived relationship between the political and physical body of the king.

5. Though Martin's world is not solely based on 12th-century Europe, both the period's upheaval and its general conception of self create opportunities for comparison.

6. Bynum notes the way in which economic and urban growth created new opportunities of employment, brought people of different customs into contact with one another, and made certain texts more widely available. All such opportunity for change, she argues, created anxiety and interest over ideas of change itself.

7. O'Keefe argues that late Anglo-Saxon England used mutilation to mark one's crime upon the body and serve as a deterrent.

8. By contrast, the preserved bodies of saints were often taken as a sign of their spiritual purity. They were believed too virtuous for decomposition (Westerhof 87).

9. Khal Drogo is perhaps the only sympathetic character to suffer from infection, and it is unclear what particular wrong is attached to his wound.

10. Attebury uses the terms *acteur* and *actant* to refer to character as individual and character as function respectively (73).

Works Cited

Attebery, Brian. *Strategies of Fantasy*. Bloomington: Indiana University Press, 1992. Print.

Baldwin, Thomas, ed. *Reading Merleau-Ponty: On Phenomenology of Perception*. London: Routledge, 2007. Print.

Brooks, Terry. *The Sword of Shannara*. New York: Little, Brown, 2012. Print.

Brown, Elizabeth A.R. "Death and the Human Body in the Later Middle Ages: the Legislation of Boniface VIII on the Division of the Corpse." *Viator: Medieval and Renaissance Studies* 12 (1981): 221–270. Print.

Bynum, Caroline Walker. *Fragmentation and Redemption: Essays on Gender and the Human Body in Medieval Religion*. New York: Zone Books, 1991. Print.

_____. *Metamorphosis and Identity*. New York: Zone Books, 2001. Print.

_____. *The Resurrection of the Body in Western Christianity, 200–1336*. New York: Columbia University Press, 1995. Print.

Casey, Jim. "Modernism and Postmodernism." *The Cambridge Companion to Fantasy Literature*. Ed. Edward James and Farah Mendlesohn. Cambridge: Cambridge University Press, 2012: 113–24. Print.

"Cath Maige Tuired: The Second Battle of Mag Tuired." Ed. and trans. Elizabeth A. Gray. CELT: University College, Cork, Ireland, 2003. Web. 24 June 2014.

Cohen, William A. *Embodied: Victorian Literature and the Senses*. Minneapolis: University of Minnesota Press, 2009. Print.

Cristea, Leo. "Disability and Imperfect People in Fantasy." *Fantasy Faction*. 24 April 2012. Web. 5 May 2014.

Glendinning, Simon. *In the Name of Phenomenology*. London: Routledge, 2007. Print.

Iwakuma, Miho. "The Body as Embodiment: An Investigation of the Body by Merleau-Ponty." *Disability/Postmodernity: Embodying Disability Theory*. Ed. Mairian Corker and Tom Shakespeare. London and New York: Continuum, 2002: 76–87. Print.

Jacobus, de Voragine. *The Golden Legend: Readings On the Saints*. Trans. William Granger Ryan. 2 volumes. Princeton: Princeton University Press, 1993. Print.

Kantorowicz, Ernst Hartwig. *The King's Two Bodies: A Study in Mediaeval Political Theology*. Princeton: Princeton University Press, 1957. Print.

King, David S. "The Meaning of Amputation in the *Chansons De Geste*." *Symposium* 62.1 (2008): 35–51. Print.

King, Stephen. *The Gunslinger*. New York: New American Library, 1988. Print.

Kriegel, Leonard. "The Cripple in Literature." *Images of the Disabled, Disabling Images*. Ed. Alan Gartner and Tom Joe. New York: Praeger, 1986: 31–46.

Lacob, Jace. "*Game of Thrones* Comes to HBO." *The Daily Beast*. 4 April 2011. Web. 22 June 2014.

Mendlesohn, Farah. *Rhetorics of Fantasy*. Middletown, CT: Wesleyan University Press, 2008. Print.

Mendlesohn, Farah, and Edward James. *A Short History of Fantasy*. London: Middlesex University Press, 2009. Print.

Mitchell, David T., and Sharon L. Snyder. *Narrative Prosthesis: Disability and the Dependencies of Discourse*. Ann Arbor: University of Michigan Press, 2000. Print.

Moorcock, Michael. *Elric of Melnibone*. New York: Arrow Books, 1973.

Nochlin, Linda. *The Body in Pieces: The Fragment as a Metaphor of Modernity*. [London]: Thames and Hudson, 1994. Print.

O'Keefe, K. "Body and Law in Late Anglo-Saxon England." *Anglo-Saxon England* 27 (1998): 209–32. Print.

Ross, Jill, and Suzanne Conklin Akbari. *The Ends of the Body: Identity and Community in Medieval Culture*. Toronto: University of Toronto Press, 2013. Print.

Rowe, Katherine. "'God's handy worke': Divine Complicity and the Anatomist's Touch." *The Body in Parts: Fantasies of Corporeality in Early Modern Europe*. Ed. David Hillman and Carla Mazzio. New York: Routledge, 1997: 285–309.

Stemp, Jane. "Devices and Desires: Science Fiction, Fantasy and Disability in Literature for Young People." *Disability Studies Quarterly* 24.1 (Winter 2004). Web.

Thompson, Raymond H. "Modern Fantasy and Medieval Romance: A Comparative Study." *The Aesthetics of Fantasy Literature and Art*. Ed. Roger C. Schlobin. Notre Dame: University of Notre Dame Press, 1982: 211–225.

Tolkien, J.R.R. *The Return of the King: Being the Third Part of The Lord of the Rings*, 2d ed. Boston: Houghton Mifflin, 1993. Print.

Vitz, Paul C., and Susan M. Felch. *The Self: Beyond the Postmodern Crisis*. Wilmington, DE: ISI Books, 2006. Print.

Weis, Margaret, and Tracy Hickman. *The Dragonlance Chronicles*. New York: Penguin, 1988. Print.

Westerhof, Danielle. *Death and the Noble Body in Medieval England*. Woodbridge, UK: Boydell Press, 2008. Print.

A Thousand Westerosi Plateaus: Wargs, Wolves and Ways of Being

T.A. Leederman

One of the compelling, and impressive factors in George R.R. Martin's *A Song of Ice and Fire* series is its depiction of chivalric and romantic ideals as catastrophic failures, riddled with the same hubris and corruption as contemporary society, in a fashion that rings with the knell of unavoidable human truth. However, it would be too simplistic to call Martin's depiction simply dark or cynical about human nature. For every failure and descent into the ugliest corners of our nature, Martin also—but perhaps more subtly—provides portraits of compassion, heroism, and love that furnish hope even in the face of seemingly impenetrable darkness. The novels accomplish this by portraying a connection between the Stark children and their direwolves that transcends both space and time, which makes the story's scope and world-building always feel somewhat more localized, understandable and relatable for the reader. Throughout the narration, those who forget their connection and responsibility to their place and people eventually meet with systematic destruction.

Both darkness and hope are focalized through the Stark children and their direwolves, as they "fan out" through Westeros and Essos. Many of the children (Jon, Arya, and Bran, as well as perhaps Rickon) share a supernatural bond with their companion direwolves, and the wolves in turn share sibling bonds with one another that are congruous with the sibling bond between the young Starks and which connect them across the both world and narrative. The disbandment of the Starks over the continents opens up the world and the story in ever-widening circles. In addition, the Starks reveal through their supernatural ties, called here "warg" bonds, and Bran's later greensight, that there are ways of being, seeing, and relating to each other and the land beyond the short-term political games, clannish rivalries, and violence, in which the rest of the characters are enmeshed. This essay's main goal is to examine George R.R. Martin's

189

conceptions of warging and greensight, both of which invite bonded humans to look through the "eyes" of the natural world—animals, in one case, and trees, in the other—and share their knowledge. Such bonds open new venues of narrative and perception, while also illuminating essential connections between people, time, and the land. I use Deleuze and Guattari's *A Thousand Plateaus* as an interpretive lens for land, ethics, and ways of being in the series, not because I am proposing a direct influence, but in order to unlock the layers of interpersonal, inter-temporal, and inter-environmental perspectives through which Martin suggests an ethical engagement with people and the land.

"Warg" possesses a long history in fantasy literature and again an older heritage in Norse mythology, almost always as a noun used to describe a wolf or wolfish creature, usually of a fierce or prehistoric nature. Wargs appear in the *Hervarar Saga* from the thirteenth century as the children of Fenrir, two wolves chasing, "one going before the sun, the other after the moon" (Tunstall 11) and who reach toward the light that is the Sun. The choice to maintain *warg* in the text as a finer definition of a type of wolf is both interesting and prevalent among translations; the sagas' warg, though *vargr* in Old Norse technically means "wolf," is here a subtype of wolf that is part of the mythological substance of the world system. Pulling from these Norse roots, J.R.R. Tolkien created a species of semi-intelligent but evil-aligned mount wolves called wargs, on whom the orcs rode into battle. Possibly descended from werewolves of the First Age of Middle-earth, wargs shared a proto-language amongst themselves.

Wargs in the Martinverse uniquely involve the act of "warging," in which a human links to a particular animal, sees through its eyes and sometimes controls its body. At least three of the Stark children see through the eyes of their direwolves in this way, as becomes clear early in the series. Thus when the reader learns in *A Storm of Swords* that some wargs, like Varamyr Sixskins and Bran Stark, can form this same link with a limited host of animals (in Varamyr's case) or any animal up to and including humans (as in Bran's case), the concept is already familiar; it is fantasy, but not fantastic. According to a plethora of publications by Brian Hare and Vanessa Woods of Duke University's Canine Cognition Center, there is strong evidence in evolutionary biology that the human relationship with wolves and other canids, both direct and indirect, allowed both species to develop into their current landed, agricultural and technological forms ("civilized" people and "domesticated" dogs); wolves therefore constitute a natural and even comfortable place to begin fleshing out the concept, and doing so situates the verb "warging" in the literary and mythological history of humankind's relationships with other species.

"I'm not a lady," thinks Arya in *A Storm of Swords*, "I'm a wolf" (23 Arya 4: 253). The Starks begin as landed feudal lords and ladies, with a horde of bannermen at their beck and call and a fortified castle behind whose walls they may hide indefinitely. Catelyn Stark, born to the softer culture of the south, calls the North *"hard and cold"*; it *"has no mercy"* (*SoS* 21 Catelyn 3: 226), suggesting here and elsewhere that the North has ossified into an ominously unyielding form which, though it can crush, may also easily shatter and never reform. Its fragility, moreover, is constantly in evidence: Martin establishes the power of the North and its impotence in successive motions of world-building and destruction. Ned becomes Hand of the King and leaves the North; Ned is beheaded by the king. Sansa becomes future queen and promised everything she ever dreamed of; Sansa becomes a beaten hostage and orphan married to a dwarf. Robb becomes King of the North and engages in a military campaign at the age of sixteen wherein he is much feared and nearly undefeated; Robb acts like a sixteen-year-old once, marries the woman he deflowered, and is murdered at a wedding. Winterfell is a strong, ingeniously fortified and engineered castle in an unforgiving and unassailable landscape; Winterfell is penetrated and conquered by a bitter, semi-inept teenager, whose follies result in the castle's razing. All heirs to Winterfell vanish; the army splinters and many of the family's staunchest supporters die far from home; and the castle becomes the device through which the Boltons gain the North. Clearly the power of Winterfell, just as is that of most strongholds, castles and sovereigns throughout the series, is primarily a political illusion—as it is Martin's ceaseless and unrelenting goal to show us, the readers.

At the outset of the series, the power of Winterfell, and of the Starks, over the territories of the North seems secure, and the long summer days which function as a metaphorical childhood in the series seem like they will last forever. It's worth noting that for Deleuze and Guattari, this idea of "territories" is psycho- and socio-spatial, rather than metaphorical; they are concerned with the way we inhabit the world we encounter, as thinking subjects, and therefore with the ways in which we ascribe, or have ascribed for us, meaning to and in that encountered world. In this context, deterritorialization is the loss of one's own ascriptions, and over the course of *A Game of Thrones, A Clash of Kings,* and *A Storm of Swords*, the Starks are slowly and methodically deterritorialized even as they are exiled from the broken towers of Winterfell. Those who adapt to this deterritorializing by drawing from their direwolves and accepting a more nomadic existence find new and potentially powerful destinies, resisting reterritorialization, learning to inhabit the world more fluidly, while those who forget or turn away from their wolves are destroyed. The territorialized Starks do not inhabit territory in the same fashion as their sigil animal, the direwolf. The boundaries of the wolf's territory are mellifluous, ever-changing according to need and population; the wolf has no fortifications to defend, but may hunt and dig dens for its young wherever the necessity arises. The pack can move, travel, split apart and come back together, can find new territories and new sources of food, and this plasticity is key to its survival. Moreover, as Henry S. Sharp found in his *Comparative Ethnology of the Wolf and the Chipewyan*, wolf packs and nomadic human tribes can adapt to each other's presence in order to preserve the natural environment and food sources upon which they rely. He noted that pack and tribe both delimited range and population in a way that preserved the resident caribou population, and held each group well below the species' highest carrying population threshold in a given area. In consequence, humans and wolves could predate in the same areas without competing or experiencing environmental population pressures in the form of massive die-offs or higher infant and fetus mortality rates. His work strongly suggests that both wolves and tribal Chipewyan utilize social structure and culture similarly in order to achieve the same, and complementary, environmental effects (Sharp 77–79). The two groups under study represent tribal nomadism in the form most likely maintained throughout the evolutionary history of both species,[1] and more importantly establishes how the parallel ethnological study of wolf and human cultures might be more fruitful in exploring human history than the study of fellow primates, most of whom remain far more stationary and roam throughout a markedly smaller territory than wolves or humans have long inhabited. Such similarities between tribe and pack emphasize the centrality of the direwolves and their bond with the human Starks in *A Song of Ice and Fire*, and how these relationships affect our understanding of territoriality in the books. As winter draws near, forces splinter the Stark children and their wolves into groups, unto death, and almost completely apart, yet the fabric of the pack— and of the narrative—continues to connect them over space and time.

Not long before *A Game of Thrones* was published, Deleuze and Guattari released *A Thousand Plateaus*, in which they posited that we might conceptualize other modes of being through our understandings of animals and their interrelationships. Their sections on "One or Several Wolves?" (26–38) and "Becoming-Intense, Becoming Animal, Becoming Imperceptible" (232–309) gives us a lens through which we might read *A Song of Ice and Fire*; they propose that the construction of an imaginative wolf self (or even a tree self) could serve as a tool for envisioning ways out of and solutions to pernicious or dysfunctional social systems, or to deal with pain, isolation and trauma. Martin mobilizes just such an idea through the Stark children, who over the course of the novels can come, if they survive, to apprehend themselves as part of something larger, connected over the land, with access to widely varied understandings both spatially and temporally. For example, in fostering the greensight, Bran is able to see his father through the eyes of the heart trees, and recognize all time as a great, unalterable flow, a genealogical and geological history, of which he is a small but precious and irretrievable part. By contrast, the alien and threatening Others, from beyond the Wall, use the past and human indolence against itself, by raising the bodies of the dead as avatars of fear and destruction, and operating after the longest summers have lulled the world into complacency. It is notably not strictly human-created objects that can frighten, wound or defeat the Others indeed, their swords fail one by one. Rather, it is the wisdom of another species, the so-called children of the forest, which must be recalled so that their tools—dragonglass (obsidian), for example—may smite the Others once again. Any suggestion that the narrow modernity of humans, which ignores the residual knowledge preserved in legend and lore, will protect them from such dangers is rendered as unutterably foolish in Martin's world. Increasingly, *A Song of Ice and Fire* suggests that hegemonic knowledge alone cannot solve our problems; we must look back, to earlier eras now wreathed in legend, and sideways, to other species, for new conceptual tools and ways of being in the world. This supposition has in-canon support from the often incomplete (though admittedly dutiful) hegemonic monopoly of knowledge and specialization practiced by the maesters, whom Martin often portrays as unprepared and even dismissive of the world's greatest threats.

For Deleuze and Guattari, wolves represent such a new way of being. They insist that when one sees wolves—whether real or in dreams—one is never seeing one wolf, but "eight or nine, six or seven" (Deleuze and Guattari 29). The wolf is always a multiplicity, representing the social order of the pack, which they see as characterized by "small or restricted numbers, dispersion, nondecomposable variable distances, qualitative metamorphoses, inequalities as remainders or crossings, impossibility of fixed totalization or hierarchization, a Brownian Variability in directions, lines of deterritorializations, and projection of particles" (33). Such a group ranges over territory, but simultaneously deterritorializes it and is deterritorialized; the territory of the pack is not hierarchical, in other words, nor fixed, but permeable and shifting. Stripped of their territory, the Stark children may become "pack," humans organized as nomads. For Deleuze and Guattari, the units of the pack are not "nondecomposable" because their primacy is so elemental that they cannot be further divided, but because division would alter the constituent parts so greatly that they would become unrecognizable, unstable, short-lived, perhaps immediately destroyed. Therefore the elements making up the pack in this nomadic sense, while they appear to be individuals making up a multiplicity, would alter and perhaps vanish upon division.

In their chapter "1730: Becoming-Intense, Becoming Animal, Becoming-Imperceptible," Deleuze and Guattari state that "the relationships between animals are the object not only of science but of dreams, symbolism, art and poetry, practical and impractical use" and primarily "bound up with the relations between man and animal, man and woman, man and child, man and the elements, man and the physical and microphysical universe" (235). *A Thousand Plateaus'* driving concern is the various forms by which humans govern themselves, gain and use power, and the way systems of power use them in turn. These concerns are likewise the main interest in much of *A Song of Ice and Fire,* in which each household has a sigil and words which reflect that family's practical philosophy of power, how to attain it, keep it, and use it. Deleuze and Guattari create categories for these governing systems of power, of which nomads are the first.

It is not always clear which is the chicken and which the egg, but fundamentally this distinction does not matter; humans may mimic what we see in nature, the relationships between animals and with their environment, or we may see figured in nature a mirror of those relationships already established. We may learn from it or gain its validation—or both. The nomadic system of human governance and power appears to be closest to this mimesis, possessing the most confluences with these relationships and the ability to see them mirrored back. In other forms of power, that Deleuze and Guattari call "war machines" (though the first nomadic form can also be a war machine, of a revolutionary or resisting character [351–423]), humans participate less, or less knowingly, in this relationship. Such distancing arguably allows other systems to harness the human war machine in favor of governance dysfunction. Rather than preserve the life and various inter- and intra- species and environmental relationships of the human, these later war machines often to seek to collect and hoard fictitious sources of security, such as capital or some vacillating cultural conception of power.

In Martin's series, the Iron Throne, money, lands, titles, highborn marriages and balms for wounded pride all represent such dysfunctional distractions—the "summer games of a child" as Eddard Stark might call them (*GOT* 23 Arya 2: 187). These distractions only appear as such when viewed with the wider perspective at hand, that vast environmental dangers are pressing on the viability of human life in Westeros and Essos, represented by ice, cold and death in the Others or white walkers to the north, and uncontrollable fire in the dragons to the south. These two diametrically opposed elements appear to be part of the fundamental make-up of their world. Unnaturally long summers might melt the ice in the Lands of Forever Winter for a time, releasing the Others from their sleep; correspondingly, dragons awake and bring all manner of magic to the world with them. It is uncertain whether the two awakenings are related, causally or otherwise, and, if causally, which factor begets the other. However, killing white walkers with dragonglass (obsidian), or with "Dragonsteel" (possibly

Valyrian steel, brought to Westeros by the Targaryens), hints at this opposing character, as does the Essos religion of the Red God R'hllor (The Lord of Light), who opposes "the great Other" of cold and darkness with his flames and light. These great opposed and destructive powers have been kept at bay and forgotten over thousands of years, and in this peace Westeros has experienced a millennial summer, during which the dragons grew smaller, stunted and misshapen, and the wall fell into disrepair, its forts more and more unmanned, its purpose forgotten in favor of fighting the wildlings whose alliance would be an aid against the white walkers.[2] These are the squabbles that take place in summer, the divisions and playacting, the human game of thrones, which are the great privilege of carnival. The Stark words, "Winter is coming," are similar to an apt Russian proverb: *"ne vsyo kotu maslenitsa, budet i velikiy post,"* or "not every day is Carnival—soon it will be Lent."[3]

The relationship between the Stark words and this Russian proverb has, no doubt, some connection to the harshness of Winterfell and Siberian winters, but it also suggests that extremity of environment has the power of impressing upon human residents the pressure of greater truths. Winter is a spatial-temporal environment and experience that is pedagogically legible, like its culturally-imposed cousin, Lent. It is a time of privation that lasts a typically predictable period of time (in Westeros's case, a summer's length should predict in some degree the span of the following winter), during which human beings must learn discipline under privation. This period of deficit then makes the following feast days more savory, and impresses upon people the need to remain controlled and be prepared for the next time. The stark words, "Winter is coming," is not only true at all times, but also experientially real and necessary, because there are winters of the hearth as well as winters of the soul.

Appropriately, the house has a sigil (in an active sense a spirit animal[4]) that reflects these words in the direwolf. "When the snows fall and the white winds blow," Ned tells Arya in *A Game of Thrones*, "the lone wolf dies but the pack survives. Summer is the time for squabbles. In the winter, we must protect one another, keep each other warm, share our strengths.... It is time to begin growing up" (*GoT* 23 Arya 2: 187). After their lord father's death, the Stark children do not survive huddled together against the blowing cold, but each one arguably gains strength through this idea of the pack whose orbital center is shifting, invisible and mutable with time. The thing that each one strives to attain is survival, and struggles for ephemeral power or songs of chivalry inevitably end in disaster and destruction, as we will examine later in this analysis. The warg bond then allows the Stark children (excluding Sansa and increasingly excluding Robb) to envision themselves in a networked pack among others, spread across the world as they know it and growing farther distant with time. They are literally deterritorialized with the burning of Winterfell, nomads wandering over Westeros, north of the wall and the Free Cities, but their direwolves sense one another regardless, binding them magically as a wandering pack.

The pack is six strong, six reflected by a further six direwolves; this twelve/six reflects in pairs and threes, reflecting a number of physical and behavioral characteristics of both the human name-giver and the wolf receiving the name. Ghost, Grey Wind, and Shaggydog all represent physical characteristics in the wolf, often a feature that figures his advantages in battle and/or behavior in the field; Grey Wind has a gray coat and moves with fatal swiftness, while Ghost is silent and blends in with his environment (snow); Shaggydog, named by a very small boy, is shaggy and feral, dangerously protective of his human. These direwolf names reflect a preference for the physical, the practice of naming according to a wolf's abilities and appearance. In Rickon's case, this is a function of his being so very young, while Jon and Robb evince their understandings of their future roles in the state of becoming (Brother of the Night's Watch and Lord of Winterfell respectively), and these roles themselves figure, reflect and complement one another through glasses darkly.

Ghost, so named because he is a voiceless albino invisible against the winter backdrop of the north and beyond the wall, symbolically figures Jon Snow perhaps even more exactly than the other wolf pups early in *A Game of Thrones*. After sacrificing his own claims by counting the litter so that it will equal only his father's trueborn children, thereby changing his father's attitude so that Bran and Robb can take the pups home, Jon pauses the train of horses while hearing "something else." Despite Ghost's muteness, Jon hears the unhearable, the voice of a creature without a voice, and returns with Ghost. The pup had opened its eyes and wandered away, or had "been driven away," while its siblings were still blind; Jon claims him for his own, or is perhaps so claimed (*GoT* 2 Bran 1: 17). At the feasting of Winterfell after the king's arrival, Jon is relegated to a table away from his brothers and sisters, as it "might give insult to the royal family to seat a bastard among them"[5] (*GoT* 6 Jon 1: 44), as though his very presence must be obviated, rendered invisible and silent—a living ghost who must be ignored or driven away. Jon's name is also a figuration of this difficulty. He is named for Jon Arryn, dead at the beginning of *A Game of Thrones*, whose death arguably sets off the events of the subsequent novels, and which itself resulted from the bubbling up of past treacheries and scandals, and the political ambitions of cynical and embittered men. Jon Snow is thus named for one of the series's principal ghosts and for the cold ambient environment into which he must recede.

Jon's case is instructive, but changing relationships to the direwolves over time also have extreme consequences—good and bad. The relationship between human and animal is mimetic of larger structures in nature, and the human place within them. For instance, Robb's relationship to his place as commander of the northern men and House Stark is best figured in his relationship to his direwolf. In response to Sansa's letter about their father's treason, too, Robb asks what could be wrong with the girl; Bran very intelligently responds that "she lost her wolf," who has "gone south, and only her bones had returned" like so many members of their house (*GoT* 54 Bran 6: 481); the later indication is that the old gods, who watch from the heart trees, can no longer see their worshippers.[6] The south appears to strip the northerners of their power, which draws directly from the northern environment. Going south displaces one from the land and encourages displacement from sources of spiritual and physical strength, like the direwolves; it drives wedges between family members, as it does between Catelyn and her sons, Ned and his daughters, between sisters and brothers.

Robb gains great victories in *A Clash of Kings* with Grey Wind by his side; in the quick and ambiguous nature of wind or smoke, rumors often mistake or conflate him with his direwolf, and fear aids him in his campaign. His fight begins as an attempt to free the north from the tyranny of Joffrey Baratheon and to save his sisters from the Lannisters' clutches; in pursuit of this goal, he vows to wed a Frey and captures Jaime Lannister for ransom. He fails, however, to trade the Kingslayer for his sisters and to uphold his oath to the Freys, marrying Jeyne Westerling instead. After his marriage, Robb increasingly keeps Grey Wind away from himself and his wife, claiming, "I am not a wolf" to his mother and no longer keeping Grey Wind's instincts in his counsel, despite his mother's warnings that "these wolves are more than wolves.... I think perhaps the gods sent them to us. Your father's gods, the old gods of the north." It is Robb's belief that Summer and Shaggydog failed to protect his brothers that destroys his faith, and hence his life (*SoS* Catelyn 2: 162–63).

Lady, Nymeria and Summer possess names that are representative of their human's dreams of future becomings, of hope and potentialities—not *what is*, but *what could be*, *what may be*, and what may lie beyond the world's nadir of blood and darkness. Lady and Nymeria represent the female types Sansa and Arya hope to someday embody, as well as their knowledge and vision about these roles. Sansa hopes to be a lady, and has the accomplishments and sensibility for the position; her direwolf is correspondingly tame and gentle, trusting and even passive, doing as she's told instead of willfully following or traveling where she ought not to go (*GoT* 17 Eddard 3: 132). Her trusting nature blinds her to Eddard Stark's intentions when he executes her, though her brothers and sister all sharply sense such violent intentions long before surrounding humans do so; Lady is too "the smallest of the litter" (Ibid) but physically like her sister Nymeria.

Through Lady and Sansa, George R.R. Martin depicts the smallness and weakness of the wish to be, generally, "a lady" when winter is coming. Sansa's only protection is her family—most particularly her pack—and when she lies in *A Game of Thrones* in order to maintain her dream of someday becoming Joffrey's lady queen, she largely loses this protection with the death of her direwolf and the escape of Arya's. Her next step in the maintenance of this dream results in Eddard's death and that of the Stark house at King's Landing. In *A Storm of Swords*, the Lannisters take off Sansa's wolf coat (*SoS* 29 Sansa 3), the symbol of her paternal household, and she is symbolically stripped of that which she lost long earlier—the pack protection of the Stark household, her claim to power, and familial connections (*CoK* 33 Sansa 3: 366). When Lady's body returns to Winterfell for burial, her brothers howl as they sense her death; very early into the story, this event prefigures Sansa's long imprisonment under the Lannisters and Baelish, and her family's grief that will lead to Robb Stark's uprising. It begins with the execution of a single wolf and a deep misunderstanding—a wolf is never one wolf. It is always five or six.

Nymeria, by staunch contrast, receives her name from a very precise historical figure within the Westerosi world. Arya names her after Nymeria of the Rhoynar, a warrior queen who traveled over the sea with ten thousand ships and conquered Dorne alongside House Martell; this historical figure is very similar to Daenerys Targaryen in this way, and represents quite a different role model for Arya Stark than the generalized hope and docile nature of "the Lady" (a shadowy figure) for Sansa, who exists in a murky might-be, could-be, chivalric *never-was* temporality. During her time with Arya, girl and wolf occupy wild pack space; Nymeria sleeps at the foot of Arya's bed and accompanies her into the forest to play swords with the butcher's boy. A threat to the girl is simultaneously threat to the wolf, who pounces from the trees when Joffrey attacks (*GoT* 16 Sansa 1: 126). Nymeria seems to understand Arya's language signaling, staying away from the girl after being ordered to do so[7]; however, in *A Clash of Kings*, she responds to Arya's prayer in the godswood as well (*CoK* 65 Arya 10: 676), to a connection across species lines and lines of deterritorialization in space and bodily separation. While conventional lines of power and connection in territory and vows may be easier for an enemy to break, the deterritorialized Stark children maintain a near-mystical power and connection that baffles warfare and greed; they appear to be the only ones who can shrug their wolf pelts from off their shoulders and forsake the protection, even if they do not know they are doing so. The enemy cannot take these pelts away if the children do not give them up first.

It is the case of Summer and Bran Stark, however, that provides a much deeper understanding of the world's processes as seen in *A Song of Ice and Fire*, and how we might in fact relate to our own environment in time and space. There is a great lie attendant on flying south when the cold winds of winter blow; summer is not a place to which one can escape when the harsh times creep in. Summer and winter are places in *time*, whether they are figural or literal summers and winters, and no human being can hope to escape them, any more than one could hope to escape aging or the sickle of death. As the cases of Sansa and Robb indicate particularly, willful abandonment of one's land, and the values one upholds in order to survive and protect it, has severe consequences for the Starks. Retreat is not an option, and indeed it is Bran who stays rooted in Winterfell and the north until the bitter end, seeking out the last greenseer for training to use his skin-changing abilities and delving deeper into the mysteries of the land. His is a mission of hope, carrying the logical partner of the saying "winter is coming," which is the obverse "summer is coming," embodied in his wolf Summer. Through the direwolf's eyes, Bran is able to run, climb and hunt as he did before his paralysis, and he can feel the presence of the other wolves, and through them his siblings stretched out over the world. In time, Bran is able to take other bodies, possessing the half-giant Hodor to protect them both and to explore, all in pursuit of the three-eyed crow, the last greenseer in Westeros, who lives with the Children of the Forest north of the wall, surrounded by a frozen moat of the living dead.

To awaken his greensight, Bran eats of the seeds of the weirwood tree, a white paste with rivulets of blood-colored sap, whose flavor changes from bitterness to honey to abstract memories of his mother's love as he consumes (*DwD* 35 Bran 3: 456–67), signaling his shift from singular corporeal physicality to a spiritual confluence with his remembrances and emotional connections. This in turn becomes a connection across land, when his first greensight allows him to see Eddard Stark through the eyes of the Winterfell heart tree, and whisper from the future as wind through lonely leaves. Brynden (the three-eyed crow or last greenseer, now Bran's teacher) explains this troubled temporality by saying that "time is a river" and "that river does not move [the trees].... A thousand human years are a moment to a weirwood, and through such gates you and I may gaze at the past," all while "men live their lives trapped in an eternal present between the mists of memory and the sea of shadow that is all we know of the days to come" (*DwD* 35 Bran 3: 458). He promises that in time Bran will learn to see beyond the weirwoods' eyes and "beyond the trees themselves" (459).

This skin-changing is, however, literal; Brynden has slowly become one with the roots of trees, and his life has been stretched many times while he sits as rooted as the weirwoods above him, as "most of him has gone into the tree" (449) like the "singers" or greenseers before him, who "went into the wood, into leaf and limb and root, and the trees remembered" (452). The trees, in particular the immortal weirwoods, are thus the living history of mankind, a text that can be read and accessed, as well as a history of the natural wood. Their eyes have seen lives pass before them and their wood carries the stories of old singers, "their histories and prayers, everything they knew about this world" (452). In his dreams that night, Bran sees his father praying about Jon Snow and Robb Stark when they're babies; he then sees his aunt and an uncle or his father playing at swords with sticks in the godswood, before he begins to see members from his house for generations, centuries, millennia. The vision ends at a beginning, one very like the events of *A Game of Thrones*—a sickle and a beheading, a blood sacrifice at the foot of the heart tree (460).

Brynden's description of time resembles the plane of immanence as depicted by Deleuze and Guattari. Without structure or origin, "only relations of movement and rest, speed and slowness between unformed elements ... affects, subjectless individuations that constitute collective assemblages" (Deleuze and Guattari 266). Rather than man's view of the river of time or the plane of organization, denoted by houses, sigils and banners, games of thrones and clashes of kings, Bran is learning to see the world as a plane of immanence, of all people, times and happenings occurring in a web of connections, actions and reactions, atop ground soaked with the waters of time and an endless wash of blood. This is the pressing preeminence of the Real, wherein man is within and of nature, here literally always already looking from the future through the eyes of the heart trees. Bran feels the presence of a girl, a singer, within the body of a flying raven, "a woman, of those who sing the song of the earth.... Long dead, yet a part of her remains ... a shadow on the soul" (*DwD* 35 Bran 3: 451), a portion of a person that flies forever after her flesh was torn apart. Just as Arya is said to have "the wolf blood" in her[8] (*GoT* 23 Arya 2: 186), the flying raven or prowling wolf or sentinel trees possess the blood and presence of untold human generations, each within and beside the other, in an ever-greater enfolding of consciousness and reality, like the folded ripples of steel in Eddard's Valyrian-forged Ice.

This perspective on the world as multifarious ways of being and becomings is something that Martin links to the project of reading fiction itself. Jojen Reed, Bran's preeminent teacher, asks Bran if he's fond of reading, and says the words, "A reader lives a thousand lives before he dies.... The man who never reads lives only one" and "when singers die they become part of godhood" (*DwD* 35 Bran 3: 452). Jojen teaches Bran to open his eyes and learn how to unlock and read the world, even though he may never read it in the same fashion himself. In this moment, George R.R. Martin has opened up the world of Westeros and Essos, their mythologies and people and magic, as a metaphor about reading and storytelling themselves. Perhaps the biggest "punch line" in his series is that the squabbles of summer, the games of thrones, the clashes of kings, the storms of swords, are all distractions from the immanent and infinitely ignored threat of the white walkers, who threaten to storm the wall and destroy the world—i.e., the threat of total environmental apocalypse, personified in the very spirit of eternal winter. The only reason the audience has such perspective and can get a sense of the necessary priorities is through a kind of warging or greensight, which is the multiple and simultaneous POV character model furnished by the books' structure. The reader may skin-change into Arya, into Tyrion, into Bran,[9] even into the bodies of wolves, ravens and trees, seeing the land over space and time and across the networks of relationships, cause, effect, farce and foibles, love and hate, heat and cold, dark and light.

The act of reading is to see through the eyes of human time across temporal and spatial boundaries, to warg into others and discover the multiplicity of the world through its many layers, and discover alternative ways of being. This is true of the world's histories, in which "the past remains the past. We can learn from it, but we cannot change it" (458), and gain knowledge from the secret history of nature and the progression of mankind across its crust and waters. Storytelling and imagination, the ability to creatively warg oneself into the footsteps of others, to "imagine with precision" the guiding conceit of Amitav Ghosh's *The Shadow Lines*, is capable of charting endless possibilities and ways of being. Thus it is a potentially ethical and ecological perspective, implying that there are infinite lessons to learn in the flights of birds, the minds of wolves, the shadow of ancient trees, the eyes of fellow man, over time and space, and that we can learn how to live these thousand lives, put on these thousand skins, by reading and listening to stories—by letting those characters inhabit us, and we them, as skin-changers and greenseers.

Another pedagogical gift of this perspective is that the series is very much a "living into" the plane of immanence. Land and the weather teach harsh lessons; it is very plain to see in *A Game of Thrones* and *A Storm of Swords* how turning from these lessons results in personal and familial disaster. Neglect of the wall, the loss of northern fighting men to "games of thrones," and the emptying out of the northern lands also spells a future danger as cold blankets the land and white walkers roam among the living. Through the books, it is the pack that offers a site of resistance, a mode of human organization that could spell the difference between death and survival, unity and sundering, learning from mistakes or staggering blindly into the Others' grasp. These ties transcend family and blood, including in them every animal, man and tree in the world over the passage of history, all the land a text and all its denizens eyewitnesses.

Notes

1. For example, splitting into smaller groups during the hunting season before regrouping for the winter; creating strategic multi-season living spaces and food stores; splitting duties and tasks in such a way that maximizes hunting potential, and sharing child-rearing responsibilities. Both groups also protect a larger territory than strictly necessary from tribes belonging to their own species, while the human and wolf groups share it with one another. The ecology of the area thus carries the two predatory species in comparative stability (Sharp).

2. It is important to note, however, that though these forces may be opposing, they are part of the multiplicity and unity of the world environment. "If ice can burn," Jojen Reed says to Bran in *A Storm of Swords*, "then love and hate can mate. Mountain or marsh, it makes no matter. The land is one" (*SoS* 25 Bran 2: 275). We see this spatial and temporal unity at work when Bran learns about greenseeing in *A Dance with Dragons*. This love and hate in elemental form is exemplified by the Other's "embrace" of the dead to make them forget that they are dead, to make the living like themselves; their hate is certainly not avoidance. Similarly, the obsidian dragon fire embraces the Others and delivers them unto long death as flowing water, the very element of life. In both cases, the encounter between these forces—light and dark, ice and fire—spells life, makes it possible through cycles of cold and heat, destruction and rebirth, like the cycles of summer and winter.

3. My translation, though please note that "Carnival" here often translates, in fact, as Shrovetide. For practical purposes, they refer to the same practice and the same time of year, though most readers will be more familiar with the general sense of Carnival.

4. From their first introduction, the direwolves are heavy with portents and magical significations. In *A Game of Thrones*, the cold north is the location with seemingly the most magic and divination, until Maegi blood magic and dragons emerge in Essos at the end of the first book. The mother direwolf dies with "a foot of shattered antler" lodged in her throat, and it is possible that the pups were "born with the dead" (*GoT* 2 Bran 1: 15), signifying the clash between Baratheon stag and Stark direwolf, possibly in the latter's defense or need of its pups, which hence leaves them orphaned. The wolf parent perhaps should have chosen its enemies more carefully.

5. A statement of unparalleled humorous irony, given the status of the royal children and King Robert's numerous bastard children abroad, to say nothing of Tyrion's claim that "all dwarfs are bastards in their fathers' eyes" (*GoT* 6 Jon 1: 47).

6. There are still entire groves of the heart trees, known as weirwoods, north of the wall; in the northern lands, they are heart trees, the hearts of godswoods inside castles. In the south, these carved white trees with blood red sap have all been chopped down, and Northerners far from home must pray at their trunks as though kneeling before the headless body of a decapitated god (*GoT* 3 Catelyn 1: 19).

7. Though this sign language also necessitated a few rocks (*GoT* 22 Arya 2: 186–87).

8. This is only one strong and infinitely quotable example; more generally, all the great houses emulate their sigil animals to a degree in their style of governance and philosophies of power. The Lannister lions' "pride" is without equal, and they are gifted with both golden hair and golden ingots; the Arryn eagles live in an eyrie, an eagle's nest, and drop their enemies out of thin air; the Tully fish gain their strength and prosperity from the rivers; the Greyjoy squid feed on fellow predators, attack ships and often take on prey bigger than themselves at an enormous gamble.

9. There are also examples of human warging in *A Dance with Dragons*, such as Varamyr Sixskins (*DwD* 1 Prologue: 4–11) and in Bran's takeover of Hodor's mind, initially to save his life and the lives of the Reeds. The novels distinguish between the kind of imaginative identification we experience in storytelling and the forced hijacking of another person's experiences and actions, as Bran does to Hodor (*DwD* 14 Bran 2: 173–74). The equivalent in

storytelling parlance would be exploitation, when a person or group's experiences are represented under false or even violent circumstances, usually for the storyteller's benefit.

Works Cited

Deleuze, Gilles, and Félix Guattari. *A Thousand Plateaus: Capitalism and Schizophrenia.* Trans. Brian Massumi. Minneapolis: University of Minnesota Press, 1987. Print.

Fox, Michael W. *Behaviour of Wolves, Dogs and Related Canids.* Malabar, FL: Robert F. Krieger Publishing Company, 1971. Print.

Ghosh, Amitav. *The Shadow Lines.* New Delhi: Ravi Dayal, 1988. Print.

Klinghammer, Erich, ed. *The Behavior and Ecology of Wolves.* New York: Garland STPM Press, 1979. Print.

Sharp, Henry S. "Comparative Ethnography of the Wolf and the Chipewyan." *Wolf and Man: Evolution in Parallel.* Ed. Roberta L. Hall. New York: Academic Press, 1978. Print.

Tolkien, J.R.R. *The Lord of the Rings.* New York: Houghton Mifflin Harcourt, 2012.

Tunstall, Peter, trans. *The Saga of Hervor and King Heidrik the Wise.* The New Northvegr Center (NNC). 2009. Web.

Sex and the Citadel: Adapting Same Sex Desire from Martin's Westeros to HBO's Bedrooms

David C. Nel

One of the most widely-discussed features of the adaptation of George Martin's *Song of Ice and Fire* novels into the critically-acclaimed HBO television series *Game of Thrones* is the show's explicit depiction of sex and violence, but especially sexuality. So often does the television show condense character development and plotting into its numerous bathtub and bedroom scenes that journalist Myles McNutt has coined the term "sexposition" ("You Win") as a shorthand for these sequences, which graphically depict a variety of sexual combinations, including male and female same-sex couplings and incest. This essay is specifically interested in the hotly-debated same-sex relationship between Ser Loras, the favored son of the aspirational House Tyrell, and Prince Renly, a contender for the Iron Throne of Westeros, the central kingdom in Martin's fictional world. While some viewers have incredulously blogged their surprise at the show's explicit recognition of their homosexuality, others, such as reader and viewer "Brandon Stark," have recognized the "queer" content in Martin's novels. Martin's source texts do indeed provide multiple strong hints indicating a sexual dimension of the relationship between Renly and Loras, which the makers of the television series have clearly extrapolated into literal depictions of sexually-charged contact between the pair. It is the politics of this shift, from innuendo and rumor in Martin's novels, to literal depiction in the TV series, that this essay concentrates on. While there are many examples of other forms of transgressive sexuality in both novels and TV series, it is the dynamics of the *male* homosocial (and potentially homosexual) bonds of chivalry that, I will argue, reveal the contradictions inherent in chivalric masculinity. While HBO's series may appear to gesture toward a more progressive representation of male homosexuality than Martin's source novels, it remains trapped between simple representation and a radical re-imagining, because of its heavy reliance on modern stereotypes of queer masculinity.

There are, of course, other examples of alternative sexualities in Martin's novels as well as in *Game of Thrones* including incest (between Jaime and Cersei) and polyamory (Elia Martell) (*GoT* 9 Bran 2: 70–71; *SoS* 39 Tyrion 5: 433) which offer a counterpoint to Renly and Loras's affair. The lesbian pairings represented by Martin and the TV series are particularly interesting here. As historian Alan Bray observes, "there is no more revealing question about the friendship of traditional society than to ask how it encompassed women" (Bray 10). Bray's focus is on the primacy of male homosociality in chivalric relationships; he says it is only in relation to these sacrosanct bonds, always potentially queer, that women's sexuality is understood, so that, whether heterosexual or homosexual, it is always subordinated to some broader, male, heterosexual power dynamic.

The most prominent examples of lesbian pairings are the brief trysts between Daenerys Targaryen and her female servant, and between Cersei Lannister and her female lady-in-waiting. The treatment of these brief interludes contrasts strongly with the prolonged innuendo surrounding Renly Baratheon and Loras Tyrell, both individually, and together, as the longest prominent same-sex romantic pairing in both novels and television series. I will suggest, then, that there is a singularity in Martin's texts in the way that *male homosexuality* is treated, which is intimately connected with the dominant chivalric ideology in Westeros, and operates in conjunction with the television adaptation to present a tension between the entwined medievalist and contemporary discourses on homosexuality, masculinity and chivalry.

Notably, both these scenes take place within the wider context of *heterosexual* romantic plotlines: in Dany's case, she spends a sleepless night wrestling with the question of which of her three knights she actually loves, before waking up and seeking sexual solace from her maidservant Irri (*SoS* 4 Daenerys 2: 268). Cersei is merely curious: "She wondered what it would feel like to suckle on those breasts, to lay the Myrish woman on her back and push her legs apart and use her as a man would use her" (*FfC* 33 Cersei 7: 481). Both instances end in disavowal in the cold light of day. Dany's brief interlude results in Irri "[curling] back up and [going] back to sleep the instant the thing was done." "The next day," Daenerys muses, "it all seemed a dream. And what did Ser Jorah have to do with it, if anything?" Read in light of Dany's later remark in *A Dance with Dragons* that *"sometimes there is truth in dreams"* (*DwD* 44 Daenerys 7: 573), it appears that the very "truth" of her dream centers upon her *heterosexual* love interests, with the lesbian content merely serving Dany's larger, "real" heterosexual romantic life.

Some days later, when Dany is similarly "sad and lost" in thought about her love life, and Irri offers to repeat her sexual favor, Dany reminds her that "what happened that night, when you woke ... you're no bed slave, I freed you, remember?" (*SoS* 24 Daenerys 2: 270). When pressed, Dany rebuffs Irri more forcefully: "'I don't want that,' she insisted. 'I don't.' She turned away sharply. 'Leave me now. I want to be alone. To think.'" For her part, Cersei concludes: "it was no good. It had never been any good with anyone other than her brother, Jaime," before rebuffing an attempt by her maid Taena to repeat the experience, as the chapter closes with the following lines: "Dawn was breaking. It would be morning soon, and all of this would be forgotten" (*FfC* 33 Cersei 7: 486).

The formula followed by both scenes is striking: a restless or drunken night leading to lesbian sex, followed by a disavowal the following day, and a forceful refusal to repeat the experience. These refusals in the light of day to repeat the previous night's homosexual passion consign both to the realm of sexual experimentation which, ultimately, gives way to the larger heterosexual concerns of these two characters. What happens, however, when the lesbian sexuality of these trysts is translated into the visual codes of the "sexposition" sequences in the television series? In Season 1, we see Littlefinger, a Westerosi powerbroker, King's Master of Coin, and brothel owner, instruct two prostitutes working for him on how to pleasure each other sexually, for the benefit of their future male customers (*Thrones* S1: Ep. 7, "You Win or You Die"). Displeased with their lackluster performance of cunnilingus, Littlefinger shouts at them: "No, no, no!" before instructing one of them to digitally penetrate the other[1]: "you [gesturing to Ros] be the man, and you be the woman." Here Littlefinger clearly replicates the heterosexist formula, assuming that all sex acts must necessarily conform to the dynamics of male/female couplings, subsuming any suggestion of mutual (homo)sexual pleasure into a recognizably masculine, dominant, position and a feminine, submissive one. Janna Kim et al. would call such scenes part of the "heterosexual script" in prime time television, which, they argue, "compels girls/women to deny or devalue their own sexual desire, to seek to please boys/men, to 'wish and wait' to be chosen, and to trade their own sexuality as a commodity" (Kim et al. 146). In this scene, Ros obeys Littlefinger's instructions, but it is unclear whether or not the apparent pleasure this brings the penetrated partner is genuine, as they have both just been asked by Littlefinger, "Don't you realize how ridiculous you look?" Clearly, Ros and her partner don't know how they look, and this is precisely the point; their coupling is constituted solely for the visual pleasure and criticism of Littlefinger, with a view to their using this "technique" to titillate future heterosexual male customers. While

Ros and her partner proceed with another performance, Littlefinger gives "stage directions" to the participants, reminding them to bear in mind the secret desires of the intended heterosexual male audience:

> You're not fooling them, they just paid you. They know what you are. They know it's all just an act. Your job is to make them forget what they know, and that takes time. You need to ease into it. Go ahead, ease into it. He's winning you over in spite of yourself. You're starting to like this. He wants to believe you. He's enjoyed his cock since he was old enough to play with it. Why shouldn't you? He knows he's better than other men. He's always known it, deep down inside. Now he has proof. He's so good, he's reaching something deep inside of you that no one even knew was there, overcoming your very nature [*Thrones* S1: Ep. 7, "You Win or You Die"].

It is clear from these lines that Littlefinger is not fostering a space for the performance of a radical lesbian sexuality, nor merely witnessing it, but directing a performance intended for the heterosexual, male voyeur, reminiscent of Kim's "heterosexual script."

Despite the acknowledgement that this sexual interaction is an act, involving no real pleasure on the part of the female participants, Littlefinger's imagined male protagonist is evoking her pleasure "despite herself." Problematically, this is not pleasure for the woman's own sake, but an extension of the man's enjoyment of his own penis; essentially, in other words, an extension of his adolescent masturbatory fantasy. Simultaneously and paradoxically, while this imagined male consumer is aware that he is witnessing an act, a hired service performed for and upon him, his sexual prowess is somehow so compelling that, despite the "bought" nature of the intercourse, it reaches "something deep inside" of the actor, some desire contrary to her "nature," which proves he has won a competition with other men: "he knows he's better than other men." Moreover, the phrases "in spite of yourself" and "overcoming your very nature," while appearing to hint that somehow the actor achieves genuine sexual pleasure despite the commercial nature of their encounter, deploy a notion of female desire as inevitably conforming to male desire, a heterosexual male fantasy. Crucially, the performer's *own* sexuality is rooted "deep" within; thus not only might the participants come to enjoy their commodified sexual transactions, but they might also come to enjoy the pleasure of lesbian sex, in the service of their male customer's voyeuristic desire. Then, too, even as Littlefinger refuses Ros's repeated suggestions that he join in, the scene rehearses another male heterosexual fantasy of being with more than one woman.

In this scene, Littlefinger also reveals backstory that will be familiar to readers of Martin's novels: that he was fostered by Catelyn Tully (later Catelyn Stark)'s father, and fell in love with her. However, due to his relatively low social status, he was prevented from marrying her, as she was promised to the eldest son of a great House. After challenging his rival to a duel and losing, Littlefinger tells Ros that sex and money—and his control of both of these commodities in the social system of Westeros—are the only weapons he has against the system: "Do you know what I learned during that duel?" he asks Ros. "I learned that I will never win. Not that way. That's their game. Their rules. I'm not going to fight them, I'm going to fuck them. That's what I know, that's what I am. And only by admitting what we are can we get what we want" (*Thrones* S1: Ep. 7, "You Win or You Die"). Coming as Littlefinger's speeches do in the same episode, they suggest an intimate link between power, money and sex as aspects of the same social structure. More importantly, though, Littlefinger's references to the exposure of hidden desires, running deeper than—and counter to—a character's "nature," seem to speak to a more contemporary discourse related to self-knowledge and personal identity: "That's what I know, that's what I am."

In this way, Littlefinger's assertion of an essential identity recalls Michel Foucault's insistent reminder, in *A History of Sexuality*, that sexuality, in the sense of a coherent state of being, a subset of identity, emerges only in the nineteenth century, and functions in part by obscuring its own constructedness with a discourse of "essence" (Foucault 145), as indeed much subsequent 20th- and 21st-century thought has done in placing sexuality at the center of being, as a foundational category of selfhood, rather than an act or relationship in which an individual engages. The discourses of sexuality in HBO's *Game of Thrones* are essentialist in this way; they associate an individual's sexuality with "essential being," whilst also suggesting this being can be over-ridden, albeit for the pleasure of heterosexual men.

Before exploring how male-male sexual dynamics work in Martin's texts and the television series, I want to highlight the important differences between these lesbian sequences and the more publicly acknowledged, albeit derided, male-male relationship. The lesbian interludes do not take the form of a codified, socially recognized "relationship" (sexual or otherwise) in the same way that squires, kings and their Lords, do. Significantly, while there are examples of both male-male and female-female sex, and none are devoid of a certain power-imbalance, the women are commodified in a way that men are not. Their sexuality is generally associated, in these scenes, with Littlefinger—quite directly and explicitly—with an exchange economy. Whereas Loras and Renly talk about blood, sport, and war, and how Loras's family can help Renly win the Iron Throne, they are not directed, as Roz is by Littlefinger; while Loras and Renly are objects of mild derision (on one hand) and dangerous, prejudiced proscription by Joffrey (on the other), these female trysts are not even worthy of mention, let alone derision.

The self-realization and open declaration Littlefinger mobilizes in these scenes is very different from the medievalist treatment of sex and sexuality in Martin's books, where sex acts are frequently alluded to through often pointed double-entendres about sword fighting, and even occasionally described (as in the cases of Cersei and Daenerys above), but never presented as constituting a coherent identity in quite the direct way expressed in the television series. I suggest that the show is propelled by late 20th and early 21st century identity politics' emphasis on candid self-declaration, exploration and sexual representation to re-imagine the novels in terms of explicit sexualities. What is more, I contend that viewers are thus provoked to read the novels *in the light of* the television series, searching for textual "clues" that will bolster the claims made on screen.

Foucault's thesis—and the 20th and 21st-century "identitarian" politics it inspired—is complicated by other textual studies, such as Bray's, of the institution of male friendship in the eighteenth century. Bray not only suggests that friendship encompassed the possibility of homoeroticism, in its explicit exclusion of women (10), but also that there was a shift in the way that homosexual desire was configured: "in this new conception ... homosexual desire was not represented as an alternative sexuality, a different but in some way logically symmetrical choice to heterosexuality: it was a perversion of something else" (Bray 218). The important point is that this shift, unlike Foucault's model of a newly-emerged sexual "self," is a *cultural* one, drawing upon older concepts of friendship in which hetero- and homosexuality are not opposites or "alternatives," as he puts it, but two sides of the same coin.

To return to the issue of adaptation, such reimagining inevitably entails an anachronistic reading of Martin's source texts, both in returning to the texts themselves, but also in applying contemporary concepts of queer identity to Martin's medievalism. One example is the allegorical reading, from both fans and professional critics alike, of King Renly's "Rainbow Guard" as a clue to Renly's sexuality which can only be read anachronistically in the light of the contemporary gay liberation movement's rainbow flag, a signifier of "queer" presence recognizable in popular culture (Hennessey 111–115). We first encounter the Rainbow Guard in the novels after the death of King Robert Baratheon, when his brother Renly assembles a host of knights loyal to him and declares himself King, raising his own Kingsguard (*CoK* 1 Prologue: 8). David Barr Kirtley points out that the television series pays little attention to this visual signifier, suggesting the possible conflation of the rainbow flag with homosexuality as a possible reason for its omission from the television show:

> The show seems to have done away with the Rainbow Guard, which is probably for
> the best. A Rainbow Guard makes a certain amount of sense within the context of
> Westerosi society, whose dominant religion uses the rainbow to symbolize the seven

aspects of God, but a Rainbow Guard strikes many readers as a distracting, fourth-wall-breaking gag about Renly's sexuality [Kirtley].

The dominant official religion in Westeros, the Faith of the Seven (*GoT* 3 Catelyn 1: 18), to which Kirtley refers, places crystals, and the rainbow diffraction patterns they produce when light is passed through them, at the center of its symbology. Divorced from the symbolism of the Seven, viewers are left with uneasy symbolism of contemporary gay activism, and activism of identity that, in the culture at large, as in the texts under discussion, seems to center around connotation, denial and affirmation. Kirtley's analysis of the "Rainbow Guard" identifies a tension between the identity politics in which the show seems to be invested, and the medievalist treatment of homosexuality in Martin's source novels; between recognizable symbols of a coherent, alternative identity, and strong hints in Martin's fictional universe.

Carolyn Dinshaw draws our attention to the problem this tension represents for approaching medievalist source material with contemporary ideas of sexuality in mind, calling it "the contradictory discourse about same-sex sexual relations that splits discussions of the issue, medieval and postmodern: desire for it is natural and presumably innate, but seems unnatural as well, and can be taught, or even caught" (Dinshaw 11).

The novels' strongest hints that chivalric same-sex bonds are at least potentially sexual are made after Renly's death, as the Queen Regent Cersei mulls over the need for her son King Tommen to learn the arts of war. She is advised by Ser Loras that this role is traditionally served by the Master at Arms, who has recently been slain. Loras campaigns strongly for the position:

> "His Grace is almost nine, and eager to learn. At his age he should be a squire. Someone has to teach him."
>
> *Someone will, but it will not be you.* "Pray, who did you squire for, ser?" she asked sweetly. "Lord Renly, was it not?"
>
> "I had that honor."
>
> "Yes. I thought as much." Cersei had seen how tight the bonds grew between squires and the knights they served. She did not want Tommen growing close to Loras Tyrell. The Knight of Flowers was no sort of man for any boy to emulate [*FfC* 25 Cersei 5: 350–351].

This passage recalls how the chivalric bond of squiring functions, namely as a way of training knights-in-waiting (Broughton 298–99). It is indeed traditional for the knights in Martin's novels, like their historical medieval counterparts, to induct new members into their orders. Medieval chroniclers describe the process using amatory, if not directly erotic, language. Geoffrey de Charney, at 14th-century knight, for example, chronicles an intimate ritual whereby older knights disrobe, bathe and dry a novice, before all parties lie down on a bed together, signifying the knight's new life when he arises. Charney writes that after this ceremony, "the knights who confer the order [of knighthood] on novices should kiss them as a sign of confirmation of the order conferred on them and received by them" (Kaeuper & Kennedy [Translation] 171). Other medieval scholars confirm the content of the "dubbing ceremony" and add that the "accolade" (literally "neck-blow" from the Medieval French *colée*) at the end of the ceremony was occasionally substituted with a kiss (Broughton 294). Martin's Cersei, it seems, is aware that the figure of the squire, like other feudal same-sex bonds, is at least a potentially sexually charged social bond, and, if squires are capable of "inheriting" the characteristics of their lord (whether heterosexual or homosexual), they may be the source of a homoeroticism that troubles her, and disrupts her political aspirations for her youngest son.

Significantly, it is not just sexuality (including homosexuality) which might be "learned" in the bonds of the squire-knight relationship, but also the performance of a particular *kind* of heterosexuality, focused on killing, drinking, hunting and wenching. In Martin's final novel, *A Dance with Dragons*, Stannis Baratheon refers to a knight's sexual promiscuity as having been learned from his master's legendary appetites: "He once served my brother Robert as squire and acquired his appetite for female flesh" (*DwD* 18 Jon 4: 227). In Loras's case, however, despite Loras's widely acknowledged prowess at arms, his masculinity is rendered suspect by rumors about his sexuality, making him (in Cersei's eyes) "not the sort of man for any boy to emulate." The word "sort" is telling here, indicating that there is a group or "type" of man that Loras embodies, which is inferior to the dominant chivalric ideal, despite the fact that Loras is a more competent courtier and fighter than Robert's own sons. These are the grounds on which Cersei rejects him as a model for Tommen:

> "You'll need to look long and hard to find a better jouster than Loras Tyrell. Ser Loras is—"
> "I know what he is. I won't have him near my son" [*FfC* 25 Cersei 5: 355].

Significantly, what Ser Loras "is" is not discussed directly; it is the stuff of subtext and innuendo, in which rumored sexual practices are linked to his identity—what he literally "is." I use "essentialism" to mark this conflation of Loras with his homosexuality, a gesture which assumes a coherent and stable sexuality as identity, in line with contemporary identity politics. Such an essentialism need not assume sexuality is natural or innate; critically, however, it is at odds with a view of sexuality as a set of practices.

Throughout Martin's novels, the clues that Cersei has become aware of are presented. The Web archivist "Maester Luwin" has usefully summarized the most often cited textual evidence for a sexual relationship between Renly and

Loras, beginning with Queen Margaery's reputed virginity long after her wedding to Renly (*CoK* 32 Catelyn 3: 358). "Maester Luwin" goes on to remind us of snippets of dialogue in the novels describing Renly's servants as having had "a great deal of practice at being blind, deaf and mute" (*SoS* 59 Tyrion 7: 655), and finally notes Renly's fashionable clothing and his fondness for the rainbow motif, claiming that "since such fashion sense in a male is another sign of being gay in our world, this could be another clue put in to help point out Renly's doubtful heterosexuality" ("Maester Luwin" I.4). In another section entitled "Thoughts about Loras" (II), "Maester Luwin" reminds us that Loras is derisively known as the "Knight O' Pansies" (*CoK* 31 Arya 7: 349) by a fellow knight, and, more suggestively, "Renly's little rose" by yet another (*SoS* 39 Tyrion 5: 437). Moreover, on the night before Renly's death, Loras stays behind to "pray" with Renly (*CoK* 32 Catelyn 3: 362). George R.R. Martin has specifically stated, "Yes, I did intend those characters to be gay," and a commenter added, "Not that we didn't already know that, of course, but I don't believed [*sic*] it's ever been actually confirmed before" ("odiedragon"). It's worth noting that the consideration of textual "evidence" or "clues" in order to buttress a "case" that a character is homosexual assumes that everyone is heterosexual until proven otherwise, so to speak. It also suggests that any assertion to the contrary is some sort of accusation of wrongdoing, requiring solid evidence. Nor does *Maester Luwin's Archive* exhaust the text-mining enterprise. One might (and commentators have) cite Catelyn's observation of Renly whispering affectionately in Loras's ear (*CoK* 23 Catelyn 2: 263), or Loras's defense of his decision to forgo marriage and children after Renly's death to enter the Kingsguard, stating that "when the sun has set, no candle can replace it" (*SoS* 13 Tyrion 2: 137).

Such clue-dropping is not limited to the novels. The television series is similarly inclined to retrospectively reveal back story about Renly long after his death. Jaime Lannister, for example, taunts Lady Brienne for the "flame" she carries for Renly. He says: "it's all true about Renly. His proclivities were the worst-kept secret at court. It's a shame the throne isn't made out of cocks; they'd never have got him off it!" (*Thrones* S3: Ep. 2, "Dark Wings, Dark Words"). When Brienne states that she is not interested in "foul rumours," Jaime is uncharacteristically compassionate, stating: "I don't blame him, and I don't blame you either. We don't get to choose who we love." He seems here to be comparing Brienne's love for Renly to his own incestuous relationship with his twin sister Cersei, and perhaps even Renly's sexuality to his own incest. Clearly, the latter reading produces a number of ethical objections, but the main point here is the essentialist view of sexuality at work in the idea that "we don't get to choose who we love."

In a sense, the textual evidence, riddled with innuendo, is less illuminating in what it reveals about Renly and Loras's relationship than it is about the text-miners themselves, whose work relies on precisely the kind of innuendo that the critic Miller describes as the "connotative" register, whereby homosexuality is alluded to, and even strongly hinted at, but never directly shown or spoken about. Miller writes that "connotation ... excites the desire for proof, a desire that, so long as it develops within the connotative register, tends to draft every signifier into what nonetheless remains a hopeless task" (123) that is, into making a "case" for homosexuality. This is precisely the activity evident in "Maester Luwin's" summation:

> In conclusion, it seems quite likely that there was a gay relationship between Loras and Renly. Numerous characters such as Chiswyck, Oberyn, Jaime, Tyrion and Littlefinger all seem to have heard rumors of the couple's homosexuality. Even there [sic] own kin, Stannis and Garlan, seem to think that their brother might be gay. Coupled with Loras's emotional feelings and words whenever he refers to Renly, it certainly seems extremely likely that he was [sic] gay lovers with Renly ["Maester Luwin"].[2]

The transition from Martin's textual denotation to the literal, explicit depiction of the "sexposition" scenes in the television series exposes the tension in Martin's texts between the connotative and denotative registers.

The most exemplary scene in this regard is the Tourney of the Hand, detailed in Book One, Martin's first novel, *A Game of Thrones*, and adapted in the television episode "The Wolf and the Lion." The entire sequence is rendered in the episode outside of any character's individual perspective, and is instead reconfigured to focus on the sexual and wider politics at Court. This transposition has the effect of substituting Ned Stark's perspective in the book—the "correct" or knightly perspective—with the "official" or "public" perspective in the TV episode. More importantly, however, the scene functions as a set piece of homoerotic double entendre between Littlefinger and Renly, whose avid interest in the outcome of the joust between Ser Gregory and Loras suggests that they both have more than money at stake:

> LITTLEFINGER: 100 Gold Dragons on the "Mountain." Now, what will I buy with a 100 Gold Dragons, I wonder? A dozen barrels of Dornish wine, or a girl from the pleasure-houses of Lys?
> RENLY: You could even buy a friend!
> ...
> RENLY: Such a shame, Littlefinger. It would have been so nice for you to have a friend.
> LITTLEFINGER: And tell me, Lord Renly, when will you be "having" your friend? (nodding to Loras).
> LITTLEFINGER (whispering to Sansa): Loras knew his mare was in heat. He's quite crafty, you know.

SANSA: Ser Loras would never do that. There's no honour in tricks!
LITTLEFINGER: No honour, but quite a bit of gold! [*Thrones* S1: Ep. 5, "The Wolf and the Lion"].

This knowing exchange is revealing, in that it links sex, power and money, picking up the thread of associations assembled in the earlier scene in Littlefinger's brothel. Much of his wealth, as we already know, is derived from nefarious dealings, including prostitution; Renly sneers here at the commodification of intimacy we have already associated with Littlefinger. It is significant that Renly mocks not the more obvious association between Littlefinger and prostitution, but his ability to have "real" (read: male) friends, namely friends who are not bought—friendship again being the foundation of knightly interactions (Broughton 291). Littlefinger's retort turns this implication around, essentially implying that he knows Renly and Loras are *more* than just friends, suggesting that, perhaps, it is better to have no friends, or even bought friends, than to have sex with one's actual male friend.

This entire exchange suggests that male friendship, in the fraternal, intense, homosocial sense identified by Charny as the chivalric ideal, albeit an ideal that Martin challenges in many instances in the novels, occupies a separate, more elevated, sphere from other forms of social (and sexual) relations, even the brief lesbian trysts we have seen earlier. This comparison is repeated throughout HBO's *Game of Thrones*, for example when Queen Cersei, later in the same episode, jests about the "marriage" between Ned Stark and King Robert, based on their close bond forged in battle (*Thrones* S1 Ep. 5, "The Wolf and the Lion"). Zeikowitz underscores the fact that "chivalric orders developing in ... the late 14th century were based on close personal ties" (Zeikowitz 13). More importantly, however, while the novels problematically consign Renly and Loras's relationship to the shadows of innuendo and derisive wordplay, the televisual version exploits this innuendo in Martin's source material to present a more complex take, when considered together with the novels, on the relationship between homosexuality and the chivalric economy depicted in Martin's fictional universe.

Shortly after the tourney scene, we are presented with the first of the "sex-position" scenes (McNutt, "You Win") between Loras and Renly, as Renly shaves Loras while they discuss that day's Council. Renly reveals that Daenerys Targaryen, daughter of the "mad king" whom Robert deposed, has been wed to a warlord on the continent of Esteros, and is pregnant. The child could pose a threat to Robert's reign. It is possible to view in this sequence the shift from what Miller calls verbal "connotation" to relatively explicit visual "denotation," or depiction, in action. Although it features nowhere in the novels, the scene continues the theme of money, politics, and sex which is inaugurated in the earlier tourney scene. As Loras lathers up a shirtless Renly in order to shave his chest (which, Loras informs him, will make him more attractive to Loras), the two engage in part political gossip, part flirtation. At the beginning of the scene, the two are discussing Ned Stark's work as the King's new Hand, which has upset the delicate balance of power in the realm:

> LORAS: Lord Stark's lucky he still has a head.
> RENLY: Robert will rant for a few days, but he won't do anything. He adores the man.
> LORAS (playfully): You're jealous!
> RENLY (as Loras puts lather on Renly's chest and lifts a shaving blade to it): Are you sure this won't hurt? (As Loras begins to shave). If you want hairless, maybe you should find a little boy.
> LORAS (firmly): I want you! [*Thrones* S1: Ep. 5, "The Wolf and the Lion"].

This exchange reifies the double entendre made earlier in the episode by Littlefinger at the tourney concerning how, and with whom, Renly uses his "sword." Earlier I noted the work of fans in "mining" the text for potentially "queer" signifiers, which are then placed under the organizing category of a character's homosexuality, requiring confirmation which they themselves provide. Miller cautions against such "mining" for every piece of innuendo and subtext, suggesting that it can objectify the (potentially) homosexual figure by placing him at the center of suspicion and close scrutiny, a stable and coherent figure testifying to a distinct, monolithic homosexuality. In HBO's *Game of Thrones*, however, I suggest that instead a dialogue is being created, between Martin's source texts and the extended fictional space of the television series, where, as I will show, competing discourses on homosexuality and chivalry are (often simultaneously) articulated, in conflict with each other.

This scene also implicates Renly and Loras in the complex politics in the kingdom, where King Robert (Renly's brother) has recently appointed Ned Stark the King's "Hand," or second-in-command, after the suspicious death of his predecessor. That the bond shared by the King and his Hand makes his biological brother jealous is not simply a matter of fraternal jealousy, but a political slight, depriving Renly of what he sees as his rightful, familial influence over the Kingdoms' politics, though Loras conflates feudal bonds with amorous ones. Robert's shared history with Ned Stark relegates his own brother to subordinate status in the King's council:

> RENLY: My brother thinks that anyone who hasn't been to war isn't a man. He treats me as if I'm a spoiled child. [Loras appears to smirk in mock-agreement]. Oh, and you're not? "Loras Tyrell, the Knight of Flowers." How many wars have you fought in? Oh, and how much did your father spend on that armour of yours? All I ever hear from Robert and Stannis is how I'm not tough enough, how I squirm at the sight of blood.

LORAS: You *did* vomit when that boy's eye was knocked out in the melee.

RENLY: His eye was dangling out of the damn socket!

LORAS: He shouldn't have entered the melee if he didn't know how to fight.

RENLY: Easy for you to say! Not everyone is such a gifted swordsman.

LORAS (sighing): It's not a gift, no one gave it to me. I'm good because I work at it. Every day of my life since I could hold a stick.

RENLY: I could work at fighting all day every day, and still not be as good as you [*Thrones* S1: Ep. 5, "The Wolf and the Lion"].

This dialogue turns on the successful performance of what gender theorist R.W. Connell calls "hegemonic masculinity" (Connell), suggesting a hierarchy of different practices which socially inscribe masculine identity according to a largely fictional ideal. Migliaccio explains: "hegemonic masculinity is used as an ideal against which other masculine performances are judged" (Migliaccio 227). Crucially, although one of their ostensible objectives within the heterosexual "script" is to win the favor of women, these performances, to the extent that they are competitive, are ultimately performances *directed at (and against) other men*. The masculine kudos is earned (in combat by Ned Stark) or learned (in the case of Loras), but the scene also proposes as hegemonic the kind of masculinity idealized in chivalric knighthood, which requires competitive participation (and triumph) in battle, and leadership. While Renly is technically fourth in line to the throne, and therefore has a tenuous but significant claim to power, his lack of military prowess simultaneously emasculates and infantilizes him in the eyes of Robert, his brother and King, and therefore within the hierarchy of the Seven Kingdoms. Loras has the requisite skills (or at least a performance of the skills), noble birth, and money to propel Renly to the throne.

This scene also illustrates a shift from Miller's "connotation" to literal "depiction" of a clearly erotically charged scene (pace Miller 123). While it remains "connotation," however, he is quite insistent that such innuendo reinforces the idea of the closet (Miller 125). Critically, such connotation "suffers from ... an abiding deniability. To refuse the evidence for a merely connoted meaning is as simple ... as uttering the words 'but isn't it just?...' before retorting the connotation" (Miller 118; qtd. in Evans and Gamman 48). In other words, the connotative conversation about homosexuality (which can pretend to be about something else) is in the business of "denying homosexuality even as it reiterates it" (Evans and Gamman 48). We have seen this process at work in "Maester Luwin's" recruitment of the signifiers of homosexuality to "prove" its existence in a text, and other fan websites, wikis, and blogs share this feverish speculation. In terms of this scene's reception, there is a fairly broad consensus that the scene sets up, and breaks off just prior to, at the very least an act of fellatio between Renly and Loras: "Then we see them having a shave, talks of a new king, and a blowjob? Really? I don't see how that scene was needed in the least bit," complains one viewer ("Trollsbane"), while others express alarm and disbelief at this apparently shocking revelation: "Renly and Ser Loras GAY????? SERIOUSLY? ... I never pictured either of them as being gay, matter of fact, I think the books picture Renly as being VERY STRAIGHT and VERY much like Robert in the fact that he is constantly fucking whores. How did you let this happen GRRM?? I don't know if I can watch any more man on man, shaving each others body scenes" ("Dan"). These and similar remarks sparked a furious verbal war, with other fans arguing that "It's in the books. You just decided not to read it. Obviously they made it very apparent here, but GRRM hints at it quite noticeably" ("Brandon Stark"), and suggest that the surprise and disgust expressed here is homophobic. This audience response is important despite Martin's clear assertion that this was his intention for these characters ("Odiedragon"). Although authorial intention does matter, the processes both of audiences reconsidering connotations in the novels in the light of explicit denotation in the television series, and that of the producers choosing to mobilize this denotation, have diverged and followed their own trajectories. "Brandon Stark" argues, too, that such responses ignore apparently clear evidence in Martin's source texts that Renly is gay, and that he is romantically involved with Loras. Yet I would suggest that this "evidence" is only apparent in light of Martin's confirmation, which, to use Miller's phrasing, "draft[s] every signifier" into the conviction of a character on grounds of homosexuality.

Strikingly, the most explicit of the Renly-Loras scenes, the shaving scene, mobilizes a critique of hegemonic masculinity as exemplified by Renly's brother, King Robert, whilst simultaneously dispelling any ambiguity surrounding the relationship between the two.

> RENLY: Robert's threatening to take me hunting with him. The last time we were out there for two weeks, tramping through the trees in the rain, day after day, all so he could stick his spear into something's flesh. (sighs) But, Robert loves his killing. And he's the King.
> LORAS (sarcastically wondering): Hmm, how did *that* ever happen?
> RENLY: Because he loves his killing! And he used to be good at it.
> RENLY (as Loras deliberately nicks his chest with the shaving blade, drawing blood): What are you doing?! You cut me!
> LORAS (pointing to the wound): Look at it! It's just blood. We've all got it in us, and sometimes, a little spills. If you become king, you're going to see a lot of this. Go on, look! People love you (looking at Renly adoringly). They love to serve you because you're kind to them. They want to be near you. You're willing to do what needs to be done. But you don't gloat over it, you don't love killing.
> (They stand up as Loras is saying this, and he holds Renly lovingly by the arms.)
> Where is it written that power is the sole province of the worst? (Loras unbuttons

Renly's trousers) that thrones are only made for the hated and the feared. You would be a *wonderful* king. (He lowers himself onto his knees in front of Renly, and undoes Renly's pants. The camera focuses on Renly's face, which displays obvious pleasure, before the scene ends) [*Thrones* S1: Ep.5, "The Wolf and the Lion"].

While Loras acknowledges that, in the pursuit of political goals, a little blood will inevitably be spilled, a great lust for killing is not a kingly attribute. He instead appeals to the people's love of him, conflating it with his own love for Renly, as he prepares to perform a sex act on Lord Renly, arguing that Renly's ability to inspire love makes his claim superior to those of Robert's sons or his other brother Stannis, on the ethical grounds of populist, "good" kingship. In short, his claim is based on love, the same love that elsewhere characterizes the bond between feudal lord and vassal or kings and their knights. Indeed, Loras implies that Renly's homosexuality is not as much of a barrier to kingship as his lack of interest in the performative elements of chivalry. Yet in Westerosi terms Renly's homosexuality is clearly a "vice" that stretches the definition of kingship a little too far for the meta-narrative to contain.

Indeed, this is suggested by Renly's death in the television series, in which Renly is killed as he is disrobing by a spectral figure, who stabs him in the back. This stabbing may signify what the critic Miller calls "the penetrated, penetrable anus" (Miller 129),[3] especially given the numerous references to Renly sitting on swords, shoving swords up Loras, and other crude allusions to anal sex. In this sense Renly's stabbing implicates male homosexuality in a discourse of danger and risk, which it would be difficult to read as anything other than a homophobic expulsion of the figure of the gay male from the narrative. Loras is, it is true, less expelled than exiled, placed in suspended narrative animation in the novels, after volunteering for a risky raid on Stannis's island stronghold Dragonstone (*FfC* 33 Cersei 7: 477), allegedly incurring mortal wounds. However, to the extent that his relationship with Renly is terminated upon the former's death, and that Loras regards this relationship as the love to end all loves (for himself, from his youthful perspective, at any rate), I would suggest that he is effectively neutered.

Significantly, the television series invents a scene dramatizing the negotiations between the Lannisters and the Tyrells about how to dispose of their problematic children, showing Lord Tywin in a fiery battle of words with Lady Olenna Tyrell, Loras's formidable grandmother, in which Olenna confirms Loras's sexual orientation. Olenna claims that Loras is "the most desirable bachelor in all seven kingdoms," and Tywin counters that Cersei "is rich, the most beautiful woman in all the seven kingdoms, and the mother of the king," before Olenna suggests the real reason for her objection, simply stating "Old!" (*Thrones*

S3: Ep. 6: "The Climb"). As Olenna remarks, she is "something of an expert on the subject" of age, and in an interesting counterpoint to the earlier scene in which Renly is described retching at the sight of blood she implies that blood spilled in battle is mild compared to the menopause, which would "turn [Tywin's] stomach." Tywin responds blow for blow, assuring Lady Olenna that "the long years punish us [men] as well, I promise you that." Their repartee is configured in terms of bodily functions and, specifically, the functioning of gendered bodies, and the uses to which they are put. Tywin continues, arguing that what *really* turns his stomach is the "details of [Olenna's] grandson's nocturnal activities," daring Olenna to deny them. Indeed Tywin, the embodiment of patriarchal, feudal masculinity, enjoys battle, but cannot abide the thought of homosexuality.

Olenna is entirely unperturbed by the accusation, responding, "Oh, not at all! A sword-swallower, through and through," thus continuing the chain of phallic imagery initiated by Littlefinger in the tourney scene. Brushing aside Tywin's suggestion that "a boy with [his] affliction should be grateful for the opportunity to marry the most beautiful woman in all the seven kingdoms, and remove the stain from his name," she takes issue with Tywin's argument that Loras's homosexuality is pathological, asking Lord Tywin if he ever indulged in a "roll in the hay" with a stable boy when he was younger. When Tywin adamantly declares that he never did, she congratulates him on his "restraint," and states that "it's a natural thing, two boys having a go at each other beneath the sheets." Later in the same scene, she remarks that the Tyrells don't "tie ourselves up in knots about a bit of discreet buggery," countering Tywin's selective disgust and hypocrisy (which ignores incest, but balks at homosexuality) by suggesting that the *real* scandal against nature and morality is Cersei and Jaime's incestuous relationship: "where I come from, *that* stain would be very difficult to wash out."

The entire scene reproduces beautifully the tension between the competing discourses on homosexuality. On the one hand, it is a series of bodily acts not necessarily constituting a solidified, stable, or coherent sexual identity, but no more unnatural than the aging process; on the other hand, it is a social and political construction. Importantly, while Martin's novels resist any explicit discussion or depiction of male homosexuality beyond innuendo and rumor, Lady Olenna explodes this silence in the television episode by directly confirming Loras's homosexuality, namely that of a "sword-swallower, through and through." Although as a euphemism, the term "sword-swallower" bears allegiance to the regime of innuendo, the phrase "through and through" suggests that she is talking about more than a passing dalliance with stable boys. Indeed she seems to speak to an essentialized identity, in keeping with contemporary identity politics, and in her confirmation she destroys the power of the innuendo in a way that Tywin's refusal to repeat the rumors about his children's incest does not. Homosexuality and incest compete here in the hierarchy of morality and disgust, and it is interesting that Tywin sees Cersei's incest as fundamentally unspeakable, saying "I will not breathe further life into a malicious lie by discussing it."

In the end it is Tywin who arguably "wins" the contest, succeeding in compelling the match between Cersei and Loras by threatening to appoint Loras to the Kingsguard: "'I'm sure you're familiar with the Kingsguard's vows. He will never marry. He will never have children. The Tyrell name will fade, and Highgarden will go to the children of Joffrey and Margaery.'"

The most crucial aspect of this alliance, for both Lannisters and Tyrells, is its issue, which has little to do with Loras's homosexuality, and more to do with Cersei's diminishing fertility. When Joffrey dies, Cersei becomes Queen Regent, and Loras does indeed go into the Kingsguard. Ultimately he doesn't seem to have a problem with this. He argues first that third sons don't need to reproduce. Second, he implies that any other relationship than his with Renly would not be "natural" for him, or in some way would be a "second choice" of sorts for him. In a way, this mimics contemporary discourse on homosexuality, which focuses less on sexual behavior, proscribed or not, and more on a loving relationship in a discourse linked to personal identity, fulfillment and satisfaction, a core, internal identity.

It is in this discursive territory—of personal identity, fulfillment and satisfaction—or rather, the lack of them, that Martin's novels leave Ser Loras. In the latest book, *A Dance with Dragons*, it is reported that Loras has been seriously wounded leading the assault on Dragonstone, and there is unconfirmed speculation about his death. The narrative's longest and arguably most significant queer relationship is effectively expelled from the text, first by the curtailment of his sexual activities in the celibate Kingsguard, and, secondly, by his exile and wounding, both of which happen offstage.

In a critical scene in the novels, Tyrion Lannister sympathizes with Loras, but sees him as visually out of place in the Kingsguard, so closely allied has he been with the now-dead Renly's Rainbow Guard. He wonders, too, what has motivated a young, attractive knight at the height of his career to join a celibate order:

> *Seventeen, and beautiful, and already a legend. Half the girls in the Seven Kingdoms want to bed him, and all the boys want to be him.* "If you will pardon my asking, ser— why would anyone choose to join the Kingsguard at seventeen?"
>
> "Prince Aemon the Dragonknight took his vows at seventeen," Ser Loras said, "and your brother Jaime was younger still."
>
> "I know their reasons. What are yours? The honor of serving beside such paragons

as Meryn Trant and Boros Blount?" He gave the boy a mocking grin. "To guard the king's life, you surrender your own. You give up your lands and titles, give up hope of marriage, children...."

"House Tyrell continues through my brothers," Ser Loras said. "It is not necessary for a third son to wed, or breed."

"Not necessary, but some find it pleasant. What of love?"

"When the sun has set, no candle can replace it" [*SoS* 13 Tyrion 2: 137].

Tyrion here echoes Sansa's much earlier description of Loras as "beautiful." Significantly, however, Loras's exploits have assured him a place in "legend," making him—contrary to Cersei's opinion about his fitness as a role model—a fantasy figure both for male Knights-in-training, and for starry-eyed young women. Significantly, Tyrion shifts the discourse here to a more 21st-century understanding of sexual identity and personal satisfaction, and Loras responds allegorically that his first or "real" love is gone, so there can be no other lover. While Loras's melancholy trope of sunset can of course be attributed to the hyperbole of youthful romanticism, the comparison of a natural source of light, the sun, to an artificial light source again suggests, as does Lady Olenna in the show, that his love for Renly was natural, while a conventional marriage would be unnatural and thus no substitute.

Here again, the novels mix ideas about what is exemplified in romantic tales, and what is politically and socially acceptable or even necessary. When Tyrion compares Loras's melodramatic metaphor of the setting sun to a song, he consigns Loras's experience with Renly to the realm of "legend." But Tyrion regrets his disparagement: "'No. If I've given offense, forgive me. I had my own love once, and we had a song as well.' *I loved a maid as fair as summer, with sunlight in her hair*" (*SoS* 13 Tyrion 2: 137). Loras's love and loss, therefore, is not singular, as Tyrion provides another example of a "true" love lost, from whom he was cruelly separated by his father, who commanded Tyrion's brother Jaime to lie, saying that his bride Tysha was hired to initiate Tyrion sexually (*SoS* 78 Tyrion 11: 871). I suggest that Tyrion's move is both sympathetic and symbolically inclusive, equating Loras's queer love story to his own. He effectively situates both kinds of "queer" romance within the discursive space of the romantic lyric. He thus equalizes the hetero- and homosexual romances and reminds us that the conventions of romance are encoded as much by the surviving cultural form of the lyric, perhaps even more so, than the historical context of their production.

Renly's death does not, in HBO's *Game of Thrones*, quite bring Loras's romantic life to an end, despite his romantic protestations. Seduced by Olyvar, who squires for him in a contest, but who is in fact one of Varys's spies, Loras naively confesses his own role in the complicated marital plots put about by the

Lannisters and the Tyrells (*Thrones* S3: Ep. 5, "Blessed by Fire"). In this sense the show continues Loras's romantic plots beyond where the book arrests them, with the death of Renly, though as I have suggested, it attempts to contain Loras's desire within the "cover" of an arranged marriage.

At the time of writing, there are two gaps between the romance of Ser Loras and Prince Renly and "our" world; firstly, the time lag between the five novels already published, and the four television seasons, each roughly based on a corresponding book; and secondly, the narrative gap between the last volume, *A Dance with Dragons*, which leaves Ser Loras in narrative suspended animation, apparently preparing to subside, like many other lost loves in Westeros, into the timeless realm of legend: "seventeen, and beautiful, and already a legend." It would, of-course, be fruitless to speculate on the outcome of this particular narrative arc in the light of the incomplete novel(s) and television adaptations. Rather, I have attempted to sketch out the contribution of this queer romantic sub-plot to Martin's broader critique of chivalry, which I suggest are thrown into relief through the adaptation process. More importantly, I have argued that this adaptation process itself illustrates some of the political and narrative issues involved in the discussion of male homosexuality, namely that, despite the presence of potentially liberating discourses seeking altruistically to neutralize and thereby equalize the figuration of sexual difference in fiction, the cultural "scripts" which are handed down to us dictate the very terms in which this debate about representation is framed.

Notes

1. Thus perhaps playing on Littlefinger's monicker.
2. Miller calls this practice "the signifying process of homophobia" (Miller 119). I disagree, along with Evans and Gamman, that this necessarily constitutes homophobia per se (48). I will discuss the reasons for this later.
3. I owe this reading to Miller's analysis of Alfred Hitchcock's *Rope*, in which he maps out the features of homophobic discourse. Miller draws our attention to the film's frequent allusions to a pervasive phobia of anal sex, culminating in the brutal slaying of a friend and former lover by stabbing him from "behind."

Works Cited

Benioff, David, and D.B. Weiss, prods. *Game of Thrones*. HBO. 2011–2014.
"Brandon Stark." "RE: Episode 5—The Wolf and the Lion—Recap." Comment # 103598. *Winteriscoming*. 15 May 2011. Web. 29 May 2014.
Bray, Alan. *The Friend*. Chicago: University of Chicago Press, 2003. Print.
Broughton, Bradford B. *Dictionary of Medieval Knighthood and Chivalry: Concepts and Terms*. Westport, CT: Greenwood Press, 1986. Print.
Connell, R.W. "Hegemonic Masculinity: Rethinking the Concept." *Gender & Society* 19 (2005): 829–859.
Crider, Paul. "Fantasy, Feminism, and *A Song of Ice and Fire*." *Quitting Providence*. Blog. 27 August 2011. Web. 26 June 2014.

"Dan." "RE: Episode 5—The Wolf and the Lion—Recap." Comment # 103591. *Winteriscoming*. 15 May 2011. Web. 29 May 2014.

Dinshaw, Carolyn. *Getting Medieval: Sexualities and Communities, Pre- and Post-Modern*. Durham: Duke University Press, 1999. Print.

Evans, Caroline, and Lorraine Gamman. "The Gaze Revisited, Or Reviewing Queer Viewing." Ed. Paul Burston and Colin Richardson. *A Queer Romance: Lesbians, Gay Men and Popular Culture*. London: Routledge, 2005. 12–61. Print.

Foucault, Michel. *The History of Sexuality*. Vol. 1. New York: Random House. 1978. Print.

Hennessy, Rosemary. *Profit and Pleasure: Sexual Identities in Late Capitalism*. New York: Routledge, 2000. Print.

Kaeuper, Richard W., and Elspeth Kennedy. *The Book of Chivalry of Geoffroi de Charny: Text, Context, and Translation*. Philadelphia: University of Pennsylvania Press, 1996. Print.

Kim, Janna L., et al. "From Sex to Sexuality: Exposing the Heterosexual Script on Primetime Network Television." *Journal of Sex Research* 44. 2 (2007): 145–157. Print.

Kirtley, David Barr. "This Week on *Game of Thrones*: No Drowning, Urination or Rainbows." *Wired.com*. 16 April 2012. Web. 12 May 2014.

"Maester Luwin." "Are Renly and Loras Gay?" *Tower of the Hand: Maester Luwin's FAQ*. Web. 20 August 2013.

McNutt, Myles. "*Game of Thrones:* 'The Night Lands' and Sexposition." *Cultural Learnings*. 8 April 2012. Web. 27 May 2014.

_____. "*Game of Thrones*: 'You Win or You Die.'" *Cultural Learnings*. 29 May 2011. Web. 27 May 2014.

Migliaccio, Todd. "Men's Friendships: Performances of Masculinity." *The Journal of Men's Studies* 17.3 (2009): 226–241. Print.

Miller, D.A. "Anal Rope." *Representations* 32 (Fall 1990): 114–133. Print.

"Odiedragon." "To Be Continued—Report from Chicago, IL, May 6–8." *The Citadel: So Spake Martin*. 6 May 2005. Web. 17 August 2013.

Sylvester, Louise M. *Medieval Romance and the Construction of Heterosexuality*. London: Palgrave Macmillan, 2008. Print.

"Trollsbane." "RE: Episode 5—The Wolf and the Lion—Recap." Comment # 103619. *Winteriscoming*. 15 May 2011. Web. 29 May 2014.

Vane, Violetta [Solace Ames]. "Gay Representation in *Game of Thrones*: The Problem with Loras and Renly." *LGBT Fantasy Fans and Writers*. 16 July 2012. Web. 20 August 2013.

Whitley, David. "More buzz over 'Bows." *Orlando Sentinel*. 9 August 2000. Web. 17 August 2013.

Wrather, Matthew. "Don't Believe your Eyes: *Game of Thrones*, Narration, and Adaptation." *Overthinkingit*. 27 April 2011. Web. 14 April 2013.

Zeikowitz, Richard E. *Homoeroticism and Chivalry: Discourses of Male Same-Sex Desire in the 14th Century*. New York: Palgrave Macmillan. 2003.

Beyond the Pale?
Craster and the Pathological Reproduction of Houses in Westeros

D. MARCEL DeCOSTE

"I was never very safe in my father's castle either"—*CoK* 7 Jon 1: 96

Featured in but two chapters of George R.R. Martin's multi-volume *A Song of Ice and Fire*, brutish Craster may seem a minor character, peripheral to the larger thematic concerns of Martin's sweeping and bloody Game of Thrones. Indeed, entrenched in his ramshackle keep in the Haunted Forest, well north of the Wall that marks the end of Westerosi civilization, defined by a predatory incest that leaves him with nineteen daughter-wives and no living male heirs, Craster appears in every way a figure beyond the pale, the very antithesis to the more courtly domains of Starks and Lannisters. Yet even if he is, in the words of Dywen of the Night's Watch, "a kinslayer, liar, raper, and craven" (*CoK* 24 Jon 3: 268), such crimes fail to distinguish him from leaders of Westeros's noble families. Lannisters, Freys, and Tullys do not balk at stratagems or kin-murder; cravens can be found in the white of the Kingsguard. Even in his incest, Craster breaks taboos wildlings acknowledge (*SoS* 27 Jon 3: 302), only to emulate both Targaryen rulers who "married brother to sister" (*GoT* 4 Daenerys 1: 26) and the scandalous love of Jaime and Cersei Lannister, whose illegitimate fruits become the seeds of the *Song*'s protracted wars. It may well be true, then, as wildling Ygritte tells Jon Snow, that "Craster's more your kind than ours" (*SoS* 27 Jon 3: 302).

It is precisely this hypothesis I propose to take seriously here. Indeed, I maintain that Craster, far from being a minor addition to Martin's formidable gallery of grotesques (on par, say, with Vargo Hoat), is a crucial cue to what the novels treat as the pathological self-regard of the Westerosi dynasties. In its endogamous self-reproduction and its dedication to cruel self-culling, the House of Craster discloses, I argue, the true economy of the Game of Thrones, high-lighting how the great Houses' insistence on purity and power sees them not only devouring their own, but reducing the realm to a feast for crows. Craster distils the truth of great seats like Riverrun or Casterly Rock, not just because his paternal incest evokes a fraternal form central to such great lines as Lannister or Targaryen. Rather, the Craster who takes all his female issue to wife and leaves the sons he sires on them to "[t]he white shadows" (*CoK* 24 Jon 3: 279), reveals a deadly social narcissism that lies at the heart of Martin's great families, one that establishes them as institutions at odds with themselves and as effective allies to the forces that threaten Westeros.

What lies at the heart of the Houses' strife and the realm's ruin, Craster's example teaches, is not merely incest nor even the Oedipal strife of fathers and sons, but a foundational narcissism that can imagine both family and society as only the pure extension of self. Martin offers Craster as a stark illustration of this phenomenon so as to highlight how the whole of Westerosi society is rooted in and ravaged by this violent narcissism. It is not only Craster who refuses to brook any rival master, or libidinal agent, under his roof; it's not just he who enforces an identification of self with House, with society, through familial bloodshed. If the Targaryens wed their siblings, it was in service to purity of blood, after all, and if Tywin's twins are pledged to one another, it is because, as Cersei says, "Jaime and I are ... one person in two bodies" (*GoT* 46 Eddard 12: 405). In both cases, love of kin only as self involves ready violence against both relations who thwart such identification and those alien to the bonds of blood: Dany must fear waking the dragon, and Bran's fall is very long, indeed. The narcissistic cast of familial ties and its tendency to ruin both Houses and the realm is, I argue, the very pith of the bloody Game of Thrones, a fact well delineated by three consequential instances: Samwell's repudiation and near-murder at the hands of his father, Randyll Tarly; Tywin Lannister's sadistic dis-solution of Tyrion's marriage to Taesha; and Hoster Tully's destruction of his grandchild, Lysa's unborn bastard, for the crime of having lowly Petyr Baelish as sire. In each case, a drive to purity tears Houses apart. Moreover, the latter two examples highlight how such narcissism stokes civil war and so abets the mortal threats of rising winter and the Others' return.

Against such pathological understandings of social bonds, Martin presents a set of alternative, other-seeking definitions of kinship and kingdom both. As Brent Hartinger claims, the perspectives of the impure and outcast "prove impor-tant to both the structure of the novels and the workings of the plot" (159). Indeed, it is those who have been un–Housed, ejected from their familial econ-omy, who offer hope for the realm. I will conclude, then, by looking to two key entities that articulate a vision of self and society rooted in complementarity and duties to the genuinely other: the Night's Watch and the brotherhood of Maesters. Both serve the realm, abjure fealty to and the rights of noble Houses, and affirm kinship with the disparate community of their sworn orders. More importantly, both champion a view of the kingdom that transcends the self-love of lowly Craster and mighty Tywin alike. Only by reforging the bonds of family and of the kingdom itself upon such lines, Martin suggests, can Westeros hope to survive as something more than Craster's gilded imitator.

That said, Craster himself seems, initially, the quintessential other and outsider, looked down upon even by the outcasts of the Night's Watch. Whipped by bitter rains in his ranging, Lord Mormont may thank the gods that Craster's Keep and its promise of shelter still stand in the Haunted Forest beyond the Wall, and Craster himself may insist he is "a godly man" (*CoK* 24 Jon 3: 273; *SoS* 34 Samwell 2: 365), but the black brothers for the most part ally him with darker forces, muttering of his traffic "with slavers and demons" (*CoK* 24 Jon 3: 268). Whatever the aid he offers them, however much Thoren Smallwood vouches for him as "a friend to the Watch" (*CoK* 24 Jon 3: 273), most of the men who have taken the black speak of Craster as "a terrible savage" (*CoK* 24 Jon 3: 268), and when we first encounter him, we are unlikely, as readers, to demur. A "squalid, foul-smelling hall," Craster's so-called keep is but a single room stinking "of soot, dung, and wet dog" (*CoK* 24 Jon 3: 271). Jon Snow, bastard son of Winterfell, dismisses it as "[a] midden heap with a roof and a firepit" (*CoK* 24 Jon 3: 270). The man who rules this dreary outpost seems no more healthy or appealing than his lodgings, with his eyes "cold and mean" and his "mouth of brown rotten teeth" (*SoS* 34 Samwell 2: 366; 373). Yet he is still a forceful figure, as jealous of his rank and rights as peevish Walder Frey in the South. He is "the only man to enjoy his own chair," seated above the hall's lone fire (*CoK* 24 Jon 3: 271), and he threatens with expulsion those who cast a critical eye on the thin beer and tough horsemeat of his grudging hospitality (*SoS* 34 Samwell 2: 377).

But it is in how Craster treats not his guests, but his own, that his power and ostensible otherness are most keenly expressed. Ahead of their first arrival, Mormont warns his men that he wants "no trouble about Craster's wives" (*CoK* 24 Jon 3: 268), and we quickly learn that this harem of nineteen represents his claiming his own flesh and blood as his exclusive erotic property. Such libidinal in-turning is, indeed, the very badge of his lordship; as Samwell Tarly reports to Jon, then, "[Craster] marries his daughters and obeys no laws but those he makes himself" (Ibid). Chief among those laws is his sole right to sexual proprietorship over his own issue and over all the fruits that spring from his exercise of this right. If this incestuous law threatens the men of the Night's Watch with violent sanctions—"Any man lays a hand on my wives, he loses the hand" (*CoK* 24 Jon 3: 273)—its consequences for Craster's own house, for his own kin, are grimmer still. As the example of Gilly makes clear, his daughters are raised in servitude to become sexual chattel—"wives" and breeders of more of their kind—at the onset of puberty:

> A girl of fifteen or sixteen years, he judged, dark hair plastered across a gaunt face by the falling rain, her bare feet muddy to the ankles. The body under the sewn skins was showing in the early turns of pregnancy. "Are you one of Craster's daughters?" [Jon] asked.
> She put a hand over her belly. "Wife now" (*CoK* 24 Jon 3: 275).

Yet an even more unnatural fate awaits the sons born of Craster's paternal incest. Gilly is desperate to flee with the Night's Watch, less to escape her father's "rights," than to save her child from worse yet. The black brothers note that Craster is the only man in the keep, and they wonder, then, how he manages to protect his holdings (*CoK* 24 Jon 3: 277). Gilly tells Jon how this comes to be: "He gives the boys to the gods.... The ones in the night. The white shadows" (*CoK* 24 Jon 3: 279).

The substance of Craster's lordship, then, is his unchallenged management of his own family, his assertion of self in both the sexual domination and brutal extirpation of his own kin, his own children. While his daughters are kept to birth him more servants and sex slaves, his sons are abandoned to the Haunted Forest, to the true Others, "white shadow[s] in the darkness" (*GoT* 1 Prologue: 7), whose stirring opens Martin's epic and poses the greatest, if neglected, threat to the realms of men. Craster founds his power on both an erotic prizing and a murderous rejection of kin. He secures his keep, his hold on nineteen wives and counting, with his sons' blood, a sacrifice that eliminates them as sexual rivals/ others and keeps those more demonic Others at bay: "There had been no attacks while they had been at Craster's, neither wights nor Others. Nor would there be, Craster said" (*SoS* 24 Samwell 2: 368). It should be noted, however, that this immunity, won by Craster's bloody form of "godliness," serves to fuel this greater threat, not only by feeding the Others themselves, but by providing them with more undead wights with which to menace the lands of living: "They'll be here soon, the sons" (*SoS* 34 Samwell 2: 380), says the old woman, when the keep falls.

In his incest and infanticide, then, Craster appears not only other—judged beyond the pale by the black brothers even Martin has dubbed "a bunch of scum" (Ippolito)—but in league with the Others; his lordship seems to set him at odds with the mores and the very survival of Westeros. What's more, he would seem to fill this role of taboo-breaker and unholy lord insofar as he exists beyond, or even prior to, the foundational prohibitions of civilization itself. Indeed, the portrait of Craster recalls nothing so much as Sigmund Freud's theory of the primordial patriarch in *Totem and Taboo*. As a means to account for the two phenomena of his title, the two pillars, in his view, upon which all human societies rest, Freud proposes an originary paternal tyranny. Accepting Darwin's hypothesis, based on the supposed social organization of the great apes, of a "primal horde" centered on a "violent and jealous father who keeps all the females for himself and drives away his sons" (*Totem* 141), Freud suggests primitive culture is born when these outcast sons enact an Oedipal rebellion and successfully slay the despotic father and claim as their own the sisters and mothers he has held as his exclusive sexual property (141). From their subsequent remorse, Freud argues, they erect a series of sexual prohibitions and pious observances that make a god of the murdered father and taboos of their own most deeply felt libidinal desires: "They revoked their deed by forbidding the killing of the totem, the substitute for their father; and they renounced its fruits by resigning their claim to the women who had now been set free. They thus created out of their filial sense of guilt the two fundamental taboos": incest and patricide (143).[1]

Yet while Craster will indeed fall victim to a group of angry young men— a faction of mutinous Watchmen coveting the hidden stores they assume Craster's keep holds (*SoS* 34 Samwell 2: 377)—these men are not his kin, but the sons of Westeros, and what follows is not the institution, but the dissolution, of order and civilization. With Craster slain, the chaste Lord Mormont himself soon falls victim to these rebels, "[a]nd then the whole world went mad" (*SoS* 34 Samwell 2: 378). Craster's death brings not an end to, but indeed the proliferation of, taboo conduct: the breaking of one's vows as a Watchman, of the prohibitions against rape and murder, and of the law of guest-right. As Mormont uselessly reminds these black renegades, they are, by their treachery, putting *themselves* beyond the pale, profaning the most sacred laws of community: "'The gods will curse us,' he cried. 'There is no crime so foul as for a guest to bring murder into a man's hall'" (Ibid). And, indeed, their actions succeed in bringing forth, if not the gods' curse, then at least those demonic forces, wights and Others, Craster has successfully warded off. My point, then, is that Craster is not, in this world, some precursor or antithesis to a civilization dependent on his extinction. Rather, as we will we see, he and his besieged keep mirror, both in what threatens them and in their own gruesome crimes, the world south of the Wall, a world which, as much as his own sordid midden-heap, needs to be reformed if a truly human culture is to be saved.[2]

But if Craster as lord is not quite Freud's atavistic patriarch, he does nonetheless betray the power of certain Freudian pathologies at work in Martin's Westeros. The founding and maintenance of Craster's "godly" House is enacted as a form of self-love and self-reproduction. In Craster's view, his keep stands firm as an outpost of the civilization of the South, distinct from the wildling clans (who know that a "true man steals a woman from afar, t' strengthen the clan" [*SoS* 27 Jon 3: 302]) and at odds with the Others it helps, in a sense, to keep at bay. But it achieves this standing primarily through an economy of radical self-preservation. Craster's Keep literally reproduces itself by means of his taking his own flesh and blood, his own image, as his libidinal object and by his refusing the possibility that any should wield power there, should even love Craster's kin, but he himself. As such, the deep dynamic of his household is less Oedipal than narcissistic. Freud applies this term to the in-turning of a subject's erotic gaze, the "cathexis" of libido not on some external object, but on the ego itself (*Lectures* 465). While it is true that eros tends to confuse the distinction between ego and object, lover and beloved, since "[a]t the height of being in love the boundary between ego and object threatens to melt away" (*Civilization* 13), narcissism's version of such merger is more radically assimilative and foundational. For Freud, in fact, "it is probable that this narcissism is the universal and original state of things, from which object-love is only later developed, without the narcissism necessarily disappearing on that account" (*Lectures* 465). That is to say, we begin as lovers and pleasers of self, taking ourselves not just as our chief concern but, in that very process, as sources of gratification, and we only emerge from infantile narcissism provisionally as we conform either to the "attachment type," which leads to mature object-love, or to the "narcissistic type," "where the subject's own ego is replaced by another one that is as similar as possible" (477).

Clearly, the latter development represents an extension of the infantile state and the emergence of an adult ego driven to find doppelgangers upon which to fix its erotic gaze. Coupled with Freud's insistence that progress beyond the originary narcissistic state is always vulnerable to psychological backsliding, this means that pathological narcissism can define more than the immature psyche. Indeed, to the extent that Freud holds that "social instincts ... are themselves derived from a combination of egoistic and erotic components" (*Totem* 73), narcissism would seem to have a definitive part to play in larger socio-cultural formations, given that narcissism is itself nothing but the eroticization of egotism (*Lectures* 466). And, in fact, a primary arena in which such self-love plays itself out, for Freud, is that of kinship. The family as structure opposes itself to, as much as it serves as the foundation for, the broader society, and it does so through an economy of self-prizing and self-love, by holding to itself object-selves that most resemble and extend its generating agents. Family, for Freud, is by nature a jealous lord: "family will not give the individual up. The more closely the members of a family are attached to one another, the more often do they tend to cut themselves off from others" (*Civilization* 50). As such, the narcissistic bent of the family may, Freud notes, fuel social strife, by keeping hostage prized images of itself and by seeking to impose its image and its goods upon the world at large. Narcissism, indeed, is linked, for Freud, to our primordial inclination to violence, as the assertion of self through force, the reduction of the other to self by their subordination to our will, may be a source of "an extraordinarily high degree of narcissistic enjoyment" for those who have not achieved or been able to maintain the standards of the attachment type (65).

Now, it's worth noting that Martin's Craster exemplifies, in the manner in which he constructs his family and sets it against its world beyond the Wall, the narcissistic type; what's more, it's precisely in the way he does so that he helps reveal the pathologies of Westeros itself. Craster, as patriarch, rules the household so as to entrench, exalt, and gratify his own ego. No individual escapes the family he rules; all there are assimilated to himself through eroticism or aggression. He proudly takes to wife only those images of himself his daughters provide, seeking as love-objects others as near his own self as can be. Rather than have these erotic rights threatened by potential rivals, Craster pursues the self's pleasure by the destruction of his sons, his narcissism thus expressing itself in explicit aggression, as well as in sexual coercion. The upshot of both forms of narcissistic lordship is that the institution of the family, the House, becomes coincident with the ego of its governing figure; it exists to serve and preserve, to mirror back to him, the will and identity of the lordly self. As such, it not only stands in ready opposition to its larger social context; it also, inevitably, is at war with itself, geared toward the enslavement and elimination of those forms of difference that the distinct egos of the family structure themselves represent.

In these narcissistic tendencies to self-love and self-mutilation both, the House of Craster, I argue, reveals for us the savagery of Westeros' most esteemed families and helps pinpoint precisely what threatens the realm with final defeat. Craster's Keep is a House on the Westerosi model, that is, insofar as it cleaves to the ideal of purity, an insistence on kinship, and ultimately on kingdom, as homogeneity, the narcissistic replication of and service to self. As it does north of the Wall, so in the South, this dynamic can play itself out in terms either of a radically endogamous eroticism, an incestuous in-turning, or of a kin-slaying refusal of alterity within the family, the destruction of one's own kind in service to the image and power of one's own self. Certainly, though vassals might insist that "the gods hate incest" (*CoK* 17 Bran 2: 195), the mighty occupants of castles and keeps much more impressive than Craster's seedy hall offer their own version of Craster's incestuous narcissism. The deposed Targaryens, rulers of the West for centuries, have for centuries "married brother to sister, since Aegon the Conqueror had taken his sisters to bride" (*GoT* 4 Daenerys 1: 26), for as Viserys, their vagabond heir, informs us, "[t]he line must be kept pure ... theirs was the kingsblood, the golden blood of old Valyria, the blood of the dragon" (Ibid). Such exaltation of self in blood and bedding becomes, indeed, the very foundations of their House's power, as the example of Maegor the Cruel and his Red Keep makes clear. When once his mighty keep was finished, Maegor "had taken the head of every stonemason, woodworker, and builder who had labored on it. Only the blood of the dragon would ever know the secrets of the fortress the Dragonlords had built" (*GoT* 19 Catelyn 4: 142).

If the Targaryens have at last been driven from the Iron Throne, though, their history of situating eroticized self-regard at the heart of the Westerosi system of great Houses has scarcely fled with them. Viserys may be willing to sell his sister, to let Khal Drogo's "whole *khalasar* fuck [her] if need be, ... all forty thousand" (*GoT* 4 Daenerys 1: 31), in order to secure the army he thinks will make him King again, but the cleaving to one's own that is his pedigree has not been rendered obsolete. Most consequentially, it still reigns at King's Landing, in the love between Jaime Lannister and his twin, Cersei, King Robert's Queen. Offering the Targaryens as her warrant, Cersei admits to Ned Stark that she has taken her brother as lover and more, as her alter-ego, underscoring again the narcissistic cast of Westerosi incest: "The Targaryens wed brother to sister for three hundred years, to keep the bloodlines pure. And Jaime and I are more than brother and sister. We are one person in two bodies" (*GoT* 46 Eddard 12: 405). This is love of the sibling as the eroticized projection of self, a point made once more when a much weathered Jaime remarks upon his changed appearance: "*I don't look as much like Cersei this way. She'll hate that*" (*SoS* 2 Jaime 1: 20). This identification between them is such that Jaime has never had another lover, and Cersei, in his absence, seeks out such consanguine substitutes as her cousin Lancel. As Tyrion reflects, "*even a poor copy of Jaime is sweeter than an empty bed*" (*CoK* 30 Tyrion 7: 335). In love with one another precisely as the not-other, as their own persons available for erotic assimilation, the Lannister twins have always been more profoundly committed to their incestuous treasuring of their own flesh and blood even than Craster, brooking no delay or bar to their union: "Even as children, they would creep into each other's beds and sleep with their arms entwined. *Even in the womb*. Long before his sister's flowering or the advent of his own manhood" (*SoS* 22 Jaime 3: 236). Indeed, neither the eyes of the Seven nor the nearness of their own son's corpse can keep them from each other in Baelon's Sept (*SoS* 63 Jaime 7: 701). Indeed, between them, they cuckold a king, achieve his death, and bring civil war to the Seven Kingdoms in order to keep the blood of their longing pure and its fruit upon the throne.

Yet Westerosi echoes of Craster's lordship are not restricted to such examples of fraternal eroticism. Indeed, the Southern House that most resembles his Keep is one free of incest. The Twins, family seat of Lord Walder Frey, offer their own reflections of conjugal and generational relations north of the Wall. Past ninety years of age, the irascible Walder does not take sisters or daughter to wife. But both the pedophilic cast of his serial marriages and the composition of his household recall Craster's narcissistic imposition of himself on and through bloodties. Walder may not have nineteen living daughter-wives, but he has just celebrated his eighth marriage to a new Lady Frey who is a "pale frail girl of sixteen years" (*GoT* 60 Catelyn 9: 538). And though she is not kin, Walder is as jealous of her youth and charms as Craster is of his own young brides: "Sixteen she is, a little flower, and her honey's only for me" (540). He doesn't reduce family to self only by collecting wives who could be his grand-daughters or great-granddaughters, however, but also by keeping captive in the castles he governs— "under my roof, my rule" (*SoS* 52 Catelyn 7: 577)[3]—nearly the whole of his clan. Thus he meets Catelyn Stark "surrounded by twenty living sons…, thirty-six grandsons, nineteen great-grandsons, and numerous daughters, bastards, and grandbastards" (*GoT* 60 Catelyn 9: 538). Though now "too gouty to stand unassisted" (Ibid), he still exerts this hold on family as the substance of his dominion, an extension of self through the despotic structure of the great house. Walder "believe[s] in taking care of his own. *All* of his own" (*SoS* 82 Epilogue: 917), but he does so as a means to ensure that they remain only that, gratifying reflections to himself of his own power. He delights in the frustrated ambitions of his myriad heirs almost as much as in his exclusive title to his girl-wife's honey, taunting sons and grandsons with his longevity, and toying with their hopes as he plays coy on the matter of his successor. The narcissistic nature of such games is revealed in the sycophantic responses they elicit, in the fact that "there were bunches of Walders at the Twins, all named after … Lord Walder Frey" (*CoK* 5 Bran 1: 57), as jockeying scions seek favor by making their own sons sops to his vanity. And if Lannister narcissism will go to war to defend its incestuous issue, so Walder will violate his oaths to House Tully and the sacred taboo of guest right to salve his wounded pride with the blood of the Red Wedding.

But if these august families reveal the currency of Craster's self-love in the in-turned desires of Houses south of the Wall, more common yet is an emulation of his household culling in service to the unchallenged supremacy of the ego. The South, too, is a land of repudiated and abandoned sons, as the tale of Samwell Tarly, source of my epigraph, makes clear. No babe offered to the Others, Sam is nonetheless punished, then threatened with murder, and finally exiled to the Wall for the sin of otherness, for failing to reproduce his father, Randyll Tarly, Lord of Horn Hill.[4] Proud bannerman "to Mace Tyrell, Lord of Highgarden and Warden of the South" (*GoT* 27 Jon 4: 225), Lord Randyll seeks an heir of his own martial stamp, another self to ensure the identification of House and ego extends itself through the generations. Yet in his eldest son he sees his antithesis, a corpulent, tender-hearted craven: "I fear I'm a coward," Sam confesses to Grenn of the Night's Watch, "my father always said so" (*GoT* 27 Jon 4: 221).

By his own account, Sam is fearful of everything: heights, cold, combat, the sea, and especially blood. Lover of music and song, "his passions [are] books and kittens and dancing" (225), his truest ambition, not to inherit "a strong keep and a storied two-handed greatsword named Heartsbane" (225), but to study at the Citadel (*FfC* 6 Samwell 1: 82). For these failures to reflect back to Lord Randyll his beloved self-image, Sam is raised to mockery, drills, and sadistic punishments. As a boy, he is "cursed and caned, slapped and starved" (*GoT* 27 Jon 4: 225), and when he dares suggest he might help others by forging a Maester's chain, he is left to "[sob] himself to sleep, manacled hand and foot to a wall" for three days and nights (*FfC* 6 Samwell 1: 82). Indeed, while Rickard Karstark and Tyrion Lannister agree that "no man is so accursed as the kinslayer" (*SoS* 21 Catelyn 3: 232; see also, *CoK* 45 Tyrion 10: 482), Lord Randyll is ready, like Craster, to sacrifice his heir to the higher end of purity, defined in the South, as at Craster's Keep, as the ongoing coincidence of family with the rights, powers, and character of the lordly self. Fearful Sam agrees to take the black only when his father has promised as his alternative a fate reminiscent of that of Craster's sons: "If you do not, then on the morrow we shall have a hunt, and somewhere in these woods your horse will stumble, and you will be thrown from the saddle to die ... or so I will tell your mother" (*GoT* 27 Jon 4: 226).

If the incestuous love of kin as self leads to a defense of purity that sees the great Houses make war upon the realm, here a similarly narcissistic desire leads such families to turn on their own. Nor is Samwell's the most notable example of this cruel economy; loftier names than Tarly deal out the same wages for relations that disappoint the ego's hunger for itself. Like Sam, Tyrion Lannister is scorned by his father for his crime of failed likeness. Even after he has, through his planning as Hand of the King, saved King's Landing for his nephew Joffrey, Tyrion's request that his father, Tywin, "stand up before the realm and proclaim" Tyrion his "son and lawful heir" is met with a swift and resolute "Never" (*SoS* 5 Tyrion 1: 53). Though Tywin has lost his favored eldest, Jaime, to the Kingsguard, and so has no heir to succeed him as Lord of Casterly Rock, he will not see his title fall to a dwarf he castigates as vilely other, "an ill-made, devious, disobedient, spiteful little creature full of envy, lust, and low cunning" (Ibid). Tywin goes to war to reclaim the Imp from Catelyn Stark but only because what befalls the son impinges on the power and glory of the father: "Lord Tywin cared not a fig for his deformed son, but he tolerated no slights on the honor of his House" (*GoT* 32 Tyrion 4: 277). This jealous regard for his name extends to more terrible designs than this repudiation of Tyrion as heir. In the matter of Tyrion's marriage to Tysha, it sanctions lies, humiliation, rape, and the destruction of homes that might be built on other lines.

Tyrion recounts how his brother Jaime and he came upon a lone girl set upon by highwaymen, how between them they effected her rescue, and how she became his first lover and then his wife, through the services of a drunken septon (*GoT* 43 Tyrion 6: 382). When the septon sobered, however, he brought news to Lord Tywin, and, as Tyrion succinctly states, "That was the end of my marriage" (383). Informed by Jaime that Tysha was a maiden whore bought to make a man of him, Tyrion then hears his sham marriage cannot stand and is forced to watch his first love violated by his father's men: "Lord Tywin brought my wife in and gave her to his guards. They paid her fair enough" (Ibid). Worse still, Tyrion tells the sell-sword Bronn, "Lord Tywin had me go last" (Ibid), wreaking the will of the father in a final, loveless unmaking of any bonds that reach beyond that will. Yet more ties than these will be severed to serve Lord Tywin's narcissistic reduction of kin to the power of the self. When he comes to save his brother from the dungeons of the Red Keep and his imminent execution for the murder of Joffrey, Jaime confesses the story he told of Tysha years ago was a fiction of his father's devising. No purchased rite of passage, Tysha was what she appeared, "a crofter's daughter" (*SoS* 78 Tyrion 11: 873), and her love, her willingness to wed herself to a dwarf reviled by his own father, sincere. Tyrion's heart, as much as their marriage and her body, had to be broken, for a crofter's daughter is other and no acceptable wife for any man, even a loathsome half-man, who bears the name of Tywin Lannister. This union had to be unmade through the cruelest of means, because "[s]he was lowborn, you were a Lannister of Casterly Rock" (Ibid). Tywin's honour must not be sullied, the wholesale equation of one's flesh and blood with one's own person must not be disturbed, by any reaching beyond the circle of one's own kind. To defend that equation, all manner of brutalization of others, of one's own children, is permissible and right. And yet the crimes this narcissistic defense of homogeneity mandates do not end when a bloodied Tysha is sent packing with her coin. Having learned the truth, Tyrion makes one last stop before fleeing Westeros, intruding on his father's privy to murder the man who still declares him "no son of mine" (880). Yet that Tyrion here insists on their likeness—"Now, that's where you're wrong, Father. Why, I believe I'm you writ small" (Ibid)—is apt, for it is this very insistence on family as self that has yielded such bloodshed.

The narcissistic desire for the self's endless reproduction that characterizes the great Houses as much as Craster's Keep thus leads to the rough excision of the heterogeneous, to a history of families grievously wounding themselves in the name of purity. And as the eroticization of this desire in incest leads to ruinous conflict between Houses, indeed, to a civil war that threatens the kingdom itself, so does this in-turned aggression work to tear apart the realm and not just individual families. This is clearest in the sad story of House Tully. Home to the future Ladies Stark and Arryn, the Tully seat of Riverrun also plays host, in their girlhood, to Petyr Baelish, Lord Hoster Tully's ward. Treated as a brother by young Catelyn, Baelish, for his part, falls in love, so that, when her betrothal to Brandon Stark is announced, "Petyr challenge[s] for the right to [her] hand" (*GoT* 19 Catelyn 4: 141). As Catelyn relates, "It was madness. Brandon was twenty, Petyr scarcely fifteen. I had to beg Brandon to spare Petyr's life. He let him off with a scar" (Ibid). Disappointed in his first love, Petyr finds a more willing Tully in Catelyn's sister, Lysa, who loves him and gives him her "maiden's gift" (*SoS* 81 Sansa 7: 913). This love bears illegitimate, if ill-fated fruit: "We made a baby together, a precious little baby," Lysa tells Sansa Stark (910), but one that never lives to be Baelish's heir. Scion of a backwater family whose "modest holdings were on the smallest of the Fingers" (*GoT* 19 Catelyn 4: 140), Petyr, Littlefinger, as he is called, is unacceptable as Hoster Tully's son by marriage, as unimaginable a husband for Lysa as for Catelyn before her. Thus to secure for the dignity of his name a proper match for his "soiled" daughter (*SoS* 81 Sansa 7: 910), Hoster, like Craster, is ready to make a sacrifice of his own flesh and blood, a decision which haunts him still on his deathbed two decades on: "Forgive me ... the blood.... Oh, please ... Tansy" (*SoS* 3 Catelyn 1: 29).

While the Catelyn who hears these words intuits part of their significance—an illicit pregnancy, a lost child prior to Lysa's marriage to a much older, but still heir-seeking Lord Arryn (31)—she misses their darker import: namely, that her father forced an abortion on his daughter to keep his line free from the base Baelish and to secure a marriage with a great House desperate for a fertile bride. While a delirious, dying Lord Hoster speaks to this long-lost Lysa, promising she will "have others ... sweet babes, and trueborn" to make up for this lost first (Ibid), it is clear that for Lysa and Littlefinger there can be no recompense. As Lysa tells Petyr, in a profession of her undying love years later, "I would have given you a son, but they murdered him with moon tea ... I never *knew*, I only drank what Father gave me" (*SoS* 81 Sansa 7: 913). The grandson that fails to reflect Hoster's eminence may be long since destroyed, but the bloody ramifications of this rejection of Baelish's otherness have not yet ceased. For the union between Lysa and Petyr, though doomed to unlawful shadows, has not been sundered, but has continued to yield its own deadly fruit. From it, we learn, has sprung both the death of Jon Arryn, poisoned at Petyr's command and by Lysa's hand, and the fateful letter accusing the Lannisters of this crime that he directs her to write to Catelyn at Winterfell (Ibid). Between them, these two acts effectively bring about the terrible ravages of the War of Five Kings. They bring Eddard Stark to King's Landing to serve as Hand, spur Catelyn's seizure of Tyrion following Baelish's implication of the Imp in an attack on her son, and initiate the conflict between Winterfell and Casterly Rock that swells to engulf the whole of the Seven Kingdoms.

One might ask why Petyr would seek such a conflagration, how he might profit thereby. I maintain that Westeros burns as part of his long-studied program to destroy the noble families that have spurned him and the whole system of dynastic great Houses which has elevated Starks, Tullys, Lannisters, above lowly Littlefingers. What this means, then, is that the jealous, purity-seeking, fundamentally narcissistic nature of Westerosi feudalism serves not only the self-love and self-culling of certain great families; it threatens the very existence of the realm. Between them, Lord Hoster's choice and Petyr's revenge upon it, on the one hand, and Cersei's arranging a King's death so as to defend her incestuous offspring, on the other, unleash devastating war. Indeed, they drive the kingdom itself to that in-turned process of self-mutilation suffered by the Houses, precisely as each great seat seeks to preserve itself through violent assertions of its self-image and power. Nor is the peril this involves only that which attends unchecked human predation, though this is amply chronicled by Martin's saga. As Lord Rodrik of Harlaw observes, "We had one king, then five. Now all I see are crows squabbling over the corpse of Westeros" (*FfC* 12 The Kraken's Daughter 1: 167). But that this ruin might be more final than any past conquest or rebellion is also underscored throughout. As the words of House Stark proclaim, Winter is coming, with disastrous consequences for a land that has razed its shelters, incinerated its crops, and slain so many of its laborers and defenders. As a dying Maester Luwin despairs at the fall of Winterfell, "war everywhere ... and winter coming ... such folly, such black mad folly..." (*CoK* 70 Bran 7: 727). Yet the folly is darker and direr than Luwin, doubter of tales of giants and other races (*GoT* 67 Bran 7: 616),[5] knows. As Susan Johnston rightly observes, "much of the tragedy of these books lies in the Westerosi's absorption in the clashes of kings, while beyond the wall winter is coming" (144). While the Houses play their bloody Game of Thrones so lordly egos might impose themselves with and beyond their own dynastic lines, the Others Craster sought to appease are moving south with the cold, driving wildlings, wights, and the promise of another Long Night before them.

Thus it is certainly the case, as Stacey Goguen observes, that the code of chivalric honour embodied in the great Houses "does not promote human flourishing" (209); indeed, just the reverse. The specific pathology which makes this so is, I contend, strikingly highlighted by Craster and his sorry keep. While they may seem at odds with the values of the Southern nobility, they in fact reveal the destructive narcissism at the heart of Westerosi feudal structures. As Joseph Strayer has argued, the definitive feature of European feudalism was its treatment of political power—juridical, executive, and military—as a private, a household, possession: "It can be divided among heirs, given as a marriage portion, mortgaged, bought and sold. Private contracts and the rules of family law determine the possessors of judicial and administrative authority" (12). It is precisely because this is so, and because the Westerosi structure of family rule follows the Craster model, that the kingdom bleeds and bids fair to become a feast not just for crows, but for the inhuman white walkers. Craster's role, then, is usefully diagnostic, and by pointing us to the disease that renders the Seven Kingdoms so vulnerable, he helps indicate, too, the realm's need to move beyond the bloody, self-reproducing confines of the great House and toward more heterogeneous conceptions of self, kin, and kingdom. In this vein, the maesters, though compromised by their role as servants to the feudal seats of Westeros, embody a vision of the polity necessary to the land's survival, one rooted in service to something other than oneself, one's clan, or one's clan solely *as* oneself, and thus in an understanding of the kingdom as the vital interplay of difference. When Jon, seeking to save Sam from the sadistic Ser Alliser Thorne, asks Maester Aemon to take Tarly under his wing, he appeals to the maester's chain itself, what it teaches concerning the true constitution and needs of society, needs that the self-seeking Crasterism of Westeros, in fact, frustrates: "The collar is supposed to remind a master of the realm he serves, isn't that so? Lords are gold and knights steel, but two links can't make a chain…. A chain needs all sorts of metals and a land needs all sorts of people" (*GoT* 42 Jon 5: 376). Only by a union of genuine difference, by a process of service to, rather than megalomaniacal erasure of, the other, can a united kingdom capable of withstanding the Others be forged.

What the Seven Kingdoms require, then, if they are to survive the coming winter, are servants made strong by their lack of purity, defenders who stand outside, indeed beyond the confining pale of, destructive House loyalties. While there are a few such communities of service in Martin's Westeros—apart from the order of maesters themselves, there's also the Kingsguard, who have "no wives or children, but [live] only to serve the king" (*GoT* 9 Bran 2: 65), and so remove themselves from the reproduction of Houses—many such examples remain significantly circumscribed by the small world of Craster-like self-seeking: drawn typically from the nobility alone, maesters and knights of the Kingsguard both remain significantly bound to one House or another, even if not their own: the maesters to a particular family seat, if not to a single occupant thereof, the kingsguard to the person of one ruler drawn from a great House, if not to that House per se. So while Maester Luwin insists that his role as maester is to serve "[t]he realm … and Winterfell" (*CoK* 67 Theon 6: 691), the latter loyalty significantly limits the former. Indeed, the organization which best serves the kingdom by defending it against both Craster's emblematic refusal of otherness and his concomitant abetting of the Others is, I argue, exactly the one which avows such a defense as its very *raison d'être*: the Night's Watch.

Manning the Wall to defend the realm from the incursion of wildlings and worse, those Others who threaten absolutely the kingdom of men, the Night's Watch, by the very nature of its composition defends also against the bloodily divisive economy of familial narcissism that threatens to destroy Westeros from within. That is to say, the Watch best defends the Seven Kingdoms, and best points toward a future that might escape their debilitating Game of Thrones, by its serving as the antithesis to the clannish self-love and strife of Westerosi great Houses. Far from wedding itself to one lord, one name, one seat, the Watch forms a family of loyal service that transcends mere family loyalty. As Abraham Schwab remarks, then, "the men of the Night's Watch are an ecumenical bunch" (151), as likely to be drawn from the dungeons of the South as from the illustrious lines of Stark or Targaryen. The men who take the black repudiate their past, their clan commitments, so as to be made ready for the most comprehensive of loyalties. As Commander Mormont tells new recruits about to take their vows to "father no children" but to be "the shield that guards the realms of men" (*GoT* 49 Jon 6: 435), they are pledging themselves not simply to die for the realm rather than for one banner or king, but to live for a family that embraces all families and all conditions of family: "Some of you bear the names of proud houses. Others have only bastards' names, or no names at all. It makes no matter. All that is past now. On the Wall, we are all one house" (431).

Swearing one's oath to the Night's Watch, then, is not simply a matter of un–Housing oneself, though it is significantly just that. Nor is it only about pledging one's service to all the Houses of Westeros, though this again is part of it. As Mormont continues, a Brother of the Night's Watch does not live for "the honor of this house or that house ... but for the *realm*, and all the people in it" (Ibid). More than this, the new Brother pledges himself to his brothers, to a brotherhood that includes within it all the peoples of Westeros, all the kinds that make the maester's chain, to a House, one might say, that transcends Houses as it embraces all. As Johnston maintains, this pledge is personally transformative as it both establishes and reconfigures family: "It is covenantal, in that it is a bond of kinship, of sworn brotherhood, but its binding is not the tribal loyalty of House against House, each against each" (150). It is, instead, a forging of flesh and blood solidarity with, life and death service to, the genuinely different, something other than one's own flesh and blood, and one's own narcissistic reflection. Precisely as such can the Night's Watch be "the fire that burns against the cold, the light that brings the dawn" not just of continued life, but of a future that promises more than Craster's and Westeros' Other-serving, fratricidal self-love.

Now, it is true that the latest volume in Martin's as yet unfinished epic presents this family as being as at odds with itself as the Houses of Lannister,

Baratheon, or Greyjoy have been, rising up a second time to slay its Commander, Jon Snow, and to halt his plans for a unification with difference, even the difference that is the wildlings: "When the third dagger took him between the shoulder blades, he gave a grunt and fell-face into the snow. He never felt the fourth knife" (*DwD* 70 Jon 13: 913). It is further true that the normatively celibate and exclusively male Night's Watch cannot, in every particular, provide a precise model for a newer, healthier future kingdom. Such a kingdom, in order to have a future at all, must embrace also the generative difference of woman. I nonetheless remain unconvinced that the cliffhanger ending of *A Dance with Dragons* marks Jon's final ending, or the end of the Night's Watch's potential to serve and even save the realm. Nor does the Watch's removal from the business of producing and raising families mean it has nothing to teach the realm about how to curtail the pathological obsession with kin and blood-purity. Indeed, Martin has clearly moved certain outcasts and orphans of the great Houses—bastard Jon, for example, with his mysterious parentage, Dany with her dragons, whose fire may be as sure a bane to the Others as the "glass" named after them—into positions which suggest some merger or détente, some overcoming of the impermeable borders of kinship, will ultimately save the realm from the doom of the white walkers.

Be that as it may, it is certainly true that Craster's own kinship with the Walder Freys and Tywin Lannisters of Westeros highlights how desperately the realm needs something like the Watch's alternative to the sordid narcissism that defines Casterly Rock as much as the solitary Keep of the Haunted Forest. Craster, in the end, lives not so much beyond the pale as on the frontier, not the border between chivalrous Westerosi lords and barbarian wildling chieftains, but that which exists between the bloodily self-loving nobles of the South and the voracious Others of the Land of Always Winter. In his readiness to reduce society to kin, and all kin to a coincidence with his will and appetite, Craster both emulates and, in his obvious squalor, condemns the great Houses of the Seven Kingdoms. What's more, in his eager sacrifice of his own, and the manner in which it feeds and strengthens the true enemies of the realms of men, he reveals how the narcissistic Game of Thrones, the great war for the supremacy of self, aids and abets the victory of the Others. Yet in his significantly liminal role, Craster points us to that other family that straddles the border of the Wall, the all-inclusive Brotherhood of the Night's Watch, which more than Craster's appeasement or the nobles' obliviousness, stands against the truly inhuman Other and for the life of the kingdom and all its peoples. In this way, I suggest, Craster is crucial to Martin's diagnosis of a pathological feudalism and to his suggesting the more heterogeneous and endogamous form of society that can, in the end, cure it.

Notes

1. Needless to say, this account of the origins of the totem and incest taboos detailed by anthropology has not itself gone uncontested. Freud's contemporary, ethnographer Lord Raglan, rejects this hypothesis as an explanation for the near-universality of incest-prohibitions in "primitive" and "advanced" cultures alike. Of Freud's primal horde theory he states, "the difficulties in the way of its acceptance are insuperable" (Raglan 72), not least because neither sexual possessiveness (and thus sexual jealousy) nor the Oedipal complex on which Freud's whole reading of this originary event depends are particularly evident in those "primitive" cultures closest to this horde, purportedly motivated by just such things (37; 74).

2. Such a blurring of margin and center, of outcast and norm, of taboo despot's keep and rightful throne of kings, is very much in keeping with Martin's avowed hopes for *A Song of Ice and Fire* as a contribution to the genre of epic fantasy. Endorsing William Faulkner's definition of literature as the duty to write "about the human heart in conflict with itself" (Brown), Martin wants his saga to be about the struggle between good and evil, yes, but about that struggle as one waged not between clearly discrete good guys and bad guys but within the confines of the single human heart (Gevers). While repeatedly affirming his admiration for Tolkien's work, even dubbing *Lord of the Rings* the "great landmark [that] looms over all of fantasy like a mountain" (Ippolito), Martin also judges that his innovations, in the hands of much lesser imitators, have become "terrible weights on the field of fantasy" (Shindler 37), particularly in the reduction of the great moral contest to the proportions of cartoon. His approach to the genre, Martin insists, is about demonstrating that the struggle between good and evil "is not waged against dark lords with evil minions. It's waged within the individual human heart" (Shindler 37). Certainly, the degree to which Craster's own gruesome crimes reflect those committed by more ostensibly heroic and esteemed figures, characters who, it seems, will play a key role in defending the realm from the evil Others, would speak to his being sincere in this aim.

3. Indeed, Frey's comments here echo rather pointedly Thoren Smallwood's acquiescence to Craster's own claim to lordship in his keep, most particularly his exclusive title to his wives' charms: "'Your roof, your rule,' said Thoren Smallwood, and Lord Mormont nodded stiffly" (*CoK* 24 Jon 3: 273).

4. Lord Randyll's contempt for any disturbance of the norm to which he cleaves and upon which he grounds his exalted sense of self, particularly the ideal of specifically masculine warriors and martial males, is revealed, too, in his hatred for Brienne of Tarth, the great questing lady-knight of Martin's saga. When he first meets Brienne at Maidenpool, Tarly instructs her in the proper way of things and so, too, in her status as freak and affront: "The gods made men to fight, and women to bear children.... A woman's war is in the birthing bed" (*FfC* 15 Brienne 3: 211). That he views her defiance of this law as worthy of the same scorn, and of the hunting "accident," he offers his own heir is made clear in his farewell to her: "Some men are blessed with sons, some with daughters. No man deserves to be cursed with such as you. Live or die, Lady Brienne, do not return to Maidenpool whilst I rule here" (*FfC* 26 Brienne 5: 365).

5. As Archmaester Marwyn informs Samwell Tarly on his arrival at Oldtown, the order of Maesters is radically and programmatically at odds with common beliefs in magic, monsters, or oracles, because its aim is to supplant such forms of power and knowledge as threats to the realm and to itself: "The world the Citadel is building has no place in it for sorcery or prophecy or glass candles, much less for dragons" (*FfC* 46 Samwell 5: 683).

Works Cited

Brown, Rachael. "George R.R. Martin on Sex, Fantasy, and *A Dance with Dragons*." Interview. 11 July 2011. *The Atlantic*. Web. 17 January 2013.

Freud, Sigmund. *Civilization and Its Discontents*. Trans. and ed. James Strachey. New York: Norton, 1962. Print.

____. *Introductory Lectures on Psychoanalysis*. The Pelican Freud Library, Vol. 1. Ed. and trans. James Strachey. Harmondsworth: Penguin, 1974. Print.

____. *Totem and Taboo: Some Points of Agreement Between the Mental Lives of Savages and Neurotics*. Trans. James Strachey. London: Routledge and Kegan Paul, 1972. Print.

Gevers, Nick. "Sunsets of High Renown: An Interview with George R.R. Martin." Interview. 3 February 2001. *Infinity Plus*. Web. 18 January 2013.

Goguen, Stacey. "'There Are No True Knights': The Injustice of Chivalry." *Game of Thrones and Philosophy: Logic Cuts Deeper than Swords*. Ed. Henry Jacoby. Hoboken, NJ: Wiley & Sons, 2012. 205–222. Print.

Hartinger, Brent. "A Different Kind of Other." *Beyond the Wall: Exploring George R.R. Martin's Song of Ice and Fire*. Ed. James Lowder. Dallas: BenBella, 2012. 153–168. Print.

Hodgman, John. "George R.R. Martin, Author of *A Song of Ice and Fire* Series." Interview. 19 September 2011. *The Sound of Young America*. Transcribed by Sean Sampson. Web. 17 January 2013.

Ippolito, Toni-Marie. "George R.R. Martin Talks to Fans About the Making of *Game of Thrones* and What Inspired His Best-selling Book Series." Interview. 13 March 2012. *The Lifestyle Report*. Web. 17 January 2013.

Johnston, Susan. "Grief Poignant as Joy: Dyscatastrophe and Eucatastrophe in *A Song of Ice and Fire*." *Mythlore* 31.1/2 (Fall/Winter 2012): 133–154. Print.

Raglan, Fitzroy R.S., Baron. *Jocasta's Crime: An Anthropological Study*. 1933; New York: Howard Fertig, 1991. Print.

Schwab, Abraham P. "'You Know Nothing, Jon Snow': Epistemic Humility Beyond the Wall." *Game of Thrones and Philosophy: Logic Cuts Deeper than Swords*. Ed. Henry Jacoby. Hoboken, NJ: Wiley & Sons, 2012. 142–153. Print.

Shindler, Dorman T. "Of Hybrids and Clichés: *PW* Talks with George R.R. Martin." Interview. *Publisher's Weekly* 252.33 (October 31, 2005): 37. Print.

Strayer, Joseph R. *Feudalism*. Princeton: D. Van Nostrand, 1965. Print.

ADAPTATIONS

The Hand of the Artist:
Fan Art in the Martinverse

Andrew Howe

In his 1996 book *A Game of Thrones*, George R.R. Martin introduced a fictional world filled with unfamiliar creatures and customs but governed by the same instinctive drives for dominance and desire found in our own. The book was unsettling, particularly in the violent and premature death meted out to Eddard Stark, whom many perceived to be the main protagonist, but also in the ambiguity and chaos that appeared to reign. However, Martin did not remove all markers of stability, populating this world with rich, three-dimensional characters and allowing readers to enjoy points of stability on which to center their reading experience. Given the quality of the writing and the complexity of the storyline, it is not surprising that a deeply loyal fan base quickly emerged following the book's debut. Slowly but surely this group of admirers, which grew larger with the publication of each subsequent novel, began to contribute to a developing movement where the boundaries between the artistic product and its consumer began to blur. "Fan Fiction" is a process whereby communities of like-minded individuals produce and share their own artistic products linked to a particular source narrative. This essay examines the aesthetic, cultural, and political dimensions of some selected pieces of visual artwork associated with *ASOIAF* and its television adaptation. Relevant to this study will be the arm of fan art involving contributions to a shared community of like-minded individuals rather than art designed to sell in online stores. Martin's narrative is largely character-driven, and thus the vast majority of such artwork focuses upon specific characters.

Examined will be artistic depictions of three characters from *ASOIAF*: Daenerys Targaryen, Jon Snow, and Cersei Lannister. These three are by far the most popular figures depicted in Fan Art, perhaps due to the fact that each has received quite a bit of character development throughout the series. They are also three of the more beautiful characters as both written by Martin and cast by HBO. Youth and beauty are prized, both by the characters in Martin's medievalist world as well as the communities in which artists produce their art. It is no surprise then that Daenerys, Jon, and Cersei should be so commonly portrayed. Other characters will be drawn into the discussion, but only as they are associated with one of these three. There will also be brief discussions of fan art involving animals and environments, but again only as they interface with these three characters. The fact that Daenerys, Jon, and Cersei exist primarily within very different parts of Martin's fictional world—the deserts of Essos, the frozen North, and King's Landing—lends a diversity to the backdrops in which they appear and the objects and other characters with whom they interact. Between them, these three intersect with a wide variety of plots, themes, and locations in Martin's fictional world. Thus, an analysis of all three will also allow for a broad examination of the way in which fan artists react to a variety of different textual components. The essay will focus on fan-created, graphically designed pieces, mostly color drawings but also costumes and other media, due in large part to the sheer volume of artifacts fandom offers, the greater diversity of depictions, and the hopes and desires to which these character arcs point. Images commissioned or at least sanctioned by Martin and/or HBO, which have exploded in popularity since the success of the television show and subsequent marketing boom, have tended to exist within a fairly narrow band of depiction. It will be instructive to explore the manner in which fan art deviates from these official images, particularly in the aspirations or desires that are reflected by non-sanctioned work. For instance, that some depictions of Jon Snow seem to anticipate him as a Targaryen, or the sexualization of Cersei Lannister—who is often portrayed as younger than she is described in Martin's text or as played by Lena Headey in the television show—suggest something intriguing, whether it be a reflection of an artist's private aspirations for the character or as a response to desired outcomes as negotiated publically on "Tower of the Hand" and other online fan communities.

As Henry Jenkins notes, such a phenomenon represents a nexus of complex binaries, such as the manner in which traditional and stable modes of art are updated with fluid forms of technology. The key tension driving fan response, however, is its situation between the poles of fulfillment and dissatisfaction: "Fandom, after all, is born of a balance between fascination and frustration: if media content didn't fascinate us, there would be no desire to engage with it; but if it didn't frustrate us on some level, there would be no drive to rewrite or remake it" (Jenkins, *Convergence Culture* 258). Visual representations constitute a sub-set of fan fiction most often referred to as "Fan Art."[1] Despite the difference in manifestation, fan motivations for producing visual art are identical to the more common written story. According to Jenkins, "Fans write stories because they want to share insights they have into the characters, their relationships, and their worlds" (Jenkins, "Fan Fiction"). Although many of the same features evident in fan fiction apply to this more specific branch, working within the visual register requires more specialized skill, yet allows the artist an emotional simultaneity of connection to a viewer. The act of creation allows the artist to vicariously occupy the narrative space, even if the result deviates from the vision of the original producer. Historically, the process of establishing parallel, non-canonical storylines for popular texts was well established in small fan communities by the late 1960s, particularly as applied to sci-fi, fantasy, and other popular art forms in narratives such as *Star Trek*.[2] The growth of the internet in the 1990s, however, gave a much larger platform for fans to share their own artistic renderings of characters or plot points. Although *Star Trek* and other cultural texts from a previous time continued to play a prominent role in fan driven content, it is no surprise that the Harry Potter series was at the center of the fan fiction explosion beginning in the late 1990s, as the technology solidified as a cultural force at about the same time the J.K. Rowling novels and film adaptations were at the height of their power.[3] There were other online communities participating in this phenomenon, however. Fans of *A Game of Thrones* began to slowly but surely post artistic renderings of their favorite characters and plot developments, in many cases to augment the narrative during the multi-year wait between Martin novels. It was not until the success of HBO's television adaptation *Game of Thrones* (2011), however, that a true cult of images arose, with visuals from the show achieving a certain level of cultural penetration and even iconic standing in popular culture.[4] Whereas the official merchandise sold by HBO merely excerpts images from the show, thus serving to solidify canon, by contrast fan art, in its introduction of new ideas and promotion of individual flourishes, pushes the extra-canonical narrative in new and interesting directions.

Although most fan-created images are solely meant to share with like-minded fans, some can be attributed to a system of capital whereby graphic designers meet the needs of a fan base willing to spend money in order to align themselves with the novels or television show. Due to the proliferation of t-shirts, mugs, posters, and other objects available for sale on the internet (most of which have no sponsorship by or official agreement with either Martin or HBO), the loyal fan can now, through the act of consumption, proudly display their affiliation with the narrative. To a large degree, the items chosen become markers of identity primarily among the faithful. For instance, shirts that depict krakens signal something very different than ones featuring dire wolves. The politics of belonging can be measured by the houses, characters, or narrative elements with which consuming fans choose to associate themselves. Thus, fashion and fan response combine to create a market-driven economy of visual items, a market that perhaps serves to influence future narrative developments. Martin is best viewed as above reproach in this regard, having previously killed off characters that were popular and most likely profitable in such arenas. However, the same cannot necessarily be said about the show-runners at HBO (David Benioff & D.B. Weiss), who have already deviated in substantive ways from the books, and have admitted to writing more scenes for popular characters such as Margaery Tyrell.[5] In the multi-million dollar world of merchandising, it is a fact that some *Game of Thrones* products will out-sell others.[6] HBO identifies *Game of Thrones* as both their largest and fastest growing commodity, commanding up to 75 percent of the market in Europe (Sacco). However, nothing indicates which *items* have sold the best, leaving the fan art generated for each character as perhaps the best indicator of popularity.

Daenerys Targaryen (commonly referred to as Dany) is one of the key point-of-view characters in the series, and one of only a few who could be considered a primary protagonist. In her early teens, she is suddenly thrust into a world of statecraft and political maneuvering when her brother marries her off to Khal Drogo in order to buy the warlord's help in retaking Westeros for House Targaryen. With the death of both her brother and Drogo, Dany comes into her own, leaving behind her caution and timidity and embracing the game of empire building as she slowly begins to form an alliance that will back her claim to the Iron Throne. The Targaryens are known for their silver-blonde hair and violet eyes, and Dany is no exception. However, the majority of fan depictions of this character illustrate her with varying hues of light blonde hair (jekaa), and it is almost jarring to come across one that is truly silver (AcidBanter 7) or white (Noto).[7] As far as illustrations of Dany as blonde, some of these predate the 2011 television show; others were posted online after the show first aired, and are clearly influenced by the actress chosen to portray this character in the series (velocitti). Emilia Clarke, a natural brunette, wears a light blonde wig for the show. The show-runners haven't said why they chose blonde over silver, although it perhaps has something to do with silver hair typically marking old age. It is interesting to note that, onscreen, Dany's brother Viserys (played by Harry Lloyd) has even lighter hair than does she. Viserys' locks only achieve a decidedly yellow hue moments before his death, when molten gold is poured over his head. This character's demise is ironic not only in that he finally receives his "crown of gold," but in that his death suggests that he is not a true Targaryen: "*He was no dragon*, Dany thought, curiously calm, *Fire cannot kill a dragon*" (*Got* 46 Daenerys 5: 418).

Another key difference between Dany as established in Martin's text, and in fan art, is her age. In the story, Dany is thirteen years old at the beginning of the narrative; furthermore, it is clear that she has recently had her first menstruation and is thus newly marriageable (*Got* 3 Daenerys 1: 27). Both Viserys and Khal Drogo are impatient men, and Viserys wants to marry his sister off to the Dothraki lord at the earliest possible moment. Illyrio and his ally in King's Landing, Varys, would have needed plenty of time to set their plans in motion and are aided in that a Dothraki lord would have no use for a child bride—as were often used to solidify bonds in Westeros—instead preferring a woman with whom he could produce an heir. Indeed, a short time after meeting Drogo, Dany is wed to him and taken out onto the prairie to consummate their bond as part of the marriage rites (*Got* 11 Daenerys 2: 88–90). Over the next several months and with tutoring from her handmaiden Doreah, Dany learns to take control of her sexuality. Her insistence upon a different sexual position, for instance, suggests that she is asserting herself as an equal in her relationship with Drogo: "When he tried to turn her over, she put a hand on his chest. 'No,' she said. 'This night I would look on your face'" (*Got* 23 Daenerys 3: 198). Over the next several novels, Dany continues to explore her sexuality and the manner in which it can be put toward the ultimate goal of winning the Iron Throne. In this distinction, she parallels Cersei Lannister, who is willing to employ her sexuality in order to secure the throne for her offspring. Clearly, a sexualized thirteen-year-old Dany could not be portrayed in fan art, as that would risk accusations of child pornography.[8] Fan depictions do exist featuring Dany as an early teenager (Petarsaur), but these are few and far between and never sexualized. Most fan artists have done the same thing that the HBO show-runners have: advance Dany in age until she is clearly in her *late* teens. This change has allowed the television show to film sex scenes, and has also allowed fan artists to illustrate character sexuality and employ nudity without fear of censure. Indeed, in online fandom, Dany is often depicted with some nudity. Sometimes, she is portrayed as entirely naked, although in most of these cases (but not all) either her dragons or her hair are conveniently placed so as to cover both of the areas charged with societal anxieties regarding female nudity (Rzhevskii).[9] One of the most common illustrations is Dany with a single breast exposed (Best; Oh; Luthien90). This portrayal is rich in meaning, perhaps conflating the following readings, two of which are textual and two contextual: (1) Daenerys the adaptive conqueror, taking on the Qartheen fashion for women, which leaves one breast exposed (*Cok* 27 Daenerys 2: 318); (2) Daenerys the woman warrior, calling to mind the classic, female warrior society of "Amazons"; (3) Daenerys the nurturing mother, nursing her dragons at her bosom until they grow old enough to eat solid food; and (4) Daenerys the beautiful goddess, calling to mind the famous Roman sculpture "Venus Genetrix" housed in the Musée du Louvre in Paris.[10]

These are four roles that Dany has played or will need in order to win the Iron Throne, as there are numerous individuals and groups she will encounter in her quest for that goal, each of whom will respond differently to dominion by a Targaryen and female.

Another interesting aspect of fan art featuring Dany is the great variety of situations and backgrounds in which she appears. Unlike Cersei, who spends most of her time in the Red Keep, and Jon Snow, who although a bit more mobile finds himself at or beyond the Wall, Dany crosses a large stretch of Essos. Her extreme mobility throughout Martin's text gives fan artists a wealth of different scenes on which to draw, ones set in disparate locations such as Pentos, Vaes Dothrak, and Qarth. Perhaps largely due to this mobility, Dany is often portrayed in the midst of some action. Although static pictures of her are common, there are also plenty of her riding a horse through the Dothraki Sea, eating a horse's heart in the Stallion Ceremony, and engulfed in flames upon Khal Drogo's pyre (Teitku). In such scenes, no longer does Dany appear in the silk gowns of Pentos; she is now a Dothraki mother and leader of her khalasar, and her wardrobe depicts that, becoming rougher and featuring the riding leathers of her adopted kin (guillemhp).

Martin has linked the War of the Five Kings to a historical antecedent in the War of the Roses (Miller). The Wall recalls Hadrian's Wall, dividing England and Scotland, and the feudalism and chivalry of Martin's medievalism is likewise evocative of Western Europe. It is not a stretch, then, to view Essos as evocative of points further east, such as Eastern Europe or the Near East. Although he eschews one-to-one comparisons, Martin himself has admitted specific references, including the Dothraki as "amalgam of a number of steppe and plains cultures" that includes both Huns and Mongols (Martin). Not surprisingly then readers and fan artists alike note the more exotic elements of Dany's surroundings as she travels to Qarth, Astapor, and Meereen and once again takes up more formal dresses made of silk and other fine materials. Yet these gowns differ from what she wore for her first encounter with Drogo in Pentos. Fan art deriving from the later novels signals this shift with various markers of exotic fashion, such as crystallographic dress patterns, beads, and bare midriffs (Amoka).[11] A few artists take Dany's transformation to an extreme, as her costume and the way it falls almost makes it appear as if she has a tail or wings (uialwen), transforming her into a dragon as she becomes more and more powerful. Indeed, her dragons round out the exotic turn undertaken by this character. There is a large variability in the manner in which the dragons are depicted (Behemotik, Chaotic-AlterEgo), and as noted earlier they often serve to mask her nakedness, becoming almost a cloak of power she wears in her quest to take the Iron Throne. Surrounding Dany with non-western markers signals the distance from her notional rule of Westeros, despite her growing empowerment. The tension between her increased distance, both geographically and culturally, from her desired endpoint of King's Landing, and the military and political coalition she has begun to put together, have provided rich terrain for fan artists seeking to produce extra-canonical representations of this character.

Unlike Dany, whose fan depictions can often be associated with a particular book based upon her clothing or background, Jon Snow is often a bit more ambiguous in fan art. Jon is the only character in *ASOIAF* that has been depicted more often than Dany. As is always the case where different artists illustrate the same character, the illustrations vary dramatically, including outlier renderings where Jon looks like a younger brother of Howard Stern's (Snow) and another where he looks like Edward Scissorhands (Taylor). However, the band of character variance is much narrower than with either Dany or Cersei Lannister. Narratively, the novels place Jon within a specific color scheme that, for the most part, fan artists maintain, with pen and ink drawings recalling what was denied to him as a name: Stark. These black and white ink drawings show Jon to be dark, brooding, and mysterious (juelshaness). The white of his direwolf Ghost and the snow in scenes north of the Wall provide a visual and narrative contrast with his black cloak and the black raven that often sits upon his shoulder (guillemhp). In many cases, the only real color of note is red, and then only minor touches: Ghost's eyes, the leaves of a Weirwood Tree, Ygritte's hair, etc. This general lack of color is in direct contrast to depictions of Dany and Cersei, whom are often illustrated with colorful costumes.

Indeed, numerous differences between Jon and Dany are evident. Strangely, Jon enjoys fewer action shots than does Dany. This may be because there is no shortage of male characters in *ASOIAF* who can be depicted in such scenes, whereas Dany is one of few female characters that Martin routinely places in such situations. Another possibility is that many of Jon's struggles are internal ones, as he deals with his bastardy, keeping his oath to the Night's Watch despite his family being at war, and his love for Ygritte compromising his vow of celibacy. Although in the text Jon is involved in plenty of battles and other significant events, has most common pose in fan art is static: brooding while staring off into the distance (Haruko). Even though he is usually depicted in a serious fashion, fan artists do occasionally inject some humor into their portrayals. Dany is almost always drawn straight, but Jon appears in several spoof-like cartoons, as well as some more outlandish depictions, such as the one where he wears sunglasses, has the phrase "I am the sexy watcher on the wall" written behind him, and is accompanied by a dialogue caption "Deal with it!" (lucy). The most significant difference between the depictions of Jon and Dany, however, is in their age. Although the Jon of fan art is often portrayed as older than fourteen, he is not aged to quite the same degree as Dany. Perhaps this is because he is not overtly sexualized in the narrative, or that he is male and thus not subject to the same levels of sexual commodification, or because the winterlands, where he dwells, mean that he is fully clothed most of the time. At least one demographic study of FanFiction.net has suggested that female members are more prevalent than males by a wide margin (FFN Research). Very likely, demographics such as gender play a large role in which characters tend to be illustrated and how they are portrayed, although such a specific study would be quite difficult as avatars and nom de plumes often obscure the gender of the artist. Regardless of their backgrounds, artists have almost uniformly taken the tactic of aging Dany for her often semi-naked travels throughout the Essos desert. With Jon, however, other than his tryst with Ygritte, there is little sexualization in the text where adaptation in fan art might run afoul of perceptions of taste. Indeed, Jon is often slightly feminized in such portrayals (moartestea), either because of his youth or in anticipation that Martin will eventually reveal him to be the son of Rhaegar Targaryen, who is noted for being "beautiful" in an Arianne Martell sample POV chapter released by Martin in early 2013 ("Excerpt from the Winds of Winter"). Although fan illustrations of Jon do exist depicting features tradi- tionally considered more masculine—square jaw, facial hair, etc.—he is more often illustrated with finer, more feminine features, and in one case could be mistaken for Arya were it not for the title given to the piece by its artist (eirlis). There appears to be no textual basis in Martin's work for Jon's femininity, although in his various depictions of Varys, Martin does indicate his awareness of gender as both performed and in the eye of the beholder (for an interesting contrast, see *Cok* 8 Tyrion 2: 98 & *Cok* 15 Tyrion 3: 180).

Some fan artists take things a step further, entering into the world of alter- nate timelines and histories in producing the extra-canonical. This is particularly true of the "R+L=J" phenomenon, the theory that Jon Snow is actually the son of Rhaegar Targaryen and Lyanna Stark, which is commonplace on "Westeros. org," "Tower of the Hand," and other sites of online fandom. At this point, this origin story is extra-canonical. However, impressive supporting evidence has been compiled by its adherents, much of it surrounding not only Ned's recol- lection of his sister's death and the promise he made to her (*Got* 39 Eddard 10: 355; *Got* 58 Eddard 15: 527) but also the prophecy that a reborn Azor Ahai (*Cok* 10 Davos 1: 113–115) and/or "Prince that was Promised" will return during a harsh winter to defeat the Others ("Tower of the Hand" and "A Forum of Ice and Fire"). Fan art reflects this theory in scenes depicting an infant Jon Snow next to a dead or dying Lyanna Stark, often unambiguously captioned, for exam- ple as "The birth of Jon Snow" (Arashell). Such birthing scenes represent a departure from the source-text, involving instead the hopes and dreams of a reading public raised upon rags-to-riches type stories. Indeed, innovations like these mark the blending of fan art and fan fiction, where the creative impulse merges with reader aspirations in order to carry the story forward into alternate plots or anticipated revelations. That fans should be supportive of Jon's ascendancy should come as no surprise, as foundlings, orphans, and bastards abound in fantasy literature.

Perhaps the 20th century text that best laid the groundwork for the modern veneration of those with low, uncertain, or problematic birth was *The Sword in the Stone* (1938), the first story published in what would become T.H. White's opus updating of the Arthurian Legend: *The Once and Future King*. In this text, Wart is an orphan who has been adopted by a knight, although he is not treated as well as his foster brother Kay, who dubs the orphan "the Wart." After having many adventures and suffering personal setbacks, all of which prepare him for eventual leadership, Wart is revealed to be the son of Uther Pendragon and rightful ruler of England when he pulls a legendary sword from a block of stone. The similarities to the case of Jon Snow are notable: a high noble raised in a house of lesser nobility, a lower station held despite full acceptance from the adoptive family, tribulations and the acquisition of skill sets that lead to seasoning, and a sword out of legend that signals the truth about the hero's origins (in Martin's text, Lightbringer). If Martin's text complies, then *ASOIAF* will eventually be situated within a sub-genre of high fantasy that celebrates the accomplishments of those who combine the power of fate with the hard work and constancy learned from their humble upbringings,[12] a trope that extends back beyond even the earliest Arthurian tales to the Greek tragedies of the 5th century BCE. More than any other classical story element, 20th century fantasy has mined the sub-plot of uncertain parentage in Sophocles' play *Oedipus Rex*. It is no surprise then that some will portray Jon's birth as the "secret" behind Lyanna's bloody death.

In this popular view, Eddard Stark proclaimed Jon his own in order to protect him from the wrath of Robert Baratheon. This reading of the character brushes aside the fact that Jon has black hair, instead focusing upon other supposed clues.[13] However, as other characters demonstrate, mixing Targaryen blood has occasionally produced dark-haired offspring, such as the quarter–Targaryen Robert Baratheon or the half–Targaryen Aegor Rivers. Indeed, Jon's dark, brooding nature as often noted in fan art may resonate with a statement Barristan Selmy makes about the Targaryens, that the gods flip a coin whenever one is born, with madness and greatness the possible outcomes (*Sos* 71 Daenerys 6: 811). Furthermore, fan art foregrounds other physical features that suggest such a lineage, such as the fine or feminized features noted prior. In the blogosphere, Jon's potential identity as a Targaryen is widely discussed, and serves to align him with Daenerys: one blogger notes, "Can't stop thinking about Jon Snow and Daenerys Targaryen becoming the Brangelina of Westeros" (suicideblonde). These characters are both young and attractive, and their kinship would not preclude a liaison given the Targaryen tradition of inter-marriage. These associations are reflected in depictions of the two apparently dressed for a wedding, with Jon in a tuxedo and Dany in a dress of fire, as well as a drawing of the two each attended by their animal protectors, Ghost and Drogon. The latter, inked with ballpoint and pentel pens, includes the caption: "Daenerys and Jon—Hoping these two will meet eventually..." (zenlang). Dany does not appear, however, in all of the images that serve to construct Jon as a Targaryen. Fan artist a-chelsea-grin shows Jon sitting on the Iron Throne, anticipating that at some point he will come into his full birthright as a Targaryen. Indeed, images of Jon on the throne are more common than those of Dany, which is ironic, as this is her sole ambition whereas Jon has to be forced to accept authority. Fan artists who portray Jon with more ambition than he has heretofore exhibited in Martin's text perhaps view him as the hero of the entire narrative, anticipating a potential character trajectory.

One other aspect of Jon Snow fan art bears scrutiny, and that is the fact that he rarely appears alone, often attended by either animals (Ghost and/or raven) or other characters (Ygritte, Val, or Sam Tarly). An important distinction between Jon and Cersei Lannister can be drawn here. Her POV chapters indicate that, much like Jon, Cersei is introspective and brooding. Unlike Jon, however, whose connection to others helps him deal with his problems, Cersei's only positive interactions are with her children, who are not equipped to converse with her as equals, and her brother Jaime, who spends much of the narrative apart from her. Perhaps in reflection of this isolation, fan art rarely depicts her interacting with anyone else, unlike Jon, who is often paired with Ghost. Intriguingly, the dire wolf, although commonly shown with Jon, is more diversely represented than is his human companion, sometimes the size of a large dog, but on other occasions the size of a horse, nearly dwarfing Jon (Darkalia). Sometimes, the wolf is drawn realistically, but on other occasions is highly stylized. In many depictions, Jon is touching or leaning against Ghost, suggesting the intimacy between them cultivated throughout the text with their narrative doubling. Moreover, while Jon is usually portrayed as emotionless, Ghost is often shown growling, occasionally with a face distorted by anger or rage (Daemon). In these cases, the fact that Jon often touches Ghost seems to represent a restraint, almost as if Jon is holding back some aspect of himself, keeping his baser instincts in check. The same is true in the rare instances where he is portrayed with another character, most notably Ygritte or Val. Ironically, although Ygritte becomes his lover and he certainly has a similar interest in Val, in most cases fan art does not depict the same level of intimacy as between him and Ghost. Nor are there the number of Jon/Ygritte depictions as there are of Jon/Ghost, perhaps not even one-tenth. While portrayals of Ygritte are rarer, there is still a large variation in the way she is depicted, from sexualized to buffoonish, from a mature woman with flowing auburn tresses to a seeming caricature of Orphan Annie replete with bright and curly, carrot-colored hair (pebbled, Gali-miau). Even less common are Jon/Val depictions, although part of this may be that by the end of *A Dance with Dragons* their relationship has not yet been fully developed.

Daenerys and Jon are largely embraced as protagonists in a fictional world where characters are portrayed as morally complex, if not ambiguous.[14] There are exceptions, however. Although not nearly to the same degree, Cersei Lannister joins Gregor Clegane, Ramsay Snow, and a few other figures in that she is rarely humanized in Martin's text, at least until her POV chapters in *A Feast for Crows* lend dimensionality to her character, exposing her hopes and fears and reasons for her actions. For the first three books, Cersei appears as a self-centered schemer, instrumental in the capture of Eddard Stark and established as a foil against her brother Tyrion, one of the more popular characters. When she is granted POV chapters in the fourth book, her interior monologues reveal her to be petty and jealous but also show her fretting about Tyrion's power despite the fact that he's locked up and awaiting execution, worrying about the safety of both Jaime and Tommen, suspecting the Tyrells and Varys, feeling rebuffed by Jaime, and considering individuals, all of whom she distrusts, to fill vacancies on the Small Council (*Ffc* 3 Cersei 1: 54). Descriptions from the novels indicate her physical appeal, but Martin also hints that her legendary beauty is well into a decline. Take, for instance, the horror she endures during her atonement walk, when her sense of humiliation turns not on being pelted with rotten vegetables and dead cats, or even her public nakedness, but on her fear that they will see that she is older than they realized and that the youthful persona she projects will be exposed as artifice:

> She did not feel beautiful, though. She felt old, used, filthy, ugly. There were stretch marks on her belly from the children she had borne, and her breasts were not as firm as they had been when she was younger. Without a gown to hold them up, they sagged against her chest. *I should not have done this. I was their queen, but now they've seen, they've seen, they've seen. I should never have let them see.* Gowned and crowned, she was a queen. Naked, bloody, limping, she was only a woman, not so very different from their wives, more like their mothers than their pretty little maiden daughters. *What have I done?* [*Dwd* 65 Cersei 2: 858].

Nor is her fear surprising. She lives in a medieval gendered setting and derives part of her power from the mystique of her beauty. Even before her penance walk, Cersei's age comes into sharp relief as she is exposed to the young and naïve women who will eventually replace her in power. Given her increased age and vulnerability as her father is murdered and Jaime both physically and emotionally incapacitated, her unpleasantness to Sansa Stark (*Cok* 57 Sansa 5: 616) and plots against Margaery Tyrell (*Ffc* 39 Cersei 7: 476) are understandable. Yet fan illustrations of Cersei have not shown this side of her, choosing instead to depict her as young and beautiful. She is often illustrated with long, flowing, blonde tresses and wearing elegant, colorful dresses, often in the red and gold of House Lannister.[15] These depictions do not focus on an earlier period of her life, since many artists depict her with her crown. The reasons for making her appear younger are understandable, as physical beauty is valued in visual art. Thus, making her younger serves to empower her, although quite differently from the empowerment that age seems to bring her in the novels. Indeed, the trope of a beautiful woman employing her sexuality as a weapon extends back to the classical letters of numerous regions. In England, the trope finds its origins, at the very least, in several of the women of Arthurian legend (Lady Guinevere, Morgan le Fay, etc.), and the lead up to the printed story in England.[16] As a sorceress who in many Arthurian stories is antagonistic, le Fay perhaps most fully prefigures the character of Melisandre. However, as a woman of extreme beauty who must rely upon that beauty in order to compete with the powerful men who surround her, Lady Guinevere best serves as progenitor to several other characters from *ASOIAF*, including Cersei Lannister.

The sexual commodification of Cersei is slightly different than that of Dany, however, above and beyond the treatment of their ages. Cersei's only nude appearance in the text, in her walk of atonement, is anything but sexual. However, in fan art she is routinely sexualized, often scantily dressed (Hear Me Roar) or in the process of disrobing (Arashell). Cersei is on average more overtly sexualized than Dany. She is invariably depicted with long hair, which often flows over or around an impressive bosom (pardoart). Her hair color ranges in these depictions from golden to dirty blonde, but is always beautiful (Vojngat). Her eyes are usually green, occasionally almost unrealistically so (Clark). In addition to resonating with Martin's comparison of Cersei's eyes to wildfire (*CoK* 60 Sansa 6: 637), this detail also underscores the envy she has for the positions of power held by the males who surround her, most of whom she perceives to be far less capable: "Cersei sniffed. 'I should have been born a man. I would have no need of any of you then. None of this would have been allowed to happen. How could Jaime let himself be captured by that *boy*? And Father, I trusted in him, fool that I am, but where is he now that he's wanted?'" (*Cok* 20 Tyrion 5: 242).

Not all focus on her beauty; a few make her appear almost girlish, while others show her to be quite a bit older and beginning to lose her looks (Cristina). She is also, but rarely, caricatured, made to look shrewish and cross, and even dressed in drag (the-savage-salad). The latter is a definite outlier but shows that fan artists incorporate their own feelings about characters into their artistic vision, including attempts to humiliate or demonstrate transgression. Generally, however, Cersei is portrayed as both beautiful and sexual. Indeed, the mixture of heightened sexuality and posing in beautiful, flowing robes almost seems as if pin-up meets high medieval fashion. Although in these illustrations Cersei tends to be static, her seductive power is specifically highlighted in a subset of fan depictions that have her reclining on a bed, or with a bed visible in the background (Komarck). Such pictures imply seduction is a weapon Cersei is well trained to wield. Indeed, unlike Dany, who is often depicted on horseback or in some other action scene, when Cersei's surroundings can be determined they are almost always domestic. She needs neither dragons nor armies of Unsullied; instead, she uses her beauty and her intelligence as weapons. Show-runner David Benioff has said as much during an interview prior to the season two premiere:

> Cersei is frustrated by the constraints placed upon a woman in medieval society, even the most privileged woman in the land. She wishes she were born a man so she could fight her enemies in the open. But she can't—and so she chooses other methods of combat [Boucher].

It is interesting to note here that Cersei is almost always depicted alone, rarely appearing with another character. Single pieces of fan artwork often focus upon a single character, but often lovers or family members are depicted together. Although they do occur (Emily84), illustrations that include Jaime and demonstrate the true nature of their relationship are few and far between. Although incest-themed fan writings can be easily found on FanFiction.net and other sites, the stakes change with *visual* portrayals, perhaps explaining why the fan artists who do draw Cersei and Jaime together usually keep things relatively tame. Another explanation may be the popularity of fan-paired Jaime Lannister and Brienne of Tarth and the anxiety fans sometimes express over whether or not these two characters will become romantically linked.

More than in fan depictions of Dany or any other female character, Cersei seems imbued with a level of feminism applied by the fans. Although all Lannisters share the motto "Hear me Roar," Cersei is most associated with the phrase in the blogosphere, perhaps because she emerges at the end of *A Storm of Swords* as the only Lannister who still enjoys real power, perhaps due to the enduring cultural resonance of Helen Reddy's feminist anthem "I am Woman (Hear me Roar)." There is also something interesting and provocative in the way that Cersei, in many of these depictions, interacts with the viewer. It is rare for characters to acknowledge the "Fourth Wall" by invading the proscenium space between actor and audience. As Aja Romano notes, in Fan Fiction the Fourth Wall also refers to the manner in which the producers of fan art protect themselves from accusations involving taste and even potential litigation by purposefully obscuring their identities (Romano). When juxtaposed with representations of Cersei Lannister this reading of the Fourth Wall suggests something revolutionary about the entire system, where a female character engaging in an oppositional gaze underscores the project of guerrilla art undertaken by the illustrator. Cersei often performs just this transgression by looking directly at the viewer. She looks proud in some depictions, dangerous in others, and even cruel in a few.[17] Unlike Dany, whose look seems to veer between innocence and experience, Cersei nearly always appears in control of the situation. It is ironic, however, that despite the fact that she is often shown wearing a crown, she is only occasionally depicted sitting upon the iron throne.

Although there could be some gender implications, such as fan artist misogyny, explaining why Cersei is rarely portrayed holding the reins of patriarchal power, most likely this notable absence is because neither Martin's novels nor the television show portray her in a positive light. Indeed, accusations of misogyny have followed Martin, both because some of Martin's female characters enjoy very little agency, and because of the frankly described rape scenes and other aspects of life in his medieval world that prove sexually humiliating for women. These voices, however, became much more forceful with the first season of the HBO adaptation. Although there were those such as Scott Meslow who noted "the difference between depicting misogyny and endorsing misogyny," some critics decried both Martin and the show-runners for their treatment of women (Meslow). The television show may have made for a larger target, but more significant was the visual nature of the adaptation, which renders such scenes more graphic and visceral. Nor do the publicity shots and posters advertising this season empower Cersei appreciably. Male characters are more prominent, as with the iconic depiction of Eddard Stark on the Iron Throne. Although he did occupy the throne briefly as the Hand of Robert Baratheon, it was Cersei who outwitted Eddard, who gives the book its name when she talks about playing "The Game of Thrones" (*Got* 45 Eddard 12: 408), and who, by the end of *A Dance with Dragons* has outlasted two Kings and four Hands. Whether Eddard was chosen to sit upon the throne for the iconic poster (as well as the covers of the book reprint and Season 1 DVD) due to the fact that he is male, was perceived by viewers as being the primary protagonist, or played by Sean Bean, the most recognizable actor, only the PR people know.

Jon, Dany, and Cersei are by no means the only characters whose renderings yield rich possibilities for interpretation; other characters play an important role in the corpus of fan art, although they do not always follow the straight and serious depictions that typically predominate with Dany, Jon, and Cersei.

Tyrion Lannister is often portrayed in a humorous and light-hearted fashion, although a poster where he replaces Jesus Christ in a clear reference to Leonardo da Vinci's painting *The Last Supper* (Sheila 2912), despite its comic overtones, has the ability and perhaps was even designed to offend. Arya Stark is often depicted holding her short sword Needle (kimsol), reflecting the empowerment this character begins to enjoy as she strikes out on her own and endures, but overcomes, numerous hardships. Some illustrations are politically motivated, such as a graphic design that places Robb Stark's visage into the red & blue background of the Obama "Hope" poster made famous by Shepard Fairey during the 2008 U.S. Presidential election (Schmidt). This mash-up is ironic for two reasons. First of all, employing a notable icon from a recent election is incongruous considering the contrast between the Westerosi game of thrones and democratic elections. And secondly, the poster is anachronistic in that it uses a contemporary meme to propose Robb as the hope for Westeros despite the fact that the novel in which he dies (*A Storm of Swords*) was published eight years prior to the first Obama election. The Robb Stark "Hope" poster is a perfect example of how fans have, through their creative energies, served to advance the narrative of George R.R. Martin's *ASOIAF* by continuing to merge it with contemporary issues. Characters such as Daenerys Targaryen, Jon Snow, and Cersei Lannister first existed within Martin's fictional world; however, to a certain extent they have outgrown that world, adapted by fans to reflect societal fears, desires, and values. The entrance of fans into such popular texts is not new, extending in any sort of organized form back to the original *Star Trek* series in the late 1960s. However, at this point in history the phenomenon of fan fiction, and its visual arm fan art, enjoys increased visibility and therefore purchase upon the consciousness of the casual fan. In a world where the construction of meaning is increasingly shared by producer and consumer, rigid divisions between them begin to collapse under their own weight. The sanctity of a narrative's canon is thus overwhelmed by the creative reader and what he or she can bring to the table, particularly in a series such as *A Song of Ice and Fire*, which in its eventual 20–25 year span will appeal to several generations of fans, every single one of whom has the ability to add their unique vision to the narrative.

Notes

1. See the PBS documentary short *Fan Art: An Explosion of Creativity* (Brown).

2. Followers of the original *Star Trek* television series pioneered the visual art form of cosplay, creating and wearing costumes to fan conventions. Some were replicas of costumes from the show, whereas others exhibited more artistic license or were even extra-canonical to series creator Gene Roddenberry's imagined universe. *Star Trek* fans also pioneered "slash fiction," in which fan authors explore transgressive romantic and sexual encounters between characters. See Penley for a treatment of *Star Trek*'s importance to the development of fan fiction.

3. Cyber-archive *Fanfiction.net* filters fan fiction by book series and thus can be used to gauge quantitative popularity. The Harry Potter series has by far the most stories archived at 656,000, considerably more than its closest competitors at 212,000 (*Twilight*) and 49,500 (*The Lord of the Rings*). *A Song of Ice and Fire*, by way of comparison, has 3300 stories archived ("Books").

4. The advertising campaign launched in Manhattan prior to the show's third season debut (March 31, 2013) traded on this cultural penetration. Iconic characters and animals from the show appeared upon buses, benches, billboards, and other sites, all in anticipation of not only the new season but also the New York opening of a traveling exhibition of artifacts from the first two seasons (*HBO Connect*).

5. See Sean T. Collins' often irreverent musings on the ten biggest changes between the books and the television adaptation, as well as Daniel Fienberg's Interview with Natalie Dormer (Fienberg).

6. The quantity of items for sale in the online HBO store may serve as markers of house popularity. The sigil of House Stark emblazons the largest group of items, with House Targaryen definitely the next most popular. Surprisingly, the sigil of House Greyjoy appears as often as do those of House Lannister and House Baratheon.

7. Markers of beauty in American culture have typically favored Western and especially Northern Europe, where fair skin and hair and blue eyes have historically been favored. Actresses such as Marilyn Monroe contributed to this ideal during the post World War II period, and it is only as subsequent waves of immigration from Asia and particularly Latin America have continued to change the face of American beauty norms that brunette models and actresses have come to outnumber blonde ones. However, as Sheryl McCarthy reminds us, despite a greater diversity in what it means to be "beautiful," American society still suffers from the legacy of "the blonde mystique": "Beauty standards are driven by racial and gender politics, by Caucasian image-makers who promote their own physical attributes as symbols of their superiority to other groups, and by male fantasies of what makes women desirable. When women are being highly sexualized in the popular culture, it's not surprising that the old standards of beauty hold sway" (McCarthy). It is interesting to note that fan illustrations depicting Daenerys often include two other features that jell with western notions of beauty but are not typically compatible, at least naturally, with very fair hair and skin: darker eyebrows & eyelashes, and red lips. Strikingly, Dany is often portrayed with fair hair, skin, and eyes, but darker eyebrows and eyelashes and full, red lips as one might expect in a fashion model (Jimenez). In the HBO adaptation, these features seem to have been darkened slightly between Seasons 1 and 4.

8. Early teen sexuality may have been commonplace during the late medieval period to which Martin's tale most closely relates. Although in 2002 the United States Supreme Court ruled that sanctions against "virtual" pornography in the Child Pornography Prevention Act of 1996 were unconstitutional, these waters continue to be murky, with the most recent legal battle involving comic book collector Christopher Handley, who although avoiding a charge of possession of pornographic material featuring minors, pled guilty to obscenity charges and was sentenced to six months in prison for owning a collection of Japanese "Manga" comics depicting early teen sexuality (Kravets).

9. Hair so employed can refer to Aphrodite or her Roman equivalent Venus, such as in Botticelli's "The Birth of Venus," or to English legend Lady Godiva.

10. Cleopatra is often commonly depicted as having a single breast exposed, but these are death scenes and so Aphrodite is a more relevant forerunner.

11. Harold Koda and Richard Martin, respectively current and former curators of the Costume Institute of the Metropolitan Museum of Art, note that clothing and fashion contribute to the western misrepresentation of the east known as Orientalism: "Orientalism is not a picture of the East of the Easts. It represents longing, option, and faraway perfection. It is, like Utopia, a picture everywhere and nowhere, save in the imagination" (Koda).

12. Other notable high fantasy characters of low or troubled birth who complete heroic quests include Ged from *The Wizard of Earthsea*, Taran from *The Chronicles of Prydain*, and the title character from the *Harry Potter* series.

13. An ancient prophecy contends that mythical hero Azor Ahai will be reborn to combat the Others from north of the wall. Astute readers have noted ways in which Jon Snow fits this prophecy, although at least 3–4 other characters do as well. Bolstering the claim for Snow are other textual hints that Jon Snow is actually a Targaryen, the most fundamental of which appears in Ned's recollection of his sister's bloody deathbed (*Got* 4 Eddard 1: 35–36). The most recent of such possible hints comes at the end of *A Dance With Dragons*, when after being stabbed by mutinous members of the Night's Watch, his body "smokes" (*Dwd* 69 Jon 13: 913).

14. Negative fan art portrayals of these characters may exist, but my online research uncovered no examples in which artists were clearly portraying negative qualities.

15. Cersei Lannister seems to have given rise to the most costumes designed and worn by fans. In cosplay—costume/play—communities of fans gather to dress up as characters from a specific series, such as *ASOIAF*. Cersei's ornate costumes make her the character of choice for many Cosplay aficionados, with the red and gold of House Lannister the most common colors (Visenya).

16. The Arthurian cycle of stories left England for France, where they were more fully imbued with chivalric codes. Marie de France brought these stories back to popularity in England with the publication of *Lanval* during the late 12th century. Although writing in England, Marie's tales were written in a dialect of French. It would take another 300 years, and the arrival of the printing press in England, until the Arthurian tales would become codified in their largely current form. *Le Mort d'Arthur* was a collection of Arthurian tales compiled by Sir Thomas Malory and printed by William Caxton in 1485 CE. As one of the first printed pieces to gain any sort of popularity in England, this collection became the benchmark for print Arthurian legend; in Malory's version, Morgan le Fay is an enchantress who attempts to foil Arthur by throwing his magical scabbard into the lake and bewitching Sir Lancelot.

17. Many of these depictions deploy one of two different looks, both of which suggest power and dominance. The first is the so-called "Kubrick Stare" (Kubrick Stare), from his use of it with Malcolm McDowell's character in *A Clockwork Orange* and Jack Nicholson's character in *The Shining*, although it was first used to highly dramatic effect at the end of Alfred Hitchcock's *Psycho*. Here, the head is tilted down but the character looks straight ahead, ominous, unsmiling, beneath lowered eyebrows, imparting simmering danger. Kubrick famously used this cinematic device in most of his films. Employed for Cersei, however, it highlights her sexuality as dangerous and fetishizes her as a femme fatale (Amoka). The second look is essentially the opposite, with her head tilted up at a slight angle but her eyes again looking straight ahead (Dinger). Here, the effect is one of haughtiness and pride instead of danger, but still of dominance over the viewer. Indeed, Cersei's interior monologues beginning with her POV chapters in *A Feast for Crows* suggest that she feels superior to just about everyone, including her own kin. As show-runner D.B. Weiss notes: "Of all the Lannister siblings, she's the one best suited to exercise power in this harsh, unyielding world—but one of the features of this harsh, unyielding world is that it won't let her exercise power openly" ("Game of Thrones" Duo).

Works Cited

a-chelsea-grin. a-chelsea-grin.deviantart.com/art/Game-of-Thrones-Jon-Snow-298651037. February 25, 2013.

AcidBanter 7. www.fanpop.com/clubs/women-of-westeros/images/31894234/title/ daenerys-targaryen-fanart. February 15, 2013.

Amoka. adwd-reread.blogspot.com/2011/09/cersei-ii.html. March 1, 2013.

____. awoiaf.westeros.org/index.php/File:Daenerys.jpg. February 15, 2013.

Arashell. arashell.deviantart.com/art/ASoIAF-Lyanna-Stark-and-Jon-291832400. February 25, 2013.

____. arashell.deviantart.com/art/Cersei-Lannister-270035666. March 1, 2013.

Behemotik, Ann. annbehemotik.deviantart.com/art/Daenerys-Targaryen-307706020. February 15, 2013.

Best, Carrie. awoiaf.westeros.org/index.php/File:Daenerys_by_carrie_best.jpg. February 15, 2013.

"Books." *Fanfiction.net.* August 1, 2013.

Boucher, Geoff. "Game of Thrones" Duo. *Hero Complex.* 3 June 2013. March 1, 2013.

Brown, Kornhaber. "Film Art: An Explosion of Creativity." Squaresevilleseries.com. No date. March 1, 2013.

Chaotic-AlterEgo. chaotic-alterego.deviantart.com/art/Daenerys-Targaryen-322694108. February 15, 2013.

Clark, Johnny. johnnyclark.deviantart.com/art/Cersei-Lannister-189403084. March 1, 2013.

Collins, Sean T. "Game Changers: The 10 Biggest Differences Between 'Game of Thrones' and the Books." *Rolling Stone.* 15 May 2012. March 1, 2013.

Cristina. beentheredrawnthat.blogspot.com/2011/04/cersei-lannister.html. March 1, 2013.

Daemon, Chris. www.newgrounds.com/art/view/chrisdaemon/jon-snow-ghost. February 25, 2013.

Darkalia. darkalia.deviantart.com/art/Jon-Snow-and-Ghost-332237826. February 25, 2013.

Dinger, Katherine. towerofthehand.com/essays/top30affc/24.html. March 1, 2013.

eirlis. eirlis.deviantart.com/art/Jon-Snow-324148311. February 25, 2013.

Emily84. emily84.tumblr.com/post/26500865791/game-of-thrones-freaks-jamie-and-cersei. March 1, 2013.

"Excerpt from the Winds of Winter." *Georgerrmartin.com.* 27 January 2013. August 10, 2013.

Feinberg, Daniel. "Interview: 'Game of Thrones' co-star Natalie Dormer discusses her Margaery Tyrell." *Hit Flix.* 31 March 2013. April 1, 2013.

FFN Research. "Fan Fiction Demographics in 2010: Age, Sex, Country." *Fanfiction.net.* August 1, 2013.

"A Forum of Ice and Fire." asoiaf.westeros.org/index.php/topic/79404-rl-j-v-38/. July 10, 2013.

Gali-miau. galleryofthrones.tumblr.com/post/27782978393/you-know-nothing-jon-snow-by-gali-miau. February 25, 2013.

guillemhp. guillemhp.deviantart.com/art/Daenerys-Targaryen-264231855. February 15, 2013.

____. guillemhp.deviantart.com/art/Jon-Snow-and-Ghost-264232412. February 25, 2013.

Haruko, Histerica. histerica-haruko.deviantart.com/art/You-know-nothing-Jon-Snow-314617581. February 25, 2013.

HBO Connect. "Exhibit." March 28, 2013.

Hear Me Roar. imgur.com/gallery/68Ks7. March 1, 2013.

Jekaa. jekaa.deviantart.com/art/Daenerys-Targaryen-64633193. February 15, 2013.

Jenkins, Henry. *Convergence Culture: Where Old and New Media Collide.* New York: New York University Press, 2006.

____. "Fan Fiction as Critical Commentary." *Henryjenkins.org.* 7 September 2006. August 1, 2013.

Jimenez, Brissia. dribbble.com/shots/831135-Daenerys-Targaryen?list=tags&tag=face. February 15, 2013.

juelshaness. juelshaness.deviantart.com/art/Jon-Snow-316372908. February 25, 2013.

kimsol. kimsol.deviantart.com/art/Stick-them-with-the-Pointy-End-344957341. March 30, 2013.

Koda, Harold, and Richard Martin. "Orientalism: Visions of the East in Western Dress" *Metropolitan Museum of Art.* October 2014. August 1, 2013.

Komarck, Michael. hieloyfuego.wikia.com/wiki/Archivo:Cersei_Lannister_by_ Michael_ Komarck,_Fantasy_Flight_Games©.jpg. March 1, 2013.

Kravets, David. "'Obscene' U.S. Manga Collector Jailed 6 Months." *Wired*. 12 February 2010. March 1, 2013.

"Kubrick Stare." tvtropes.org/pmwiki/pmwiki.php/Main/KubrickStare. March 1, 2013.

lucy. nym-winchester.tumblr.com/image/7299894732. February 25, 2013.

Luthien90. luthien90.deviantart.com/art/Daenerys-Targaryen-from-ASOIAF-312100346. February 15, 2013.

Martin, George R.R. <http://www.westeros.org/Citadel/SSM/Entry/6040/> July 28, 2013.

McCarthy, Sheryl. "Blond is Beautiful Mystique." *USA Today*. 18 February 2006. July 28, 2013.

Meslow, Scott. "'Game of Thrones': Making Sense of All the Sex. *The Atlantic*. 25 April 2011. August 1, 2013.

Miller, Laura. moartestea.deviantart.com/art/One-dance-308116940. February 25, 2013.

____. "The real life inspirations for 'Game of Thrones.'" *Salon*. 4 April 2012. March 1, 2013.

Noto, Phil. robot6.comicbookresources.com/2011/07/gallery-of-game-of-thrones-awesome-a-song-of-ice-and-fire-fan-art-from-around-the-web. February 15, 2013.

Oh, Lauren. robot6.comicbookresources.com/2011/08/gallery-of-game-of-thrones-vol-2-more-fan-art-from-around-the-web. February 15, 2013.

pardoart. pardoart.deviantart.com/art/Concept-Art-Cersei-Lannister-331388788. March 1, 2013.

pebbled. pebbled.deviantart.com/art/you-know-nothing-jon-snow-337196044. February 25, 2013.

Penley, Constance. *NASA/Trek: Popular Science and Sex in America*. London: Verso, 1997.

Petarsaur. petarsaur.deviantart.com/art/Daenerys-Targaryen-312687158. February 15, 2013.

Romano, Aja. "The Crumbling of the Fourth Wall: Why Fandom Shouldn't Hide Anymore." *Daily Dot*. 8 January 2013. August 1, 2013.

Sacco, Dominic. www.licensing.biz/news/read/game-of-thrones-is-hbo-s-fastest-selling-merch/027730. July 20, 2013.

Schmidt, R.J. www.fanpop.com/clubs/robb-stark/images/32234870/title/robb-westeros-election-fanart. March 30, 2013.

Sheila 2912. io9.com/5949671/tyrion-plays-jesus-in-the-game-of-thrones-last-supper. March 30, 2013.

Snow, Jen. www.redbubble.com/people/jensnow/works/9257723-jon-snow. February 25, 2013.

suicideblonde. suicideblonde.tumblr.com/post/24491278309/cant-stop-thinking-about-jon-snow-and-daenerys. August 12, 2013.

Taylor, Luther. luthertaylor.deviantart.com/art/Concept-12-Jon-Snow-309431779. February 25, 2013.

Teitku. www.comicvine.com/forums/battles-7/hermione-granger-vs-bella-swan-vs-daenerys-targary-638185. February 15, 2013.

the-savage-salad. the-savage-salad.deviantart.com/art/Cersei-Lannister-295103070. March 1, 2013.

"Tower of the Hand." towerofthehand.com/essays/chrisholden/jon_snows_parents.html. July 10, 2013.

uialwen. uialwen.deviantart.com/art/Daenerys-253423482. February 15, 2013.

velocitti. velocitti.deviantart.com/art/Winter-Is-Coming-259101776. February 15, 2013.

Visenya. www.cosplay.com/costume/339936/. March 1, 2013.

Vojngat, Calinn. calinnvojnngat.deviantart.com/art/Cersei-Lannister-portrait-II-214045943. February 25, 2013.

White, T.H. "The Sword in the Stone." *The Once and Future King*. New York: Ace Books, 1987.

zenlang. zenlang.deviantart.com/art/Daenerys-Targaryen-and-Jon-Snow-30893200. February 25, 2013.

"A reader lives a thousand lives before he dies": Transmedia Textuality and the Flows of Adaptation

ZOË SHACKLOCK

> "'A reader lives a thousand lives before he dies,' said Jojen. 'The man who never reads lives only one'"—*DwD* 35 Bran 3: 452

According to Jojen Reed, a weirwood forest is a forest of stories. Much like the human reader, the trees listen to, remember, and embody the many narratives sung to them by the children of the forest. Jojen's words have much to tell us about the nature of the contemporary media consumer, and more importantly, the fate of narrative texts in today's mediascape. As an adaptation of George R.R. Martin's epic fantasy series *A Song of Ice and Fire*, HBO's *Game of Thrones* follows a long tradition of adapting literary texts for the screen. However, while such texts have "adapted" to new media contexts and new structures of engagement, our understandings of them have not. Debates surrounding adaptation remain mired in highly charged notions of fidelity, and focus almost exclusively on the textual flows between literature and cinema,[1] thus translating poorly to the contemporary televisual context.

André Bazin's definition of adaptation—"the refraction of one work in another creator's consciousness" (20)—offers a new theoretical paradigm for adaptation studies. Just as adaptive works refocus their source texts, so too should our theoretical frameworks, refracting existing theories through the lens of new ideas. Today's narrative television is defined by complex, sprawling storytelling, extending beyond the borders of the medium. For example, *Lost* used numerous interactive alternate reality games to flesh out its mythology, *Heroes* unfolded simultaneously on television and in graphic novels, and a diverse array of shows, from *Community* to *Doctor Who*, expand their narratives through online webisodes. Henry Jenkins terms this new narrational framework "transmedia storytelling," in which a narrative unfolds across a variety of media forms, and must be pieced together by an active audience (20–1). Transmedia and adaptation studies share a common interest in transtextuality and an interdisciplinary position, meaning that there is strong potential in refocusing screen adaptation through the lens of televisual transmediality.

Rather than continuing to assert the authenticity of a single source text, this approach repositions the "original" and adapted texts as nodes in a greater transmedial network, or what Sara Gwenllian-Jones terms the "transmedial metatext" of cult television (86). In the networked narrative of *A Song of Ice and Fire*, the novels, the television program, the alternate reality game "The Maester's Path," and fan-created texts such as memes exist alongside one another and unfold together. Rethinking adaptation as content flow within a continuing narrative, rather than the re-iteration of a single original text, allows us to better account for the more flexible positions of narrative, authorship and consumption in the contemporary mediascape. Consequently, it allows us to celebrate the "thousand lives" of the narrative, rather than continuing to promote the authenticity of "only one."

"Our way is the old way": Adaptation Theory at the Crossroads

For most of its relatively short history,[2] the study of adaptation has been locked in something of a stalemate. Caught between literary, film, and cultural studies, the discipline seems to regard its liminal positioning as a hazard, desperately dealing in absolutes in the hope of establishing solid ground. Discussions of adaptation continue to revolve around the traditional binaries long dismantled in other disciplines—original versus copy, literature versus film, author versus consumer, and so on. These frames of reference form the core of the everyday definition of adaptation—a screen version of a literary work, best discussed in terms of its faithfulness to that single, original source.

Much discussion surrounding HBO's *Game of Thrones* exemplifies this model, focusing intently on the differences between the text of the novel and the television program. One of the most pronounced changes is the replacement of Robb's wife, from Jeyne Westerling in the novels to Talisa Maegyr. Responses varied from outrage at the change to attempts to reconcile it—for example, the so-called "Lannister Honeypot" theory, in which Talisa was a Lannister spy infiltrating and undermining Robb's campaign. These ideas follow the familiar template of adaptation criticism: Talisa's character either betrays the "spirit" of the text or honors it. Her eventual death at the Red Wedding is either a needless addition that reflects the violence of television (*The Atlantic*'s Christopher Orr described it as "just the kind of dialling-up-the-cruelty in which Benioff and Weiss specialise"), or adds an extra layer of emotional trauma that remains true to the horror of the scene in the novels (Richard Madden suggested that the scene was "more tragic that there's nothing left over" [Schwartz]). These either-or possibilities establish a rigid binary that persists in adaptation criticism. As Thomas Leitch concisely states, binaries retain "the power to direct discussion even among analysts who ought to know better" ("Twelve Fallacies" 150).

In treating the transactions between the cinema and the novel as its analytical blueprint, theorists of adaptation have turned something of a blind eye to the changing context surrounding its objects of study. James Naremore recognizes this issue, calling for the need for an approach that "takes into account the commercial apparatus, the audience, and the academic culture industry" (10). Despite the fact that this plea is increasingly prevalent in adaptation discourses, it has been poorly realized. Simone Murray, in taking up Naremore's challenge, argues that the focus on poststructuralist and reception theory in the 1990s shifted attention away from the conditions of cultural production (7). In this sense, adaptation theory could perhaps learn something from its etymological sibling, Darwinian evolution. In Darwin's work, adaptation operates according to best fit with the environment—a gene's fitness is wholly determined by the particular environment of the reproducing organism. Similarly, textual adaptations always exist within particular commercial, production, and reception contexts, and operate according to those conditions.

Henry Jenkins succinctly defines the contemporary mediasphere as a "convergence culture," epitomized by the horizontal organization of both media companies and texts across a whole suite of media formats (2).[3] Convergence culture also tightens the relationships between a text and its paratexts[4]—those elements that surround the body of a text, such as introductions, titles, commentaries, promotional material, reviews, and so on (Genette, *Paratexts* 5). Indeed, Jonathan Gray argues that contemporary media texts cannot be analyzed in isolation from their proliferations, which increasingly come to live with and influence the meanings of the texts themselves (2). By refocusing our attention on what are commonly disregarded as "peripherals" (6), Gray demonstrates that we can usefully unsettle the distinctions between primary and secondary texts, and between central and marginal elements—a feat that adaptation studies has never been able to achieve.

The promotional campaign for HBO's *Thrones*' third season reflects the important role paratexts play in the processes of adaptation. The first teaser trailer for season three, "Chaos," depicts close-ups of the main cast against a black background. The actors are lit dramatically, cloaked and twisted by the plays of shadow and light that dance across their faces. To tie in with this trailer, HBO released a set of twelve character posters for the main cast, each depicting an extreme close-up of the actors' faces, again lit with dramatic contrasts of light and shadow. Yet in the posters, this contrast takes on a coloured hue: each face lies half in warm light and half in cool blue shadow. Therefore, while the trailer traps the characters between the forces of light and dark, the posters place them in the interplay between ice and fire, a subtle allusion to the novels. Furthermore, the "Chaos" trailer includes a voiceover by Littlefinger, who tells us that chaos is a ladder, and while people may try to "cling to the realm or the gods or love ... only the ladder is real." While Littlefinger's speech at first evokes a sense of an endless climb upwards, neither the ladder nor the climb has a directional bias—both can either go up or down. And importantly, they can also go sideways, for if you turn a ladder on its side, it becomes a bridge. Of course, neither the posters nor the trailer fit our traditional definition of an adaptive text. Yet they mediate the textual flows between the larger adaptive nodes of the novels and the television series, drawing from and providing access to each equally. They cannot be disregarded as mere peripherals, for they bridge the adaptive nodes, holding the whole network together.

Paratexts play a crucial role in what is commonly known as transmedia storytelling. "A transmedia story," as Henry Jenkins defines it, "unfolds across multiple media platforms, with each new text making a distinctive and valuable contribution to the whole" (95–6). By "distinctive and valuable," Jenkins is referring to a model whereby a story is distributed evenly amongst the various transmedia elements, with the narrative emerging only through the comprehension of the entire collection. Transmedia storytelling is thus perhaps the prime example of the logic of convergence, and provides an important example for adaptation studies. It exploits its interdisciplinary position by acknowledging new, complex story structures, the fallacy of the single author, and the powerful role of the audience. Of course, *A Song of Ice and Fire* does not fit the central definition of transmedia storytelling, for George R.R. Martin did not set out to construct a multi-platform narrative. However, from the point of view of adaptation studies, what makes the relationship between the novels, the television program, and other textual elements unique is that the novels are as yet unfinished. Consequently, as the narrative continues to unfold across multiple media formats at once, the horizontal network model of transmedia clearly offers new possibilities for discussing the adaptive processes at work.

Shortly before the first season of *Game of Thrones*, HBO released an online game called "The Maester's Path." This game was created by the transmedia production company Campfire, most famous for the viral campaign for *The Blair Witch Project*. The purpose of this game was to introduce viewers to the world of Westeros, and was pitched to appeal to both those familiar and unfamiliar with the novels. The game had five sections, each corresponding to a particular human sense. The sight component involved traversing an online version of the Wall; the sound section required players to identify the houses of Westeros by listening to stories in an online "tavern"; and touch introduced a "winter is coming" iPad app. In the smell section, a collection of "influencers" were sent packages containing small scent vials from regions of Westeros. The journalists shared their information and experiences online, and the fan community worked together to identify the scents and solve the accompanying puzzle. The final section of the game was by far the most publicized and innovative. In order to approximate the taste of Westeros, food trucks travelled around Los Angeles and New York, serving up cuisine inspired by the series. The menu varied according to which particular region of Westeros was featured, including dishes such as roast squab, trout, and the ever-popular lemon cakes. While each section of the game could be played in isolation, all five had to be completed to win, and thus to experience a complete sensory immersion into the world of Westeros.

"The Maester's Path" complicates the theoretical maxims of adaptation theory. It does not have a single source text, but rather draws from both the television program and the novels alike. The food truck provides a culinary adaptation of the dishes described in Martin's prose, a very literal example of the great sin of adaptation: the word made flesh. Yet at the same time, it adapts the aesthetics of the television program. HBO is famous for its graphic representations of sex and violence, epitomized by the short-lived series *Rome*.[5] By forcing a visceral, bodily confrontation with the world of the narrative, "The Maester's Path" infuses Martin's descriptions with the carnality of HBO's visual aesthetic. In doing so, it lives up to HBO's famous slogan: "It's not TV. It's HBO." The world of Westeros is not simply translated to television, to be read in a new format, but is entirely fleshed out. This transmedia text can be touched, smelled and tasted, incorporated into our physiological constitutions. Therefore, it finds its life through the many bodies of the audience—a life that is, of course, open to a thousand different incarnations.

However, although transmedia and adaptation studies share a common transtextual focus, they seem to differ fundamentally at their core. Elizabeth Evans argues that "transmedia elements do not involve the telling of the same events on different platforms; they involve the telling of new events from the same storyworld" (27). Geoffrey Long is even more concise, explicitly establishing the two as mutually exclusive: "retelling a story in a different media type is adaptation, while using multiple media types to craft a *single story* is transmediation" (22, emphasis added). It needs to be stressed that adaptation and trans-media cannot be collapsed into one another; adaptation is not automatically an example of transmedia storytelling, and transmedia texts do not fit our traditional idea of derivative works. However, while Evans and Long are correct, their definitions return to the singular terminology that transmedia storytelling is well-equipped to dispense with altogether. Evans' discernment between "the same" and "new" events is insidious to the degree that it appears self-evident, but repetition can never simply be dismissed as replication. Similarly, Long's understanding of the singularity of the story, either retold or dispersed across media, fails to recognize that any text always possesses multiple incarnations. Therefore, refracting adaptation through the lens of transmedia storytelling allows us to properly exploit the mobile, multi-directional potential of both areas of study.

It is significant that "The Maester's Path" takes the world of Westeros as its focus, rather than the characters or plot mechanics. Long argues that trans-media narratives are "the story of world," held together by the coherence of the textual universe (48). While strict theorists of transmedia storytelling, such as Evans, would argue that "The Maester's Path" contains no significant narrative structure and thus cannot be true transmedia storytelling, the contributions it makes to our understanding of Westeros—a world as vital to the narrative as the mechanics of the plot—fulfill Jenkins' "valuable and distinctive" criteria. A world is not subject to the same strict criteria of innovation: you can visit the same place over and over again without it feeling stale. In ThinkHero TV's YouTube report on the food truck, fans swap fluidly between discussing their favorite parts of the novel, their expectations for the television series and their responses to the food. One fan enthusiastically describes the lemon cakes as representing Sansa's innocence, signifying "that part of the book where everything's fancy and princes exist" (ThinkHero TV). The food truck thus encourages a pleasurable temporal and spatial revisitation of the Westeros of the novels, as well as a sense of anticipation for a new encounter in the form of the television program. For the audience, therefore, the vast narrative is big enough to encompass multiple versions and incarnations.

Transmedia paratexts such as "The Maester's Path" harness the liminal power of adaptation, reconfiguring the adaptive text as one of many concurrent lives of a sprawling narrative. All textual elements are thus in some way paratexts, depending on where we are in the network at any one time. As Gerard Genette recognizes, paratexts are thresholds, zones of transition and transaction (*Para-texts* 2). Campfire described the food trucks as sites that "brought *Game of Thrones* fans and HBO's target audience face to face," a space in which different audiences with different textual knowledge come together, transforming one another in the process. Therefore, rather than looking back only at established theories and "original" texts, we should perhaps take a lesson from the Starks, bound by the old ways of the North but still forward-looking: in the vast narrative world of *A Song of Ice and Fire*, texts always relate in multiple ways, adaptive processes always operate across the whole network, and winter is always coming.

"I saw the White Walkers": Transmedial Synaesthesia and Adaptation

Repositioning the adaptive text as a node in a vast, transmedial network requires a similar rethinking of the modes of expression and consumption of that text. If adaptive processes always flow both ways, then they are never simply a translation between word and image; rather, the vast narrative is formed across all sensory modes. In *A Dance with Dragons*, almost every main character at one point speaks or thinks the same pithy maxim: "words are wind." While the characters are referring to distrust of what people say, Martin's repetition of the phrase undermines the entrenched logophilia in Western culture. The love of the word, and its twin fear of the image, makes up perhaps the most pervasive binary underpinning adaptation studies—the strict distinction between the written word and the screen image. Yet in the transmedial networks of contemporary adaptations, words are not the sacred gospel, but may be picked up and scattered in a thousand different animations. And they are never simply read, but are experienced synaesthestically; like the wind itself, they are felt on the skin, heard by the ears, and tasted in the back of the throat.

As with fidelity discourses, the sanctity of the word-image binary, and its associated value judgments, have been largely discredited by adaptation scholars.[6] Yet again, the transformations between written description and visual depiction remain at the forefront of the discipline; for example, Verlyn Flieger, writing on Peter Jackson's *The Lord of the Rings* as recently as 2011, states that the job of a film adaptation is to "translate words into pictures" (47). Consequently, discussions tend to revolve around the cinematic actualization of literary imagery, and the shift from imaginative visualization to perceptual presentation.[7] This pernicious visual bias remains a massive hurdle for the field.

The opening scene of "Winter Is Coming" (*GoT* 1.01) provides a compelling example of the complexities of multimodal adaptation processes. The scene refuses to establish a clear visual translation of the written text; rather, it subverts the primacy of vision, forcing the audience to turn to other cues to interpret the scene. As the gate to the tunnel slowly rises in the opening shot, the screen remains mostly obscured, directing the audience's attention to the creaking and clanking of the gate. The sound of horse hoofs, burning flames, and the pulley systems of the tunnel gates occupy the foreground of the sound-scape, unusually loud and crisp. This creates a sense of the isolation of The Wall, as the sound seems to ricochet around a barren, solemn, and cruel landscape. Furthermore, the camera work in the first few shots is deliberately slow and steady, and the actors betray little emotion and move only minimally. By them-selves, these shots provide little narrative information. However, in conjunction with the soundscape, the visual scarcity neatly codes the starkness and solitude of life at The Wall. Therefore, the scene fulfills Robert Stam's assertion that in the multi-track medium of screen media, the "possible contradictions between tracks are an aesthetic resource" (60).

These productive contradictions are exemplified in HBO's *Thrones'* use of subtitled languages, such as Dothraki and Valyrian. Subtitled speech relies on the cooperation between the eyes and the ears; comprehension comes from read-ing the text, but tone and character are communicated through sound. These juxtapositions allow for complex constructions of meaning. In "And Now His Watch Is Ended" (*GoT* 3.04), Daenerys reveals to Kraznys mo Nakloz that she speaks Valyrian fluently. However, her triumph over the slave master is simul-taneously a triumph over the audience. The audience have been privy to Kraznys mo Nakloz's Valyrian insults through the subtitles, enjoying a powerful feeling of knowing more than Daenerys and her retinue. However, by speaking in an unfamiliar language, Daenerys reclaims this power, becoming unknowable to us on the level of sound. This doubled experience of comprehending, yet not understanding, Daenerys' speech creates a strong sense of disorientation, enhanc-ing the power of the scene.

HBO's *Thrones'* use of the spaces that open up between image and sound reflects the way both adaptation and transmedia storytelling exploit the "gaps" in other texts (Long 53).[8] However, while we tend to understand adaptation as working to fill in the thinner parts of its source narrative, transmedia storytelling fleshes them out, "demand[ing] sensory play" across the whole suite of its textual nodes (Ndalianis 165). The transmedial flows of adaptation are thus best under-stood as operating across *sensory* gaps, rather than strictly narrative ones; indeed, "The Maester's Path" organized itself around the five senses, suggesting that each element of a transmedia text foregrounds a different sensory experience. Rethink-ing adaptation in this sense allows us to see adaptive texts as simply occupying and exploring different sensory niches, and thus to situate them alongside one another in a complete sensory experience. And it allows us to understand adaptive textual flows not comparatively or aesthetically, but precisely *synaesthetically*.

Synaesthesia is a particularly powerful way of approaching adaptation. It can be understood as a process of adaptation in its own right—the adaptation of one sensory mode by another. It suggests an experience that exceeds the limits of a single sensory modality, just as the transmedia text extends beyond any one medium. Brian Massumi describes synaesthesia as a "hinge" between two senses (184), again reflecting the adaptive text, which always occupies the junction where various texts and media modes meet, facilitating the smooth movement between them. A synaesthetic mode of engagement thus allows us to fully explore the way the adaptive text exists liminally, always in a process of transition and transportation, without attempting to privilege one particular text, sensory mode, or media property above others.

One of the most obvious points of difference between the novels and the television series is the renaming of "the Others" to "the White Walkers." While this change is undoubtedly pragmatic (it distinguishes them from the villains in *Lost*), it points to the synaesthetic nature of adaptive texts. "White Walkers" suggests a merging of color and movement, a mix of vision and touch that flows into a single unit. The alliteration of the name enhances this sense of a conjoined sensation—a white movement and a walking color—creating a smooth "hinge" between two senses. We can find similar sensory hinges at work in other aspects of *A Song of Ice and Fire*. The oath of the Night's Watch, as it appears in Martin's prose, has a distinctively synaesthetic quality. A man of the Night's Watch is the "watcher on the walls," the "fire that burns against the cold," the "light that brings the dawn," and the "horn that wakes the sleepers" (*GoT* 49 Jon 6: 436). Similarly, the Wall section of "The Maester's Path" invited players to "take the black," suggesting that to move through the virtual world was to handle the color of the Night's Watch. Each adaptive element picks up on a different sensory conjunction—be it the hinge between color and motion, or vision and touch—in order to illustrate life at the Wall. Therefore, the adaptive process is never simply about finding visual correspondences for written descriptions, but the fluid crossover and interaction between various sensory modes of expression, none of which can be held up as original and true.

In synaesthesia, human senses are better understood as conduits rather than containers, folding into one another and extending beyond their borders (Barker 238). This ties neatly into the importance of paratextual thresholds in the transmedia text, which implies that the meaning of any text emerges through the movements across various paratextual gateways. In order to think about the transportational qualities of the transmedia text, we need to turn to the overlooked sixth human sense—kinesthesia, or the sense of the body's position in space. In doing so, we might re-interpret Gerard Genette's "text in the second degree" (*Palimpsests* 5) not as a kind of vertical, numbered list, but as a matter of degrees on a compass. The relationship between the texts in an adaptive network thus becomes simply a matter of which texts we've already travelled through—earlier texts influence our understanding of our current location, but do not necessarily become more authentic just because they came first.

The opening credits of HBO's *Game of Thrones* epitomize the kinetic adaptive text, and the kinesthetic engagement with the vast transmedia narrative. Rather than adopting the standard focus on actors and characters, the credit sequence introduces the locations of Westeros featured in each particular episode. By attempting to physically locate us in Martin's universe, the sequence privileges a kinesthetic understanding of the narrative. Towards the end of the credits, the camera travels across the Narrow Sea to the Dothraki Sea and Vaes Dothrak. This region is positioned on its side, at a 90 degree angle to the bird's eye view framing of the other cities. It is practically impossible to read the names of the places on first viewing, and difficult to do so at all without turning your head. The overwhelming impression we get from the Dothraki lands is one of disorientation, in sharp contrast to the relatively straightforward presentation of the cities of Westeros. In HBO's *Thrones,* the land across the narrow sea is kinesthetically comprehended as a place removed from Westeros, where different rules and principles apply.

Yet as well as signaling the geography of each episode, the credits also chart our position within the broader textual universe of *A Song of Ice and Fire.* The map of Westeros is familiar to readers and non-readers alike as a key trope of fantasy literature. As the camera zooms across the map, geographically orienting the viewer, the cities rise up from the map's surface like an elaborate pop-up book. The map is animated by the movement of the camera, rising from the flat surface to occupy a third dimension. The credits reflect the common description of the adaptive text as palimpsest (Hutcheon 6)—a document that has been written over many times, but retains traces of its earlier versions. The sweeping movements of the camera provide a televisual "writing" over the top of the literary work. However, the map is not simply a televisual effacement of the written text; rather, it comes to life in the space *between* the two adaptive layers, rising up to fill the gap between literary and televisual aesthetics, between the page and the camera. The many lives of the text exist in the movement between the various textual layers of the adaptive palimpsest, rather than simply in the end products. Senses, readings, and stories are thus never confined to a single medium or text, but constantly flow between them, moving across the great map of the vast transmedia network.

"Brace yourself":
Meme Culture and Fan Adaptation

The various textual movements and passages that cross the vast narrative of *A Song of Ice and Fire* are not limited to those officially sanctioned by Martin, HBO, and their associates. Rather, the audience is entirely capable of carving their own pathways through a text, and in doing so, bringing it to life in a thousand new ways. However, in most discussions of adaptation, the role of the audience is recognized only to the extent that they can interpret the text as a derivative work. While this does acknowledge the audience's ability to place a text within its intertextual context, it continues to rest on traditional ideas about authorship—the audience can interpret texts and organize intertextual networks, but have no power to contribute to these networks themselves.

Yet fan activities constitute a particularly powerful and important example of adaptive practice, particularly in the context of transmedia television. Transmedia storytelling depends on active fan engagement for the continued survival and propagation of the narrative. "The Maester's Path" was a collective experience, relying on shared information and communication. While only a select number of audience members participated directly in the taste and smell sections, they shared their sensory experiences with the wider fan community. This created a communal sense of sensory immersion, once more reflecting a synaesthetic modality in which senses are open and shared. Furthermore, Long argues that transmedia storytelling is formed through the transportation of both text and audience, as the latter "are expected to follow a narrative across media forms" (19). The movements of the audience thus hold as much creative potential as the narrative flows of adaptive texts.

Jonathan Gray recognizes that of the many paratexts circulating around a text, audience-created texts outnumber those fashioned by the industry (143). He suggests that fan-created paratexts are a powerful means of traversing new textual pathways, "multiplying the text into various versions" (174). The sheer number and diversity of fan texts is staggering, and all would provide interesting case studies. Yet perhaps the most productive example is the contemporary Internet meme. The term "meme" was coined by Richard Dawkins to describe the cultural equivalent of the gene. Dawkins argues that cultural evolution occurs through the replication of particular ideas (192), which seek stability and persistence in a crowded cultural environment, bounded by the limits of human attention (197). Consequently, in today's popular lexicon, "meme" is often used interchangeably with the term "viral," referring to a particular artifact that gains a foothold in popular culture, spreading rapidly and broadly across the cultural sphere.

Inside fan cultures, however, "meme" tends to be used as shorthand to refer to a particular artifact which has a tendency to "go viral"—the image macro, in which images are edited with humorous captions. This meme follows a simple but strict blueprint: a still image with two superimposed text lines—one at the top of the image which tends to be descriptive, and the punch line at the bottom. Memes encourage endless variations on the central theme, but the theme remains paramount, and variations without thematic consistency are rejected by the meme-making community. Not all memes are related to fandom—many are based on everyday phenomena and social interactions—but fan cultures increasingly include image macros in their broader collection of creative output. Memes are generally easy to understand and simple to construct, making them a fast, accessible, and popular means of participating in creative fan culture.

While there are a number of memes related to HBO's *Game of Thrones*, two will serve as illustrations. "Hipster Game of Thrones" appropriates the popular hipster meme, in which large rimmed glasses are superimposed on faces, and captions mock the twenty-first century "hipster" counterculture, composed of young adults with progressive politics, creative sensibilities, and a strong aversion to mainstream taste. "Hipster Game of Thrones" employs this theme to put a modern spin on the fantasy text. The text on one version of hipster Daenerys states "I ate the heart of the horse / 100% organic," mocking the contemporary organic food obsession. Jon Snow proclaims "I worship the Old Gods / you probably haven't heard of them," employing the meme's familiar punch line to satirize the love of the unconventional. And hipster Jaime tells us that he "Served in Aerys' Kingsguard / like, ironically." A second meme is commonly known as "Stupid Ned Stark." An image of Ned sitting on the Iron Throne provides the base, and the text humorously criticizes his decisions: "Littlefinger tells you not to trust him? / Trust Littlefinger"; "Investigating mysterious death of your predecessor? / Follow his exact steps precisely so everyone can see what you're up to." "Stupid Ned Stark" thus re-interprets Ned's actions, calling his honour into question in a way the official narrative does not.

The congruence between Darwin, Dawkins, and derivative textual processes means that meme theory holds much potential for approaching adaptation. Linda Hutcheon recognizes this point, arguing that as stories are retold again and again, they mutate and adapt to their environment, much like genetic or memetic material (31). She suggests that some stories are "fitter" than others, in terms of their reproductive output (the wealth of adaptive material they encourage), and their persistence in the cultural environment (32). Following Darwinian logic, the life of a story thus depends on its ability to reproduce itself; by definition, a successful story will always be open to a thousand lives.

In this respect, fan-driven meme culture does much to progress contemporary adaptation theory. Firstly, memes explicitly acknowledge their position within a complex web of different texts and intertextual references, and exploit numerous flows of adaptation. "Hipster Game of Thrones" at once adapts the popular hipster meme as well as the images of the television program and the content of the novels. Consequently, the meme acts like any other paratext, a multi-directional threshold between various aspects of the textual universe. Those familiar with the world of *A Song of Ice and Fire* may follow the pathways leading from the meme to engage with other fan paratexts; those familiar with other instances of the "hipster" meme may travel in the opposite direction, encountering Westeros for the first time. Secondly, a meme has no single known origin or creator, but instead reflects the way transmedia storytelling relies on the collective intelligence of its audience (Jenkins 4). In an open and accessible meme culture, the "refraction" of adaptation extends through all those who participate. Meme culture thus encapsulates the diffuse textual ownership that exists across the entire vast network of the contemporary transmedia narrative. Finally, meme culture demonstrates the importance of looking at paratextual adaptations alongside larger adaptive texts. In an article on the Stupid Ned Stark phenomenon, Scott Wampler from *Examiner* hoped to see the meme "continue for as long as HBO's *Game of Thrones* continues to enthrall us each week." This statement neatly reflects the way adaptive texts are organized laterally, sitting comfortably alongside one another, and how much of the meaning and pleasure arises through the audience's movements between them.

By encouraging new ways of accessing and moving through texts, memes breathe new life into their characters and their narratives. Despite its irreverent surface, "Stupid Ned Stark" functions as a relatively detailed character study. The starkly pragmatic interpretations of his actions encourage us to go back through the text, more critically interrogating his decisions, and questioning the heroic representation of his strict sense of honour. The meme creates a version of the text in which Ned becomes a bumbling buffoon, off-setting the more official incarnations it orbits around. Similarly, "Hipster Game of Thrones" brings the world of Westeros and twenty-first century society together, refocusing the former through the lens of the latter. Here, it reflects the familiar need to adapt according to context; indeed, its contemporary imaginings of fantastical characters and places is not so dissimilar to the modernization of classic novels. "Hipster Game of Thrones" thus creates a contemporary version of *A Song of Ice and Fire*, in which the doppelgängers of the characters transcend the boundaries of the fantasy text to operate within the contemporary cultural context.

While fan texts lack the resources and capital of the more official nodes of the narrative, they must not be dismissed as powerless peripherals. Rather, such texts stand as valuable sites for adaptation in their own right. The web series

"School of Thrones" functions as a parody of the television series, repositioning the narrative and characters within the familiar trope of the cut-throat world of high school social politics. The series clearly parodies the structures of HBO's *Game of Thrones*; the characters mirror their televisual counterparts in costume and appearance, and the opening sequence redraws the map of Westeros as a sketch of a school on a lined notepad, complete with an upbeat guitar version of the television series' theme music. However, "School of Thrones" also very obviously adapts "Hipster Game of Thrones." Robb and Sansa Stark wear the quintessential thick glasses of the meme, and Robb proclaims "we are Starks. Our way is the vintage way." In "School of Thrones," meme paratexts and HBO's *Thrones* are equally positioned as source material, parallel lives of equal standing in a networked narrative.

The strictly consistent composition of a meme is also of interest to adaptation studies. Each meme uses identical (or very similar) images, with the thematic variation operating through the text. The first line of the text is always descriptive—all of the examples of both "Stupid Ned Stark" and "Hipster Game of Thrones" start with a statement entirely consistent with the program and the novels—and the bottom row of text refracts the existing material into a new reflection. As such, the two lines of text operate as two layers of the adaptive palimpsest, with the punch line effectively rewriting the description by casting it in a new light. However, in between these two lines of text lies the consistent image, usually a promotional shot from the television program. Framed neatly by the text, the image seems to occupy the focal point of the meme; however, its familiarity and repetition negates this focus. Indeed, after seeing one or two examples of a meme, the audience stops looking *at* the image, and starts looking *through* it. Any meme encourages the audience to imagine new examples and variations, sending them on new pathways through the text. The image becomes the doorway through which we can travel to access other parts of the vast narrative. However, because the various versions of a meme are linked through the consistency of the images, the meme itself seems to be held together precisely through the alignment of its doorways. The central aspect of any meme is thus its shared portal to other texts. In engaging with memes, we once more occupy the space between the layers of the adaptive palimpsest, constantly moving back and forth through the paratextual threshold, always in a state of transition.

Conclusion: The Song of Ice and Fire

It is fitting that Jojen Reed's analogy of the reincarnated reader describes the singers of the forest, who had "no books ... no ink, no parchment, no written language," only songs remembered by the weirwoods (*DwD* 35 Bran 3: 452). Martin's vast narrative is, after all, a ballad: a hymn of gods and kings, and a *song* of ice and fire. In 2012, comedy duo Paul and Storm had a minor internet hit with their own song of ice and fire, "Write Like the Wind," an impassioned plea to Martin to finish *The Winds of Winter*. The clip for the song begins with a man turning the final page of *A Dance with Dragons* with a heavy sigh. Paul and Storm enact various encounters with the text—reading, playing board games, singing a vocalized version of HBO's *Thrones* theme music, and fighting one another for the Iron Throne in a live action role-play. They appear in a range of different costumes, from modern clothing to various medieval outfits, at one point even dressed as Martin himself.

The clip for "Write Like the Wind" epitomizes the value of seeking a new approach to adaptive texts. While the lyrics to the song place authorship solely with Martin, the clip demonstrates the thousand other incarnations of fan engagement with the text. Rather than an anchor weighing down the adaptive text, the novel here becomes simply a threshold for new movements into other parts of the narrative—the closing of the physical page segues neatly into a paratextual performance. The novels are positioned equally alongside other aspects of the narrative—the television series' signature theme, the physical encounter with the text as in "The Maester's Path," and the song itself as a fan creation. In such a multifaceted narrative experience, rather than simply reading the novels, watching the television show, or participating in paratextual elements, the "reader" of *A Song of Ice and Fire* lives the text. We embody it across multiple senses and multiple incarnations, just as Paul and Storm wear the skins of fan, character, and creator through their costume changes. In this song, the various aspects of the text simply form different components of the music, from beat to lyric to melody, all working together to create the sound of the story.

Opening up adaptation theory, in order to consider the whole network of texts that form a narrative, has huge implications for the way we understand both theory and text in the contemporary mediasphere. Focusing on the transmedial nature of a text such as *A Song of Ice and Fire* allows us to transcend the limited axes of established adaptation studies, and to consider the thousand lives of both the text and the reader, formed in the intersections between the various elements that make up the narrative. While Cersei may insist that there is no middle ground in the game of thrones, the various texts suggest otherwise, better supporting Littlefinger's belief that "even the humblest pieces can have wills of their own" (*FfC* 24 Alayne 1: 335). Each of the textual elements that make up the transmedial narrative of *A Song of Ice and Fire* offers a life and a power of its own. Each piece contributes to the narrative through their movements across the board, movements that may be defined in relation to other pieces, but are never simply copies. Ultimately, while all men must die in the game of thrones, the thousand incarnations of the narrative suggest that there may be multiple ways to live.

Notes

1. Thomas Leitch's work provides an excellent interrogation of this debate. He clearly outlines the tenets that adaptation critics continue to reiterate: the focus on literature, an assumption that media forms have essential properties that determine the features of their texts, the overwhelming visual nature of screen media, and above all else, that a close investigation of a text's fidelity to its source remains the most appropriate critical framework ("Twelve Fallacies"). While he recognizes many attempts to criticize these rigid terms, the almost obsessive focus on fidelity criticism means that its principles continue to form the foundation for all theoretical work; as he elegantly asserts, "adaptation studies has been haunted by concepts and premises it has repudiated in principle but continued to rely on in practice" ("Adaptation Studies" 63).

2. Most reviews of adaptation theory establish three main waves. In the 1960s, attention was focused on comparing screen and literature texts; in the 1970s and 1980s, critics used the principles of structuralism and narratology to create different categories of adaptive text, depending on the degree of fidelity to the source; and the 1990s saw a more pluralist approach, which used feminist and cultural theory to open up the text to intertextual meaning and the agency of the audience (Cardwell 44, 60; Murray 6–7).

3. Jenkins' definition is a three-pronged assertion of increased mobility on the part of the text, the industry, and the audience: the textual "flow of content across multiple media platforms," increasing mergers and cooperation between companies, and "migratory" audiences who actively seek out the material they desire (2). In a convergence culture, companies have stakes and interests in all manner of media types: film and television, games, web content, traditional print media, amusement parks, and more. Consequently, textual universes operate across these various media formats.

4. Paratexts are the focus of the third part of Gérard Genette's ambitious study of transtextuality. Genette is no stranger to adaptation theorist, yet they have largely ignored paratexts in favor of his theory of hypertextuality, defined as "any relationship uniting a text B ... to an earlier text A" (*Palimpsests* 5). Once again, this reiterates the unidirectional flow of textual material from an original "hypotext," to its derivative "hypertext" (5). While Genette does rely heavily on categorization, he stresses that these can never be understood as autonomous and bounded; rather, there is always a high degree of overlap and blurring. His work recognizes not groups of texts, but aspects of textuality, and thus must be considered more broadly.

5. *Rome* is often presented as the clear predecessor to *Game of Thrones*; they share sprawling storylines, explicit sex and violence, high production values, and huge budgets. Martin has been generous in his praise for *Rome*, and his comments on the show often extend to praise for the network as a whole. In a blog post from 2005, he compared *Rome* with ABC's *I, Claudius*, suggesting that the former was superior precisely because of HBO's talent for storytelling that was "rich, layered, authentic, sexy and engrossing."

6. Most significantly, Kamilla Elliott demonstrates how images and words occur freely in both print and screen media, arguing that if we rethink our belief in literature as text and cinema as image, "categorical differentiations unravel and new interdisciplinary dynamics emerge" (16).

7. Brian McFarlane's assertion that the cinema's "high iconicity" precludes the "imaginative activity necessary to the reader's visualization of what he reads" (27) epitomizes this ocularcentric argument.

8. Drawing on the work of Wolfgang Iser, Thomas Leitch suggests that the gaps in any

text are a key source of pleasure for the audience, because they allow us to extrapolate the explicitly presented parts of the narrative ("Twelve Fallacies" 158). He also notes that because novels and films tend to rely on different kinds of gaps, derivative works are able to pick up and fill the spaces left by their source texts (159).

Works Cited

Barker, Jennifer. "Out of Sync, Out of Sight: Synaesthesia and Film Spectacle." *Paragraph* 31.2 (2008): 236–251. *Humanities International Complete*. Web. 24 March 2013.

Bazin, André. "Cinema as Digest." *Film Adaptation*. Ed. James Naremore. New Brunswick: Rutgers University Press, 2000. 19–27. Print.

Benioff, D.B., and David Weiss, prods. *Game of Thrones*. HBO. 2011–2014.

Campfire. "HBO/Game of Thrones." *Campfire NYC*. Web.

Cardwell, Sarah. *Adaptation Revisited*. Manchester: Manchester University Press, 2002. Print.

Dawkins, Richard. *The Selfish Gene*. Oxford: Oxford University Press, 1989. Print.

Elliott, Kamilla. *Rethinking the Novel/Film Debate*. Cambridge: Cambridge University Press, 2003. Print.

Evans, Elizabeth. *Transmedia Television: Audiences, New Media and Daily Life*. New York: Routledge, 2011. Print.

Flieger, Verlyn. "Sometimes One Word is Worth a Thousand Pictures." *Picturing Tolkien: Essays on Peter Jackson's* The Lord of the Rings *Film Trilogy*. Ed. Janice M. Bogstad and Philip E. Kaveny. Jefferson, NC: McFarland, 2011. 46–53. Print.

Game of Thrones. "Game of Thrones: Season 3—Chaos Preview (HBO)." *YouTube*. YouTube, 10 February 2013. Web. 24 March 2013.

Genette, Gérard. *Palimpsests: Literature in the Second Degree*. Trans. Channa Newman and Claude Doubinsky. Lincoln: University of Nebraska Press, 1997. Print.

____. *Paratexts: Thresholds of Interpretation*. Trans. Jane E. Lewin. Cambridge: Cambridge University Press, 1997. Print.

Gray, Jonathan. *Show Sold Separately: Promos, Spoilers, and Other Media Paratexts*. New York: New York University Press, 2009. Print.

Gwenllian-Jones, Sara. "Virtual Reality and Cult Television." *Cult Television*. Ed. Sara Gwenllian-Jones and Roberta E. Pearson. Minneapolis: University of Minnesota Press, 2004. 83–97. Print.

Hutcheon, Linda. *A Theory of Adaptation*. Hoboken: CRC Press, 2006. *EBL*. Web. 29 January 2013.

Jenkins, Henry. *Convergence Culture: Where Old and New Media Collide*. New York: New York University Press, 2006. Print.

Leitch, Thomas. "Adaptation Studies at a Crossroads." *Adaptation* 1.1 (2008): 63–77. *Film & Television Literature Index*. Web. 23 June 2013.

____. "Twelve Fallacies in Contemporary Adaptation Theory." *Criticism* 45.2 (2003): 149–171. *JSTOR*. Web. 12 January 2013.

Long, Geoffrey. "Transmedia Storytelling: Business, Aesthetics and Production at the Jim Henson Company." MSc Thesis. Massachusetts Institute of Technology, 2007. *MIT Comparative Media Studies/Writing*. Web. 5 May 2014.

Martin, George R.R. "Rome." *George R.R. Martin.com*. George R.R. Martin, 7 October 2005. Web. 5 May 2014.

Massumi, Brian. *Parables for the Virtual: Movement, Affect, Sensation*. Durham: Duke University Press, 2002. Print.

McFarlane, Brian. *Novel to Film: An Introduction to the Theory of Adaptation*. Oxford: Clarendon, 1996. Print.

Murray, Simone. "Materializing Adaptation Theory: The Adaptation Industry." *Literature Film Quarterly* 36.1 (2008): 4–20. *Arts & Humanities Citation Index*. Web. 23 June 2013.

Naremore, James. "Film and the Reign of Adaptation." Introduction. *Film Adaptation*. Ed. Naremore. New Brunswick: Rutgers University Press, 2000. 1–16. Print.

Ndalianis, Angela. *The Horror Sensorium: Media and the Senses*. Jefferson, NC: McFarland, 2012. Print.

Orr, Christopher. "Some Spoilery *Game of Thrones* Speculation About Robb and Talisa." *The Atlantic*. Atlantic Monthly Group, 19 May 2013. Web. 24 June 2013.

Paul and Storm. "Write Like the Wind." *YouTube*. YouTube, Jun 22. 2012. Web. 26 June 2013.

School of Thrones. "Prom Night is Coming." *YouTube*. YouTube, March 10 2013. Web. 24 June 2013.

Schwartz, Terri. "'Game of Thrones': Richard Madden Cried A Lot Over the Red Wedding." *Zap2it*. Tribune Media Services, 2 June 2013. Web. 1 May 2014.

Stam, Robert. "Beyond Fidelity: The Dialogics of Adaptation." *Film Adaptation*. Ed. James Naremore. New Brunswick: Rutgers University Press, 2000. 54–76. Print.

ThinkHero TV. "Game of Thrones Food Truck Experience." *YouTube*. YouTube, 6 April 2011. Web. 9 Apr 2013.

Wampler, Scott. "'Game of Thrones' Fans Sure to be Unamused by the 'Stupid Ned Stark' Meme." Examiner.com. Clarity Digital Group, 3 June 2011. Web. 28 February 2013.

About the Contributors

Jes **Battis** teaches in the Department of English at the University of Regina. His teaching and research focus on intersections between fantasy and sexuality as they occur across a number of historical periods. He has published academic articles on the fantasy literature of J.R.R. Tolkien and Samuel Delany, as well as the young-adult fiction of Diane Duane and David Levithan.

Brian **Cowlishaw** is an associate professor of English at Northeastern State University in Oklahoma. He writes about and teaches Victorian literature, fantasy and science fiction, and Indian literature.

D. Marcel **DeCoste** is an associate professor of English at the University of Regina, where he teaches twentieth-century British and American literature. He is the author of essays on Richard Wright, Malcolm Lowry, Graham Greene, Ford Madox Ford, Graham Swift and Cormac McCarthy, and he has also published on Evelyn Waugh, in such venues as *Style*, *Renascence*, and *Papers on Language and Literature*.

Karin **Gresham** is an instructor in the Department of English and Philosophy at the United States Military Academy, West Point. She received an M.A. in human relations from the University of Oklahoma and an M.A. in English from Washington State University.

Charles H. **Hackney** is the chair of the Psychology Department at Briercrest College and Seminary, where his research interests include positive psychology and the psychology of the martial arts. He has trained with the Academy of European Medieval Martial Arts, is the founding instructor of the Caronport Bartitsu Society, and is the author of a book and several scholarly articles on the philosophy and psychology of warriorhood.

Andrew **Howe** is an associate professor of history at La Sierra University. Recent publications include articles on race and racism in *Star Wars* and Maya Deren's portrayal of the female body in her avant-garde films. Research projects involve the rhetoric of fear employed during the 1980s killer bee invasion of the American Southwest, as well as the recent debate over the rediscovery of the ivory-billed woodpecker in Arkansas.

Susan **Johnston** is an associate professor of English at the University of Regina, where her courses include George R.R. Martin, J.K. Rowling, and literary historiography and theory. She is the author of *Women and Domestic Experience in Victorian Political Fiction*, articles on textual and filmic adaptation, fantasy, and teaching.

Beth **Kozinsky** is an instructor at the University of Georgia, where she received an M.A. in English for her work on *Wuthering Heights* as a revenge tragedy. She is a member of the Town & Gown Players in Athens, Georgia, where she has acted in and directed a variety of productions, including Matthew Barber's *Enchanted April* and *Lysistrata*. Her research interests focus on masculinity and disability.

T.A. **Leederman** is an avid environmentalist and ecocritic, specializing in new theoretical approaches to late twentieth and twenty-first-century literature and popular culture, utilizing interdisciplinary tools from anthropology, ethics, biology, environmental science, and economics. Her research interests include the problem of capitalism and over-consumption in the United States today.

Marc **Napolitano** is an assistant professor at the United States Military Academy, West Point, where he teaches composition, literature, and film as well as serving as advisor to the Opera Forum. His primary interests are in Victorian literature, the British novel, and adaptation theory. He is the author of numerous articles on Dickens and adaptation, specifically, on the use of music in film and stage versions of Dickens's novels.

David C. **Nel** is interested in literary, cultural, gender and communication studies, heavily slanted toward the fantasy/science fiction end of the spectrum. He has published critical chapters on such diverse areas as the fiction of Jeanette Winterson, gender politics in *Buffy, the Vampire Slayer*, and encyclopaedia entries on "Psychoanalysis" and "Homosexuality" in the Greenwood *Encyclopaedia of Love, Courtship and Sexuality*.

David J. **Peterson** is the creator of the Dothraki language for HBO's *Game of Thrones* and is the alien language and culture consultant for SyFy's *Defiance*. He received undergraduate degrees in English and linguistics from UC Berkeley, and an M.A. in linguistics from UC San Diego. He has been creating languages since 2000 and serves as the president of the Language Creation Society, a nonprofit dedicated to promoting the art and science of language creation.

Zoë **Shacklock** is a Ph.D. candidate in the Department of Film and Television Studies at the University of Warwick. Her research examines structures of engagement with contemporary narrative television, focusing on affective and meta-sensorial experience. She has also published on *Breaking Bad*.

Jessica **Walker** is an assistant professor at Alabama A&M University, where she teaches courses in Renaissance literature and the history of the English language. Her research interests include early modern historiography, women's writing, the Gothic, and the intersection of pop culture and Renaissance texts.

Ryan Mitchell **Wittingslow** is a Ph.D. student in film and philosophy at the University of Sydney, researching the relationship between material culture and the ontology of film. He also writes about genre fiction.

Michail **Zontos** is working on his Ph.D. dissertation entitled "American Perceptions of Europe in the Intellectual Arsenal of the Progressive Era: A Study Case of Frederick Jackson Turner, Charles A. Beard, Herbert Croly and Edward A. Ross" at Utrecht University. He is a published short-story author in Greece.

Index

Note: Page numbers with *f* refer to figures; page numbers with *t* refer to tables.